12/04/03
FOR

COL. RUSS WOINOWSK –

WITH OUR VERY BEST REGARDS – !

NOW YOU'LL READ THE TRUTH !

THANKS & TELL YOUR FRIENDS

[signature]

Elizabeth Addabbo

TARGET
JFK

FINAL CHAPTER IN THE
ASSASSINATION

NUNZIO and ELIZABETH ADDABBO

THIRD MILLENNIUM PUBLISHING
TEMPE, AZ

ISBN 1-929381-86-7

vi, 473 pages

Printed in the U.S.A. by Third Millennium Publishing

Available exclusively from:

N. & E. Addabbo, 300 Meridian Ct., New Bern, NC 28562

2003 Updated Edition

Also available on the INTERNET at:
http://www.target-JFK.com/
http://3mpub.com/addabbo/

Third Millennium Publishing
1931 East Libra Drive
Tempe, AZ 85283
mccollum@3mpub.com

Table of Contents

INTRODUCTION

Those of us who love to read new books are blessed occasionally with a special treat! So it has been for me as my good friends and co-authors, Nunzio and Elizabeth Addabbo, invited me to read and comment on their latest effort: *TARGET*JFK**.

My wife and I became acquainted with the Addabbos when we moved to North Carolina from Washington State. Nunzio and I soon discovered we shared common interests, as did our wives. We had both seen military service and a love for flying that went back many years. As we shared personal histories, I soon came to know of Nunzio's technical expertise in mining engineering and his extensive projects over many years throughout South America and the Middle East. It was while following his profession in these far flung areas for decades that he became aware of, and involved in, the story that unfolds throughout these pages. Over time, Nunzio told me bits and pieces of his incredible experiences but only just enough to make me want to know more. And, believe me, when I was finally privileged to read this truly gripping exposè of intrigue, treachery, ruthlessness, murder, passion and enduring love, my fondest expectations were realized. Here, at last, we have an account of the death of JFK supported by facts-hard evidence in the form of diaries, photos, documents, phone records, and more!

The reader will become acquainted with Tony Berlotti, who innocently took a photograph shortly before the assassination of JFK, a photo that revealed some of the major players in that conspiracy, thus making Berlotti himself a target when the conspirators learned of the photo's existence. The ruthless and savage attempts by the killers of JFK to gain possession of the photo and negative and to kill Berlotti led him to form a group of dedicated men and women committed to finding and eliminating these assassins. The suspense builds for the reader as this true story of the plot to kill JFK, the act itself, and the decades following is finally told. A full grasp of this involved conspiracy and the years following is afforded to the reader through detailed charts and chronologies of events.

As author of this introduction, I highly recommend this historically significant read.

— Col. David C. Andre, USMC (Ret.)

AUTHOR'S NOTES

Elizabeth Addabbo

Although this author was never personally involved in any of the "action" involved in this conspiracy and its resolution, my complete commitment to Nunzio Addabbo and this project necessitated my participation in the writing of the book. As I told him when I first learned what the book was about, "Nunz, it is an historical imperative that you publish this book. The world must know that the Warren Commission was wrong. They must finally be able to confirm that this was a conspiracy to assassinate President Kennedy". The facts are his- and probably not known to anyone else in this country. It was only a few weeks before we were married that the last assassin was "eliminated", in Bolivia in 1994. When Nunz told me he almost cried in relief. Until that time Nunzio was justifiably paranoid and very security conscious. He has steadfastly refused to tell me Tony Berlotti's real name because he never wanted me to be put in a situation where I would be unduly pressured to reveal it. I have seen Tony's photograph. I know family members and friends who met Tony over the course of their long friendship. I was aware of sudden trips to Los Angeles or Santa Barbara while we were dating and learned that these trips were to meet with Tony for the transfer of tapes and notes from Tony to Nunz.

Among the many sources we have examined in correlating Tony's information, we have seen Oliver Stone's movie *JFK* that was based on Jim Garrison's book *ON THE TRAIL OF THE ASSASSINS*. I hope that Nunz (and I) will not be subject to the kind of ridicule and disparagement that was heaped on Garrison. I can only know the facts as they are contained in Nunz's book. We would never presume to go beyond these facts and cannot prove or disprove some of Mr. Garrison's theories as to the government's involvement in a cover-up and President Johnson's coup d'etat, although I personally believe these may have some validity. We will probably never know for a certainty as so many of the critical players are dead. But we have finally put to rest all the questions about who murdered President Kennedy, who financed it, all the details about how the assassination was committed, how Tony Berlotti became involved and how he finally eliminated all of the assassins - although it took over thirty years and at an incredible cost to Tony.

Although all the information in our book is based on personal experience, we find we have opened a Pandora's Box that has led us to other important sources with additional observations. 1. Pulitzer Prize Winner for Journalism, Seymour Hersh, in THE DARK SIDE OF CAMELOT, details the facts leading to the nomination of Lyndon B. Johnson as Vice President on Kennedy's 1960 ticket. LBJ evidently blackmailed his way into the nomination with the explicit help of J. Edgar Hoover. Hoover had secret files on Kennedy's sexual liaisons, some of which could have proved very dangerous to our country. Hersh further states that Bobby and Jackie believed it was a conspiracy to kill JFK and not by the Communists. 2. In his book, JFK, CONSPIRACY OF SILENCE, Dr. Charles Crenshaw, Resident Trauma Surgeon at Parkland Hospital, confirms many of our facts regarding the bullet wounds, directions, etc. A Texas Democrat, Dr. Crenshaw also states it was well known that LBJ was to be dropped from JFK's ticket in 1964. 3. ACT OF TREASON by Mark North, details Hoover's involvement in what North calls an "Act of Treason." It was also known that JFK was going to insist upon Hoover's mandatory retirement and that Hoover was completely unwilling to retire. Hoover had too much power and liked to wield it whenever it suited his purposes. His contant ally in his poitical machinations was LBJ. 4. Readers should make note of a new book scheduled for release in October 2003, BLOOD, MONEY & POWER, HOW LBJ KILLED JFK, by Barr McClellan.

All of the above are well worth reading. Finally, after reading our book, we pose the question: *"Who had the most to gain by President Kennedy's death?"*

Elizabeth H. Addabbo

AUTHOR'S NOTES

Nunzio Addabbo

Readers should understand that this book is not another theory about JFK's assassination. It's the true story of how my friend, Anthony "Tony" Berlotti, accidentally uncovered the conspiracy and assassination of President Kennedy, why he and others, including this author, became assassination targets and why he dedicated his life and fortune to track down the assassins. You will learn in chilling details his compelling reasons to eliminate the killers.

If you are one who has accepted the Warren Commission Report and the theory that "lone gunman" Lee Harvey Oswald fired the "magic bullet" which zigzagged through President Kennedy, then miraculously zigzagged through Governor Connally, you are either incredibly naive or brainwashed. Open your mind. Read the unfolding events and evidence as presented by the witnesses, then, as stated in line one of John, chapter 8, verse 32: "AND YE SHALL KNOW THE TRUTH".

Due to the complex nature of the conspiracy, Tony could not risk seeking government assistance. He was forced to conduct an extremely expensive clandestine operation spanning several continents.

You will recognize most of the names, places, dates and activities throughout this book because they have been in the public domain many years. Per agreement with Tony, his name, along with a few others, has been changed. The changed names are indicated by asterisk in the index. Most of the dialogue from Chapter One to chapter Five has been created from diaries, notes, photos and Tony's familiarity with those individuals. Almost all of the dialogue thereafter is from tapes from Tony or members of Tony's Capture Team. The conspirator's "thoughts" come from Tony and others and are based largely on surveillance tapes providing insight into the character of those individuals. We have eliminated much of the foul language although some was necessary to preserve authenticity. Limited literary license was taken in reconstructing some private conversations to preserve the sense of the story and the motivation. Having known Tony for more than 45 years and listening carefully to him, George, Jamshid and Rashid, seeing the photos, hearing the tapes and reading the many diaries, charts and logs, I assure you that the events, as bizarre as they may seem, occurred as reported.

Readers need to know how I met Tony and why I'm writing this book.

In mid December 1953, I was on a Pan Am flight from Brazil to the U.S. Somewhere between Belem and Trinidad, I developed a headache. I went to the galley and asked the stewardess for an aspirin. She was in conversation with a big man holding a drink in his hand. He smiled and said, "Hell, a scotch and soda is always better than aspirin. Hello, I'm Tony Berlotti."

I agreed, then introduced myself. As the stewardess mixed my drink, Tony and I discovered we had many things in common. We were born in New York, were Italian, WWII Army Air Corp officers, going home for Christmas and in the engineering/mining business.

Two minutes later the Captain announced an emergency. "Sorry, folks, we're having an engine problem and will be forced to land at Port of Spain, Trinidad."

Tony and I spent the next two days getting better acquainted at the Pan Am "Guest House" in Port of Spain and promised to keep in touch. We have been close friends ever since, having met frequently at engineering and mining conventions, airports, hotels and vacations. As well as I know Tony, it was not until we met at the Los Andes Airport in Chile on Sunday March 24, 1968, that I suspected he was involved in a clandestine operation. (Chapter 8).

On July 6, 1974, Tony and I met at a duplicate bridge game in the American Club, Tehran, Iran. He appeared devastated. When I inquired as to his health, he told me of the tragedy that had befallen his family and that it was no accident. (Prologue). Without his saying so, I knew he was in danger. (Chapter 11). On Friday May 3, 1985, while Alex Steiner, M.D. and I were having lunch at the Pizza Nostra Restaurant in Santiago, Chile, we overheard a conversation targeting Tony for assassination. I saved him from the hit. (Chapter 25). It was not until January 3, 1990 in Antofagasta, Chile, that I learned of Tony's long kept secret. (Chapter 28).

On February 11, 1990, when a conspirator's hit-man attempted to assassinate me in Coloso, Chile, I knew I was also a target. A dog saved my life. (Chapter 29). I learned later that the passport I reported missing to the U.S. Consulate in Santiago, Chile in 1986, was stolen by one of the assassins. The reader will be surprised to read where the photo from that passport was found. (Chapter 35).

From 1989 to 1991, I was managing the 800 man fast-track port facility construction operation in Coloso, Chile, ten miles south of Antofagasta, for the one billion dollar Escondida Copper Project.

In early 1990, I began sifting through Tony's briefcase full of notes, photos and tapes, recording the conspiracy data on my lap-top computer, knowing full well that two assassins were still at large and that my wife and I remained targets.

Tony had a Montico security system installed in our apartment in Antofagasta, Chile and provided us with small automatic weapons. Additionally, we had trained police dogs and two-way radios with us twenty four hours a day. The remainder of our stay in Chile was uneventful.

With my project completed, we returned to the U.S. in early 1991. I decided to retire and concentrate on writing Tony's story. By mid year my wife developed severe myelodysplastic syndrome, later diagnosed as a-plastic anemia, requiring many hospital visits, tests and blood transfusions, from U.C. San Francisco Medical Center to Scripps Clinic in La Jolla, CA.. She died on January 17, 1992.

I resumed writing in early 1992 and received frequent conspiracy updates from Tony, George (his son) and Jamshid (his bodyguard). I met Elizabeth in 1993 at a duplicate bridge game. Both widowed, we started dating and married on Valentine's day 1994. We sold our California homes, moved to North Carolina, designed and built a new home in 1995. In February 1998, Elizabeth underwent surgery. The lab report showed stage three ovarian cancer. Her Taxol and Carboplatin chemotherapy treatments began on April 9, 1998 and lasted until the last quarter of 1998. In late 1998, I was diagnosed with prostate cancer. I underwent prostate surgery in February 1999. In May 2000, Elizabeth's cancer returned. Her next chemotherapy treatments began on June 9, 2000, ended on October 23, 2000.

The above, coupled with several other cross-country emergencies and deaths in the family, should explain to the reader why this book was not published sooner.

Had I not been Tony's close friend, this book would probably never have been written and the truth surrounding JFK's assassination never revealed. As a trusted friend and for saving his life in 1985, Tony gave me carte blanche to write his story. We dedicate this book to history, to the Kennedy family, to all the families who lost their loved ones in the conspiracy and especially to Tony Berlotti, one of life's true heroes.

Nunzio P. Addabbo

PROLOGUE

The gracious two-story home in this affluent community was a scene of wanton destruction. All that remained of the house were portions of the two brick chimneys, fireplaces and a scorched refrigerator incongruously standing sentinel in the ashes of the kitchen. The police had already cordoned off the property with the official, ubiquitous yellow ribbons. The house could be replaced. The charred bodies of Tony's wife and two daughters were already in the morgue. Eventually, when he could stand it, he would have to try to identify them.

The six-foot-five, two-hundred-thirty pound man was kneeling in the gravel driveway in front of his suburban home. Rocking back and forth on his haunches, he pounded his bloodied fists in the gravel, sobbing with the harsh, rasping breath of a man who has had the wind knocked out of his lungs. Just a few short hours before, in the cool autumn evening of 1973, Tony had exchanged words of love by phone with his beloved wife, Gloria.

"Everything's good, Tony. Nancy and Mary are upstairs doing their homework and I'm ready to watch for news about Chile. When are you coming home, darling? We miss you!"

"I miss you, too, sweetheart! I'll be home in four or five days. You know I love you, baby."

"And I adore you, big guy."

Dr. Monti stood mute, too shocked to cry as he looked at the horrific scene before him. All he could do for his friend was to pat his shoulder in empathy. He could not trust his voice nor would he insult Tony by overtures of meaningless platitudes. Nothing could possibly ameliorate Tony's agonizing pain; his own was excruciating.

Tony Berlotti raised lifeless, red-rimmed eyes to his friend, his right hand raised in a hard fist.

"The bastards have attacked my family, in my home. By God, I'm taking the battle to them. I'll get every one of the sons-of-bitches where they live, no matter where it is. They can't hide from me. I'll kill them if it takes the rest of my life, every ounce of energy I possess, every cent I own. They'll have to kill me to stop me."

The passion, the flame of Tony's heart and soul had been extinguished. All that remained in the frozen core of what had been was the unremitting, overpowering covenant to avenge his innocent family. He knew who they were. He would find them.

Nothing else meant a damn now.

CHAPTER 1

THE ASSASSINATION ORDER

FEBRUARY 15, 1963, DESERT INN CASINO, LAS VEGAS.

A short, rosy-cheeked fat man, masticating a long cigar and wearing the obligatory large diamond pinkie ring, leans against a pay phone next to the cigar shop. The phone displays an OUT OF ORDER sign. In the strident, ear-blasting noise of the casino, amid a swirling kaleidoscope of flashing colored lights and smoke permeated air, the phone rings. He looks at his Rolex, another requisite of his status. It's 8 PM. On the fifth ring, Sammy Shickarian removes the sign and picks up the phone. He listens without speaking.

"Hello - Sammy?"

"Yeah - Jimmy?"

"Yeah - So, Sonny got to you about this call?"

"Obviously - What's up, Jimmy?"

"Listen, word came down from the Lansky group. You should get down to Puerto Rico tomorrow. Meet with Bruno and Kovar at the El San Juan. Usual time and place."

"Jesus! Tomorrow? What the hell for?"

"Hey! It's a 500 thou cash deal. That's what the hell for! Okay?"

"Yeah. Sounds promising. Does Dan Hill know about this?"

"Of course, but I don't know where he is. Check with Roselli. He can locate Hill."

"I'll do that. By the way - how are you guys makin' out with young Bobby?" (Kennedy)

"That sonofabitch is breakin' my balls. He's a real pain in the ass...there's no gratitude in that Kennedy bunch."

"Want me to have the little prick wasted?"

"No, hell no! Just get down to the El San Juan tomorrow. The weather there is great now."

Sammy hangs up the phone, replaces the OUT OF ORDER sign, lights his cigar and walks out into the cold night air, wondering what deal worth $500 thousand awaits him.

*FEBRUARY 16, 1963 - 10:15 pm - EL SAN JUAN HOTEL
CASINO, PUERTO RICO*

As soon as Sammy enters the casino he spots Bruno and
Kovar, side by side, at the first roulette table. It's their designated
meeting place.   Sammy stands behind them for about fifteen
seconds, then blows a billowing cloud of grey smoke between the
two men.

As the offensive smoke drifts past them, Bruno looks at Kovar
and, in a stage aside meant for Sammy, growls, "There's only one
guy I know that blows Havana smoke like that - and the fatso is
late!"

Without turning around, each man places another bet.

"Where the hell you been, Sammy?" asks Bruno.

"Now is that the way to talk to an old friend?" responds
Sammy, jabbing his index finger, with thumb extended, into
Bruno's back, then continuing, "How you doin'?"

"Good - like always, Sammy.   How are things in Vegas?"
Bruno still does not turn around.

"Oh, man. I'm makin' a killin'. Why? You guys lookin' for
a job?"

"Hell, no!" Kovar answers in a gruff whisper. "We're here to
make you a deal you can't refuse."

"That's right," adds Bruno. "Let's take a walk."

They exit the casino into balmy tropical air and walk along the
sidewalk with Sammy in the middle.   "Ok," says Sammy
conspiratorially. "Hoffa says there's a $500 thou cash deal comin'
up."

Bruno lights a cigarette and motions for a huddle. "We got
word from Sonny that the Finance Committee wants a hit on
President Kennedy before the end of the year. Can you handle it?"

"Holy shit! We're goin' to the top? You bet your ass I can
handle it."

"Good," continues Bruno. "When we get back to our room
you get fifty grand start-up money. The balance after Kennedy is
hit. No...not hit. After he's dead."

The gravelly voiced Kovar adds, "And you know what
happens if you blow the deal!"

"Don't threaten me, pal. I know the game rules. So...the
money is comin' down from the Lansky organization?"

"We don't know that and don't care," barks Bruno. "Hell, you know all our bosses are like Howard Hughes. We never meet 'em. We get our orders and cash envelopes every month. No questions asked; no information given. If we find out we might tell you."

Kovar gives Sammy a humorless smile. "So tell us...who you gonna' get to make the hit?"

Sammy grins. "No questions, remember? But don't worry. It'll be a professional. I just might tell you after I collect the balance. And you know what happens if you don't come up with the balance. My organization knows where you and your families live."

It was the wrong thing to say. Bruno jabs his knuckles into Sammy's ribs.

"Don't try to intimidate us, you fat little sonofabitch, or you'll leave Puerto Rico in a fuckin' box. You were nothin' but a two-bit bookie when we met. And remember, it was our dough that got you started in Vegas. Don't ever forget it...Hear?" Another poke in the ribs.

Sammy's rosy cheeks blanch but he remains as cocky as a bantam rooster and fires back.

"Listen, the reason I was picked for this job is because they know it'll get done - not like the Bay of Pigs fiasco you mothers butchered."

"We didn't butcher anything," interrupts an angry Kovar. "It was Kennedy and the CIA who fucked up the deal. A lot of our guys got killed. Our casinos are down and the bosses say the Committee has a serious cash flow problem."

"Yeah. And another thing," adds Bruno. "After Sam (Giancana) and Hoffa broke their asses to win the election for Kennedy by swingin' the votes in Chicago, the Kennedys turned their chicken-shit backs on 'em. Old Man Kennedy said he'd see that Bobby became Ambassador to Ireland. Now he's the trouble-makin' Attorney General. Just a couple of the reasons for the hit - understand?"

"Sure - and what are the other reasons?"

"Who knows? But, for starters, how about oil, banks, politics, the CIA! Come on - let's get back to the hotel. We'll give you the dough and then get a bite to eat. I'm hungry."

Ten minutes later, back at El San Juan, the three proceed to Bruno's room. Upon entering Sammy spots two burly men playing cards.

"Who the hell are they?" shouts Sammy.

"Don't get excited, Sammy." Bruno silkily waves off the players. "OK, boys. Tell Sonny we made the connection. We'll be back in Miami in a couple-a-days."

The bodyguards leave without a word. Kovar unlocks an overnight suitcase, opens it slowly, points to stacks of $100 bills and declares, "Here's your down payment, Sammy. Wanna' count it?"

"Do I wanna' count it? You bet your sweet ass I'm gonna count it."

Sammy picks up and counts stack after stack with the finesse of a professional money handler. Within seconds, he blows cigar smoke into the last stack.

"Yeah, boys. It's all here, so consider the job done."

Sammy locks the suitcase, walks briskly to the door, opens it, blows an obligatory final cloud of smoke into the air and proudly announces, "Consider it done, boys. Consider it done."

When Sammy leaves, Kovar asks, "Hey, Bruno...You think Sammy is crazy enough to try the hit himself?"

"Come on, Kovar. There's no way he could pull it off alone. Besides, he'll soon find out that the Committee wants an outsider for the hit. That's why they picked Sammy to arrange it. He's got direct connections to the best foreign 'mechanics' (hit men). Come on. Let's pack, get a bit to eat and head back to Miami."

"What's the hurry, Bruno. We did our job. Why don't we eat and then make a run out to Bayamon and visit our little lady friend?"

"Forget the broads this trip. Let's go, Kovar."

Bruno's word is always final. They pack, eat and take a cab to the Eastern Airlines Terminal. En-route, Bruno breaks the silence by making the most profound statement of his life.

He whispers, in awe, "Kovar, do you realize we just set wheels in motion that will make history?"

CHAPTER 2

HIT-MAN and PATSY #1

Sammy remains in San Juan, spending most of the next two days in El Yunque Rain Forest contemplating who should get the Kennedy contract. Overwhelmed by the magnitude of his assignment, he weakens to a bottle of Don-Q rum and, still unable to reach any definite conclusions about a "mechanic", returns to Las Vegas with a monumental hang-over.

FEBRUARY 20, 1963, 9 PM, DESERT INN, LAS VEGAS.

Same pay phone. Sammy removes the OUT OF ORDER sign, dials, blows cigar smoke into the mouthpiece, then speaks: "Hello, John?"

"Who's this?" answers John Cerrone.

"It's Sammy. What, you don't recognize my voice?"

"Hey, Sammy. No, I didn't recognize your voice."

"Well, I just got back from San Juan and I got a cold. Listen, I got a job for you."

"Yeah? What?"

"Come to Vegas in a couple-a-days and we'll talk."

"I don't travel 'til I know how much is in it for me."

"John, listen - I'll make it worth your while."

"Don't jerk me off, Sammy. How much?"

"Thirty or forty grand start-up, John. OK?"

"Well, I gotta' go to the Dominican Republic this weekend. I can come later."

"OK. So, what are you doin' down there?"

A long silence before Cerrone answers. "Sam (Giancana) don't want me to talk about my trips. I'll call ya' when I get back."

After Cerrone hangs-up, Sammy tries unsuccessfully to contact Dan Hill. He replaces the OUT OF ORDER sign, lights a cigar and goes to the bar for a double martini. After another double, he heads downtown to the Horseshoe Casino in search of Hill, who isn't there. Sammy drives home.

A week later, Sammy is at his usual pay phone. A casino security guard approaches and greets him with a handshake. Sammy palms the guard a $100 bill and the guard continues his walk. Sammy removes the OUT OF ORDER sign and finally contacts Hill. "Hello, Dan. You were on vacation in Acapulco - or what?"

"Sammy, you know I seldom take vacations. And when I do, it's not Acapulco."

"What's wrong with Acapulco?"

"It's much too busy. There are no hassles in Viña del Mar. (Chile) That's where I usually go. I hear you've been in San Juan. We need to talk. Ferrie tells me he has someone for us."

"No need, Dan. I've already contacted Cerrone."

"You what? Now listen, Sammy, this contract needs to be a coordinated joint effort without people like you making unilateral decisions. Remember, I'm the only one who knows all the players. I need to tie up loose ends and avoid duplications. Don't try and play Mister Bigshot or you'll get in over your head."

"Who the hell made you the boss?" shouts Sammy.

"The Finance Committee, in case you haven't heard, appointed me principal coordinator. You were ordered to find the hit-man -that's all! I'll see you in Vegas in two weeks after I return from my meetings with the Committee. So long."

MARCH 16, 1963, LAS VEGAS

Dan Hill arrives at Sammy's residence. Sammy answers the door and leads him into the den. Sammy prepares two drinks. Hill is middle age, about 5'-10", 160 lbs., blue eyes, black receding hairline and is always dressed in Brooks Brothers clothes one size too small. He speaks with a distinctive Bostonian accent, is an articulate but a pompous and sarcastic individual who claims to be CIA. When Sammy returns with the drinks, Hill asks, "Are you alone?"

"Alone, as usual. My wife's down in Saint Croix again with her bitch of a sister!"

"Good.   Now listen, Cerrone is out of the picture. The Committee emphatically insists on a foreign mechanic and you don't have much time."

"No problem. I have three or four top notch guys who can handle it. But I'm curious - who did David Ferrie have in mind?"

"A guy in New Orleans. Lee Harvey Oswald. Ferrie says he's politically active but a cagy odd-ball eager to make a name for himself. He's also unhappy with the administration's policy toward Cuba and handy with a gun."

"I never heard of Oswald. Ferrie must be off his friggin' rocker!"

"You may be right, but I'm thinking we may be able to use Oswald as a patsy."

"Man, you C.I.A. guys are always schemin'... But I must admit, it has possibilities. Anyway, I'm leaning toward Carlo Perez. He's the best shot in South America. Know him?"

"No, but I've heard of him... I hear he's good. Also very independent."

"You got that right. He made big bucks workin' the Havana casinos with the Lansky group, settin' up high rollers. Roselli used him on some of his priority offshore contracts. He's in Bolivia now - runnin' drugs."

"What else should I know?" asks Hill.

"Carlo Perez is a skilled mountain climber and a dead-eye-dick on a movin' target. He's also a mean motha'-fucker with ice water in his veins."

"Good. Can you arrange a meeting?"

"It'll be difficult, but I know Marcello (in New Orleans) can arrange to have Ferrie fly him to us."

"Forget Marcello. I know Ferrie. I'll have him arrange the meeting so we can deal directly with Carlo."

"No way, Dan! Carlo won't come unless he gets the green light from a senior Committee member, so don't get any ideas. Like you said - this is a joint effort, remember?"

"Very well, but don't waste time. We have a tight time table."

"I know. So tell me, Mister C.I.A., how do we use this guy Oswald?"

"We'll let Carlo work it out if he accepts the patsy idea. I'm going to New Orleans next week to have Ferrie keep him on the hook until Carlo meets him."

"Sounds good to me. Come on, let's go to the strip."

Arranging to meet Carlo is difficult indeed. Meetings must be arranged through his number one man and communications manager, Jose Martinez. Carlo spends much of his time keeping his six foot, 190 pound muscular frame in shape at his private rifle range or mountain climbing with Los Machos, who call him El Padrino (the godfather).

Carlo speaks fair English with a heavy Spanish accent, has deadly black eyes, and a Latino mustache. He is utterly humorless and has a Gestapo type mentality. He drinks red wine with every meal, doesn't smoke and has never used drugs. His mother and father were killed in an earthquake when he was a teenager and he has no siblings. He deals mostly with Lansky, Trafficante and Roselli and brags about the size of his Swiss bank account.

Jose Martinez is a brilliant electronics and explosives expert. He is Carlo's number one man and runs Carlo's heroin operation in Oruro, Bolivia. The heroin plant is disguised as a sulfur refinery. Jose's English is fluent. He also coordinates operations with Las Vegas operative Sammy Shickarian, is a big eater, smokes Cuban cigars and drinks straight Pisco[1].

Carlo's hit-men are the four Los Machos. They are experienced killers, arsonists, mountain climbers and card sharks. Their favorite pastimes are drinking Pisco sours and availing themselves of call-girls. Manuel Sanchez, their leader, is an experienced helicopter pilot and speaks fair English. The others, all Bolivian, are Poncho Rivera, Gabriel Torre, and Pepe Torrijos, all of whom speak little English. Enrique "Hank" Palma is a Cuban/American living in Las Vegas. Hank speaks fluent English with a slight Spanish accent. He sets-up high rollers for Los Machos, is a flashy dresser, devout womanizer and often coordinates activities between Sammy and Jose.

(See Organization Chart, PLATE 1AB for Conspirators Hit-Team.)

TWO WEEKS LATER, LAS VEGAS

Dan Hill, having returned to Las Vegas, enters a private room at the Desert Inn where Sammy is waiting.

"Hello, Sammy. Is this a clean room?"

"Yeah. You know Roselli is part owner of this joint. Listen, Jose Martinez says we can arrange a meeting here on April 25, but only Manuel and Poncho will come."

"That's OK for openers. Meanwhile, I'll contact the others."

"So, what's the deal with Oswald?"

---

[1] Popular Bolivian, Peruvian and Chilean grape brandy.

"Ferrie said he, Guy Bannister and Clay Shaw guarantee to guide him to us."

"Let's hope Carlo agrees to use Oswald."

"I'm sure he will. Having a patsy is always a good back-up plan."

"All you CIA guys think alike. Come on, let's go downtown to the Horseshoe."

APRIL 25, LAS VEGAS.

Attending the scheduled meeting are Hill, Roselli, Sammy, Hank, Manuel, Poncho and Sam[2] (representing the Finance Committee).

Dan Hill is in control and opens the meeting by announcing that the Committee wants President Kennedy hit before the end of the year. They will pay five hundred thousand dollars. He then begins to outline a plan of operations. Manuel stands, motions Poncho to rise.

"Stop! Eef Don Carlo accept de contract, only he say when, where and how de hit be made!" He grabs Poncho's arm, ordering, "Vamanos! (Let's go). Adios, amigos."

The two Machos walk out.

Hill breaks the silence by announcing, "Well, gentlemen, that confirms Carlo's independence. We'll let him cool his heels - give him a week to get back to us. Agreed?"

They all agree and the meeting is adjourned.

APRIL 27, 1963, 11 AM, DESERT INN, LAS VEGAS

Roselli, Hill and Sammy are sitting around a coffee table drinking coffee in Roselli's office in the Desert Inn.

"Guess what?" Roselli asks rhetorically, " Carlo refused 500 G's."

"Why?" asks Sammy.

''He said anything this high profile will require 700 G's or forget about it. I'm waiting on a call from Sam (Giancana) to see if the Committee approves it."

"It's still a good deal," adds Hill. "Louis already told me they'll go one million if necessary."

---

[2] Listed in Hill's diary as a friend of Lansky.

The phone rings. Roselli picks up, listens, smiles, says "OK" and hangs up.

"What?" asks Sammy.

Still smiling, Roselli announces, "They approved 700 grand and we'll have meetings here starting May 10th."

"I told you it's a good deal," brags Hill.

"Come on," waves Roselli, "let's go downstairs. Lunch is on me."

Meetings are held on schedule, attended by Hill, Carlo, Jose, Manuel, Roselli, Sam[3], The Oilman[4], Ferrie and Sammy. Hill states that his friend Sam (Giancana) could not attend because he has to resolve a problem with Judith Campbell that involves President Kennedy.

Carlo guarantees the hit before the end of the year or he will forfeit his $100 thousand cash down payment. He also agrees to hear hit-strategies but with the understanding that he, and he alone, has the final word on when, where and how JFK will be eliminated as long as the timetable is met.

One scheme, by Sammy, is to have Judith Campbell place a poison ball-point pen on President Kennedy's night stand during one of their rendezvous. The pen, he states, is a refinement of the type originally planned for use to assassinate Fidel Castro.

Roselli quickly interrupts by stating, "That's a ridiculous idea! The relationship between Judith and Kennedy was finished when she told him she was pregnant. Another thing, Sam doesn't want Judith involved and finally, the plan doesn't involve Carlo."

Another scheme, by Jose, is to have a small remote controlled submarine explode Kennedy's boat during one of his jaunts off Hyannis port. This plan is considered too costly, time consuming and with no guarantee that President Kennedy will take a boat ride there before the end of the year. Jose argues that it's worth a gamble and not expensive since he already has an operable remote controlled mini submarine loaded with powerful explosives. He loses the argument.

Roselli announces that Oswald is ruled out because he's an American and not good enough to be the number one hit-man; however, the Committee would like to know how he could be used in the contract.

---

[3] From Hill's charts: Sam, representing Mr. Louis.
[4] The Oilman, representing the Oil Syndicate.

Hill responds: "I have Oswald's dossier. He's no sharpshooter, but the fact that he's continuously involved in some form of political activity leads us to believe he's a not- so-naive, double agent. Carlo might want to interview him as a possible patsy."

"I like your idea, Señor Hill," responds Carlo, "but I want to meet heem in Mexico before I decide...".

"Very well," states Hill, "I'll get things moving, then you can...".

Carlo slams his hand on the table, glares at Hill and coldly announces: "You get nothing moving. I call and make all dee moves. Eef I use Oswald as dee patsy, I want someone to keel heem afterwards and it must to be one of your men. Comprende?"

Taken aback by Carlo's combative and dictatorial attitude, the now agitated Hill develops an intense dislike for the man he needs to work with before the end of the year. Always cool, however, he maintains his composure and advises Carlo: "Finding someone to eliminate Oswald won't be difficult. I have several unique individuals in mind. It will depend on where you plan to hit Kennedy."

"So," concludes Carlo, "you must to work it out after I peek dee site. Keep me informed on everything you do."

Carlo stands, motions to Sam and asks, "And, now Señor Sam - dee money?"

"Carlo, we'll have $100 thousand in your hands in 48 hours. Thereafter, Sammy will have Hank hand deliver you $50 thousand cash each month until you make the hit and the balance after you complete the contract. Agreed?"

Carlo nods his agreement. He does not say "goodbye", "adios", "thanks" or "kiss my ass". He just walks out, followed by Jose and Manuel. Roselli rises and follows them out. Meeting adjourned.

CHAPTER 3

PATSY #2

JULY 10, 1963

Sammy calls Hill. He has just received word from Jose that Carlo prefers the hit be made on foreign ground; Mexico, if possible, and that Hill is to provide him with the President's latest travel plans.

In mid August, Hill calls Sammy: "Get word to Carlo that Governor Connally is maneuvering to have Kennedy travel to Texas. He might go for that area since he and his men can move freely across the Mexican border."

"Yeah, Texas would be the best option after a foreign city," agrees Sammy, then continues, "So, what are you doin' about Oswald?"

"I'm going back to New Orleans to have Bannister[5], Shaw[6] and Ferrie arrange a meeting in Mexico between Carlo and Oswald."

"And who've you got to knock-off Oswald?"

"Sammy, you ask too many questions. I'll talk to you later. So long."

SEPTEMBER 13, 1963

Hill calls Sammy to advise that President Kennedy will travel to Texas before the end of the year to meet Governor Connally and that Roselli should contact Carlo with the news. The next day, Carlo advises Roselli that he plans to make the hit in Texas. He wants Hill to obtain Kennedy's itinerary and arrange to have Oswald travel to Mexico City where he will interview him as a possible patsy.

---

[5] Guy Bannister, ex-FBI Chicago agent.
[6] Clay Shaw, ex-CIA and International Trade Mart Director

SEPTEMBER 15, 1963

Smugly satisfied that Carlo picked Texas, Hill travels to Tucson to meet John Richardson, his trusted ally and choice to eliminate Oswald. A narc agent and sharpshooter, Richardson knows his way around and is on-the-take with Marcello. His price to eliminate Oswald is twenty thousand dollars.

NEW ORLEANS - TWO DAYS LATER

Hill arrives in New Orleans and meets Guy Bannister to discuss when and how Oswald should travel to Mexico. While there he receives the alarming news that Richardson received serious leg injuries during a drug shakedown. He returns immediately to Tucson to assess his friend's condition. Flat on his back with both legs in a cast, Richardson agrees he can't be ready in time.

"Sorry about this, Dan. Who will you get to replace me?"

"I'm not sure. Right now I'm gambling that Connally will drive Kennedy through Dallas, so I'll start there. If I can't make a connection, I may take your place."

"You're probably right about Dallas. I have an idea... My best informant there is a guy named Jack Ruby. He runs the Carousel Club and knows all the right people there. I pay him regularly for inside information. The mob also uses him for police pay-offs."

"What should I know about him?" asks Hill.

"Jack is a street-wise strip joint operator who can I.D. law enforcement on sight. He worked in Chicago for Paul Dorfman until WWII, when he was in the Army Air Corp. He moved to Dallas in 1947. He also takes money from Nofio Pecora, a heroin pusher in the Marcello group. Ruby is friendly with Ferrie, David Yaras and Assistant Police Chief Charlie Batchelor, to name a few. And he's handy with a gun."

"Thanks for the tip. I'll pay him a visit after I figure out how to approach him."

"I have another idea. You could...". Hill hands Richardson a glass of water and they spend the next two hours discussing ways to approach Ruby.

SEPTEMBER 19, ABOUT 11 PM, CAROUSEL CLUB, DALLAS

Hill walks into the Carousel Club where he is greeted by a young, vacant eyed hostess wearing a revealing dress.

"Good evening, young lady. Is Jack around?"

"No, but if it's important we can find him. Who are you?"

"I'm John Richardson," lies Hill. "And I'll have an orange soda while I wait."

Smarter than she looks, the blonde remembers seeing the real John Richardson there with Jack on numerous occasions and knows Hill is an imposter. She smiles, leads him to a table, promises to get Ruby, then gives him a broad wink before leaving.

Thirty minutes later, Ruby enters, looks around the noisy, smoke-filled room and puts his hands in his pockets. Hill is pointed out and Ruby approaches from the rear.

"OK, smart ass! What kinda' joke is this? And who the fuck are you?"

Hill stands and extends his hand which is refused by Ruby. "A pleasure meeting you, Jack. I'm Dan Hill. Sorry I lied, but this was the best way I knew to get you here quickly. I'm with the C.I.A. and work with your best business pal. He sent me."

"Oh yeah? What for?"

"John is away working on a major case. He needs you to I.D. an individual."

"Why didn't John come or call?"

"John is in charge of a dangerous, around-the-clock sting operation. He's so busy he isn't even calling his wife. So don't feel bad, Jack."

"Dangerous, eh? What else did he say?"

"John said there's 20 thousand in it for you. I have 3 thousand for you now, for traveling, and the rest after you complete the contract." Hill pauses for effect. "If you're interested, of course.."

"I'm always interested in helping John. So, where and when am I supposed to travel?"

"I don't know yet. But it will be soon. And John said this is top-secret. Are you available?"

"I can be packed, ready to go, in fifteen minutes. John is my buddy and God help any son-of-a-bitch who does him wrong!" responds Ruby, slamming the table.

Hill reaches into his pocket, thinking, *"I believe my Patsy is hooked."* He pulls out an envelope with the money, hands it to Ruby and nods his approval. "We have a deal then. Very good!"

As they shake hands, Ruby asks, "Hey, you want a private party with one of my girls?"

Citing his early morning return to Las Vegas and the urgent need to contact Richardson, Hill gracefully declines the invitation. Standing, he puts his arm around Ruby's shoulder, eyes one of the girls approvingly and agrees to take a rain-check. *"Yes, I do believe Patsy Number Two is hooked."*

Deceiving and lying with extraordinary finesse and conviction are Hill's forte.

CHAPTER 4

MEXICO CITY PHOTOGRAPH

Hill spends the next week in New Orleans coordinating with Bannister and Ferrie to brainwash Oswald and arrange his trip to Mexico City to meet Carlo. Carlo advises he wants to meet Oswald at the Regina Hotel in the Zona Rosa at 8 P.M. September 28.

Conditioning and conning Oswald is successful. He is promised a rewarding and major role in a highly sensitive, upcoming political event. The role will be posing as a double-agent, but it's conditional on his being interviewed and approved by Carlo Perez in Mexico City. Carlo, he is told, will discuss the details with him.

Intrigued with the offer, Oswald accepts, is handed 120 dollars cash for the trip and told where and when to meet Carlo. He is to travel by bus from Houston and check into the Hotel del Comercio, near the bus station, where Manuel (of Los Machos) will meet and guide him around Mexico City.

Hill's decision to use Ruby as a patsy and bring him to Mexico City is his secret. His plan is to point-out Oswald to Ruby, then tell him that Oswald has killed Richardson.

On September 25th, Hill calls Ruby. "Hello, Jack. Dan Hill here."

"Yeah, Dan. What did you hear from John?"

"That's why I'm calling. John wants to meet you at the Maria Isabel Sheraton in Mexico City."

"Jesus! Mexico City? When?"

"10 A.M. September 29. Any problem for you with Mexico City?"

"Shit, I know a few Spanish words, but not enough to talk to a cabbie."

"Don't worry, Jack. Just tell the driver, 'El Hotel Sheraton en la Zona Rosa, por favor'."

"Where the hell is that?"

"The Sheraton is next to the U.S. Embassy, near all the Zona Rosa facilities. Don't worry, Jack. All the cabbies know how to get there."

"Well, OK. Anything else?"

"Yes. John's instructions are for you to go to San Ysidro, California, walk across the border, hop a cab to the Tijuana airport and leave from there. You won't need a passport but they'll want some other form of I.D. for a visa. Also, John won't be registered in his name. He'll meet you in the lobby. That's it, Jack. Give John my warmest regards."

"OK. Adios, amigo." Ruby's terrible Spanish accent is strictly Chicagoesque.

SEPTEMBER 25, 1963, LOS ANGELES AIRPORT

Tony Berlotti and Dr. Frank Monti are standing at an airport snack-bar eating chili-dogs. Tony is waiting for his flight to Mexico City to meet Victor Moran, his Mexican engineering consultant, to discuss a proposed improvement to the Real Del Monte silver plant in Pachuca. Dr. Monti is returning to his office and home in New York, following his meeting with Tony. Tony and Frank grew up and went to school together in New York during the great depression. Monti was the little skinny kid who always started fights. Tony was the big tough kid who always had to settle them. They were inseparable until WWII when Tony went into military aviation while Monti opted for communications.

After the war, Tony became an engineering/construction executive, formed his own company, A-TEC, and specialized in foreign mining projects. Intelligent, adventurous and ambitious, Tony has a compelling personality with a unique and rare ability to win friends and influence people. Success came quickly by way of lucrative turn-key projects. By 1961 he was a multimillionaire.

Monti, an electronics engineer, formed his own company, MONTICO, specializing in communications and surveillance. He hired Misha, an old friend he first met in Europe in 1943. Misha had worked in the "underground" movement against Hitler and later became a Mossad agent. The Montico assembly plant in New York is small, private and very successful. Tony is one of a select few who have access to Montico's hardware and often acts as Dr. Monti's agent.

The chili-dog lunch is interrupted when Dr. Monti's flight is announced. They bear-hug as Monti assures Tony that he will check on his family. Tony walks slowly to the gate for his flight to Mexico City.

SEPTEMBER 25, MEXICO CITY

Tony's American flight lands at Mexico City late afternoon. After being cleared by immigration and customs, he is met by his Mexican engineering consultant, Victor Moran. They drive directly to Victor's office at Avenida Universidad #2217 where they work on the Real Del Monte proposal until 9 P.M., then drive to their favorite evening restaurant, the San Angel Inn, where Tony invariably blows his diet at the exquisite ante-pasto table. They spend the next three days in Pachuca and Mexico City meeting with engineers, contractors and labor groups.

FRIDAY, SEPTEMBER 27, MEXICO CITY

Oswald arrives by bus the morning of Friday, September 27, one day ahead of schedule. He checks into Room 18 in the Hotel del Comercio, where he is to be met by Manuel the next evening. Oswald spends most of Friday and Saturday visiting the Cuban and Russian embassies.[7]

Carlo and his Los Machos henchmen check into the Regina Hotel on September 27. They are well acquainted with Mexico City and spend the first day in Texcoco, eating and watching amateurs fight young bulls-in-training at the Plaza De Toros. Their next day is spent discussing "hit" strategies and how to program Oswald for their assassination program.

SEPTEMBER 28

Dan Hill checks into the Sheraton Hotel. Although he has spent considerable time working in Spanish speaking countries, his Spanish is barely adequate to pass high school 1-A. He's thankful that the senior hotel staff are bi-lingual. He spends his time alone in his room contemplating how he will handle Jack Ruby's arrival. *"He's a volatile bastard. That's good, but I need to control him."*

Ruby arrives at the Sheraton on schedule and begins to pace around the lobby, looking for his friend, John Richardson. At 10:30 A.M. he opens his briefcase, pulls out and lights a long cigar. By

---

[7] *According to Tony Berlotti, arriving one day early and checking out his options was Oswald's way of developing a back-up plan in case negotiations with Carlo fell apart.*

10:45 he's pacing erratically, clock watching, nervous, talking to himself. *"Where the hell is John? He's never late. I hope he's OK."*

From a concealed position behind a large potted plant, Hill enjoys Ruby's growing agitation. Hill is a master at manipulating emotions and Ruby's escalating anxiety gives him perverse pleasure.

By now Ruby, always with a short fuse, is becoming unglued, obviously ready to walk out.

Assessing Ruby's state of mind, Hill decides, *"Now!"* and walks to intercept his pacing.

Startled at seeing Hill, Ruby shouts, turning the heads of a few onlookers, "Jesus Christ! What the hell are you doin' here? And where's Richardson?"

"Sit down, Jack. It's bad news." Hill's expression is that of a funeral director.

"Don't tell me he's dead?"

"I'm afraid so," lies Hill. "But we know who gunned him down. We intend..."

"Tell me," interrupts the emotionally volatile Ruby. "I'll kill the son-of-a-bitch!" He pulls out a handkerchief and rubs his eyes, whispering, "John was my good buddy."

Zeroing-in on Ruby's vulnerability, Hill continues: "I'm sorry, Jack. Get hold of yourself. People are staring. Listen, we have a plan to trap his killer. John told me we can always count on you for anything."

"You bet your ass you can! I was his best Dallas informant at twelve hundred a month and it's all down the fuckin' tubes! What now?"

Ruby stands, blows cigar smoke in all directions, visibly in a frenzy over Richardson's death, snarls: "Who's the motha'fucker!!"

Delighted with his progress, Hill rises, grips Ruby's shoulder and whispers, "The first thing is for you to calm down, Jack. You must be in full control and have all your ducks in a row. Come on, let's take a walk and I'll tell you how we propose to deal with John's murderer."

They take the elevator up to Hill's room. Hill turns on the radio, prepares two drinks, then goes to the bathroom. Moments later the bathroom door opens and Hill strolls into the room. He's wearing a Poncho Villa mustache, white beret, large dark glasses and a white guayabera. Startled and almost spilling his drink, Ruby shouts, "What the hell is this, Hill?"

"Simple, Jack. The guy who ambushed John is in Mexico City. He knows me, but it's imperative we get close enough to him for you to get a positive I.D." lies Hill.

The truth is Carlo doesn't know Richardson is laid-up and Hill cannot afford to be seen with Ruby. Also, Ruby is too well known in Dallas. A meeting there might have drawn attention; hence Hill's last minute arrangement to meet Ruby in Mexico City. Ruby takes the bait and luck is with Hill. Believing one of his best friends has been murdered and his steady income gone, Ruby begins pacing the floor.

Eyes glazed, face flushed and fuming, he flies into a rage, shouting, "The prick is in Mexico City? I'll kill the motha'!"

Hill reaches into the bag, pulls out a Hawaiian shirt, mustache and dark glasses, handing them to Ruby. "Not yet, Jack. Put these on. You need to be in disguise, too, when you I.D. John's killer. After that, we'll bring him to you in Dallas along with the twenty thousand Richardson reserved for you."

Ruby stands in front of a mirror, puts on his disguise and almost burns the mustache with his cigar. Hill observes, "You smoke too much. John never told me you smoked."

"I only smoke when I'm pissed-off!"

"OK, your disguise is great. Let's go."

Hill picks up his camera, they leave the Sheraton and walk to the Regina Hotel. En route, Hill decides, *"Ruby's condition is much too volatile for a confrontation. I'll just take a photo of Oswald and show it to him in Dallas."*

Hill and Ruby enter the Regina at noon. As Ruby goes to the men's room, Hill spots Poncho of Los Machos leaning against a wall pretending to read a newspaper. Poncho scans the lobby, looks at Hill but does not recognize him. Hill's disguise is perfect. While Ruby is in the men's room, Hill sees Carlo, Oswald, Manuel and Pepe walking down the stairs into the lobby.

Carlo states, "Vamanos al Restaurante Sanborn" (Let's go to the Sanborn Restaurant).

Hill wishes he had been a better student of Spanish but understands enough to know where they're going. As soon as they leave, Hill rushes into the man's room. Ruby is looking into a mirror adjusting his disguise. "Come on, Jack! You'll get a look at

John's killer soon. Just remember, no rough stuff because your man brought protection. They're armed."

Hill senses Ruby's frustrations as he automatically reaches into his pants pocket for the weapon that isn't there. Ruby's frenzy pleases Hill. He continues agitating Jack to maintain the "kill mode", correctly reasoning. *"Yes, when I show him Oswald's photo in Dallas, he'll go after him."*

They exit the hotel and walk to the nearby Sanborn. Before entering, Hill notices Poncho standing outside near a band playing "Solamente una Vez." Inside, Carlo and Oswald can be seen sitting at a corner table in front of an unusual large copper sculpture. They are seated side by side facing the entrance. Manuel and Pepe are seated side by side facing the entrance at a table to Carlo's left. Hill asks the waiter, mostly in sign-language, to seat them at the vacant table in front of Carlo. Hill has Ruby seated with his back to Carlo and he takes the seat facing them.

SEPTEMBER 29, 1963

Earlier this same Sunday, Tony and Victor complete the rough draft of their proposal and drive to the Zona Rosa where Tony wants to buy gifts for his wife and children. In one of those strange quirks of destiny, Victor invites Tony to the popular Sanborn Restaurant for lunch. In another capricious spin of fortune's wheel, the waiter seats them in front of Hill and Ruby. Tony and Victor enjoy a light lunch, alternating their conversation easily between English and Spanish, until Tony is approached by a stranger.

"Pardon me, Sir. I heard you speaking English and wonder if you'd be kind enough to take a photo of us?" Hill points to Ruby.

"Sure, no problem. Hi, I'm Tony Berlotti."

Hill does not introduce himself, but quickly hands Tony his camera and, in his distinctive Bostonian accent, states, "Thanks, Tony. Here, my camera is already set up. All you need to do is click this red button. Oh, and please be sure to include that copper sculpture in the background."

"Ah, yes, that will include Carlo and Oswald easily in the photo," Hill reasons.

While Hill returns to his table and sits next to Ruby, Tony, intrigued with the sculpture, asks Victor to go stand next to the sculpture, picks up his own camera and moves in position to properly frame the picture. He decides to first take a picture with his own camera and then with that of the stranger. This maneuver gives Ruby the time to impulsively pull off Hill's mustache and glasses and his own disguise. Tony snaps the two strangers without their disguises in a fatally damning photo. By the time Tony takes the picture with the stranger's camera, their disguises are back on and Hill is heard whispering profanities at Ruby for his untimely indiscretion. Tony returns Hill's camera, walks to his table and is joined by a surprised Victor.

"What was all that about?" asks Victor.

"Good question, Victor." Thoughtfully, Tony adds, "Those two aren't tourists."

"Perhaps they are Hollywood actors who don't want to be recognized?"

"Not a chance. Excuse me, Victor. I'm going to the men's room."

While Tony is walking to the men's room, Carlo pays the waiter and leaves with Oswald, followed by Manuel and Pepe., all oblivious to what happened at Hill's table. Ruby, enjoying his sandwich, does not see Carlo and Oswald leave.

When Carlo and Oswald are out of sight, Hill carefully adjusts his disguise, then walks to Victor, saying, "Sir, we appreciate your friend taking our picture. I would like to mail him a special gift for his kindness. Can you give me his name and address?"

"Yes, of course," responds Victor. "Here's one of his business cards."

Hill thanks Victor, quickly puts the card in his guayabera pocket and leaves with Ruby.

Tony returns, orders two espressos, then notices the two disguised men are gone, commenting, "What a weird pair!"

"Yes. And they left in a hurry."

"Good," replies Tony. "A Bostonian accent always sounds phony as hell to me!"

"Well, Tony, he came over and said he wants to send you a gift for taking their picture - so I gave him one of your cards."

"Hmmmm." Tony is thoughtful, " I'm still puzzled over the disguises."

After a second espresso with no further comment from Tony, they leave for a short walk through Chapultepec Park before returning to Victor's office. At this point, Tony does not know Hill, Ruby, Carlo or Oswald. Carlo and Oswald did not recognize Hill and Ruby and Ruby never noticed Carlo and Oswald. Carlo,

Oswald and Los Machos return to the hotel where Carlo continues interrogating and brainwashing Oswald for an assassination, but does not tell him the target will be President Kennedy.

Hill and Ruby return to the Sheraton where Hill continues to admonish Ruby, "Goddamit, Jack, don't be so impulsive!"

"What now?" asks Ruby.

"Removing our disguises was not only stupid, it was outright dangerous. You see, Richardson's killer was sitting at the table behind you and me... "

"And you didn't point out the sonofabitch?"

"You're so damn impulsive you might have gotten us both killed. I told you they had protection! That's why I asked the big guy to take our picture... with John's killer in the background."

"Well, I didn't know that," the feisty Ruby was unrepentant. "The only reason I pulled off the disguises was to have a photo of the real you and me. Another thing, I couldn't make trouble...I didn't bring my 'piece'."

"That's certainly fortunate!" Hill comments sarcastically. "Well, now I need to get my film developed and the picture of Richardson's killer in your hands. You return to Dallas the same way you got here and wait for my call. Don't worry, Jack. I know how to locate John's killer."

"Bring me the picture. I'm gonna' kill the bastard!"

Pleased with himself for successfully manipulating Ruby, Hill arranges to have his Patsy #2 driven to the airport. Then he looks at the card in his shirt pocket. It reads, "Pescaderia Antonio, Avenida La Playa #22, Acapulco. Looking at the card, Hill ponders, *"that big guy didn't look like he owns a fish market."*

Wondering if he may have been given the wrong card, Hill rushes back to the restaurant hoping to find the man who introduced himself as Tony Berlotti, but to no avail. Tony and Victor are gone. He looks at the card again, deducing, *"Hum, Antonio is Spanish for Anthony or Tony and pescaderia means fish market. I guess he does own a fish market in Acapulco."* Wasting no time, Hill makes a deal with an English speaking driver and leaves immediately for Acapulco, a busy city he dislikes. Luckily, Hill's taxi driver once worked in Acapulco and drives directly to Avenida La Playa #22. "Bueno," announces Hill, "This is the place. Come with me."

As they enter the fish market. Hill asks the cashier, "Señor Antonio Berlotti?"

The cashier looks surprised and yells across the room to a busy butcher, "Antonio, venga por favor." (Please come, Antonio).

The butcher wraps a large huachinango (a red snapper), hands it to a lady and walks quickly to Hill, asking, "Si, Señor?"

Obviously, this little butcher is not the big Tony Berlotti he met in the restaurant as Hill musters his best Spanish, "Por favor, que es su nombre?" (What's your name please?).

"Soy Antonio Rodriguez, el dueño." (I'm Antonio Rodriguez, the owner.)

Realizing he was given the wrong business card, Hill walks out without a word and orders the driver to rush him back to Mexico City. He spends the next two days checking hotels and walking the streets in the Zona Rosa searching for Tony Berlotti. Frustrated and angry, he books a flight to Viña del Mar, Chile, his favorite place to plan, unwind and visit his wife. His only thoughts during the long flight revolve around Ruby and Tony Berlotti, *"Ruby is an impulsive bastard. Showing him Oswald's photo must be timed perfectly. But suddenly my major problem is this Tony Berlotti. I've got to find him and destroy that incriminating film!"*

CHAPTER 5

THE PRESIDENT'S ASSASSINATION

OCTOBER 6, 1963, LAS VEGAS

Hill returns to Las Vegas and calls his fat friend. "Hello, Sammy."

"Christ, Hill, where the hell were you? Everybody's been lookin' for you!"

"Business, Sammy. I'm C.I.A., remember?"

"Big fuckin' deal! You spooks are all alike! Never give a straight answer. Anyway, Carlo wants to know who you got to hit Oswald."

"I gave the contract to a sharp shooting double-agent for twenty thousand and you don't know him. He's a narc agent who's also on Trafficante's payroll for special favors. His name is Richardson. All I need from Carlo is when and where he's supposed to hit Oswald."

"Everybody knows Kennedy is going to Dallas. What Carlo needs is the date and route.

"One of the favored destinations is the Trade Mart. That will pretty much establish the general route. I'll obtain the motorcade route soon and clue Carlo."

"Good. By the way, I haven't heard how Carlo is makin' out with Oswald. Do you know?"

"According to Roselli, Carlo gave Oswald a hundred dollars and promised to get him a twenty thousand dollar shooting job in Dallas."

"Very good. Now it's up to you to get Kennedy's agenda, the timing and motorcade route. According to Hank, the Macho boys are already in Dallas obtaining street maps, locating police offices, noting police frequencies and escape routes."

"Yes, Sammy, I know. I'm leaving for D.C. in three hours. I'll call you tomorrow. So long."

OCTOBER 7

Hill calls Sammy. He advises that the Trade Mart, as predicted, will be one of Kennedy's stops. Sammy immediately contacts Roselli with the news.

"Johnny, according to Hill, Kennedy is definitely goin' to the Trade Mart."

"I like that. I may go to Dallas on hit-day myself to be sure nothin' goes wrong."

"Don't go. You know the Committee doesn't want any local involvement."

"We'll see. I'll talk to you later, Sammy. So long."

Roselli's ultimate decision to go to Dallas turns out to be fatal.

OCTOBER 8, 1963, DALLAS

Carlo and Jose arrive and are briefed by Manuel while driving them to proposed ambush sites. Two ambush sites are ruled out: The Trade Mart because security there will be heavily concentrated and the storm drains because the throngs of people expected could obstruct difficult low angle shots and escaping through the tunnels would be slow, if not impossible. Two days later, Hill calls Ruby, advising that he will arrive in Dallas in a few days with the photo of Richardson's killer. "The killer will be in Dallas for a big event. We want you to I.D. him."

OCTOBER 11, 1963, DALLAS

Carlo meets Oswald and assures him of a job soon. "Stay home. Wait for the job offer."

OCTOBER 12, 1963, DALLAS

Hill arrives and tells Carlo that the F.B.I. are watching Oswald because of his possible double-agent status, his defection to Russia, his association with Cubans and his unpredictable behavior.

"Also," states Hill, "It would be wise to put a tail on James Hosty, the F.B.I. agent assigned to track Oswald."

Carlo instructs Oswald to maintain a low profile. Poncho is assigned to tail agent Hosty and to stay away from Oswald.

"Jose," states Carlo, "will arrange to have others notify Oswald of a job offer."

OCTOBER 14, 1963, DALLAS

Oswald's wife, Marina, is notified by her neighbor that there is a job opening at the Texas School Book Depository and that Lee (Oswald) should go there to apply. The next day, Oswald is hired on the spot by Roy Truly, the Depository superintendent.

Truly instructs Oswald to report for work at 8 A.M. the next morning. Oswald is impressed with Carlo's ability to secure this position for him but is frustrated because he feels his isolation is leaving him out of the loop. He follows instructions, however, and is looking forward to his twenty thousand dollar contract. Dan Hill, concerned over Ruby's volatile personality, decides it's not the right time to show him the photo of Oswald. *"If he has the picture and accidentally runs into Oswald, he may kill him before Kennedy gets to Dallas. I'll wait and just keep him on edge until the time is right."*

OCTOBER 20, 1963

Hill issues instructions to all participating conspirators that, effective immediately, Carlo will control all Dallas activities. Hill will coordinate and keep everyone advised. Carlo, in his usual dictatorial manner, advises Hill to pass the word that anyone interfering with his operation will be eliminated.

With the President's motorcade route established, Carlo and Jose zero-in on Dealey Plaza as the assassination site. Foremost in Carlo's mind is establishing several prime vantage points for the ambush. He's a sharpshooter on moving targets and prefers firing from elevated positions. Jose, the explosives and communications expert, advises Carlo and Hill that he is pleased with the Dealey Plaza layout and is planning a Grassy Knoll surprise. Carlo, Jose, the four Los Machos and Hill hold several strategy and planning meetings. Hill advises that the slowest motorcade speed will be the left turn onto Elm street. Carlo decides that their mountain climbing experience will be employed for the ambush.

"I soon weel tell you which buildings we use."

"Yes," adds Jose, "And all of us will use radios."

Carlo orders that Oswald is to remain in the Depository with Gabriel, one of the Machos.

"Gabriel weel tell Oswald to shot dee President's driver to start dee ambush," states Carlo. "Immediately after dee shooting, Oswald must to go out dee back door to our car behind the store. Then, Señor Hill, your John Richardson is to keel Oswald when he come out."

Hill throws two thumbs-up. "Brilliant, Carlo. Just brilliant. Everyone will believe Oswald, our patsy, is justifiably killed trying to escape. That will make Richardson a hero. Absolutely brilliant!"

"That's why they gave us the contract, Mister Hill. And make sure," continues Jose, "that Richardson is waiting at the back door!"

NOVEMBER 15, 1963, LAS VEGAS

Giancana, Roselli, Sammy, Sam (representing Louis), Ferrie (representing Marcello), The Oilman (representing the Oil Syndicate) and Hill hold a meeting to determine who will eliminate Carlo if he fails to assassinate President Kennedy. The vote is unanimous: Dan Hill.

In Dallas, the hit-team, excluding Oswald's participation, silently rehearse their ambush until Carlo is satisfied. Hill assures Carlo that Richardson will gun-down Oswald as he leaves the back door of the Depository. Jose assures that his Grassy Knoll surprise will be executed with precision. Manuel assures everyone that they will all escape with ease.

NOVERMBER 22, 1963, DALLAS

On the fateful Friday morning, Hill meets Ruby. Hill sees that Ruby is still agitated over Richardson. *"Yes, now is the time to show him Oswald's photo."* "Well, Jack, your man is here and about to make his move. This is going to be a very busy day so I'll explain all the details tonight after President Kennedy leaves Dallas."

"Good. In that case I'll watch the motorcade today. I kinda like Kennedy."

"So do I. Oh, by the way, Jack, here's the photo of Richardson's killer. He's the little guy at the table behind us."

Ruby does a double take, then shouts, "Jesus Christ! I know this guy!"

"You what?" Hill acts astonished.

"Yeah! That's Lee Oswald. He's been to my club a few times; a real cheapo! He's usually alone. I saw him once with a white haired guy I don't know. And he's the bastard who killed my buddy John?"

"Absolutely, Jack. He's your man."

Ruby slams his right fist into his left palm, shouting, "Oh yeah! I'm gonna' kill this motha! It'll be the sweetest twenty grand I'll ever make!"

Initially taken aback when Ruby recognizes Oswald, Hill decides it really doesn't matter because he has decided to kill Oswald himself when he exits the rear door of the depository.

"Yes, I'll be the hero in this episode." "Take care, Jack. See you tonight."

At 11 A.M., Hill meets Jose and lies, "I'm returning immediately to Las Vegas as planned. Advise Carlo that Richardson is here and ready to gun-down Oswald. Good luck."

NOVEMBER 22, DALLAS - NOON

The ambush on President Kennedy is executed with precision. At 12:29:38 P.M., according to Jose, as the President's motorcade drives slowly along Elm Street past the Texas School Book Depository, a series of shots begin at Dealey Plaza. Onlookers are startled by the shots. Some run for cover, others duck. A few brave observers hold their position and scan the area between the County Records Building, Dal-Tex Building, Texas School Book Depository and the Grassy Knoll. Those frozen in position stare at the motorcade and watch in horror at President Kennedy's violent reaction to the shots. Mrs. Kennedy scrambles on to the rear of the open limo. Governor Connally is seen doubling-over and Secret Service men draw their weapons. At 12:29:44, after seven rapid shots, (again according to Jose), he transmits his signal to begin the escape. The motorcade speeds away under the RR overpass to Parkland Hospital as police and Secret Service agents rush to secure suspected gunfire areas. Hill, in disguise and acting as a Secret Service agent, rushes to the back door of the Depository and waits for Oswald to exit. Pepe, of los Machos, also in disguise, is standing at the rear corner of the Depository on Houston Street near an idling car. Hill knows this is where Pepe is waiting for Gabriel. Pepe does not recognize Hill since he's supposed to be in Vegas. He assumes the stranger is John Richardson waiting to hit Oswald.

They don't speak. In less than one minute, reasoning correctly that Oswald is not coming out in the allotted time, Hill draws his weapon and checks the rear door. It's locked. He curses and walks quickly away from the building along Houston Street towards the R.R. yard. Pepe draws his weapon but decides to hold fire as Gabriel rappels down the rear wall. At a safe distance, Hill stops and sees Pepe and Gabriel quickly drive away making a sharp left between the Dal-Tex and County Records buildings. (See Plate 2AB).

"Why in hell didn't Oswald exit as planned? And where is he? I wonder if Gabriel killed him before leaving the building." Hill leaves the area in confusion.

At this point, Hill does not know that Oswald exited the front door of the Depository and Carlo does not know that Oswald is not dead. (The facts surrounding the ambush will not be revealed until the hit-team's reunion at the Varian Casino in Iran in July 1974.)

Hill remains in Dallas with a back-up plan. He monitors radio and TV coverage for status reports on the President's assassination. First he hears what he believes is good news: the President is dead. Then comes the bad news: Lee Harvey Oswald is alive. He was captured in the Texas Theater with a gun and presumed to be the President's killer.

"What the hell went wrong? Why didn't Oswald come out the back door as planned? Carlo will now be on my ass for sure. It's time to goad my patsy number two into action."

AFTERNOON, NOVEMBER 22, 1963

Hill meets with an extremely explosive Ruby.

"Jack, you heard the news?"

"Everybody heard the news! That sonofabitch, Oswald killed my buddy John, cut-off my monthly income and now the mother-fucker killed the President? Oh yeah - he's as good as dead!"

"Yes, Jack. They're interrogating him now. Find out from your police friends when he'll be moved so you can plan your access to him. Oh, yes, and here's some money you may need for information. I'll give you the twenty thousand after you complete the contract. Deal?"

"Yeah, deal. I'll contact my source right away. But how am I gonna' be protected?"

"Don't worry, Jack. The law and C.I.A. work in mysterious ways. Keep this our secret. We'll arrange everything through our Washington contacts. Oh, you'll get arrested, but you'll only get a light sentence, perhaps even a suspended one. You still want the contract?"

"I gave you my word, didn't I? Get the money ready!"

"You're a good man, Jack. I'm on my way to Washington to arrange your protection. Don't miss. You have no reason to worry. Trust me," lies Hill.

Hill does not go to Washington. Instead, fearing Carlo will come after him because Oswald is still alive, he flies directly to Santiago, Chile and checks into the Orly hotel in the fashionable Providencia District. The Orly is away from downtown and tourists. He will be safe while he waits for breaking news on the assassination. Hill's wait is short.

NOVEMBER 24, SANTIAGO, CHILE

Radio broadcasts and "El Mercurio", Santiago's major newspaper, alert the public that on November 24th, Jack Ruby shot and killed Lee Harvey Oswald. Relieved that Oswald is dead and proud of himself for having masterminded the Ruby coup, he immediately books a flight to the U.S.

NOVEMBER 27, LAS VEGAS

Hill arrives and checks into the Desert Inn. He calls Sammy and tells him to come there immediately. Sammy arrives in about an hour.

"Well, Sammy, we did it!" boasts Hill.

"Bullshit! Carlo did it and he's already called. He's pissed-off and wants to know why Oswald wasn't hit as planned and why Ruby, instead of Richardson, made the hit two days later."

"Because, at the last minute, Richardson got whacked and I had to scramble for another gunman. Ruby guaranteed he could hit Oswald. I believed him and I was right!"

"You were lucky! Another thing, Hill. Carlo said he thought he saw Ruby in a Mexican restaurant in late October when he was there with Oswald. Do you know anything about that?"

"No idea. Carlo must be mistaken," lies Hill, thinking, *"That restaurant episode was a close call. I must find that big guy and destroy that incriminating photo. Anyone with half a brain could put together the whole scenario from that damn picture!"*

"So, how much did you pay Ruby to knock-off Oswald?"

"Twenty thousand," lies Hill again.

"Wow! A cheapo contract. And he did one hell of a good job. Only one shot!"

"I knew Ruby could do it. Carlo should be pleased that Oswald can't talk."

"I'm sure he is. Anyway, he sent word that when things cool off, he wants to meet us to discuss his drug trafficking business. Interested?"

"I'm always interested in making money. Set it up."

Sammy lights a cigar, blows smoke at Hill, and asks, "Now tell me, Dan, just between you and me, how were you gonna' hit Carlo if he blew the contract?"

Hill smiles, pats Sammy on the shoulder, "Now that's a trade secret, Sammy. I'm C.I.A. and we have our ways - remember?"

"Go to hell, Hill! You spooks are all alike. Always evasive. Well, since you're not gonna' talk, let's celebrate. Yeah, man. It's the biggest news of the century and we pulled it off! The whole world is talking about it..."

CHAPTER 6

WELCOME TO THE CIA, TONY

JANUARY, 1964, LAS VEGAS

Roselli, Carlo, Jose Martinez, Hill, Levinson (representing Lansky), Ferrie (representing Marcello), Sammy and Hank meet at the Desert Inn and Roselli announces that the Committee is pleased with Carlo's contract and that the political climate will now surely improve under Lyndon Johnson. Hill reports that J. Edgar Hoover will continue protecting the Committee by supporting the "Lone Assassin" theory and denying a Mafia presence.

"Lansky," explains Hill, "has photos of Hoover dressed in drag and in intimate positions with his fag buddy, Clyde Tolson. Hoover received copies of those photos. So don't worry, gentlemen, he'll never expose us."

"Our big problem now," warns Sammy, "is Bobby Kennedy. He's still after Hoffa and Marcello."

"He's no problem," states Hill. "Without his big brother and no support from Hoover, Bobby has an uphill road ahead. Hoover hates all the Kennedys."

"Never mind all them fucking people," orders Carlo. "Let's talk business."

Within months they form a strong working relationship in drug trafficking. Business is exceptionally good and tax free. Women and booze are plentiful. What more could a cabal of conscienceless gangsters want? Hill remains tormented but silent with his knowledge that Tony Berlotti possesses the photograph that can expose the entire conspiracy. *"It's odd that Berlotti hasn't gone public with that photo. Has he examined it? I must find that man."*

Locating Tony is difficult, time consuming and extremely frustrating for Hill. Tony is constantly on the move, state to state, country to country, negotiating, financing and overseeing his mining projects. He frequently flies his own aircraft to stateside projects, sometimes landing at private and remote fields, making it virtually impossible to be tracked. Additionally, he also drives rented cars, compounding the problem.

EARLY 1967

Between his continuous contact with the Committee and trying to locate Tony, Hill's juggling act consumes three years. His search is rewarded when he reads in a business journal that Anthony Berlotti, President of Berlotti Company, is financing a contract for design and construction of a sulfur refinery in the Tacora area of northern Chile to begin in April. Tony had promised his wife, Gloria, he would take her there some day. Upon learning of Tony's new project, Gloria wastes no time in agreeing with Tony to take their three children, George, Mary and Nancy, to Chile They secure their New York home, leave the keys with their best friends, Dr. Monti and wife Gina, and depart. Tony rents a penthouse apartment in Santiago overlooking Cerro Santa Lucia, and opens an office on Avenida Alameda (now O'Higgins), a short walk from the apartment. They enroll the children in the Nido de Aguilas school, outfit them in Chile's standard navy blue uniforms and Tony mobilizes his work force.

There is continued speculation about Kennedy's assassination with many conspiracy theories advanced. Some are very close to hitting the mark, leading to Hill's mounting paranoia over Tony's possible exposure of the conspiracy but he is faced with a serious dilemma. Should he remain actively involved with Carlo and crew or should he make a move to Santiago, Chile? With all the recent publicity and theories regarding JFK's assassination, Hill fears that Tony may suddenly appear and drop his bomb. *"That,"* reasons Hill, *"will certainly end my career and probably my life."* Hill's decision is Santiago, Chile. His decision to move to Chile receives little resistance. His Conspiracy associates believe him to be a C.I.A. agent and understand that such sudden moves are common. Hill promises to keep in touch with the Las Vegas clan and will continue providing insider information as needed. Hill relocates to Santiago and opens an office at Agustinas #1235, near the U.S. Embassy.

JULY, 1967, SANTIAGO, CHILE

Tony Berlotti is a master at public relations and could have written the book on how to win friends and influence people. He is a non-stop, brilliant business man. His Tacora sulfur project is on the drawing boards, financing a copper concentrator project in

Talagante is underway and discussions begin for design and construction of another sulfur refinery and gold refinery near the city of La Serena.

In less than three months after his arrival in Chile, Tony's name is well known to important business, government and military personnel. Eduardo Frei, a Christian Democrat, is President and business is good. Tony and Gloria are invited to countless functions and their children are learning Spanish with ease. Unlike many American families who venture into foreign lands, the Berlotti's suffer no culture shock. Tony does not play golf, but, for political reasons, joins the Santiago Country Club where he and his family often dine on Sunday afternoons. He joins the Tobalaba Aero Club, presents his U.S. commercial pilot license and within weeks receives a permanent Chilean pilot license.

In August one of Tony's flying friends, the Comisario (police chief), calls him to the Comisaria (precinct). To Tony's surprise, the Chief presents him with a Carnet de Identidad Especial (special I.D. card). The Comisario explains that this card is as good as Diplomatic Immunity. To show his appreciation, Tony has a fully equipped jeep delivered to the Comisario's home. To round out their social life, Tony and Gloria join the local bridge club and play every Tuesday night when Tony is in town. Their circle of friends call them "muy simpatico" (very appealing). The Berlottis are a remarkably close knit family and very happy, totally unaware of the existence of Dan Hill and the danger he represents.

Dan Hill worked several years in Mexico and Guatemala but failed miserably in conversational Spanish. He decides, correctly, that locating Tony will require more than his usual sign-language for communication. He enrolls in a crash Berlitz program to learn Spanish and devises a plan to bring Tony into his world. Three months later, armed with basic Castellano (Castilian or Chilean Spanish), Hill decides to locate Tony and implement his plan.

OCTOBER 27-28-29, 1967

First, however, Hill travels to Mexico to visit Sam Giancana, in exile. Sam heard a rumor that Carlo was involved in Che Guevara's assassination in Bolivia on October 9th and asks Hill to investigate. Hill agrees, then returns to Chile, determined to locate Tony.

NOVEMBER, 1967

Hill's search ends in late November when his friend, Rusty Thompson, provides Tony's office address.

DECEMBER 19, 1967, SANTIAGO, CHILE

Tony receives an unexpected early morning phone call. "Hello, Mr. Berlotti?"

"Yes."

"Good morning, Sir. I'm Rusty Thompson, Commercial Attaché, U. S. Embassy. I know this is short notice, but I'd like to invite you for lunch today to discuss an important business matter. Can you squeeze that into your busy schedule?"

There is a long silence. Tony has already attended several business meetings at the Embassy and does not recognize the caller's name. Always curious, he decides to accept.

"Rusty, I can always make time to discuss important business. Where and what time?"

"Great! Meet me pool-side on the roof of the Hotel Carrera at 1300 hours. I'm bald, 40 years old, six feet and I'm wearing a black pinstripe suit with white shirt and red tie. I've already reserved a table in my name."

"I look forward to our discussion, Rusty. See you at one."

With only a couple of days before the start of Chile's summer season, the weather in Santiago is ideal. A warm, gentle breeze ripples the fringes of the pool-side umbrellas as the sun plays hide-and-seek with the clouds. Tony arrives on time and the maitre d' immediately greets him by name. Tony spots Thompson, seated at a table with a stack of mini empanadas (small fritters stuffed with meat, cheese and spices) and a pitcher of Pisco sours (popular grape brandy cocktail). He removes his jacket as the maitre d' escorts him to Thompson's table.

After exchanging pleasantries and ordering their main course, Tony wastes no time asking Thompson: "So, Rusty, how long have you been in Santiago?"

"I'm starting my second year. Why?"

Tony knows it's a lie. Annoyed, but deciding he has to find out why he was summoned to this meeting with an obvious imposter, he asks Thompson: "OK, Rusty. Now why am I here?"

"Tony, some of our people have been watching you and, I must say, they're impressed with your connections and freedom of movement in Chile. One of them wants to discuss the possibility of providing us with a special service. Interested?"

"Hell no! I want no part of bureaucratic red-tape, party-goers or ass-kissers. Sorry, no offense intended."

"I'll forget you said that. But seriously, this man won't take no for an answer. He has clout, knows how to pull strings and wants to meet you tonight."

"Rusty, do you have a hearing problem? I said I'm not interested. Period!"

"Well then, Berlotti, he also said if you don't come tonight, you may have some serious business problems and he..."

Rusty doesn't have a chance to utter another word. The table is abruptly turned over, dishes fly into the air and Tony grabs Rusty and throws him head first into the pool. Then he calmly walks to the nearby wall phone and makes a call. By the time Thompson climbs out of the pool and tries to collect himself, two security guards are on hand. They handcuff Thompson in front of horrified diners.

Tony snarls at the humiliated man: "Tell your associate, whoever he is, that I wrote the book on intimidation! And another thing," grabbing Thompson's tie at the collar, "I want you to bring your friend to my office tomorrow at 6 P.M. sharp! If not, forget it!"

Tony signals security to release Rusty. Thompson, soaked, embarrassed and in a state of shock, makes a rapid exit, staggering to the elevator without a word.

Tony thanks the security guards, the maitre-d' escorts him to a clean table and Tony calmly orders another entrée.

DECEMBER 20, 1967

At exactly 6 P.m. Tony's secretary announces the arrival of two gentlemen:

"Mr. Thompson and Mr. Hill are here to see you, Sir."

"Show them in, Patricia. Thank you. You can go home now. Buenas noches."

Rusty Thompson is followed into the room with the man he introduces:

"Tony Berlotti, meet Dan Hill. He needs your help and wants to make you an attractive offer."

Tony shakes Hill's hand, looks him over and comments: "Mr. Hill, you look familiar. Have we met somewhere?"

"I doubt it," lies Hill, thinking, *"Does he recognize me from the photo he took in Mexico City?"*

Tony invites them to take seats, but Rusty, visibly nervous, declines, stating: " I've introduced you. My job is finished now. Call me tonight, Dan. So long." He walks out.

"OK, Hill, what's on your mind?" Tony frowns, trying to remember where he saw him before.

"We'll get to that in a minute, Berlotti," snarls Hill, sarcastically. "First let me tell you, Rusty clued me on what happened yesterday at the hotel. I'm telling you, if you accept the job offer I'm about to make, we don't tolerate strong-arm tactics against our diplomats. If Ambassador Korry finds out about your fracas, he'll blow a fuse! Do I make myself clear?"

Hill's sarcasm together with his offensive Bostonian accent and wearing a Brooks Brothers suit one size too small as well needing a good shoe shine, cause Tony to dislike everything about him, thinking: *This slob needs to be taken-down a couple of notches."* He lights a cigar, blows smoke in Hill's direction. "Now let me tell you something, Mr. Hill. You came to me and are the one who says he needs help. If I decide to help you, you'll accept me as-is, strong arm tactics and all, or you can walk out now. Do I make myself clear?"

"Now calm down, Berlotti. OK., but you must learn to control your temper."

"Really? Why?"

"Because it's company policy. That's why."

"What company?" blowing more smoke at Hill, guessing: *"This guy is C.I.A."*

"Are you interested?"

"It depends on who you are, who you represent and what you expect of me; so, stop beating around the bush. I'm busy."

"As you may have surmised, the company is the C.I.A. I've been assigned as your recruiting and controlling agent. We'd like you to attend a 45 day crash program at our Remote Farm in Virginia. Then you'll return to Chile, resume your normal work schedules and await my instructions."

"That isn't good enough. What do you want from me, Hill?"

"We want you to record and photograph certain individuals. Since you seem to have a foot in every door, it should be a piece of cake. So, we hope you will be a good American and join us."

"Might be interesting but what is my motivation?. And what are the risks?"

"We're dealing with professional killers and the risks are high. Still interested?"

"I can handle challenges. Who are you looking at and why?"

"We have a number of prime targets, but how does President Kennedy's real assassin sound for openers?"

"Real assassin? You mean Oswald wasn't the real killer?"

"That's right. He was just a patsy, like he tried to tell everyone. The real killer is still out there and we have some clues." Hill lies with his customary conviction.

"What makes you think I can help?"

"There's a strong possibility he's hiding in the south of Chile. Another thing, we're taking a hard look at Dr. Salvator Allende, right here in Santiago. He's a Marxist and has a staff of advisors from Cuba. He's receiving large sums of campaign funds for his presidential run from an unknown source via a bank in Zurich. He's bad news for the U.S. and worse news for Chile. Jim Noland, one of our people here, doesn't think he can win, but we need more data. That's where you come in."

"Can't win? Ha! He's chummy with Señor Tomic and word is out that Allende and Tomic have a deal in their three man race. If Tomic is low man, which he will be, he'll throw his votes to Allende. So, you see, Allende will probably win."

Hill maintains a moment of silence, savoring a pleasant thought, *"Very interesting. Here I am ready to pay for this kind of information and he's giving it to me, free."*

As Hill hesitates, Tony asks, "What's the matter, Hill? Don't you believe me?"

"Tell me, Berlotti, how reliable is your information?"

"You can make book on it. Like you said, I have a foot in every door."

Hill's offer gets down to the specifics, offering Tony a part-time assignment as 'Contract Agent' at two hundred dollars per day commencing after his 45 day training period, with the understanding he must withhold his C.I.A. involvement from everyone, "Including your wife," states Hill.

"Well," Tony gazes thoughtfully out a window as Hill becomes restless. *"This is really important to this guy."* he tells himself. *"And that's got me really curious. There's more to this..."*

Then, blowing smoke in the air, "You know Hill, I served in World War II and consider myself a good American. I don't like the idea of a killer running loose, especially the one who killed our President.   And I want to see the political situation in Chile stabilized for purely selfish reasons. So - OK. Count me in."

CHAPTER 7

THE REMOTE FARM

After learning of the C.I.A.'s botched attempt to assassinate Fidel Castro, and the failure of the Bay of Pigs invasion, Tony is convinced that associating with the C.I.A. cannot only involve personal danger, but deceit in the form of dissemination of disinformation, establishing plausible denial stories to divert attention away from them, sponsoring foreign coup d'etats and much more.

Tony spends the next few days preparing for his trip. Realizing his family could also become exposed to danger, he hires around the clock security for Gloria and the children and briefs them on the operation of their penthouse Montico security system, split-paraboloid antenna and single-sideband transceiver for communication with Dr. Monti. He obtains a 'poder especial' (special power of attorney) for his second in command to conduct business in his absence and orders that his family be chauffeured by his security people at all times. To diffuse Gloria's anxiety he explains it is just because, with Marxist Allende's power apparently ascending in Chile, political unrest could get out of hand.

Tony flies his family to a private airfield at Lago Ranco (Lake Ranco) for Christmas.

JANUARY 1,1968,USA

During his flight to Miami, Tony keeps thinking about Hill: *"There's something about this guy I don't like. I've seen him somewhere before Santiago. But where?. I wonder if I made the right decision. Why did they choose me? That's what I really need to know. But I would like to help find Kennedy's real assassin and keep Chile free of a potential Marxist regime."*

Then, on a final ILS approach to the airport, still agonizing over Hill, he snaps his fingers:

"I've got it! It's that damn Bostonian accent I can't stand. He's the stranger who asked me to take his picture in that Mexico City restaurant in 1963. That was Dan Hill! Is this just a

coincidence? Or what? Why were Hill and his friend wearing disguises in the restaurant? What's the connection?"

After a 90 minute layover in Miami, Tony boards his United flight to New York. Years of experience in the service, foreign travel in high risk areas, flying his own plane and protecting his multi-million dollar enterprises have made Tonay very security conscious. That instinct is warning him now that he must find the photo he took of Hill in Mexico City. The United captain announces they will go into a holding pattern because New York is socked-in. Tony pulls out his Montico HX-88 mini transceiver, another Monti invention, and calls his best friend, advising that he hopes to be on the ground soon and will go directly to Monti's penthouse apartment.

Ten minutes later, after another ILS landing, Tony is glad to be on the ground at Kennedy International. It's windy with a freezing rain just starting, causing Tony to curse about it to the taxi driver all the way to Monti's apartment.

At 6 P.M., as Tony enters Monti's spacious apartment, he is greeted with a big bear-hug by Peter, Monti's only child, "Uncle Tony! Welcome home and Happy New Year!"

Dr. Monti's wife, Gina, rushes into the foyer, hugs and kisses Tony, also announcing: "Happy New Year, you big lug. Take off your coat and go sit with Peter. I'm making hot rum toddies. Frank (Dr. Monti) is just getting out of the shower."

A few minutes later, the four are standing in the living room toasting the New Year.

"Well, Gina, you invited me for dinner. What are you making?" asks Tony with a thumb up.

Gina, unlike her formal and studious Frank, is always open, lovable and full of fun. She looks at Tony, licks her lips and proudly announces: "I'm making my favorite thing tonight!"

"Great! What is it?"

"A reservation at Luigi's! I want to celebrate with my loved ones and dear friend instead of working in the kitchen. Luigi's it is!"

After dinner, they return to the apartment. Peter goes into the office to assemble a new computer and Gina tactfully decides to take in a late TV show in the bedroom, leaving the men to talk. Comfortably settled in the den, sipping brandy, Tony relates what happened in Chile.

Dr.. Monti was thoughtful, then, "Tony, I'm not surprised. You're a highly visible person, you have money, connections and, obviously, something they want!"

"You may be right. One thing bothering me is the photo I took of Hill in Mexico City. The S.O.B. was wearing a disguise. That's why I can't stay here tonight. That photo is nagging at me. I've got to go home and find it, then pack for my 45 day program at Hill's Remote Farm."

"Well, OK, but I'm suspicious. Keep in touch with your HX-88 and be sure you don't take any other Montico units with you. If they're C.I.A., they will go through your things. Another thing, don't use any of their pay phones to call me. They'll have them bugged like everything else. Be careful, Tony."

Tony bids them good night and promises to see them before returning to Chile. After a long taxi ride, Tony arrives home after midnight. He turns off the security alarm, makes a pot of coffee, moves into the office and searches for his 1963 photo files. Ever since he was introduced to Dan Hill, Tony knew there was something about him that seemed familiar. His interest intensified when he recognized Hill's voice. *"Why would he recruit me, an outsider, when the Embassy is crawling with agents? It doesn't make sense. I've got to find that photo."*

Finally, when the grandfather clock strikes 4 A.M., Tony discovers the photo in a pile not yet cataloged. He looks at the photo under his desk lamp. *"Yep, this is the photo and that's Dan Hill with his friend without their disguises. And there's Victor standing in the background."* But he fails to examine the faces of the other three men in the photo.

Bleary-eyed and very tired after a long day, he puts the picture in his briefcase. Setting the clock for a 7 A.M. wakeup, Tony, exhausted, falls asleep on the sofa. Up quickly at the sound of the alarm clock, Tony reheats last night's coffee, takes a quick shower, packs his bags, calls a taxi, sets the house alarms and is on his way at 9 A.M.

JANUARY 4, 1968, VIRGINIA

Dan Hill meets him at the Williamsburg airport at noon. They drive a winding road along the James River, then turn on a narrow gravel road leading to a secluded, gated and armed campsite, posted PRIVATE PROPERTY.

"Here we are," announces Hill. "This is the Camp Peary annex we call the Remote Farm."

Nonplussed with what he sees, Tony comments coolly, "Certainly remote all right."

"Everything here is temporary, but very much action oriented. You'll change your mind after our people bring you up to speed on surveillance, explosives, martial arts and all that other good stuff."

As they drive by a row of tents, Tony cannot believe the C.I.A. would set-up such a shoddy looking campsite. Not one to mince words, Tony declares: "Looks like this camouflaged tent city was set up by a bunch of drunks. I mean this is really Mickey Mouse!"

"I'm sorry things aren't up to your high standards, Berlotti. But, like I said, you'll change your mind."

Tony doesn't respond, thinking, *"Jesus, it's my own fault that I'm stuck with this sonofabitch. I don't trust him. This place can't really be C.I.A. And why was Hill wearing a disguise in Mexico city?"*

Hill stops in front of a tent marked MESS HALL. "It's 2 P.M. Let's have lunch."

Except for a short, fat cook, peeling onions, the hall is empty. Tony orders a ham on rye and coffee. Hill eats a greasy looking cheeseburger with fries and a milk. During their brief lunch, Tony notices there is seating for approximately 20 people. After lunch they enter a tent marked ADMIN. Tony is photographed, fingerprinted, signs a secrecy agreement and fills out a questionnaire. The lights in the tent flutter often as Tony hears the sound of a nearby generator.

At 4 P.M., Hill drives Tony around the compound, then stops at a log cabin located about 200 feet beyond the last tent and escorts him to a private room in the cabin. "It's late and I need to check-in at Langley. Dinner will be between 6 and 7 and a drill instructor will meet you at breakfast. I'll return in a few days to check your progress."

Relieved that Hill is gone, and noticing that he appears to be alone in the cabin, Tony quickly pulls down the shades, checks the room for 'bugs', opens his briefcase in the bathroom and pulls out the photo of Dan Hill, wondering, *"Why were he and his friend in disguise? Why did his friend pull off the disguises? Why did he want that copper sculpture in the background included in the shot?*

And why did he tell Victor he wanted to send me a gift? Let's take a look."

Tony looks at the photo, sees Hill seated next to his friend, sees Victor standing in the background next to the copper sculpture behind two men seated between Hill and Victor. Nothing registers. He reaches into the briefcase and pulls out his miners loop to get a very close look. The first look is followed by a double-take. One of the men sitting in front of Victor draws his immediate attention: *"What the hell?"* He rubs his eyes, cleans the loop and looks again. *"Jesus! It's Lee Harvey Oswald! What the hell was he doing there? And who was he sitting with? It was no coincidence that he asked me to include the sculpture in the background."*

Totally psyched-up with an adrenalin rush, he looks at Hill's friend and rubs his eyes again.

"Bingo! Unbelievable! It's Jack Ruby sitting with Hill."

Tony splashes cold water on his face and behind his neck. He examines the photo again, shaking his head in disbelief.

"Hill with Ruby and Oswald with an unknown? Who is this Mister X with Oswald? What were they doing in Mexico City? Wow! Oswald shot Kennedy and Ruby shot Oswald. So where do Hill and Mister X fit into the picture? Is this the answer to all the speculation about a conspiracy?"

He curses as he showers in lukewarm water, shaves, puts the photo in his jacket and walks to dinner. Back in his room at 8 P.M., he labels the back of the photo 'Mexico City, September 1963, Negative with Luigi', puts the photo in a small photo package with other photos, sets a 'hair-trap' in the booklet, locks the booklet in his briefcase and retires for the night. *"The photo must be what Hill wants from me. Who is Kennedy's real assassin? Is there more than one? Was it a conspiracy?"*

The next morning, an instructor meets him for breakfast. Tony counts 12 men in the Mess Hall. Four are instructors dressed in camouflaged suits and eight are trainees, all dressed differently.

The first day is introduction to the instructors and trainees, a briefing on programs for the next 45 days and preliminary surveillance photography and recording equipment. Tony finds working conditions deplorable but is impressed with the instruction and equipment. His mind keeps returning to the photograph; why he was recruited.

"Hill knows Kennedy's real killer, I'm sure. Why are Oswald and Ruby in that restaurant but seated at separate tables? Who else was in on the conspiracy?"

Tony remembers all the advice Dr. Monti gave him about the C.I.A. before he came to the Remote Farm. When dinner ends, several trainees start a poker game in the Mess Hall. Tony is invited but declines. He walks quickly to his room, opens his briefcase and examines his photo package.

"Sons-of-bitches! Monti was right! They took a look and know I've got the photo. But they have no clue where I'm keeping the negative. Hill was in on the conspiracy all right. Destroying the negative will be his primary goal. I'm in deep shit and all because of a damn photo. They won't let me go now."

Tony activates the Montico HX-88, punches-in his 5 digit code and calls Dr. Monti.

"You were right, Frank. They opened my briefcase, saw the picture, replaced it and have probably already contacted Hill. I'm the real target for these guys. What do you advise?"

"They won't do anything yet. They have to figure out where you have the negative. I'd play along like you don't know they saw the photo."

Tony takes Dr. Monti's advice. During the next few days he receives instructions on code technology, explosives, weapons, lock-picking, photography, recording, communications and physical training.

During one of the explosives lessons the other trainees learn that Tony knows more about implosion techniques than the instructor. Another day, the main generator fails and it is Tony who tells the camp mechanic how to put it back on line.

Tony maintains nightly communication with Dr. Monti advising on his progress and receiving status reports on his family. During one communication, Dr. Monti reports he has established that the C.I.A. calls Camp Peary "The Farm" and there is no C.I.A. annex called the "Remote Farm".

A month passes with no word from Dan Hill. The administrative manager advises Tony that Dan Hill is usually there during the last two days of the training program. The last days of training involve various assassination techniques. Tony has found that one of the commando instructors, a crew-cut, neo-Nazi type, is not only sarcastic but sadistic. On one of the last afternoons, this instructor, standing on a high platform with bull horn in hand, announces:

"OK, men, you've learned how to handle guns, explosives and a lot of other things. Then we got you in shape. It's cold out here this afternoon but you'll soon get warm. Today you learn the real world of martial arts."

He climbs down, removes his jacket, flexes his muscles and glares at the men, announcing:

"Anybody here think they can take me?"

A young, tough looking trainee steps forward and removes his jacket, declaring:

"Yes, Sir. I think I can take you." and he promptly attacks the instructor. Within seconds, the trainee is bruised, battered and semi-conscious on the ground. Tony rushes to the young man and kneels beside him to check his condition. As he looks into the trainee's eyes, the instructor grabs Tony behind the collar and jerks him away, violently. Tony gets up, removes his jacket, then smiles at the instructor. "You shouldn't have done that."

The instructor glares at Tony. "OK class, you're about to see how 'The Bigger They Are, The Harder They Fall'!"

Unfortunately for the instructor, Tony did not indicate on his admission questionnaire that he is a fifth degree martial-arts master. The instructor makes the first move and is quickly thrown to the ground.

He rises, with fire in his eyes, shouting: "OK, big guy—wanna' play rough, eh? Get ready!"

And he attacks.

The next moments are violent. Tony shows no mercy. The instructor is beaten into unconsciousness as the trainees give Tony a standing ovation. An instructor, trained in paramedics, is summoned, and rushes the battered instructor away in a four-by-four. Hill finally arrives on the last day of training, addresses the trainees with a boiler-plate commencement speech, then escorts Tony outside for a private talk.

"I'm proud of you, Tony. I see you graduated top of the class. But we discovered that you lied on your application. You didn't indicate you're an explosives expert or that you're a martial arts master."

"No one asked and, frankly, you should have guessed about the explosives due to my work."

"So, are you proud of putting our instructor in the hospital with a broken jaw and dislocated shoulder?"

"Check the facts. That son-of-a-bitch had it coming!"

"As I told you in Chile, we don't tolerate strong-arm tactics."

"And I told you in Chile - take me as-is or forget about using me. Is that clear?"

"We'll see, Berlotti. Just remember, I'm your control agent and you answer to me. Now, let's get a bite to eat. We're out of here tomorrow morning."

Upon leaving Hill, Tony meets Dr. Monti for lunch at Luigi's. They discuss their respective families as they order the house specialty: gnocchi Neapolitan. The conversation turns to Dan Hill.

"Well, Frank, we're sure now that Hill was involved in a conspiracy to assassinate Kennedy and he knows that I know. That's why he wants the negative to my photo. And I sure as hell never wanted to be part of anything like this."

"Yes, but the note you wrote on the back of the photo must be driving him nuts."

"Good! I can play their game, too, if I have to. Psychological warfare has always intrigued me." Thoughtfully, Tony continues, "Frank, since they're never going to let me off the hook, I've decided to play along. We've got to find out who else was involved. Why did Hill tell me we need to search for Kennedy's real killer? Why did Ruby kill Oswald? Who was sitting next to Oswald? And who started the conspiracy?"

Frank was more serious than ever. "This is very risky business, Tony. But the world needs to know what really happened that November 22nd. I'll give you my complete support. I have six of my new X-Mit bugs ready for you to take back to Chile. You'll need them; your life may well be for sale, Tony.

"I know." Tony was still thoughtful, then, "How's your new Electrodot system coming along?"

"Terrific. It's so much better than Microdot. The C.I.A. and F.B.I. would kill to have it. But, for now, it must remain a trade-secret. Here, let me pick up the tab."

At home that night, Tony packs for his return to Chile, secures the house and taxies to Kennedy International in the morning. Dr. Monti meets him there for lunch, provides the six new bugs and they establish a communications schedule. By late afternoon, Monti leaves and Tony checks through security for his late flight to Chile.

MARCH 4, 1968, LAGO RANCO, CHILE

Late in the afternoon, Tony arrives by jeep at a rented lakeside cabin on Lago Ranco, in the south of Chile. He toots the horn and is immediately greeted by happy sounds:

"Daddy's here! Daddy's here!"

After loving embraces, the children brag about the big fish they caught and Gloria starts to cook the fresh bass. As the children help their father unpack, George asks all questions:

"Dad, how are Uncle Frank, Aunt Gina and Peter? What did you do in Virginia? Did you stop in Lima as planned? And what did you bring back?"

Tony tells them that the Monti's are fine, his Virginia trip was successful, that he had a good business meeting in the Hotel Bolivar in Lima and saw a military exercise at the Plaza San Martin. He then opens a wrapped box and hands each child a new alpaca sweater.

The children immediately try-on their sweaters. As Tony unpacks two bottles of Pisco, Gloria's happy voice is heard from the kitchen: "Wash up, gang. Dinner will be ready in five minutes."

Six days later the Berlotti family is back in their Santiago penthouse, unpacking. It's late and everyone is tired, but George, the family inquisitor, continues his barrage of questions:

"Dad, you didn't tell us what you did in Virginia for 45 days. What did you do? What is Peter doing with his new computer? Is Uncle Frank coming to visit us? And when are we going back to the lake?"

Tony politely brushes aside the questions. "I have a headache, son, and must get some rest. I have an early morning meeting." Tony hugs his son as he says, "Goodnight, George."

CHAPTER 8

SPYING IN CHILE

MARCH 15, 1968, SANTIAGO, CHILE

It's noon and Tony is alone, standing at the counter in the popular and always crowded HAITI coffee shop in downtown Santiago. While a young lady prepares his cappuccino, his thoughts keep drifting back to Dan Hill: *"Strange I haven't heard from Hill. He surely knows I'm on to the conspiracy and expect he'll want to try and destroy my photo."*

As the young lady places the cappuccino on the bar, Tony receives a sharp jolt and firm grip on his shoulder. His action is swift and devastating. He has the unfortunate aggressor on the floor, totally disabled, before realizing it's Dan Hill. Most of the other coffee drinkers make a quick exit. Those remaining back away, waiting for more action. On the floor, in a daze, Hill attempts to get up.

Tony places his foot on Hill's chest, inquiring: "Now, is that the way to make your contact?"

Looking up, Hill groans: "God Damn you, Berlotti ! I warned you about strong arm tactics."

Looking down, Tony releases his foot and grins disarmingly, "How about a cappuccino?"

Hill rises slowly, brushes himself off, adjusts his tie and jacket, then glares at Tony, issuing an order: "Let's go! The boss wants to meet you."

Tony smiles, walks back to the counter and orders another cappuccino. Hill, embarrassed and angry, but without recourse, walks out to the sidewalk and waits for Tony. A half hour later they walk up Paseo Ahumada onto Agustinas and then to Hill's office. Hill picks up a briefcase and escorts Tony to a room occupied by three men and two women seated around a conference table jammed with briefcases, papers, sodas, coffee cups and assorted pastries. Hill, still nervous and disheveled, introduces Tony to the white haired man sitting at the end of the table.

"Tony Berlotti, this is Mr. Louis."

Mr. Louis nods, then, with a Henry Kissinger accent, asks Hill: "Dan, why are you in such - uh - disarray?"

Still outraged over how Tony embarrassed him in public a half hour ago, Hill makes his second mistake of the day, announcing, "This smart ass WOP had the nerve..."

Calling Tony a WOP has always been tantamount to a declaration of war and suddenly his tolerance level goes ballistic. Within seconds the conference room looks and sounds like a war zone. Tony slams Hill onto the table, sending food, plates, papers and briefcases crashing to the floor.

He grabs Hill at the collar and, as the others stand and watch, calmly states: "Ever since I was a kid growing up in New York, I creamed everyone who called me a WOP. You obviously are ignorant of the fact that WOP is an acronym that originated at Ellis Island many years ago when Italians, like my mother and father, came to the U.S.. It has two meanings: With Out Papers or Work Or Pay. Now, I was born in New York. I'm no WOP and if you ever call me WOP again I'll tear out your bigot tongue!"

Tony releases Hill and takes a seat. Hill, in great pain, slowly rolls off the table, adjusts his tie and jacket and stands, dazed. The others quickly pick up items from the floor and sit down quietly. Mr. Louis puts on his glasses and addresses Hill: "Take a seat, Dan. I'll deal with this outburst, later." He then looks at Tony, introduces the others and states: "Now let's get down to business, Mr. Berlotti. Take a good look at all of us and remember our faces. We're all C.I.A. and you'll be seeing us from time to time at various functions around Chile. Do not make contact with any of us and, if anyone asks, deny you ever saw us. Your only contact is Dan Hill."

Tony asks each to walk around the room as he studies their faces, body language and dress. The brief parade ends. "OK, I've identified the agents. Mr. Louis, why isn't this office in the Embassy?"

"Deception, of course. The Chilenos think we're venture capitalists. Just another one of our plausible denial stories." Louis dismisses everyone except Hill and Tony, then addresses Hill: "I heard what happened to Rusty at the Hotel Carrera. Dan, you've got to stop trying to win through intimidation. Now, come off your ivy-league high horse and get down to earth. We need Mr. Berlotti. He's now one of us, so shake hands and let's get to our priorities."

As the two men shake, the hostility is as palpable as sparks from an electric probe.

MARCH 24, 1968, (SUNDAY), CHILE

The Los Andes Chile Aero Club is holding a fly-in asado (barbeque). About 25 pilots are gathered around the clubhouse, cooking steaks, watching aircraft on final approach, listening to Chilean music. Nunzio Addabbo[8], a resident member of the club, chatting with three friends, watches a Cherokee Six land and taxi to the tie-down area. Tony Berlotti and Dan Hill exit the low wing aircraft, tie it down and walk towards the clubhouse. Nunzio looks at them and does a double-take.

He tells his friends, "Well, I'll be damned! Here comes my old buddy, Tony!" Then he shouts and waves, "Tony, what a surprise!"

Tony spots Addabbo, raises his arms and shouts, "Nunzio!"

They bear hug in greeting and Tony says, "I heard you were here. What are you doing?"

"I'm Chief Resident Engineer on the Rio Blanco project. What are you doing and how did you find out about our asado?"

Before answering, Tony introduces Dan Hill, then Nunzio introduces Jimmy Santelli, Bert Renzetti and Buck Yancey. "I just started a couple of mining projects. Dan, here, said a girl at the Embassy, Francene, who's dating one of the flight instructors at this club, told him this will be the best fly-in asado in Chile. So, here we are."

"She got that right. Come on, I'll show you our new club house - it's still under construction. Then let's have some grilled 'lomo" (beef). As they walk to the club house, pilots, women and children are seen enjoying their lomo, salads and drinks as strains of "Granada" are heard from the loudspeaker in the small wooden control tower.

An hour or so hour later, Tony and Nunzio are standing alone, alongside CC-KAD, a Cessna 172. With his arm around Nunzio's shoulder, Tony whispers, "Terrific asado. I'll get seconds later. But first, now that we're alone, I have something important to tell you. I've known you a long time and trust you to keep this confidential. Several years ago, in Mexico City, I took a photo of four men involved in a monumental conspiracy that will make history. This guy Hill may be involved so I've got to be careful. When the time is

---

[8] this author.

right, I'll show you that photo so you can be witness to their identity."

"But you can't tell me now?"

"I'm still doing detective work on two of the men. It's dangerous, Nunzio, and wouldn't be fair to involve you. I promise to clue you in after it's safe.

"Is that why I haven't heard from you lately?"

"Of course. Come on, let's get more of that good steak! I'm still hungry."

FOR THE NEXT FEW YEARS

During the next couple of years, Hill's intensified involvement in Carlo's heroin operation, coupled with Mr. Louis' unrelenting pressure to provide insider information on Marxist Allende, leave him little time to locate Tony's conspiracy photo. He does not report Tony's plans nor predictions concerning Chile's three man presidential race. Instead, he agrees with statements made by Station Chief Jim Noland that Allende cannot win. Hill's frustration mounts when he learns that Allende does in fact win the congressional runoff and that Berlotti was right. Soon after the shocking and disastrous election of Allende, U.S. officials in Santiago begin moving around like pieces on a chess board. Noland is replaced by Henry Hecksher, Hecksher is replaced by Ray Warren in 1970 and Ambassador Korry is replaced in 1971 by Nat Davis, a Nixon yes-man. During this period, Richard Helms is C.I.A. Director. Bill Broe, the C.I.A. Inspector General, carefully documents activities in Chile. Tony learns, from Hill and an I.T.T. official in Santiago, that Richard Nixon is not pleased with a Marxist in power in Chile.

When Tony realizes his fast-track mining projects are keeping him too busy to investigate Hill's activities and associates, he asks his Police Chief friend for help. The Chief reports that Mr. Louis left Chile soon after Allende's victory, leaving Hill in charge and that Hill never goes to the U.S. Embassy.

The Police Chief also reports that sizeable deposits are being made in Hill's Santiago bank account, that Hill's alcoholic wife spends most of her time in a rented beach condo in Viña del Mar and that Hill travels frequently to Bolivia and the U.S. Tony knows, from Hill's bugged phone, that Hill is seeing a man named Carlo and Jose Martinez in Bolivia and Johnny Roselli and Sammy

Shickarian in Las Vegas. He is still unaware that Carlo is the man sitting next to Oswald in the Mexico City photo or of Carlo's involvement in the conspiracy. After numerous deciphered "electrodot system" conversations with Tony, Dr. Monti sends Misha[9], ex-Mossad agent and his number two man, to bug Sammy's residence in Las Vegas. Dr. Monti reports that Hill, Carlo and Sammy agreed to cut Roselli out of their heroin operation and that Dan Hill visited Sam Giancana, in exile, in Mexico on October 27, 28 and 29, 1967; purpose unknown. Tony and Dr. Monti agree that Dan Hill probably has more than one allegiance, none of which appear to be in the best interests of the U.S. Tony is convinced that Hill is not C.I.A. Dr. Monti is not so sure who's pulling Hill's strings and suggests that Tony, with his projects nearing completion, train and keep a team in Chile to monitor Hill and send another team to Bolivia to locate Carlo. He suggests each team be husband and wife.

JANUARY, 1970, CHILE

With his projects completed and husband and wife teams trained in surveillance, Tony advises Hill he is leaving Chile. "You can't go!" states Hill. "We need to do something about Allende! If you leave now I'll see you never work for the Company again!"

"Whatever, Hill." Tony ignores the threat.

He sets-up a husband and wife team to operate out of their home in Santiago, sends the second team to La Paz, then packs up and returns to New York with his family.

"My only regret in leaving Chile," rues Tony, *"is that I may lose contact with Hill. Oswald is dead. Ruby is dead. And the conspiracy still unsolved. I must identify the man sitting next to Oswald and what part he played in the assassination. And I think I'm still on the hook for that damn negative."*

---

[9] Dr. Monti met Misha in Europe during WWII when Monti was with the OSS and Misha worked for the underground.

CHAPTER 9

IRAN, SAVAK, AND ARSON

MARCH AND APRIL, 1970

After reviewing all favorable drilling reports and subsequent feasibility studies, Tony begins negotiations for the Zahedan turn-key copper project in Iran.

During a luncheon with Dr. Monti in April, Monti reports: "Tony, we just found out that Carlo has a heroin operation near Oruro, Bolivia."

"That's a break. I'll send my husband and wife geology team immediately."

Tony's team confirms that Carlo's heroin plant, outside Oruro, is disguised as a sulfur refining operation and managed by Jose Martinez. The team rents a small cabin located between Oruro and the heroin plant, and plan to visit that operation as sulfur buyers.

SEPTEMBER 15, 1970, TUCSON, ARIZONA

While on a mine-site visit outside Tucson, Tony receives word from his Santiago team, via Dr. Monti, that John Mitchell is in Santiago having breakfast with Agustin Edwards. Tony knows Edwards, Editor of "El Mercurio" newspaper and that the meeting was arranged by Donald Kendall, known around town as "Señor Pepsi Cola", a man with lots of VIP friends in Washington.

When Monti asks about the current situation in Chile, Tony replies: "It's a disaster. Allende is bad news for Chile. He's a Marxist and I guarantee he'll nationalize the big corporations, especially the copper industry. Then watch things go to hell. Another thing - I'll bet Mitchell's visit there has something to do with Allende."

OCTOBER 11, 1970, NEW YORK

Tony is packing for a trip to Iran when his secretary enters, in tears: "Mr. Berlotti. Bad news. Your team in Bolivia were burned to death while asleep. The report says it was an accident."

Tony shakes his head in denial, walks to the window and finally snarls: "No goddamn way!"

"What can I do, Mr. Berlotti?" asks his Secretary. Everyone working closely with Tony recognizes that his gruff exterior hides a generous and compassionate heart.

"Notify and arrange for their next of kin to travel to Oruro, pay all their expenses. Do whatever you can to help them. Then get Dr. Monti on the line and bring me a cappuccino."

Five minutes later, cappuccino in hand, Tony is on the phone with Monti. "Frank, the sonofabitches struck! I know it!"

"I had my suspicions, too, Tony"

"I know my team in Bolivia were burned to death in their sleep and I lay odds they were deliberately torched. Please, do me a favor. Send Misha down there to investigate. I'm leaving tomorrow for Tehran to open an office, rent an apartment and interview for an office manager. I'll be at the Intercontinental Hotel."

"I'll take care of everything. But be careful, Tony. Hill may be there to set you up."

"Don't worry, I know how he operates. See you in a few weeks."

LATE OCTOBER, 1970, TEHRAN, IRAN

At the Intercontinental Hotel, Tony is in his room, sleeves rolled-up, smoking a cigar, and drinking, as always, a cappuccino, when the phone rings. "Hello."

"It's me, Tony and this needs to be secure."

Tony recognizes Dr. Monti's voice, hits the scrambler button on a unit attached to his hotel phone, puffs on his cigar and tells his most trusted friend to continue.

"Tony, you were right. Misha confirms it was arson. Reports are that three men, known locally as Los Machos, torched the cabin on orders by Jose via Carlo. Carlo, as you know is Sammy Shickarian's friend in Vegas. Hill was not in Bolivia at the time."

"How convenient! But I'm sure he was involved. Now we need to find out what part Carlo played in the conspiracy. I'm interviewing an ex-SAVAK agent tomorrow. I may form an investigative and protection team."

SAVAK, the Iranian acronym for Security Organization of the Country, better known as the Secret Police, was formed in 1957 under Shah Muhammad Reza Pahlavi. SAVAK agents were trained by the CIA and Israel's Mossad. They are known to have used CIA, Mossad and FBI methods for investigation and interrogation, but also practiced torture and murder to intimidate those opposed to the Shah.[10]

Tony's interview with the ex SAVAK agent begins in Tony's office at 118 Elizabeth II Blvd. at 11 A.M. A husky, middle aged man, bushy mustache, wearing the typical SAVAK uniform of black suit, white shirt and black tie, greets him with a firm handshake and perfect English: "Good morning Mr. Berlotti. I'm Jamshid and it's a pleasure meeting you after our phone conversation yesterday. Here is my résumé."

Tony looks him over and sees a powerfully built, well mannered and apparently self assured man. He asks Jamshid to sit down, and studies the résumé.

"Your record as a SAVAK agent is impressive. When and why did you leave the Shah's secret police?"

"I left about six months ago. It was because of a disagreement with a superior."

"What was the disagreement?"

"My superior wanted me to assassinate an American for personal reasons. I investigated and found the American did nothing wrong. When I refused the assignment, he began making my work difficult. I quit and took several agents with me. As my résumé indicates, I lived and studied in the United States. Americans are some of my favorite people."

---

[10] For example, when this author was working in Iran in the mid seventies and applied for an Iranian Commercial Pilot License, SAVAK investigated me. I learned from Tony Berlotti that they not only had copies of my work history and 201 file, but also checked with my friends and the history of my parents and family in Italy and the U.S. After six months of investigation, I was approved, checked-out in a military trainer by Colonel Vakil Mosafari, one of the Shah's personal pilots and issued Commercial License Number 508.

Tony looks him over again, lights a cigar and continues reading. He stops, opens a small box on his desk, the asks: "How about a cigar, Jamshid?"

"Thank you, but no, Sir. I don't smoke and except under unusual circumstances, avoid alcohol."

"No problem. Now, if I hire you, it will be long hours and dangerous. Can you handle that?"

"Mr. Berlotti, I've always worked long hours and danger is my profession."

"That's good. I'd like to know more about you. Let's go for lunch."

Two weeks later, Tony attaches a Montico scrambler to the phone and calls Dr. Monti. "Frank, I lucked-out. I hired Jamshid and four other ex SAVAK agents. They know what's going on around here, have big-time connections and swore, on the Koran, to protect me. Jamshid will be my personal bodyguard. The others, under Jamshid, will tail Dan Hill."

"Are you sure you can trust those agents?"

"Not yet. But don't worry, I'll set some bait. To tell you how good they are, Jamshid already found out that Hill called Sammy in Vegas and told him to warn Carlo to stay away from the mob in Chicago because FBI agent Bill Roemer is tailing Sam Giancana."

"That's certainly fast work, Tony, but I encourage you to set bait."

"Stop worrying, Frank. Listen, please have more X-MIT bugs ready for me on my return. Another thing, I finally installed Addabbo's split-paraboloid antenna[11], so let's go on the air at ten."

The next morning, after last night's conversation with Dr. Monti, Tony, convinced that Hill and others are determined to destroy his conspiracy photo, makes a quick trip to New York to pick up his new Montico electronic bugs and spend the year end holidays with his family. During the Christmas week, Tony calls Nunzio Addabbo, also on vacation in New York. "Nunzio, I'm home for a few days. How about meeting me for lunch tomorrow; the usual place. I have something to tell you."

---

[11] This antenna remains a "Trade Secret" because the Army Ballistic Missile Agency requested full disclosure as an unsolicited proposal without financial considerations. Addabbo refused their request.

The meeting takes place, but Tony does not reveal any conspiracy details. He does confirm that he has a conspiracy photo that will make history, that Dan Hill was involved and he will show it to Nunzio soon. He warns Addabbo to avoid Hill and asks him to report if Hill tries to contact him. Addabbo has known Tony well since 1953 and trusts him. They meet frequently at business conventions, social functions and have vacationed together. While he's convinced that Tony is involved in a dangerous clandestine operation, Nunzio has no clue it has anything to do with JFK's assassination. He knows Tony will, in his own time, confide in him. Nunzio is curious but content to wait.

THE YEAR OF 1971

Tony spends much of his time shuttling between New York and Iran, frustrated with his unsuccessful attempts to obtain satisfactory mining contracts for the Zahedan copper project. As an aggressive but principled mover and shaker, Tony is not pleased with the procrastination involved and invariably rejects negotiating with middle-men and their none-to-subtle requests for "baksheesh" (bribes). Subcontractors soon learn that he will negotiate only with their managing directors. His frustration mounts when negotiating conditions don't improve. He decides to put the project on hold and begins exploring other proposed mining projects in Iran. He joins the local bridge club for a little diversion.

As the months pass, Tony continues to shuttle between Iran and the U.S., balancing his various commitments and priorities. His security chief, Jamshid, reports that Dan Hill has been traveling to the U.S., Bolivia, Chile and Mexico.

"Dan Hill told Carlo and Sammy," states Jamshid, "that his wife is still in Chile, that Allende has already put his Marxist plans in motion and that something needs to be done about it."

"Carlo told Hill, from Bolivia," continues Jamshid, "that with Johnny Roselli in prison, they'll make no assassination deal against Allende unless it comes down to him directly from the Committee. We also know Hill has been seeing a Manuel in Mexico but don't know why. And he has never, since we started monitoring his calls, mentioned a Mexico City photo to anyone."

Tony thanks Jamshid and explains that Hill wants to keep the conspiracy photo a secret to avoid his exposure in the conspiracy.

"Hill wants to destroy my photo, and probably me as well" states Tony, "because it appears to be the only evidence of who was involved with Oswald. Hill told me in Chile that one of my assignments would be a search for President Kennedy's real assassin. I strongly suspect he was involved in the assassination and said that to lure me into one of his traps."

"You mean," asks Jamshid. "Oswald was not the assassin?"

"According to my friend Dr. Monti, nitrate tests conducted on Oswald showed no evidence of gunpowder anywhere on his face or neck."

"That would prove Oswald didn't fire a rifle."

"That's right, Jamshid, and therein lies the mystery. Who killed Kennedy and why?"

"Don't worry, rais (Farsi for boss). We have him covered."

JULY 15, 1973, TEHRAN, IRAN

Hill answers the phone in his office. "Hello."

The voice on the other end, the one that sounds like Henry Kissinger's, is firm, "Dan, this is Louis in Geneva. Your lack of progress with Berlotti is worrying us. What seems to be the problem?"

"The problem is keeping up with him. He's constantly on the move, in and out of the city and country promoting his business ventures. And now that he's evidently on to us, he often uses aliases, rents cars and airplanes to evade me. Additionally, we're unable to tap into his phones because he has a scrambling system unknown to us. We trained him, remember?"

"Yes, and it was your brilliant idea to contract him, remember?"

"It's the best way to keep him in my sights."

"Well, you're not doing a good job and we hold you responsible for destroying that photo. Spend more time on Berlotti and less on your drug deals with the Vegas bunch."

"They don't know anything about the photo. You're the only one that knows."

"Then you should consider telling them. There's strength in numbers. Goodbye."

SEPTEMBER 11, 1973, LOS ANGELES AIRPORT

Late at night, Tony is at the Los Angels airport waiting for his flight to New York. He calls Dr. Monti. "Hello, Frank. I was in a meeting earlier when news broke about the coup in Chile. Is it true Allende committed suicide?"

"Not true. According to your man Tomas, Allende was shot by a young Army officer during the assault on the palace immediately following the saber-jet attack. General Augusto Pinochet Ugarte is now in command. Your predictions were right-on."

"Well, I hope some of the data I passed on to Hill had an effect on Allende's downfall, but you know I had absolutely nothing to do with the coup. But here's another prediction for you, Frank. Conditions will improve dramatically with Pinochet in the drivers-seat. Oh, there's my flight. Gotta' go."

SEPTEMBER 15, 1973, LAS VEGAS, NEVADA

At the Horseshoe Casino at about 10 P.M., Sammy Shickarian, downstairs in the restaurant, finishes a hamburger, lights a cigar and looks at his watch. Seconds later, Hill walks in, spots Sammy, walks over and sits down.

"Hello, Sammy. That Iran Air flight was a disaster."

"So, what else is new. Listen, we got a report that an ex CIA agent knows who shot Kennedy. Jesus, if Carlo finds out you're in deep shit. Know anything about it?"

"Sammy, I hear rumors like that all the time. Everybody with a theory on the assassination is writing a book on it. It's become a fucking cottage industry! Another thing, what do you mean, if Carlo finds out I'm in deep shit? You're in this as deep as all of us!"

"If Carlo finds out, he'll finger you as the snitch. You know Carlo, he doesn't like witnesses."

Hill closes his eyes, rubs his chin, then taps his fingers on the table.

He leans over confidentially and whispers, "Sammy, I just got a brilliant triple whammy idea!"

"OK, Mr. Genius. What's your brilliant idea this time?"

"Look, we all know FBI agent Roemer is putting heat on Giancana. I'm sure Roemer is getting his information from that ex CIA agent in New York."

"How do you know that?" asks Sammy.

"Because that agent," lies Hill, " was involved with the mob to eliminate Castro. Giancana doesn't trust him after their relationship turned sour. We'll negotiate with Carlo to torch him at home. Carlo will appreciate the tip. It'll take the heat off Giancana and there's your whammy!"

"Hill, that's only a double whammy!"

"Yeah, Sammy. The third whammy is my secret."

"Oh, fuck! Why do you spooks always have to have so damn many secrets?"

"You know we always operate on a need to know basis. And you don't need to know. Anyway, get word to Carlo. I'll provide the agent's address tomorrow. Then I'm back to Iran for important work."

"Come on, Hill," wheedles Sammy. "What's the third whammy?"

"Good night, Sammy." *"There's no way I'm going to tell him,"* concludes Hill as he leaves, *"that destroying the conspiracy evidence is my primary goal and third whammy. Yes, in a couple of days, Berlotti, his house, family and photo will be history."*

With these hardened assassins, criminals and drug smugglers, killing innocent 'civilians' like Tony's family doesn't impact them at all. They are of a sub-human species without a conscience.

SEPTEMBER 15-16, 1973

Dr. Monti and family join Tony and his family for two fun packed days at Tony's beach house. The young adults spend hours racing around on their dune buggies while the seniors play bridge. Before leaving, they plan a Thanksgiving reunion at Dr. Monti's summer home in New England. On September 17, Tony's son, George and Dr. Monti's son, Peter, return to their respective colleges and Tony's daughters resume their high school studies. Days later, Tony flies to Los Angeles for meetings with geological consultants regarding proposed mining projects in Chile and Arizona.

SEPTEMBER 18, CHICAGO

Hill calls Sammy from Chicago. "Well, did you get word to Carlo?"

"Yes. He said he'll do it because he owes Giancana a favor.

"Excellent. Sam will appreciate less heat from the Feds. I'm on my way to Iran. Call me after it happens."

"You got it."

Tony's Los Angeles meetings are productive, necessitating a trip to Phoenix to meet a prospective client. Before leaving Los Angeles he arranges to have a king-size silver samovar engraved for Gloria for their upcoming 25th wedding anniversary. The engraving reads: "FOR GLORIA, MY QUEEN". Tony's abiding love for Gloria, and his generosity, are known to all. It is as much a part of him as his gruff, machismo image.

He once told Nunzio, "If Gloria wants to retire in Shangri La, I'll build a palace for her there."

As the sun begins it's southern declination, foliage on the East coast is a riot of color with varying shades of flame, gold, bronze and burgundy. Rural New York and New England are an adventure to treasure for sightseers. The large two-story Berlotti home at the end of a quiet cul-de-sac, surrounded by tall oaks, maples and fruit trees, is such a sight to behold.

During her nightly call from Tony, Gloria comments, "Everything's good, Tony. Nancy and Mary are upstairs doing their homework and I'm ready to watch for news about Chile. When are you coming home, darling? We miss you!"

"I miss you, too, sweetheart! I'll be home in four or five days. You know I love you, baby."

"And I adore you, big guy."

After a late dinner in downtown Phoenix, Tony returns to his hotel and tries to call Gloria again. The line is busy. One hour later, after three tries, the line is still busy. *It can't be one of the girls. They should be in bed. Bet someone left the phone off the hook. Guess they'll discover it in the morning.*

As Tony falls asleep in Phoenix, a car arrives and parks in front of an empty "For Sale" lot next to the Berlotti home. In the cool serenity of this east coast neighborhood, now in total darkness, men's voices can be heard whispering in Spanish. Seconds later, one man whispers, "Ahora" (now). Three silhouettes exit the car, carrying small cases, and move quickly around the house. The whispering continues. Moments later a tiny flash is seen and a voice whispers, "Vamanos" (let's go). Seconds later ignition is heard and the silhouetted car pulls away from the cul-de-sac. The tiny flash suddenly bursts into flames and within seconds the house is engulfed in a violent blaze.

In Phoenix the next morning, before breakfast, Tony tries to call Gloria again. The line is dead. He calls Dr. Monti. Gina answers, "Hello?"

"Gina, it's me. I haven't been able to reach Gloria. Last night I got a busy signal. This morning the line is dead. Could you have Frank check it out?"

"He's already at the shop. I'll call right away. Don't worry, he'll send someone to your house."

Hours later, in front of a blackboard explaining a metallurgical flow-diagram to six men seated around a conference table, a secretary enters the room and asks Tony to pick up the phone for a call from Dr. Monti.

"Hello, Frank."

As Tony listens, initially in stunned silence, he suddenly makes a fist, curses, pounds the table and slams down the receiver. He tersely excuses himself, picks up his briefcase and rushes out of the room. The six men look at one another in bewilderment.

"What the hell?..." one of them mutters to everyone in general.

At approximately midnight the same day, Tony arrives by taxi to be confronted by a sight he will never forget: what was once his home is now the sight of rubble and ashes surrounded by yellow police ribbon. Dr. Monti receives Tony with a long bear-hug, unable to speak.

"Frank! Where are the girls?"

Holding Tony tighter, he cries, "Oh, God, Tony, I'm so sorry. Gloria and the girls never got out."

Tony drops to his knees and pounds his fists in the gravel until they are bloodied. His sobs are those of a man who has taken such a blow that all of the air is knocked out of his lungs. He raises red-rimmed eyes to his friend.

"I'll kill the bastards if it takes the rest of my life, every ounce of energy I possess, every cent I own. They'll have to kill me to stop me."

Tony stands and walks around in circles, crying, cursing, kicking dirt. "Sons-a-bitches!! It was them, Frank!"

"Yes, I'm sure," Frank agrees sadly. "The investigation continues tomorrow."

"I don't need an investigation! I know! It was arson-just like the one they pulled in Bolivia!"

"Yes, Tony," Frank takes him by the arm. "Let's wait for George and then have some coffee. I've called him at school."

A car races into the cul-de-sac and slams on its brakes behind the taxi. George gets out and runs to his father. "Dad! Uncle Frank told me about the fire. Where are Mom and the girls?"

"He didn't tell you?"

"Tell me what? What, Uncle Frank?"

Tony grabs his son, smothering him in his arms. "We're all that's left, son, just you and me."

The next morning, two police cars and two fire department cars are at the scene. Officials are behind the ribbon taking photos, inspecting rubble and making notes. Tony, George and Dr. Monti arrive. When they move under the ribbon, an inspector waves them off.

As they continue, he approaches, shouting, "Are you guys blind? I waved you off!"

"It's Okay, officer. I'm Tony Berlotti. This was my..."

The cocky inspector interrupts, sarcastically, "I don't care who the hell you are. I told you..."

Tony slams the inspector to the ground and, within seconds, the trio is confronted by a police officer with his gun drawn. "Freeze!" he commands.

Tony steps slowly away from the stunned inspector on the ground and addresses the officer with the assuredness that comes from leadership, "Put your gun away. I'm Tony Berlotti."

The officer recognizes the name, expresses concern for Tony's loss, holsters his weapon and introduces himself. "Mr. Berlotti. I'm Police Chief Cox. We're all sorry for your loss. Fire Chief Witherspoon advised me it was arson. Any clues on who may have done this?"

"Absolutely none," lies Tony.   *"That bastard Hill had something to do with this!"*

Chief Cox tilts his head and gives Tony a tight-lipped, superficial smile. It's obvious he's thinking, *"I'm not sure I believe you."* Then shaking Tony's hand, "Very well, Mr. Berlotti. You need to file police and fire reports as soon as possible. Again, I'm very sorry."

That night at Dr. Monti's apartment, Tony, George, Dr. Monti, Gina and Peter are sitting around the dinner table, silent, pushing food around on their plates in a futile attempt at eating.

Gina breaks the silence. "Come on, guys! Eat something."

George pushes his plate away. "Sorry, Aunt Gina." Then, abruptly, "Dad, do you know who did it?"

"I think so," Tony is thoughtful. "But this is not the time to tell you. As soon as we take care of the funeral arrangements, you need to leave school."

"Leave school? Why?"

"What I mean is - you need to change schools and your identity."

"Change my identity? Why?"

"Because I have an idea who was responsible and you'll probably be the next target. We'll get you a new name and into a different school. Then I'll go after the arsonists."

"Okay, Dad, but, if you know who they are, I want to get the bastards who killed Mom, Mary and Nancy!"

Tony looks at his son with tenderness. Everyone's emotions are raw.

"You'll get your chance, son, but first things first. You must finish your education."

"Your father is right, George," adds Dr. Monti. "Don't worry, Tony. After the burial services, I'll make arrangements for George's new identity and you can return to Iran. And, George, this is important. You must sever relations with everyone at your existing school, girlfriends included."

George nods his head in agreement and understanding.

"Uncle Tony," shouts Peter, "I want to get the arsonists, too!"

"Yes, and I make it unanimous," states Gina, pounding the table. "But for now, let's eat."

One week later, sitting in first class during his late night flight to Tehran, Tony pulls out a photo of his wife and daughters. He rubs his eyes, kisses the photo and holds it to his chest. *"Dan Hill, if you were responsible... and I'm damn sure you were... I'm going to kill you. I don't care if you are C.I.A., F.B.I., or a Five Star General. You'll pay for this, you bastard!"*

Two weeks later, Tony enrolls in a "Learn to Speak Farsi" class at the Iran-American Society. At the first class session, Tony picks a front row seat, sets-up a tape recorder and waits, along with six women and four men, for the instructor to arrive. Tony's bodyguard, Jamshid, acting as a newspaper photographer, is sitting in the last row next to the door. The instructor enters, introduces himself, identifies each student from the sign-up sheet, then gives a puzzled look at Jamshid.

"Sir, are you Mister Spencer?"

"No, Sir. I'm here to take publicity photos for the American newspaper."

Seconds later, the door opens, a man enters, looks around, then makes his way quietly to a seat behind Tony. Jamshid identifies the man, palms the weapon in his shoulder holster under his jacket and watches.

"Sorry I'm late. It just started raining and I waited in the car until it let up," the newcomer says.

The voice and distinctive Bostonian accent identify Hill, but Tony does not turn around. The instructor looks at the sign-up sheet and asks, "You must be Mister Spencer?"

"That's correct," lies Hill.

Two hours later, the instructor dismisses the class. Jamshid remains at the rear of the room watching Hill. Tony knows who is seated behind him but he rises slowly, turns and acts surprised. "Well, Dan Hill! What's with the Spencer bit?"

"Never mind, Berlotti. I've been trying to reach you for weeks. Listen," whispering, "I have an important assignment for you."

"Of course. You only come around when you need a favor. What is it this time?"

"Meet me tomorrow at 0900 at Ghalehmorgi Military Air Base main gate. It's a surprise."

"OK, I'll be there."

The next morning, as Tony is alone drinking coffee, looking at a flight chart in the Pilot Lounge, Hill enters at 0915 with a surprised look. "They told me at the gate that you were already in here. How did you get in?"

"I have connections. You told me in Chile that I have a foot in every door, remember?"

"So I see. Anyway, I'm making arrangements for you to get an Iranian pilot license."

Tony finishes his coffee, then pulls out his Iranian pilot's license. "You mean like this?"

"How the hell did you get that license?"

"Never mind, Hill. Now, what favor do you want this time?"

"We want you to fly up to Bandar Pahlavi on the Caspian Sea. There's an Armenian up there in paper mill construction by the name of Vosarikian who is also an arms dealer. We need to get him on our team. Meet and befriend him - you're good at that. Also, we're keeping an eye on Ayatollah Khomeini. He's been hiding out in France but reports indicate he's mounting a strong campaign to overthrow the Shah. Let us know if you hear anything on this. Contacting Vosarikian is urgent."

Tony takes his time, then, "Don't count on it. I'll give you my decision next week."

"You have a contract with us! Louis says they are counting on your help!"

"I operate on my terms, remember? Tell Louis I'll think about it. Have a nice day. Bye."

CHAPTER 10

HIT-TEAM REUNION

JULY 4, 1974, IRAN

Four months later Tony is on his secure phone with Dr. Monti in New York.

"Frank, have you uncovered Mister Louis's organization?"

"Sorry, Tony. Not yet. But Misha says, 'don't rule out the MOSSAD'. Louis seems to have a connection with an ex-MOSSAD agent called Max Stein; probably a code name. Another thing, my friends at the CIA deny knowing Dan Hill. Interesting?"

"Yes, very interesting but I'm not surprised. I have an idea to..." Tony's conversation is interrupted by the buzzing of his walkie-talkie and the Morse code: JAM#1. "Frank, I have Jamshid calling me with an important message. I'll get back to you soon."

Tony cradles the phone and keys his mike: "Go ahead, Jamshid"

"Good news, Rais. You don't mind being addressed Rais?"

"Not at all. I learned it means Boss at my first Farsi lesson - remember?"

"Yes, Sir. Well, Rais, you may want to cancel your bridge game tonight."

"You know I will if it's important. What's up?"

"Dan Hill met some of his 'friends' yesterday at the Varian Casino. My cousin is in charge of security there. One of the men is the one sitting next to Oswald in your Mexico City photo. We have photos and a cassette tape."

"Good work, Jamshid! Come right over."

A half hour later, Tony lights a cigar and begins pacing.

"Ah, let's hope we hit pay-dirt!"

Minutes later the voice of Tony's secretary is heard on the intercom announcing Jamshid's arrival.

"Here, Sir, are the photos and cassette tape of the men. We followed Dan Hill and, incredibly, this is what happened."

Tony looks at the photos, puts on headphones, puffs on his cigar and starts the tape. The Varian Casino is small and elegant.

On this night, the blackjack tables, roulette wheels and baccarat tables are mostly occupied. All the men wear jackets, ladies in long gowns or suits; never shorts or jeans. A man plays soft background music on a baby grand and there are fresh flowers everywhere. Rials are the local currency. Dan Hill is seen as he enters the casino, looks around and spots Sammy Shickarian, Carlo Perez and Jose Martinez at the bar. Carlo's two bodyguards are seen observing from a distance. Jamshid and the cassette provide the narrative explaining the photos. "Here, Hill walks to the bar and acts surprised," Jamshid explains.

"Sammy! What a surprise seeing you here."

"Dan, how you been, pal? Meet Carlo and Jose." They shake like it was their first meeting.

"Get us a table, Sammy," orders Carlo. "I'm hungry."

Sammy blows cigar smoke into the air, pulls out a roll of rials, flags the maitre-d', then winks and palms him a bill. "Hey, pal, get us a nice quiet table and send over our drinks."

"Yes Sir. I have a corner table where no one will bother you. Follow me, gentlemen."

The polite maitre-d' escorts them to the table. Carlo looks around, nods his head in agreement, then signals his bodyguards who take seats at a nearby table. Carlo sits with his back to the wall between Sammy and Hill. Jose sits next to Sammy. The maitre-d' flags a waiter and leaves.

"Yeah," bellows Sammy, "this is the perfect table. Hey, waiter bring us another round before we order and make mine a double."

The conspirators begin a conversation. The maitre-d' is seen nodding at Rashid, one of Jamshid's agents, observing the action from a distance. Rashid nods at Mehdi, another of the agents sitting alone at a table in view of the conspirators. Sammy chugs his drink, waves for another, blows cigar smoke across the table and looks at Carlo. "So, Señor. How are things in Bolivia?"

"Good. You breeng dee money?" Carlo goes right to the point of the meeting.

"Jesus Christ! We're here five minutes and he's talkin' money already. Relax, Carlo. Enjoy yourself. This isn't Vegas, but you gotta' admit it's pretty nice. Want a girl? Bet I can arrange to get you a pretty Iranian chick. I hear they're hot stuff." It's vintage Sammy.

"Never mind dee fucking broads. You not in Vegas now. Beside, if I want some ass, I make dee arrangements. I said - you breeng dee money?"

Sammy takes another drink, then looks at Hill. "See, Dan, all he thinks about is money, drugs and killin'. Carlo never enjoys himself. But maybe he enjoys killin'." He lights a fresh cigar, waves for another drink, pulls out a large envelope and waves it at Carlo. "Yeah, I brought the dough. Here, Carlo. Go ahead - count it. And how about you, Hill? Did you bring my money?"

"Only half, Sammy. You didn't finish the job. You'll get the rest when Berlotti goes!"

Hill passes an envelope to Sammy. Sammy slams it on the table. "Now listen, you spy bastard! You never said anything about Berlotti. You said, 'torch his house'. Carlo had his Los Machos boys torch it. What the hell else do you want?"

Carlo taps the table and motions that they whisper.

Hill leans forward. "Sammy, you fucking idiot. It was to be torched with Berlotti in it! I made it clear to you that he knows our connection to Oswald, Ruby and the assassination! The guy is dangerous. He has proof, connections and plenty of money. He's a mean sonofabitch! And now that you killed his family, he's really on the war path! I know him - I work with him."

Sammy waves his arms, orders more drinks, then glares at Carlo. "It was your dumb-ass Machos who blew it! I told you Berlotti had a make on you and Hill!"

Carlo pulls on his mustache, then crosses his arms. His voice is icy. "Tell me, Señor Hill. How dis Berlotti know about us?"

"Hey - I've been a spy for twenty-five years. When I tell you he knows, you better believe he knows. It was a damn lucky fluke that put him on to us."

Sammy interrupts by waving his arms, then blows smoke at Hill. "A lucky fluke? What fluke?"

"Let's have another drink and I'll tell you."

Carlo slams the table. "Never mind dee dreenks. We order and you esplain when we eat!"

José flags the waiter. After they order, Carlo and Sammy go to the men's room, followed by one bodyguard. Hill engages Josè in conversation. Rashid and Mehdi nod as Carlo and Sammy return.

As they begin eating, Carlo waves a steak knife at Hill. "OK, Señor Hill. What eez all dee fluke sheet?"

They all stare at him as Hill leisurely finishes his glass of wine. "Well, Carlo—back in early 1963, the Finance Committee made the decision to hit President Kennedy and insisted on an outside cut-out. Why they chose Sammy to pick the hit-team I'll never know!"

Sammy picks up his soup bowl. "Don't be a smart ass, Hill or you'll get this God damn soup in your face! What's this fuckin' fluke crap and wha..."

Dishes jump and wine spills as Carlo slams the table, glaring at Sammy. "Shut up, you 'tonto-huevon' (Spanish for dumb-ass) and make Hill finish. You gettin' drunk!"

No one crosses Carlo. Sammy looks like a petulant child but remains silent as Hill continues.

"In any case, Hoffa was told to have Sammy make a money transfer. Sammy went to Puerto Rico and received instructions and a down-payment from Lansky's men. Then he tried to get..."

Carlo interrupts by sticking his index finger on Hill's chin, shouting:

"Stop you stalling and get to dee fucking fluke! I losing mi patience."

"Don't shout and don't stick your finger in my face! You're on my territory now!"

Carlo fingers Hill's chin again. "I talk to zee people on my payroll any way I want and you ain't no esception! Comprende?"

"Careful, Carlo. One phone call from me and you'll have trouble leaving Iran!"

Carlo glares. "And you a 'tonto-huevon' too! One word to my men and you never leave dees table. Remember, Señor Hill, I pay you mucho dollars and keep you people supply with dee white stuff that make you rich. You nobody without me."

"And you remember, Carlo, I gave you Kennedy's itinerary for the hit. You couldn't have pulled it off without me. So, let's stop quibbling and concentrate on how to handle Tony Berlotti."

"Very well, Hill," adds José, "explain the fluke. And who is Tony Berlotti ?"

"Carlo, remember when you were in Mexico City the last week in September 1963?"

"I remember. So?"

"As you know, the plan was to have John Richardson I.D. Oswald so he could make the hit when Oswald exited the rear door of the Book Depository. When Richardson got killed, I was forced to make a last minute decision to replace him. Jack Ruby was the man! When I knew you would meet Oswald in Mexico, I arranged to meet Ruby there. We were in disguise when you and Oswald were having lunch. I had stirred up Ruby until he was in a killing mode. I was afraid he'd make trouble, so I had a stranger take a photo of us with you and Oswald in the background. That way I could show him the photo later. But first, the stranger took a photo with his camera before using mine. That stranger, Señor Carlo, was Berlotti. So, you see, he can now I.D. you, too, and has the photo to prove the conspiracy."

As a waiter distracts Carlo's bodyguards, Rashid and Mehdi take photos of the conspirators. The maitre-d' enters a private room and gives a thumbs-up to another agent monitoring a recorder. Carlo refills his wine glass, takes a drink, looks around, then makes a thumbs-down gesture.

"We keel heem before I leave Iran!"

"Don't be ridiculous, Carlo. You could never pull it off here. Berlotti is on to us. He has money, connections and protection. And he has the proof of the conspiracy. We must get the negative of that photo. Don't worry, as long as I know where he is, we can set him up. But not in Iran. I assure you, if he discovers that your Machos torched his family, we're all in deep trouble, big time!"

Carlo snarls at Hill, livid with rage. "Why you have heem take dee photo? For CIA, you fuckin' stupido! What you propose to do now, Señor Hill?"

"We wait. I'm being transferred to Las Vegas. We'll set him up after he leaves Iran. I already have a plan to ambush him in Mexico."

"Vegas is my town," brags Sammy. "Get him there and I'll have him bumped-off!"

"Shut up, Sammy! Eat dee rice pudding," orders Carlo. "Si, Hill ees right. We keel heem on our territory."

"I'm so glad you agree, Carlo," adds Hill, sarcastically. "Now you tell me - why did Oswald exit the front door of the Depository instead of the rear. Why were there shots from the Grassy Knoll? I didn't see any of your Macho men there."

Carlo takes a long sip of wine and gives José the 'Go ahead' nod. José smiles, sips his wine, leans over and whispers. "All you smart guys in the CIA, FBI, Secret Service, even the local police are still wondering? Everything worked according to plan. Carlo was not sure about Oswald's reliability, so we placed Gabriel with him on the sixth floor. Oswald was supposed to wait until the motorcade turned left on Elm, then shoot Kennedy's driver and escape from the rear door, where your man Richardson would gun him down. Shooting the driver would stop the limo and Carlo would hit Kennedy. Carlo was right about Oswald. When the motorcade turned right on Houston Street, Oswald chickened-out and ran downstairs. He never fired his rifle. When I gave the radio signal to fire, Gabriel took the first two shots. The third shot came from the Grassy Knoll. Carlo took the fourth shot and hit Kennedy from the roof of the Dal-Tex Building. The fifth and sixth shots came from the Grassy Knoll and the seventh came from Gabriel - all seven shots in six seconds."

Carlo looks at Hill. José looks at Hill. As they wait for his reaction, Hill appears puzzled. "I was at the Grassy Knoll acting as a Secret Service agent and, like I said, I didn't see anybody there. But I heard the shots. Explain that one."

"Tell us, Señor Hill, how many shots did you hear?" asks José.

"Two." lies Hill.

José looks at Carlo. "CIA men have selective hearing."

"What's that supposed to mean, José?"

"I mean - there were three shots from the Grassy Knoll. I have it on tape! Now, since you didn't see anybody else there, you fired the shots - right?"

"Absolutely not! What I heard were two other shots."

"So," smiles José, "the third shot from the Grassy Knoll was yours!"

"No," lies Hill again, "You must be mistaken." Hill somewhat changes the direction. " There's a problem here, gentlemen. You admit shots from the Grassy Knoll but you don't explain them."

Carlo gives José an approval wave. "Why you theenk José be my communications and explosives expert? José, tell heem."

"It was easy. Your experts failed to examine the Grassy Knoll trees. Several years ago I perfected a small remote controlled explosive device. We set two of them in the trees two nights before your President arrived. So, you see, all the people who said they saw or heard shots from the Grassy Knoll were correct."

"Yes," whispers Carlo, "And eef you talk about it - we keel you."

"Don't worry," responds Hill, "Nothing leaves this table. No one needs to know. I do have another important question, but first I need to visit the men's room."

Sammy gets up and staggers out behind Hill. With Hill and Sammy out of sight, José moves to Carlo's side, speaking quietly, "Carlo, you were right. Since I set only two remote charges, Hill had to have fired the third shot from the Grassy Knoll. He probably hit Kennedy from the front."

"Si! He not follow instructions. He almost ruin dee operation and espose us. I never like or trust heem. Ahora tenemos que matar el bastardo." (Now we must kill the bastard).

"I'll have Manuel take care of it after we leave Iran."

"Si! And make it luke like dee accident!"

Hill and Sammy return to the table and Carlo and José wait for Hill to ask his 'important' question. "As I was going to ask before I left... " Carlo interrupts.

"Wait! Manuel tell me when we watch dee FBI office in Dallas, he see you drive car with una señorita. Who dee lady?"

"Manuel must be mistaken. There was no lady in my car. I was with Ruby, conditioning him to hit Oswald."

Carlo and José look at each other with skepticism, no doubt thinking, *"he's lying again"*.

Sammy lights a fresh cigar and blows smoke in the air. "Lay off, Carlo. Ruby did a good job, just the way you like it. No witness!"

"Yes," adds Hill. "Now, Carlo. Why did Oswald exit the front door instead of the rear. Why did he go home, get a gun, shoot a police officer, then go to the Texas Theater?"

Carlo picks up his wine glass and leans back. "Esplain to heem, José."

Sammy blows smoke at Jose. "Yeah, José. Explain that!"

José lights a long cigar. His explanation is professorial and condescending. "As usual, the big shots are still guessing. Anyway, everything went according to plan, except for Oswald. He agreed to take the first shot at Kennedy's driver for twenty thousand dollars. We told him that right after the shooting he was to exit the back door and go to the theater, where a lady wearing a white raincoat would give him the cash."

"So," asks Sammy. "Why the hell didn't he go out the back door?"

"According to Gabriel, he chickened-out on the sixth floor, guessing he might be a patsy. Then he ran down to the lunch room, I guess to think about it. He must have figured he was being set up, so he decided to leave by the front door immediately. Since he was an employee, he could walk casually out the front door and no one would suspect anything. He was right."

"And," blowing more smoke, Sammy asks, "Why did he go to his room for the gun?"

"Simple," points José. "He correctly figured he was set up as a patsy and decided to take the money by force, if necessary. If he killed the policeman, he was probably in a panic to get to the theater before the lady departed. Of course, there was no lady and there was no money."

Tony's secure phone rings. He stops the tape, identifies the code and picks-up. "Hello, Frank."

"Some bad news, Tony." Frank's voice was weary, somber.

"What is it, Frank?"

"Gina was hit by a drunk driver. She's in critical condition."

"Oh, my God, Frank! I'm so sorry. What can I do...?"

"Nothing, Tony, but thank you. I just wanted you to know. I'll keep you posted. Anyway, let's keep our nightly communication schedule and don't worry about me. I'm OK, I guess, but Peter is taking it hard. So long."

Tony cradles the phone and rubs his eyes.

"What's wrong, Rais? Bad news?"

"Yes. Dr. Monti's wife was hit by a drunk driver. It's very serious. She's like a sister to me."

Jamshid pats Tony on the shoulder and says, "Perhaps you don't want to continue hearing the tape?"

But Tony says "Yes, play it, Jamshid."

The action resumes with Sammy. He has his arms crossed and is glaring at Hill.

"You said the guy in your car was Ruby. Are you sure it wasn't Roselli?

"Roselli? Are you crazy?"

"Hill, I might be a little drunk, but I'm not crazy. Roselli told me he might go to Dallas on the hit day to check-up on you guys. Was Roselli in Dallas on November 22, 1963?"

"If he was, I never saw him. The Committee didn't want any members involved - remember?"

Carlo turns icy stares at Hill and then Sammy. "If he was, hees own people will keel heem."

"Maybe he was at the Grassy Knoll with Hill," snaps Sammy, taking another drink.

"I told you," states Hill. "I was there alone, acting as a Secret Service agent! Now I have a question for you, Carlo. How did you and your Machos get away from the scene so quickly?"

"You a dumb fucking huevon (asshole)!" snarls Carlo. "I going to the men's room. José weel esplain."

Jose re-lights his cigar, savors a long drink of wine, smugly confident. "We did it with plenty of advance planning, thanks to your advance notice, Hill. Our timing was perfect. After we decided that the roof of the Dal-Tex Building would be Carlo's best vantage point, I acted as a supervisor for the Voice Of America. Access to the roof to obtain field strength readings for a new antenna was easy. Carlo, Manuel and me went up to the roof the first day. We had to confirm that there was a clear view of Elm Street from behind the parapet wall and adequate support for our gear. Carlo agreed that from this position he would need only one shot, so we left all our gear. Then..."

"What gear?" interrupts Sammy.

"We're expert mountain climbers, remember? We left Carlo's special design Astrolloy quick disconnect parapet wall anchor and rope, his telescopic rifle, a sleeping bag, a bottle of water and candy bars. Then on Thursday night, the day before your President arrived, Carlo accessed the roof and remained overnight. The next day, I was stationed between Elm and Main Streets, in clear view of the Dal-Tex Building and the Grassy Knoll. We timed our firing sequence to match the motorcades slowest speed, just after they turned left on Elm Street. We all had walkie-talkies. The firing didn't start until I gave the signal. According to my recorder, we did it in six seconds."

"So," asks Sammy, "I still want to know - how did you get away so fast?"

Jose was proud of their work and happy to talk. "Pepe was waiting behind the Book Depository near the car on Houston Street. Gabriel rappelled down the rear of the Depository, got into the car with Pepe and they drove between the sides of the Dal-Tex building and County Records Building. Manuel and Poncho were behind the Dal-Tex Building. When Carlo rappelled down, they all ran to the car and drove away without being stopped by anyone. From his rear view mirror, according to Pepe, the man he saw at the back of the Depository drove away in the opposite direction on Houston Street. Was that you, Hill?"

"Of course," admits Hill. "Remember, I was a Secret Service man with government plates on my car. I noticed that when Pepe first saw me he reached for his weapon, then held up. That was an extremely prudent decision."

"You didn't ask how I escaped," adds José, clearly enjoying center stage.

"Oh, yeah, José," slurs Sammy. "How did you get away?"

"In all the confusion, a lot of people ran away from the scene. I walked away quickly with some of them and met our car at the corner of Commerce and Houston. It went easier than we figured because all the action centered around Dealey Plaza[12]. That's it." Jose was clearly pleased with himself.

"That's it, escept we need to know how you, Señor Hill, got tied-up with Berlotti," states Carlo.

"It all started in 1967 when I was checking out a Panamanian by the name of Manuel Noriega. You see, he was sent first to Fort Gulick in Panama, then to Fort Bragg in the U.S. to study intelligence and psychological operations for the CIA."

"Noriega worked for the CIA?" asks Sammy.

"Indeed he did. He was gathering data in Omar Torrijos's headquarters in 1965. Anyway, later on, when I got word that Berlotti was in Chile, I got myself transferred there to stop the political moves being made by Allende. And, incidentally, find Berlotti. We heard his name mentioned at several functions. I located Berlotti and had Rusty Thompson set up a meeting with him. I've been following him ever since, but I have reason to believe that the negative of his conspiracy photo is with 'Luigi', whoever he is. Somehow, I've got to confirm that. We figured it would be easier to get our information with him on our side, so we gave him a part-time contract. Don't worry, we'll get him and the photo."

"You get to Vegas soon! I lose my patience and want heem muerto! (dead)."

"Don't worry, Carlo, I'll set him up for you after I relocate to Las Vegas."

Carlo rises and waves a farewell arm in dismissal. "Bueno, amigos. Nada mas. Vamanos." (OK friends. Nothing else. Let's go.). Sammy throws a wad of rials on the table and they all leave.

The tape ends at this point.

---

[12] See Plate 2AB for Plan of Dealey Plaza.

CHAPTER 11

TONY'S RAGE

Tony remains seated, staring at the tape. He removes his earphones, walks to the window, slams his hand on the sill, curses and turns to Jamshid. "Those no good bastards! They killed my dear wife and daughters, my team in Bolivia, President Kennedy, Oswald and probably Ruby. From now on it's war! How would you and some of your men like to come to the U.S. for a special assignment?"

"We would consider it an honor to work for you, anywhere." It was said with quiet sincerity.

"It will be dangerous."

"Rais, our entire careers have been subject to extreme danger and we are the survivors. I assure you - none of our team will refuse your assignment."

"Thank you, Jamshid. I'm in your debt, deeply! You know, I'm determined to eliminate them!"

"No need, Rais. We will kill all of them for you. What is your mobilization plan?"

The next morning in his apartment, drinking a cappuccino, still in a foul mood over last night's revealing tape, Tony prepares for a flight to Esfahan. He snarls as he answers the phone. "Yes!"

"What's wrong, Berlotti. You're not polite this morning. Have a bad night?"

Tony refrains from exploding. "No, it was actually very productive. So, Hill, what now?"

Their conversation is short and they agree to meet in Hill's office at 5 PM. Rashid invites Tony and Jamshid to join him at the Epicurean Restaurant for an important business lunch.

"Mr. Berlotti, the Montico bugs are working very well. We believe Mr. Hill wants to talk to you about Khomeini's war against the Shah. We now have Khomeini's son under surveillance because Hill is trying to get information from him..."

The lunch becomes a long strategy meeting and then Tony is driven to Hill's office at 5 PM.

"What the hell was so important that you couldn't come this morning, Berlotti?"

"You should be impressed. Even though I'm leaving Iran, I created 200 new jobs for the Iranians. It does enhance our American image, don't you think?" Tony asks rhetorically.

Hill is arrogant. "If I'm supposed to be impressed, Berlotti, I'm not. All it does is enhance your bank account. Now, what I told you about Khomeini is true. He's in France, but gaining local support to overthrow the Shah."

"I know. I fail to see how I can do anything about that."

"He has a son named Ahmed, who's about 28 years old. Ahmed's close friend is one of your engineers named Farzan. What we want you to do is get Farzan to find out from Ahmed where Khomeini is hiding and who his number one man is in Iran. Since you're now an expert in subliminal brainwashing techniques." Hill's tone was sarcastic. "It should be a piece of cake for you."

"I'm leaving soon to start a new project in Mexico." Tony states without apology.

"You can't refuse, Berlotti. We're counting on you!"

"I can refuse anything I want, Hill, and my answer is a definite 'No'! Another thing, my engineer Farzan is off limits, so don't get any ideas about using him. Do I make myself clear?"

Hill pounds the table in controlled rage. "Goddamn you, Berlotti! You have a contract with us!"

"Yes, as a Special Consultant to assist as MY schedule permits. There's no time now in my schedule, so make other arrangements. And remember, Hill, my Iranian engineer is off limits!"

Realizing he would lose this encounter and knowing Tony's volatility, Hill changes tactics.

"Look, Berlotti, I'm being transferred soon to switch hit between Vegas and Tucson. I'm to track a KGB agent named Boris Kruchenko. Perhaps you can monitor him until I arrive."

Tony lights a cigar, looks at his scheduling book, then ponders the offer, his unwavering gaze on Hill. He would like to see Hill squirm in Hell, but, for now, he needs Hill as much as Hill needs him. As he waits to answer, he thinks, *"You no good sonofabitch. I want you in my sights more than you do me."*

"Okay, Hill," Tony replies coolly. "I can handle that."

Satisfied with Tony's decision on this assignment, Hill provides him with data on Kruchenko. The next night, Tony enters the American Club in Tehran for a night of bridge. Tony joins his partner, Ali Morshid, already seated at a table. Minutes later,

Nunzio Addabbo enters, spots his partner, Ake Ramnor, at the coffee urn and walks over to him. On the way, as he passes Tony, they both do a double-take, and Nunzio calls out, "Tony!"

Tony stands and the two men greet each other with a bear hug. "Nunzio! I didn't know you were in Iran. What are you doing here?"

"I've only been here a short while. I'm Chief Resident Engineer on the Sar Cheshmeh copper project. How about you?"

The bridge director signals that play should begin.

"Nunzio, I have a lot to tell you."

"Good. Let's meet at the Intercontinental Hotel right after this session and catch up."

Three or so hours later, Tony and Nunzio are seated in the hotel lounge, drinking cappuccino. Jamshid, unknown to Nunzio, is seated nearby drinking green tea.

"Tony, old buddy, what's happened? Your play wasn't up to your usual standards tonight. And, forgive me, but you look like hell. What's wrong?"

Tony looks down at his hands outstretched on the table and his face reveals his emotions. There is naked pain in his eyes as he lifts them to Nunzio's.

"There was arson last year, Nunz. Our home was burned to the ground. Gloria and the girls died in the fire. Nunzio, It was no accident!"

Nunzio reaches over and holds Tony's arm. "My God, Tony. Gloria? Both the girls? No wonder you look so devastated. I'm speechless. Do you know who did it?"

"You bet your ass I do! And I'm gonna' get the sons-a-bitches!"

"Does this have anything to do with that photo you promised to show me?"

"Yes. You'll understand when I show you the picture. But, right now, it's too dangerous, Nunzio. Other people have been killed and I don't want to involve anyone else. I'm leaving Iran soon for a new project in Mexico, so let's keep in closer contact. It was such a surprise, meeting you tonight."

"Seeing you is always good, but your news is devastating. I can't tell you how sorry I am. Here's my business card. Try to pull yourself together, Tony, and get back in shape. And show me that photo next time we can get together."

One week later, before leaving Iran, Tony follows the maitre-d' into the dining room of the Gameroon Hotel in Bandar Abbas on the Persian Gulf. An attractive young lady intercepts them.

She dismisses the maitre-d', in Farsi, then smiles at Tony. "You are Mister Berlotti, yes?"

"Yes. Have we met? I don't recognize you."

"You may not recognize me but I once sat behind you in Farsi class. My name is Fahli. You seem to be alone. I would be pleased to have you join me for dinner."

Tony looks her over, smiling approvingly, then gives a discrete nod to Jamshid, Rashid and Mehdi, already seated nearby. He extends his arm to Fahli and she leads him to her corner table. Tony positions himself with his back to the wall.

After a couple of cocktails and small talk, Tony asks, "So, Fahli, what brings you to Bandar Abbas?"

"I'm going to my summer home on Kish island."

"I've never been there, but I hear it's Iran's best kept secret - for the rich and famous. Right?"

"Yes, it is lovely. We have so few American visitors...Since you haven't been there, I would be pleased to show you our island. We can fly to my home there in the morning, if you like."

Their conversation is interrupted by the waiter. He takes their order for Jujay Kabob (chicken on a skewer), rice and salad. Tony eyes Jamshid going to the men's room. The waiter leaves.

"I'll be happy to accept your offer, Fahli. For the moment, though, please excuse me. I'd like to wash my hands."

Seconds later in the men's room Jamshid tells Tony, "Rais, we know that woman. Mehdi saw her in Tehran with Dan Hill on two occasions."

"Thanks, Jamshid. I figured it was a set-up. Why would an Iranian come to a Farsi class? Have her Kabob spiked - enough to send her to the hospital - but don't kill her."

An hour or so later, Tony and Fahli are having dessert. Tony acts excited about flying to Kish Island with her, but thinks, *"She should be in la-la land soon."*

Moments later, Fahli looks puzzled. "Tony, I feel so bad. I'm dizzy and my stomach hurts."

As she collapses, Tony summons the maitre-d' who immediately calls for an ambulance.

Two hours later, Tony and his agents are alone in the hotel lobby, in a huddle.

Jamshid reports. "The doctors say she is in no danger. Rashid and Mehdi went through her effects. She is a registered opium addict and high-class prostitute, Rais. Hill probably uses her for special assignments such as this."

"Very good. Keep her under surveillance, Mehdi. Hill may try to use her to con my Iranian engineer in the Khomeini deal. Jamshid and I will head back to Tehran in the morning."

The next afternoon, Tony is in his office packing to leave Iran.

He answers the phone. "Hello."

"Berlotti, I called yesterday. Your secretary said you were in Bandar Abbas. I called there and they said you checked out. I didn't know you were in Bandar Abbas."

"You didn't? *Lying sonofabitch!*"

"How would I know. You never tell me where you're going."

"Well, Hill, now I am telling you. I'm leaving Iran in a couple of days. I'll keep in touch. And remember, my Iranian engineer is off limits! So long."

Tony hangs up without giving Hill a chance to protest.

CHAPTER 12

ACTION IN VEGAS

EARLY AUGUST, 1974, LOS ANGELES AND NEW YORK

Three days after Hill's attempted set-up, Tony meets his team at the LAX baggage claim. "Good luck in Vegas and Tucson, men. Jamshid and I will see you soon. Hoda Hafez." (good bye).

Tony and Jamshid fly to New York. That night Tony arrives at Dr. Monti's apartment. He is greeted by Peter, who can not hold back his tears.

"Peter, what's wrong?"

"Uncle Tony, Mom died this morning. She didn't recover from the car accident. Dad is at the hospital. We knew you were coming, that's why I'm here."

Tony smothers Peter in his arms as both remain silent in their grief. Finally, Tony leads Peter to the kitchen for a glass of water, then picks up the phone. "I'm calling George to have him meet us at the hospital. Then we'll go and try to comfort your father."

AUGUST 12, 1974, NEW YORK

Tony and Dr. Monti are at MaMa Mia's Restaurant having lunch.

"Tony, there's nothing we can do now. The drunken S.O.B. who hit Gina was from Chicago, uninsured, and he died this morning."

"I know, Frank. My men also found out he was homeless and driving a stolen car. Looks like we were destined to be early widowers. First, Gloria and the girls, now Gina."

"Tony, the only way I can cope with losing Gina is to keep busy - mentally and physically active. I need to feel I'm doing something worthwhile. Let me help you get the assassins you're after. At least I can have the satisfaction of helping to avenge your losses."

"No way, Frank! Give yourself some time, friend. You're not equipped to handle all this cloak-and-dagger crap." Tony was thoughtful, then, " But...maybe you can help, indirectly."

"Anything, Tony. Just tell me what to do and I'll do it."

"I'll work it out, and soon, I promise. But next June, Peter gets his engineering degree and George his law degree so, for now, let's concentrate on our sons. They're all we have left, Frank."

They pick-up their wine glasses and make a silent toast as they think about their losses.

AUGUST 14, 1974, NEW YORK

Two days later in his office, as Dr. Monti is at his computer, the phone rings. "Hello."

"Hello, Frank. If your offer to help still stands, how soon could you come to Las Vegas and Tucson for a couple of days to show my SAVAK team your new surveillance gear?"

"I can come anytime, Tony. But I'm not sure about showing your men my latest gear. How do you know those Iranians can be trusted?'

"They're as loyal to me as Misha is to you and I can prove it with your help. Interested?"

"Knowing they're unconditionally loyal is the only way I'll show my latest gear. When do we leave?"

"Pack your bag, Frank. You won't be disappointed.."

The next day at 42,000 feet, en-route to Las Vegas, Tony awakens from a short nap and nudges Frank. "I forgot to tell you. George called last night. He made black belt."

"That's great. I wish Peter would get more physical instead of sitting behind a computer all the time with Judy Attwater. He says she's a computer genius and would like to bring her into our organization when they graduate."

"Sounds like it could be a bonus, Frank. Computers are the wave of the future - I'd go for it. Now, let me explain my plan to set-up the Iranians. First, I sent Jamshid ahead last night and didn't tell him you'd be coming with me. None of them know. Here's what I want you to do—"

As Tony whispers his instructions, Dr. Monti raises his eyebrows and rubs his hands approvingly. "This is the kind of action I need now, Tony."

One hour later the jet makes a slow decent through the clouds and the Captain announces their approach to McCarren Field, Las Vegas.

LAS VEGAS

Three hours later, in his hotel room, Tony knocks on the adjoining room door, unlocks it and Dr. Monti enters. "All clear, Frank. Jamshid just drove me from our Safe House. I told him I'm not leaving my room tonight so he returned to our House."

"Good. Is it a go for tomorrow morning?"

"Absolutely. You still want to go through with it?"

"I'm ready."

Tony opens a suitcase and pulls out a weapon. "Here's your gun, Frank. Good luck."

The next morning, Jamshid and four agents arrive by taxi at the south west corner of Flamingo and Buffalo. Jamshid pays the driver and the taxi departs. They mill around waiting for Tony.

Dr. Monti, in disguise, is parked on Buffalo between Tropicana and Flamingo, heading north about 50 yards from Flamingo. Tony arrives by car, gets out with a roll of plans under his arm and greets his agents. The agents kneel on the ground with Tony as he unrolls the plans, explaining that he proposes building an office at this location. Dr. Monti drives up to the corner and stops. Tony turns around and looks up.

Dr. Monti, gun in hand, rolls down the window and looks at Tony. "Mister Berlotti?"

"Yes, Sir. What can I do for you?"

Dr. Monti reaches out and takes aim at Tony. Jamshid and two other agents see the gun and jump on Tony as Dr. Monti gets off three rapid shots. Seeing Rashid charging the car, Monti rolls up the window and steps on the gas. Rashid gets slammed against the side of the car, then falls to the ground. As Dr. Monti races away, the other agents quickly examine Tony for gunshot wounds.

"Rais," asks Jamshid. "Are you all right.?"

Tony gets up, brushes himself off, pats Jamshid on the shoulder and nods at the others.

"Yes, I'm fine. You men saved my life."

"Not so, Rais," states Jamshid. "The gunman was an amateur. He missed all of us."

Rashid, who charged the car, was showing considerable pain, but he proudly announces, "I got his license plate number!"

"Very good, Rashid. Thank God no one got shot! I'm proud of all of you. But we've had enough excitement for the moment. Let's leave now and all meet at the Safe House at 3 PM. I want all of you to meet Dr. Monti. He's arriving today and has important information for us."

One hour later, Dr. Monti, displaying a broad grin, enters Tony's room. "Well, Tony, you proved your team is loyal and fearless. If I wasn't firing blanks, two of your agents would be history. And I'm glad none of your agents were armed. That agent who charged my car had fire in his eyes."

"I gave Jamshid instructions that none of them are to be armed until I OK it. I was armed this morning and would have shot any agent who disobeyed my order."

"I'm so relieved! Oh, by the way, I removed the phony magnetic plates from the rented car, sprayed the interior and returned it. How did I do?"

"Frank," grins Tony, "It was an Academy Award performance. You pulled it off like a pro."

"Thanks, Tony. This is good therapy after losing Gina. For a few minutes there I could stop thinking about her. After I meet your team and demonstrate some of my new gear, I'd like to play some blackjack tonight and take some money home. More therapy," grins Frank.

AUGUST 23, 1974, LAS VEGAS SAFE HOUSE

In the Safe House at 3 PM, Tony introduces Dr. Monti to his team. The next four hours are a non-stop presentation by Dr. Monti of his latest surveillance gear, most of which are not yet on FBI or CIA drawing boards.

Jamshid asks, "How do you keep all this state-of-the-art equipment out of the public domain?"

"I don't patent my sensitive equipment. The gear I'm showing you represents Trade Secrets."

"How do you keep these secrets from your assembly people?" asks Rashid.

"No problem. Each of the major components are assembled in different States, by individuals who don't know each other, who don't know anything about the other components, where and how they are installed or for what purpose. The components are mailed to eleven different mail boxes in New York and picked-up by Misha or his son, Josh. Final assembly, testing, permanent sealing and X-raying each unit is performed only by my son, Peter, Misha, Josh and me."

"Are these units tamper proof?" asks Rashid.

"Yes. The interior will self destruct if opened, drilled into, cut or in any other way tampered with. Additionally, our transmitters avoid eavesdropping since they leave no electronic signature on the receivers. And as you now know, they only operate when properly accessed by codes I provide."

"What's the theory behind your Split Paraboloid Antenna?" asks Jamshid.

"I should make it clear it's not my antenna. It's a Trade Secret by Tony's friend Addabbo, who refused to disclose it's secret operation to the Army Ballistic Missile Agency because they wanted the secret before considering payment. The secret is the antenna's SPADE, the acronym for Split Paraboloid Antenna Driven Element. I only developed the sealing technique to protect the SPADE. It, too, will self-destruct if tampered with. The interaction between the antenna, our selected orbital satellite and Doppler-shift-effect allow us to leapfrog yesterday's technology. Now, let me demonstrate."

Dr. Monti activates one of his COM systems and within seconds is in contact with Peter in New York. He demonstrates start-up, programming, coding, decoding, recording, videotaping, relays, stand-by and shutdown. Following a long and successful hands-on operation by each agent, Dr. Monti gives Tony a nod of approval. Tony thanks his team.

"Gentlemen, what you've just been exposed to is not state-of-the-art; it's state-of-the-future. I expect you to protect it and Dr. Monti to the best of your ability. Thank you. We'll see some of you tonight."

After dinner and one hour of warm-up blackjack at Caesar's Palace, Dr. Monti, a consummate count-down player, states, "OK, Tony, let's go downtown and take their money."

At 11 PM, Tony and Dr. Monti, followed by Jamshid and two agents, enter the Horseshoe Casino. They buy chips, move to an empty table, turn up the remaining chairs and tell the dealer they'll each play two hands. The dealer looks at and gets an OK nod from the pit boss. Jamshid and one agent watch from a nearby wall. The other agent watches from the opposite wall. Ninety minutes later, with a small group watching, Tony is ahead about $2,000. Dr. Monti's take is over $8,000, at which point the pit boss moves in and changes dealers. Tony nods at Dr. Monti and calls security to carry their chips to the cashier's window. As the chips are being counted, a flashy cuff-linked dude, smoking a cigar, walks up and taps Dr. Monti on the shoulder. The dude is Enrique "Hank" Palma, an associate of Sammy Shickarian. Hank is Cuban and speaks fluent English.

"Hello there," greets Hank. "I've been watching you play. You are very good. Listen, fellas, I can take you to a private game for really big bucks. The way you play, you'd make a killing. But, I get 10% of your take. Deal?"

"What about me?" asks Tony.

"The same goes for you, pal."

Tony gives Dr. Monti a look that only two old friends understand.

"OK," agrees Tony. "You've got a deal. First, I need to go to the men's room."

Hank remains at the window with Dr. Monti. Tony walks downstairs and meets Jamshid in the men's room. "This dude may be trouble. Have your men follow him around the clock. We're not going anywhere with him tonight!"

Jamshid leaves first, followed a minute later by Tony. At the window, Dr. Monti hands Tony his winnings.

Hank moves in and announces, "OK, guys, let's go!"

"Just a minute, friend," announces Tony. "I'm not up to any more blackjack tonight. Besides, I don't have enough money for a big game. Let's make it another time."

Hank gives Tony a surprised look. "Hey, man, you've got over ten thousand between you. That's plenty for openers." With that, he grabs Tony's arm and pulls. "Come on. Let's go."

Tony looks down and quickly puts the dude's wrist in a vice-grip. "Now look, sonny, if you have a hearing problem I can clear your ears real fast. I said, we're not playing tonight! Do you hear me?"

Tony's eyes and paralyzing grip put the fear of God in Hank. "OK, OK you don't have to get pissed off about it. When can you come?"

"Next week. This place. This time. Same day. And we'll have plenty of bread. Agreed?"

"Sure thing. I'll arrange it. See you then."

Hank rubs his wrist and walks away, followed by Jamshid's agents.

One hour later in his room ready to retire, Tony receives and recognizes a coded radio signal.

"Go ahead, Jamshid."

"Sorry to call so late, Rais, but thought you should know that Sammy received a call from Carlo while we were at the casino. He wanted to know when Dan Hill was coming to Las Vegas. He told Sammy to make a deal with a hooker to lure you to Los Machos in Mexico."

"They sure like to use hookers. Apparently Sammy and Carlo don't know what we did to Hill's shill in Iran. Thanks. We'll talk about that tomorrow in Tucson. Good night, Jamshid."

Before retiring, Tony calls George to advise he is sending Lin Komatsu, martial arts master, to tutor him on advanced defense and attack techniques.

"Dad, I'm already a black belt. I'm ready for action."

"Son, you won't be ready until you can put me down. Love you! Good night, George."

CHAPTER 13

ORGANIZED IN TUCSON AND NEW YORK

AUGUST 28, 1974, TUCSON

Early in the morning, Tony, Dr. Monti and Jamshid arrive at Tucson International. Ali meets them and they drive east on Broadway, right on Old Spanish Trail and continue until they turn onto a dirt road to their Safe House. Four agents greet them. The sky is clear and for a brief moment they enjoy the view of the Catalina Mountains and towering saguaros.

"Hell," observes Tony, "It's just eight thirty and I'll bet it's 90 degrees already. Let's go inside."

By lunchtime, Dr. Monti concludes his demonstration and training session. These experienced agents, like those in Las Vegas, are impressed with the sophistication of Dr. Monti's units. Tony thanks Dr. Monti and directs the agents' attention to their latest assignment.

"Gentlemen, Dan Hill told me he will soon be shuttling between Las Vegas and Tucson to track a suspected KGB agent, Boris Kruchenko. He asked for my help in tracking the Russian until his arrival. Kruchenko was last seen at Marana Air Park just north of here. I don't trust Hill and this may well be another one of his traps. Let's determine what part, if any, Kruchenko plays in the conspiracy."

"According to our sources," adds Dr. Monti, "Marana is an aircraft repair and retrofitting base for major air carriers, domestic and foreign. Dan Hill told Tony that the CIA uses it on occasion for their Air America planes. We are going to bug the place."

"Yes," adds Tony, "And remember, right now, Dan Hill, Carlo and his hit-team are my primary concern. They're dangerous and well organized, so exercise extreme caution. Good luck."

After an Iranian snack at the Safe House, Tony, Dr. Monti, Jamshid and Ali drive to Marana Air Park. Tony, on the pretext of buying an aircraft, succeeds in securing access on the flight line and into several facilities. While Tony views and sits in various aircraft,

Dr. Monti takes notes and prepares rough floor plans of each facility while Jamshid and Ali take several rolls of photos.

Of particular interest to Tony is the lack of personnel in the large "Evergreen" hanger. The door to the unoccupied office is open and a "unicom" radio is heard intermittently. The only aircraft on the floor, a Queen Air, is in mint condition. There are six steel lockers against the wall, four large oxygen cylinders, two heavy duty dollies, a deep sink surrounded by cleaning supplies and a young man vacuuming the floor.

"Where is everybody," asks Tony.

"I don't know, but I know they're around here somewhere." states the young man confidently.

Satisfied with their preliminary site visit, Tony and his group return to Tucson.

After a short nap, shower and change of clothes, Jamshid and Ali drive Tony and Dr. Monti to the Palomino Restaurant for dinner, where they enjoy veal scaloppini marsala, fettuccine alfredo, Caesar salad and fine imported cabernet sauvignon.

"Well," raves Dr. Monti, "You're batting a thousand! You picked a superior team of agents and now a fine restaurant."

"Thank you, Frank. I knew you'd approve. By the way, take a look at the two guys sitting next to the wall. Do you recognize the one with the great head of hair?"

"No, I don't think so...but he looks familiar."

"That's Michael Landon. He comes here often. Owns lots of property around Tucson."

"He looks like a happy fellow. Any more celebrities around here?"

Tony speaks quietly, "I saw Joe and Bill Bonanno once. You know who they are, right?"

"Yes. I heard the old man is collaborating on an autobiography and understand that Bill is still serving time in California, along with Roselli and, would you believe, Gordon Liddy?"

"Frank, you're a cornucopia of information. So, all-seeing Frank, where's Boris Kruchenko?"

"Touché, Tony. Now eat your veal before it gets cold. Where are we dining tomorrow?"

"Take your pick. There's the Tac Room with a great western style t-bone cooked over mesquite or there's Scordato's for shrimp scampi with a side of rigatoni a la marinara. What's your pleasure?" *"At least he's not dwelling on Gina at the moment,"* observes Tony.

The next three days are spent placing bugs in critical areas at Marana Air Park facilities and waiting for Boris Kruchenko to arrive at his Skyline area apartment west of north Swan Road. Kruchenko does not arrive at his apartment nor at Marana.

Before retiring on Saturday night, Jamshid alerts Tony. "Rais, we got a signal from Marana. Our agent there believes Kruchenko visited locker number four at the Evergreen hanger."

SEPTEMBER 1, 1974, MARANA AIR PARK, ARIZONA

The next morning, a Sunday, Tony, Dr. Monti and Jamshid charter an aircraft and fly to Marana. "This place looks deserted," observes Dr. Monti.

"Yes," responds the charter pilot. "All you'll see today are week-end pilots shooting touch-and-goes and sky-diving at the north end of the field."

Jamshid assists the pilot in securing the plane at the tie-down area while Tony and Dr. Monti make their way to the Evergreen hanger. The large roll-up door is down. The office door is closed but unlocked. They enter, see the silent unicom radio on the desk and notice that the interior door to the hanger is open.

"Anybody around?" shouts Tony.

When there is no response, they quickly enter the hanger and move to locker number four. The Montico bug on the lower web of the steel purlin behind the locker is still operating.

"That's good, Tony."

"Yes, but look, Frank. The lock has been changed. Kruchenko was here."

As they prepare to pick the lock, Tony receives a radio alert from Jamshid on his walkie-talkie.

They hear a car door being slammed, so they move away from the lockers and begin walking around the Queen Air. A man enters and approaches them.

"Hello. I've been fueling some planes on the far end of the field and saw you land. Your people told me you were in here. Can I help you?"

"Yes," replies Tony. "I'm trying to find out if this Queen Air is for sale."

"No, Sir. It's only here for some avionics work. The owner is from Las Vegas."

When Tony hears Las Vegas, he gives Dr. Monti his 'uh huh' look.

"Who's the owner?"

"I don't know."

"Can we look at the aircraft's documents?"

"The aircraft is locked. And, like I said, Mister. It's not for sale."

Realizing it would not be prudent to continue this exchange, Tony thanks the man and they leave. After exiting, Dr. Monti notices the line-man locking the front door. As they walk to their chartered aircraft, Tony puts his arm around Dr. Monti's shoulder.

"We know he lied. That Queen Air is Mexican. Now we need to find out who owns XB-MIN."

On their return flight, Tony instructs the pilot to divert his course to fly over the Twin Buttes open-pit copper mine just 17 miles from Tucson. Circling over the pit impresses Dr. Monti and Jamshid.

"Just thought I'd show you an aerial of Twin Buttes. I'm trying to get a contract down there."

SEPTEMBER 2, 1974, NEW YORK

The next morning, after a late night briefing with his team, Tony, Dr. Monti and Jamshid fly to New York. Tony recently signed a lease and has retrofitted 8,000 square feet of penthouse space at 88 Empire Place. A 3,000 square foot section, facing Dr. Monti's office across the street, will serve as Tony's and George's apartment. The balance is a security office and living quarters for his SAVAK men. The lease permits Tony to raise the roof's parapet wall and build a plastic barrier to protect his split-paraboloid antenna and repeaters. Installation of the security system, computers and communications is being performed by Tony, Dr. Monti and Peter. Tony's retrofitted penthouse is now complete and ready for occupancy. The penthouse is leased to "A-Tec Corporation", incorporated in Carson City, Nevada as a Consulting Firm. Tony Berlotti is President and C.E.O.; Dr. Monti, Executive Vice President; George, Vice President and Secretary/ Treasurer and SAVAK agent Mehdi is the "Resident Agent".

Pleased with the new facility and living quarters, Tony calls his A-Tec organization "The Capture Team". Dr. Monti agrees to shuttle between his Montico plant and A-Tec when Tony is out of town. Before George and Peter return to college, after taking extra summer credits, Tony decides to fly them and Dr. Monti for a weekend of fun to Disney World in his new fully IFR turbo Centurion. Twenty four hours before the flight Dr. Monti calls.

"Tony, I'm sorry I can't go with you tomorrow. A rich Saudi client is coming to see me about a security problem. I know you and the boys will enjoy the trip."

The next morning, at 200 feet above the runway with gear up, Tony, George and Peter are cleared IFR to Kissimmee Airport near Disney World. Although both young men still feel the loss of their mothers, and, for George, his sisters as well, they are young, resilient and focused on the future. They enjoy the three day weekend. Tony is always heavy-hearted when not fully occupied with work but he puts a good face on the holiday for the sake of the boys. Always, in the back of his mind, is his mantra, *"Hill, Carlo, Sammy, Los Machos and whoever else was involved in the death of my family - you're gonna' die painful deaths. Each one of you!"*

SEPTEMBER 5, 1974, NEW YORK

George and Peter are off to their respective colleges. Jamshid advises Tony that Dan Hill is still in Iran, deeply involved in the anti Khomeini movement but has not made an attempt to contact Tony's engineer. Also, according to the latest reports from high SAVAK officials, the Shah appears to be in poor health and there is a strong underground anti-American movement being orchestrated by religious leaders under Khomeini. Tony selects and mobilizes a key staff from his engineering company for his new project in Mexico and asks Dr. Monti to screen and hire additional office personnel to support the A-Tec "Capture Team".

SEPTEMBER 6, SNAPPER INN, LONG ISLAND

Finishing dinner, Frank asks, "So, Tony, Dan Hill's contact in Mexico is Haldon Brooks?"

"Yes. Hill told me Brooks is an inexperienced CIA agent, but with good contacts in Mexico."

"You know you can't believe anything he tells you. Be careful! Have a good flight tomorrow."

CHAPTER 14

BACK TO MEXICO

SEPTEMBER 7, 1974, MEXICO CITY

Tony and Jamshid arrive on a Saturday afternoon and are met by Rashid, their Spanish speaking SAVAK agent. Although Tony has a furnished apartment at the south end of the city, he checks into the Maria Isabel Sheraton hotel, next to the U.S. Embassy. After a shower and shave he dials Haldon Brooks. There's no answer after eight rings.

"That's strange. Hill told me Brooks could be reached at this number 24 hours a day."

Not one to waste time, Tony calls Victor Moran. They meet for dinner at the Del Lago Restaurant and discuss mobilizing local engineers for the Rio Plata silver project. The next day, Tony and Victor lunch at the Sanborn restaurant in La Zona Rosa and recall the events that took place there on September 29, 1963. The restaurant has been modernized and the copper sculpture is gone.

"Tony, have you ever figured out why those men were wearing disguises?"

"Yes. It was part of a conspiracy. I'll tell you about it after I have all the answers." *"I wonder what they did with that magnificent copper sculpture."*

After a late breakfast on Monday, Tony calls Haldon Brooks. A female answers the phone.

"Buenos dias." (Good morning)

"Buenos dias, Señorita. Señor Brooks por favor. Soy Antonio Berlotti." (Good morning, Miss. Mister Brooks please. I'm Tony Berlotti).

"Good morning Mister Berlotti. Mr. Brooks has been expecting your call. By the way, your Spanish is excellent. I'll connect you."

"Good morning Mister Berlotti and welcome to Mexico City. Haldon Brooks here. Sorry about this lousy rain storm. Are you free to come to my office now?"

"Hello, Hal. No need to be formal. I'm Tony. And yes, I can come now. I'm at the Sheraton. Where are you?"

"I'm at Tampico #17, in Colonia Condessa, overlooking Chapultepec Park. I'll have someone waiting for you at the entrance. Even in this storm, you can be here in ten minutes."

"I'm on my way."

Fifteen minutes later, Tony, Jamshid and Rashid arrive at #17. With no sign that the rain will let-up, Tony rushes out to the main entrance. Jamshid and Rashid wait in the taxi. A doorman opens the door, greets Tony, escorts him to the elevator and up to the penthouse and an unmarked door with a peek-hole. The doorman gives a coded knock, the door opens and Tony is greeted by Hal Brooks, a strong looking, well dressed, middle aged man.

"Hello, Tony. I'm Hal."

"Pleasure meeting you, Hal."

"Come in. Take off your wet jacket and I'll have my girl prepare a fresh cup of coffee."

"That'll be fine, but this needs to be a short visit. I have two business associates waiting for me in the cab."

Brooks escorts Tony into a living room. Tony removes his jacket. Brooks looks at Tony's massive size, commenting, "Man, you're a lot bigger than Hill described to me!"

Tony smiles, "And you look a lot more experienced than what Hill told me. How long have you known him?"

"About fifteen years. He became a contract agent for Mr. Louis a couple of years before me. How do you get along with him?"

"I ignore him as much as possible. He's an Ivy League snob and a master at turning disingenuousness into an art form. Sorry, Hal, but I don't like the son-of-a-bitch!"

"Welcome to the club. I understand where you're coming from. What's your schedule?"

"Very busy. Next three days in Mexico, three days in Peru, three more in Bolivia, then back to New York."

"What does your wife say about all that traveling?"

Tony hesitates before answering, *"Strange, can it be that he doesn't know about Gloria and my girls?"* "My wife and daughters were burned to death, actually, murdered, not long ago."

Brooks looks genuinely perplexed. "I'm sorry, Tony. That's strange. It's not listed in your file. Any clues on who or why?"

"Oh yes! I know who and why. And they know I know. They have a contract out on me."

"Sounds like you need protection. Want some help while you're in Mexico? I have connections."

Tony looks at his wrist watch, lights a cigar, looks at Brooks, gets up and puts on his jacket, thinking, *"Sure, so you can set me up for Hill. Dream on."* "Thanks, Hal. I appreciate your offer and will certainly call if necessary. I'll also take a rain check on the coffee. Here's my local business card. Sorry I have to rush off."

"No problem and don't let Dan Hill bother you. He's always been a snob. Mr. Louis knows you're a valuable asset. Remember, my door is always open to you."

They shake hands and Tony leaves.

SEPTEMBER 16, MEXICO CITY

Due to settling a jurisdictional dispute between transport companies, Tony's stay is extended one week. While in his office packing for Peru, along with Victor Moran, Jamshid and Rashid, Tony receives a call from Hal Brooks.

"Tony, it's Hal. I just received word that Dan Hill was injured in a helicopter crash in Iran. He broke a leg and some ribs. He'll be out of service several months. Louis wants to know if you're working on locating Kruchenko."

"Yes, but only part-time. What do you know about Kruchenko?"

"Hill said he's a KGB agent and wants to find him. But I don't know why. That's all."

"Hal, how long have you been in Mexico?"

"Going on nine years. Why?"

"Just curious." *"If he's telling the truth, he wasn't in Mexico City in September 1963."* You've been here quite a while. Sounds like Louis is your boss, too. What exactly do you do in Mexico?"

"I collect data and support the PRI[13] and PEMEX[14] for the Committee's Oil Syndicate. They sent me here because I speak Spanish and have friends here in high social circles. I've never had a direct working relationship with Hill. He's been down here on secret missions on numerous occasions and probably to check up on

---

[13] Institutional Revolutionary Party - in control of Mexican politics for years.
[14] Mexican Oil company

me." Brooks is sardonic. "He's a sneaky SOB and I don't like him either."

"Thanks for your honesty, Hal. I'll call you on my return trip."

SEPTEMBER 23, NEW YORK

Tony and Dr. Monti are having dinner at Luigi's.

"Ahhhhh," boasts Tony. "Spaghetti with Italian sausage and cabernet sauvignon. Tell me, Frank, who eats better than us?"

"I think you'll agree," Frank's smile was sad. "We ate a lot better when we had our wives." At the look on Tony's face, Frank changes the subject. "So, what's the latest on the business front?"

"I'm bidding a job for Mineria Peru and need to send my chief geologist down there ASAP. The Bolivian sulfur project is still in limbo, pending results of ore tests. Then it's back to Mexico."

"What's your reaction to Haldon Brooks? And what's he doing down there?"

"Don't know, but I can't help but like him. He said he's supporting the PRI and PEMEX and he sure doesn't like Hill. He strikes me as being honest. Don't worry, I'll give him plenty of rope."

"Don't trust him and be sure to have your men bug his office. By the way, your agent in Tehran, Jahangir, reported that Hill is in the hospital with a broken leg."

"Yes, I know. Brooks told me the same thing. Well, shall we go?"

"No! Eat some more spaghetti. You're losing more weight, Tony. And go get your physical!"

A week later, Tony is back in Mexico and into his spacious and tastefully decorated furnished penthouse apartment on Oso Street, overlooking the elegant Liverpool department store. Rashid has a two bedroom apartment next to the elevator on the ground floor. Tony's office is a short distance away at Insurgentes Sur #2300. He calls Victor Moran and they meet for dinner at San Angel Inn.

Tony arrives and sees Victor, as excited as a kid at Christmas, waiting at the entrance.

"Victor, What are you up to? You look like a kid at Christmas."

"Tony! I have a surprise for you. Follow me into the atrium."

They make their way past several guests and into the small open garden atrium.

"Unbelievable!" shouts Tony as he gazes at the surprise. "It's the copper sculpture from the Zona Rosa restaurant in 1963."

"Yes," nods Victor. "It was so shiny when you photographed it. Now it looks old."

"Well, that photo was over ten years ago. We didn't know it then, Victor, but that photo changed my life, and not for the best, certainly." Tony was thoughtful, " I'll tell you about it some day."

The next morning, after trying unsuccessfully to associate Hal Brooks with the 1963 photo, Tony decides to investigate. He calls Brooks and they meet in Brooks's office where Brooks greets him with a firm handshake.

"Welcome back, Tony. Successful trip?"

"Well, you know, we win some; lose some. Peru was a plus. Bolivia a negative."

"I tried to call you at the Hotel Bolivar in Lima. They told me you never checked-in."

"That's right. Hill told me that's where he stays and I didn't need him around. Besides, it's next to the Plaza San Martin and very noisy. I stayed at the Caesar in Mira Flores. I signed an exploration contract with the Peruvians. The Bolivians, on the other hand, have grandiose plans but no money. "

"Batting five hundred isn't too shabby. So, Tony, what can I do for you?"

"What's the latest on Hill?"

Studying Tony, Brooks leans back in his high-back swivel chair, lights an unfiltered cigarette.

"I really don't know, except he's still in the hospital. Mr. Louis said he'll remain there until the Khomeini problem is resolved. I hope he doesn't send Hill to Mexico. Anyway, Louis still wants to know if you have any clues on locating Kruchenko."

Tony lights a cigar and studies Brooks, thinking, *"So far, this guy seems to be telling the truth."*

"Nothing yet on Kruchenko. Tell me, why is Louis involving you in this?"

"I guess only because I have easy access to you and can provide manpower support if needed."

"Kruchenko is supposedly traveling between Tucson and Las Vegas. How could you provide support there?"

"I have competent bi-lingual people who travel. Fair enough?"

"Fair enough. And I'll let you know if I need help. Fair enough?"

"Touché! Gosh, look at the time. How about joining me for lunch at Rincon Gaucho?"

"Sure. I'd like that. I've been there once and enjoyed it."

At Rincon Gaucho, after drinking two Pisco sours, filet miñons are brought out on a sizzling table-top charcoal grill, along with hot rolls, vegetables and a bottle of Argentinian wine.

"Good choice, Hal. I'm big on prime beef and good wine."

"I knew we had something in common, Tony. By the way, do you happen to play bridge?"

"I sure do. Why...you looking for a partner?

"As a matter of fact, I am. Mine always forgets the unusual no trump during duplicate play."

"Oh, oh! In a husband and wife partnership, that's grounds for divorce."

"That's right," Hal grins. "I usually play at the Club de Bridge Azteca. Would you be available?"

"Give me some advance notice and I'll play with you. I know most of the latest conventions."

"Great! Just once, I'd like to beat George Rosenkranz. He's the best player in Mexico."

"I've heard of him. Hopefully we'll have some good luck. I like a challenge. Who owns this place?"

"An ex Argentine boxer and fantastic magician. He does magic shows here."

"I'll have to catch his show one day. Well," Tony is enthusiastically spooning up the last of his crème caramel, "I'm sorry but I'm going to have to eat and run."

"Enjoyed your company, Tony. And let me know if you need protection."

That afternoon, Tony arranges to have his key Rio Plata Project supervisory staff, including Victor Moran, meet him for a business kick-off luncheon the next day at the Las Mañanitas restaurant in Cuernavaca, a one hour drive south of Mexico City. That evening, he raises his Split-Paraboloid Antenna, installed earlier by Rashid on the apartment roof, and calls George and Dr. Monti for their daily briefing session. He advises he will fly to Las Vegas tomorrow night to start joint venture negotiations with a major investor for the four hundred ton per day Geo Sierra gold mine and plant in California. He will try, as well, to obtain an update on Boris Kruchenko Before retiring, he receives a call from Rashid.

"Mr. Berlotti, Hal Brooks just ended a conversation with Mr. Louis in Switzerland. He told Louis he has you under surveillance 24 hours a day. That was a lie. No one is tailing you and all our communications are clean. He also said he and his wife are planning to retire to Maine next year. That, too, was a lie. We have found out he is, in fact, building a large retirement home on Lake Chapala just south east of Guadalajara. His wife's name is Alicia but he calls her Alice. Alice is Mexican and would never move to Maine."

"Good work, Rashid. Keep Brooks under surveillance. See you tomorrow in Cuernavaca."

Sunday afternoons at Las Mañanitas are always crowded. Fortunately, Victor, a steady customer there, made reservations directly with the manager, a personal friend. Tony's table for a party of ten, nearest the large open garden, is marked "reservado". Cuernavaca, known as the land of eternal spring, is unusually warm this day. Three large bright colored parrots, perched on swings, are chattering many recognizable words as two peacocks strut around the garden delighting guests by fanning out their brilliantly iridescent tail feathers. Everyone in Tony's party, to the delight of master chef Ramon, orders the house specialty: "pollo mole negro" (heavily seasoned chocolate chicken). The luncheon is a huge success and everyone is enthusiastic and high-spirited in response to Tony's presentation.

In the late afternoon, Tony excuses himself and returns to Mexico City for his late night flight to the U.S.

CHAPTER 15

CONSPIRATORS IN VEGAS

LATE SEPTEMBER, 1974, NEW YORK

Twenty four hours later, Tony is back in New York. After a short nap, and a meeting with Dr. Monti and talking with George at college, Tony rolls out his Centurion, pre-flights it, walks into the pilot's lounge, pulls out his Jepp charts, checks weather, notams, alternate airports, then files IFR (instrument flight rules)for the first leg of his flight to Las Vegas. The Centurion lifts off the runway in the dark, cleared by ATC for a heading of 270 degrees at 8500 feet.

In Las Vegas, meanwhile, Carlo, Sammy and Los Machos are in a meeting with Vinnie Carmona, representing Roselli, and Benjamin Silver, representing Lansky. Silver opens the meeting.

"I'm glad you all came. I got good news and bad news. The good news is Giancana is coming soon to meet us. The bad news is Lansky isn't happy with the declining cash flow here, IF you know what I mean."

"Fuck you! Fuck Giancana and fuck Lansky!" snarls Carlo. "We do only dee contract work. We don't answer to nobody. Comprende, señor?"

Carmona slams his hand on the table and glares at Carlo, "Now listen, you Bolivian asshole, you better not get out of your league or you'll end up with a dead fish in your mouth! Comprende?"

Sammy immediately tries to arbitrate the crisis, but Carlo and Los Machos storm out of the room, cursing in Spanish. Sammy knows that he, Roselli and Hill have been skimming too much. He assures Carmona and Silver he will resolve the matter.

During most of Tony's cross country flight the weather is CAVU (ceiling and visibility unlimited) and the Centurion cruises effortlessly on auto-pilot while he sips copious amounts of coffee from his thermos bottle, scans the instruments and contemplates his next move against the conspirators. He makes stops only for refueling and something to eat. The last leg of the flight to Las Vegas turns out to be solid IFR (instrument flight rules or flying solely on instruments). Tony disengages the auto-pilot and keeps a gentle grip on the control yoke. Flying on instruments is an exhilarating experience requiring full concentration on instrument behavior to maintain the aircraft straight and level on the assigned altitude and course. *"Ah—this is a piece of cake. In my next life, I'm an airline pilot."*

After almost an hour of solid and turbulent IFR, Tony wishes he could have a cappuccino. His hands become clammy on the yoke, his eyes blinking excessively and his *"piece of cake "* turns to:

"Jesus Christ, Murphy—enough already!" He puts the Centurion back on auto pilot and opens the thermos for more coffee. It's empty. *"Goddamn—Murphy strikes again!"*

Suddenly, in the dark on Victor 562 Airway out of the Peach Springs VOR, (VHF omni-directional radio) Murphy dies as the plane breaks out of the soup into VFR conditions (visual flight rules) over Lake Mead in Arizona.

The sight of the Las Vegas lights ahead light up the night sky like the aurora borealis and Tony's "enough already" turns to: *"Finally! Beautiful sight—absolutely beautiful. Yes,...next life, I'll be an airline pilot."*

With his DME (distance measuring equipment) indicating 38 miles to touch-down, Tony calls Jamshid, who confirms he is waiting at McCarren field. Tony switches to the Las Vegas Vortac on 116.9, sets his OBS to the 066 radial and continues straight-in, canceling IFR on the long final approach, touches-down at 05:05 local time, taxies to the general aviation terminal, refuels, ties-down and meets Jamshid.

"Good morning, Mr. Berlotti. How are you and how was your long flight?"

"I'm fine, had a good flight and I'm hungry. Let's get breakfast at the Tropicana."

When Jamshid pulls into the parking lot, he notices that Tony is sound asleep. He parks, cuts the engine and decides to give his boss a few winks. Tony's short nap lasts only a few minutes as a nearby car back-fires. Tony stiffens and dives to the floor, shouting, "Get the bastards!"

"It's OK, Rais, it's OK. It was only a car backfiring."

"Damn. I was having a dream that you and I were in a shoot-out with Los Machos. It sure sounded like a gunshot. Scared the hell out of me. Come on, Jamshid, let's get breakfast."

Moments later, after Tony splashes cold water on his face, they order pancakes and eggs.

"So, tell me Jamshid. How do you and your men like Vegas?"

"Mr. Berlotti, not too long ago, in Iran, we had only dreams about visiting this magic city. Now here we are living and working in it. We are eternally grateful."

"Good. I knew you'd like this assignment. What news do you have?"

"Yes, Sir. Let me start with Sammy. He spends most of the time in the Desert Inn but also frequents the Stardust, Caesar's Palace and the downtown Horseshoe. He always carries a fat roll of one hundred dollar bills, usually has one or two beautiful girls at his side, chain smokes long Cuban cigars, gambles on craps and roulette, drives a Lincoln Continental, lives with his wife on West Desert Inn Road. He has no children, his wife is a good blackjack player but frequently travels out of Vegas and Sammy often stays out all night."

"Interesting. Anything else?"

"We have surveillance gear set up in his house, phones, car, and hotel office. We have tapes of his conversations with Dan Hill in Tehran and Carlo and Jose in La Paz. He also received a call from a Benjamin Silver, representing Ed Levinson, who told him that Lansky and the Committee know that someone is skimming at the Desert Inn."

Jamshid pours another cup of tea, refers to his Farsi notes and continues: "Los Machos came to town last week and met with Sammy at the Horseshoe. There are four Machos, all Bolivian, all between 5'-6" and 5'-9", all in their thirties and all speak poor English. They are flashy dressers, big spenders, good blackjack players, are never armed in the casinos and chew what they call "chachacoma".

"I know chachacoma. It's an Andes Mountain plant. Many miners along the Bolivian, Peruvian and Chilean high altitude borders chew the leaves to improve breathing and get a quick high."

"Did you ever try it?"

"Yes but I didn't like the taste. I always take a few drops of "coramina" with a glass of water when I'm at high altitudes. Makes breathing easy and you don't get high. Any more news?"

"Yes. Remember the 'dude' card hustler from the Horseshoe?"

"Of course. What's the deal with him?"

"His name is Enrique Palma but everybody calls him "Hank". He's a Cuban with a U.S. passport and is a close friend of Sammy and Los Machos. He met the Machos at McCarren field and drove them to a large hanger at the general aviation area. After they left, we gained access and discovered that it has been retrofitted. It has a game room, efficiency kitchen, two bedrooms, two chemical toilets, heating and air conditioning, water supply tanks, generator and a large assortment of radios. It's really a neat facility."

"What? No aircraft?"

"Oh, yes Sir. There's a Queen Air in the adjoining hanger. They have two watchmen on twelve hour shifts and they maintain the plane in good condition. The Macho named Manuel is the pilot. We have the place totally bugged. They have had only two blackjack games there since we started monitoring them. Two big Texans were their pigeons. It was Hank who lured the Texans to the game after he got tipped-off by Sammy."

"How did the games go?"

"The first game was last Friday when the Texans broke even after almost eight hours of play. When the Texans wanted to play again, they agreed to resume play the following night. On Saturday night, when the Texans ran out of cash at over fifty thousand dollars, the Machos would not allow them to write checks to continue. You see, one of the Machos and the night watchman were young sleight-of-hand dealers in Havana before Castro took over the casinos. When the Texans were losing about twenty thousand dollars they asked for a new dealer and settled for the watchman. As you might expect, the watchman let them win the first few hands, then easily dealt himself winning hands until the Texans ran out of money. Hank drove them back to the Stardust Casino and left. That's it."

"Nice people we're dealing with. Well, that was a good breakfast. Now let's see the new vehicle we purchased."

Half an hour later they arrive at Tony's Safe House. Jamshid points to the shiny new 38 foot motor home parked under an oversized carport. "There it is, Rais——and we've already retrofitted it with Dr. Monti's latest "state-of-the-future" surveillance equipment."

They enter and are greeted by one of Jamshid's Savak agents who promptly offers Tony a cup of tea. Jamshid glares at the agent and reprimands him in Farsi, stating, "All of you were told the boss drinks cappuccino. Don't let it happen again!"

"Hey, it's OK. I like tea occasionally."

Tony sips the tea and begins a slow walk-through of the unit, examining each piece of gear in detail. "Great work, Jamshid. This would be the envy of the FBI and CIA."

"Thank you, Sir. Now, we will let you hear the tape of Sammy's September 13th conversation with Dan Hill in Iran."

The motor home agent starts the tape. "Hello, Sammy?"

"Yeah, Dan. How the hell are ya'?"

"Lousy. My leg is in a cast and my chest hurts. I was in a helicopter crash."

"Rotten luck, man. Does that mean you can't meet with us next month?"

"That's right. There's no way I can travel now. Have you seen or heard anything about Berlotti?"

"Hell no. He must be makin' money on one of his Latin American projects."

"Have you talked to Carlo lately?"

"Of course. He sent Los Machos to Miami on a special contract. Then they came here and ripped off a couple of dumb Texans in a blackjack game."

"That's penny ante crap. Now listen, Louis told me the Committee is concerned over skimming at the Sands and that Lansky has his men on the case. Know anything about that?"

"Yeah. They called a meeting and sent Benny Silver and Vinnie Carmona to warn us."

"I had a feeling this might happen. You need to cool it and get word to Roselli to stop his people before Lansky's men solve our scam."

"Easy for you to say. You're away, safe in Iran. I'll do the best I can to stop it. So, when are you comin' to Vegas to do somethin' about Berlotti?"

"I told you, I'm laid up. Besides, Dick Helms is the new Ambassador here and runs a tighter ship than Bill Sullivan ever did. Helms was appalled when he learned that there were no bugs in the Shah's office. According to my sources, Sullivan believed he had a lock on Savak and others around the Shah and didn't need to bug."

"I thought Helms was your CIA Director?"

"He was, but Helms knows too much about Watergate and the Chile-Allende connection so, last February, Nixon moved him as far away from Washington as possible. Helms has the secrets. He'll probably write a book about it some day."

"Interesting. What's the latest on Nixon's resignation last month?"

"It was a can of worms. Chief-of-Staff Haig conducted an investigation and there are tapes on June 23, 1972 to prove the Watergate cover-up. Nixon, Haldeman, Ehrlichman, Dean, Hunt, Liddy and others were all aware of it. Some day those tapes will be released."

"Anything else on Nixon?"

"Yes, and it's important. On December 23, 1971, Nixon had Hoffa released from prison. We can't prove it but figure they had a quid-pro-quo back in 1960."

"What the hell is quid pro what?"

"Dear Jesus! Why am I surrounded by morons? It's quid-pro-quo! They made a deal. You know. Something for something! Back in 1960, when Nixon was running against Kennedy, Hoffa arranged a half million dollar contribution that came from Lansky and Marcello to the Nixon campaign. Also, early in 1973 the teamsters provided one million for Watergate hush-money, via Tony Pro, Frank Fitzsimmons and Allen Dorfman. So, you see, Nixon owed Hoffa and the teamsters. Big time! And that, Sammy, is what is known as quid-pro-quo."

"OK, goddamn it! I don't need a friggin' history lesson. What does all that shit have to do with Tony Berlotti?"

"I give up trying to educate you, Sammy."

"Look, pal, don't bother! We all understood that you have a handle on Tony and that you'd arrange to set him up. So instead of lecturing, get off your ass and do somethin' about it!"

"You just stay put and do as you're told. I'll have Carlo contact you with instructions."

"No way, Hill! When it comes to dealin' in Vegas, you deal directly with me - got that?"

"I'm not getting into a pissing contest with you, Sammy. Bye."

The tape ends after Sammy is heard shouting, "Spook sonofabitch!"

Tony leans back, asks for a cappuccino, lights a cigar and smiles at Jamshid. "I'm so glad they love each other. It should work to our advantage some day."

When the agent arrives with the cappuccino and fresh baklava, Jamshid starts the tape between Sammy and Carlo.

"Hello Sammy. You alone?"

"Yeah, Carlo, I'm alone. What's up?"

"Where dee hell eez Señor Berlotti?"

"I think he's in Mexico. Why?"

"Good. I send Los Machos to make dee hit. Where in Mexico?"

"Don't know exactly. Hill probably knows."

"So, ask Hill and get back to me, pronto. I prefer to hit heem outside the U.S."

"That sonofabitch Hill won't give me the time of day. He's a problem."

"Theenk he coming to Las Vegas next month?"

"No. The bastard was in a chopper crash and is laid up. We're not talking. You call him."

After a ten second delay, Carlo asks, "Tell me, Sammy, what you and Hill talk about?"

"Nothing you would consider important. The spook rambled on about Nixon, Watergate, Chile and Iran. He had nothing new on Tony. I tell you, that sonofabitch is beginning to be a problem."

There is another ten second delay before Carlo asks, "You have no talk about dee skim meeting we had with Silver and Carmona?"

"No" lies Sammy. "I'm trying to figure how Roselli and me can pin the scam on him."

"You better stop dee operation. If Lansky find out he have you all killed. Like you, I no like el spook Hill, but we need heem to find Berlotti. When you know something, make Hank contact Los Machos and we arrange dee hit, comprende?"

"Yeah, I comprende. Adios amigo."

The tape ends. Tony gets a cappuccino refill, another piece of fresh baklava, then asks Jamshid, "What do we have on Boris Kruchenko?"

"Interesting Russian. He is now in Tucson at a rented condo on Skyline Drive. We followed him to the Nogales International Airport where he met two Mexicans at the little coffee shop there. Ali went into the coffee shop alone and saw an exchange of money for a very small bag, probably drugs. The Mexicans left, then Kruchenko drove up to a nearby Patagonia Lake cabin, where he spent two days."

"Was he alone?"

"Yes, sir. Then he drove up to Marana Air Park, left the bag in locker Number 3, picked up money out of locker Number 4 in the

Evergreen hanger and drove to his condo. Ali confirms that the man, with a fake limp and in disguise, placed the money in the locker. The man got away but we now have an agent stationed there as a spotter for the skydivers. He's already placed a transmitter in both lockers."

"What has Kruchenko done with the money?"

"Nothing yet. He hasn't been anywhere since and has had no visitors."

"What does Kruchenko do for entertainment?"

"He occasionally plays bridge at the Tucson Bridge Center on Saturday nights, so we checked with the Center. They don't have his name registered. He must play under an alias."

"Good work. Go to the club next time he plays and find out if he has a steady partner."

"But, Rais, none of us play bridge. How do we arrange that?"

"No problem. Have a couple of your men join the club and start taking novice lessons. That way they can watch the Saturday night games until they're ready for play. That will provide an opportunity to observe Kruchenko. If I'm in town when he plays, I'll go to the club and try to arrange to play against him."

"Yes, sir. By the way, here's the latest photo that Ali took of him."

Tony examines the photo, "Well, if he's KGB, he certainly does a lousy job covering his tracks."

"Yes, following him has been too easy. Perhaps Dan Hill is lying to you about the Russian."

"Time will tell - certainly he lies about a lot of things. Let's head back to New York to visit George and Dr. Monti, then down to my project in Mexico. Meanwhile, have Ali keep a tight tail on Kruchenko. We need to determine what part this so called KGB agent played in the Conspiracy."

CHAPTER 16

IMPERSONATION AND FRAME-UP

SEPTEMBER 27, 1974 (FRIDAY), NEW YORK

Dr. Monti briefs Tony on the operation of newly installed computers, communications and surveillance gear in Tony's A-Tec office. Dr. Monti has provided a skeleton clerical and technical staff and Jamshid has enlisted three Savak security guards for around-the-clock protection.

Over dinner that evening at Luigi's, Tony and Dr. Monti agree to bring their sons, George and Peter, into the organization as soon as they graduate from college next June. After listening to Tony's half hour, non-stop, briefing on the status of the Conspirators, Dr. Monti shakes his fork at Tony.

"Stop and listen to me, Tony. You look like hell! Go see Dr. Asti for a physical."

"What brought that on? I'm fine."

"You're not fine! You've lost too much weight and not getting enough rest. Do it. See Asti."

"Frank, you worry too much. But I'll do it as soon as possible."

"Good. Now go home. Get some sleep. Let me know how you make out with George tomorrow."

The next day, Tony arrives at George's off-campus apartment for lunch. Following their bear hugs, George steps back, looks at Tony and shakes his head. "Dad - you look like hell!"

"Is this a conspiracy...or what? You've been talking to Frank?"

"No, but I'm sure he would agree. Dad, you're working too hard. Please go see Doctor Asti."

"OK, I will." Noting George's skepticism, "Promise! Now fix the grilled cheese sandwiches."

After the sandwiches, cappuccino and biscotti, Tony "sweeps" the apartment for bugs.

"No need, Dad. I've already done it. No bugs, believe me."

"Very good. I trust you. George, after you graduate I think you should study for the bar, pass it, get some international law experience, then join my A-Tec organization. Okay ?"

"No!" George is emphatic. " I'm going to join you and Uncle Frank next June to help you track down and eliminate the assassins!"

"I had a feeling you'd say that. So, I have a special proposal for you."

"What is it?"

"George, it's extremely unusual, bizarre actually, and very risky."

"Whatever you say, Dad. I want those bastards just as much as you!"

"How would you like to take acting lessons and become a temporary female impersonator?"

"Hello? A female impersonator? Good grief, why? How would that help?"

"So you can lure the sons-a-bitches into our traps. Besides being killers, these guys are also womanizers. You're young, slim, and, like your mother, fair and good looking. I'm sure we can develop ways for you to con them and lead them to us. Of course, it's gonna play hell with your sex life, but George, it's only temporary. It's a tough and crazy assignment. Think you could handle it?"

George scratches his head, pours another cappuccino, then slams his hand on the table.

"They killed Mom, Mary and Nancy and aren't gonna get away with it! I'll do it, Dad."

"That's my boy. I'll make arrangements and give you the details next time we meet. Now, tell me about your grades, the debating team and how your martial arts lessons are going with Komatsu."

The next day, back in New York, Tony apprizes Dr. Monti of George's agreement to his proposal and then makes plans for his trip to Iran. Tony spends Sunday relaxing and being briefed by Jamshid. Late Monday morning, Tony decides to take the advice he's been getting to see Dr. Asti. Tony and his family have been Dr. Asti's patients for years. He considers the doctor a good friend and they often socialized with him while Gloria was alive. When he arrives, however, the sign on the door reads: "Richard Spooner, M.D." Entering, he recognizes the grey haired, sweet looking woman at the receptionist's desk.   Sally has been Dr. Asti's receptionist for many years.

"Hello, Sally. I'm sorry I didn't call for an appointment but thought I would find Dr. Asti here and he might squeeze me in. What's happened? Did he retire early or move to another location?"

Sally's professional demeanor vanishes and there is profound sadness in her face.

"Hello, Mr. Berlotti. Dr. Asti would have been happy to see you...but...he's gone."

"Gone!" Tony is aghast. "You don't mean he died, Sally?"

"Oh, no! Not that. Mr. Berlotti, let me get someone to relieve me here at the desk so we can talk."

Sally is nervous and furtive as she leads Tony into a conference room, closes the door and offers him a cup of coffee. She is obviously making an effort to compose herself.

"Mr. Berlotti, what I am about to tell you is in strictest confidence, but I know Dr. Asti likes you and respects you as a good friend and not just a patient. I have been beside myself and need to talk to someone. Mr. Berlotti, it all happened during the past year. Dr. Asti believes he was set up, then threatened with a malpractice suit. Then he and his family received death threats," Sally's eyes welled up with tears.

Tony takes Sally's hand in sympathy. "Malpractice? Death Threats? What in the world...what happened, Sally? You can tell me."

Sally reaches for some tissue to wipe her nose.

"Oh, Mr. Berlotti, I have to trust you. There's no one else I can trust.   Dr. Asti went to Las Vegas for a seminar on new diagnostic procedures...he always likes to keep up with the latest information, you know. He was very tense when he returned, not like himself at all. Then he told me that he and his family were moving out-of-state because of certain events that happened while he was in Las Vegas."

"Please go on..."

"He told me that he was in his room at the Desert Inn, ready to retire, when his phone rang. A man with a Spanish accent told him that he had some materials from the conference to deliver. Dr. Asti told him to come to the room. When he opened the door, a stranger stuck a gun in his face and told him to back in, get dressed and not say a word. He had to get his medical bag and follow him quietly out of the hotel and all the while his captor had a gun in his side.

Dr. Asti followed instructions. When they got in the car, the stranger handcuffed and blindfolded him, and then they drove off. As he was led out of the car he could hear metal doors opening and a lot of aircraft noise. He assumed he was being led into a building near an airport. Then they were walking on a soft carpet, into a room where he could hear, but not understand, some men speaking in Spanish. When his cuffs and blindfold were removed he found himself in a bedroom with three men and one woman."

Sally gets up and paces the floor, extremely agitated.

"Stop, Sally. Perhaps you'll give me a refill on the coffee." Tony recognizes that Sally is struggling for control. She pours more coffee for Tony and opens a diet coke for herself, taking a big gulp.

"Now the real trouble begins for Dr. Asti. They said he would have to perform an abortion on the young woman. He told them he had never performed an abortion, that it was illegal and against his religious beliefs. He said he couldn't even do it in a emergency because he didn't have the proper equipment. One of the men slapped him hard in the face, causing his nose to bleed, then knocked him down and started kicking him..."

"Obviously, these thugs meant business," Tony interjected.

"Well, one of the other men shouted in Spanish for 'Manuel' to stop; that it was enough'."

Sally takes another sip of coke as Tony shakes his head in disbelief, but warning signals are popping up like storm signals. *"Las Vegas...Spanish speaking thugs...an airport...Manuel. Is it possible? Could this have been the conspirators at McCarren with more of their dirty schemes? This doesn't sound like just a coincidence!"*

Sally takes a deep breath and continues, seemingly anxious to tell all to the sympathetic Tony. She obviously has needed someone to share this information with her for a long while.

"According to Dr. Asti, they all went into a huddle while he tried to stop his nose bleed. One of the men went into another room and returned with two cameras, a large plastic tarp, two cut-up coat hangers and a tool box. They put the tarp on the bed, told the young woman to strip, get into a robe and lie on the bed. Then Dr. Asti was told to remove his jacket, roll up his sleeves, put his black bag on the bed, his stethoscope around his neck and begin going through the motions of performing an abortion."

Sally takes a deep breath and continues. "When Dr. Asti said, 'This is insane. This could kill the girl.' Manuel punched him in the back of the head, leveled his gun at him again and shouted, 'We agree you must pretend to do dee abortion'."

"When Dr. Asti didn't respond, it was 'If you no pretend, I keel you! Comprende?' Dr. Asti recognized he had no options and nodded his agreement. They opened the girl's robe, spread her legs, placed a long hanger in Dr. Asti's hand and began taking photos of them as he faked the operation."

"This is insane!" states Tony, pacing the floor in agitation. "Then what, Sally?"

"Dr. Asti said it was all over in five minutes but then he was told he would be sued for performing an illegal abortion and that the woman would testify against him, but the girl never spoke a word the whole time."

"What about her? Did Dr. Asti say? Was she pregnant or was it all faked?"

"Doctor couldn't confirm that she was pregnant but was 99 percent sure she wasn't; that it was a set-up, but couldn't understand why. It wasn't blackmail. They didn't demand money. But Dr. Asti did say they kept referring to 'Carlo' and 'Jose' during the ordeal."

Now bells and sirens ring in Tony's head as he hears the names. It all fits. Tony raises his hand. "OK, Sally. Stop. I've heard enough. Dr. Asti was certainly set-up."

"There's no more to tell, except that Dr. Asti was frightened and a very angry man when he left New York. He disappeared with his family and no one knows what happened to him or where he's gone." Sally looked at Tony thoughtfully, then asked, "Mr. Berlotti, is it possible you know something about this?"

"Sally, it is certainly much more than a coincidence but I can't be certain. And I can't tell you everything I suspect as it might put you at risk. Trust me, Sally. You were right to be careful and please don't discuss this with anyone else. May I have your word on that, Sally?"

Tony pats Sally on the shoulder as she starts to cry again. He leaves after Sally is in control again but without any further explanation. He heads directly for Dr. Monti's office.

En route to Dr. Monti's, Tony's only thoughts are, *"Sons-a-bitches! It's not enough that you're after me and my family. You framed an innocent man just because he was a good friend! I know you bastards are sending me another message. I'm gonna' get you; I've gotta get you. No matter what!!"*

Dr. Monti is not surprised. "Tony, the odds are against it being a coincidence. They must have known Guy Asti is your doctor. They're striking out against you on all fronts, hoping to rattle you, to make you so angry you become careless and you fall into a trap. Can you recall mentioning Guy's name to Dan Hill or Hal Brooks?"

"Nope. I would have no reason to give them his name."

"Well, try not to worry about it. Now that you're going back to Iran, Misha and I will find Guy. It may take a while—— but we'll find him."

"Good. We need to find out what else he knows and protect him."

Dr. Monti's radio activates with a call from his son, Peter. Tony sips a cappuccino, paying little attention to the radio conversation while thinking about Dr. Asti. When the conversation ends, Tony remarks, "Frank, did I hear correctly— Peter has a girl friend?"

"Yes, and he's nuts about her. They met in one of Peter's electronic classes. He says she's a genius on the verge of a major breakthrough in voice synthesizers. Her name is Judy Attwater. She lives in the Bronx near Fordham but is deeply depressed over recent events in her family, too."

"What events?"

"First, her father, a private detective, disappeared. Then, in deep depression, her mother committed suicide. She's the only child, has no nearby relatives. And now Peter says he wants to marry her."

"So—what's wrong with that?"

"I haven't met her yet—that's what wrong."

"Come on, Frank...Peter's cool. He always makes good decisions. I'm sure she's a lovely girl. Besides...as Peter's wife, she'd be a terrific asset to our group. Loosen up. Tell Peter you want to meet her and that you'll undoubtedly approve of his decision."

"I probably will. But right now my decision is maybe...and that's final." Frank grins at Tony.

"You will," Tony predicts. "Now let's start locating our...wait! It just came to me."

"What?"

"Eureka!...now I remember. Not long ago I told Dan Hill I had to break an appointment with him because of my biennial flight medical with Dr. Asti."

"Ah ha,...so that's the connection."

"Yeah, I'm sure," Tony's voice is disgusted. "And he passed it on to Carlo."

"Like I said, Tony, go to Iran and take care of business. This is costing you a lot. And try not to worry...we'll find Asti. Now let's talk about George. Is he sure he wants to be a lure and does he understand the danger?"

"Absolutely. There's no way I could talk him out of it. I've outlined all the dangers; all the pitfalls and hazards. But, you know, he wants to avenge his mother and sisters as badly as I do."

"In that case, I believe we should send George to an acting school to learn his new trade, then keep his identity secret except for our own group. Don't you agree?"

"I do. By the way, since we're dealing with Bolivians, I have my Tucson and Vegas men taking Spanish lessons. Have our New York staff do the same. It's absolutely necessary. I don't think anyone will refuse...but, if they do - fire 'em!"

"They'll agree."

"Good. Now I'm hungry. Let's go to Luigi's for a bite. Then I need to pack for Iran."

CHAPTER 17

HOSPITALIZED IN IRAN

October 6, 1974, TEHRAN, IRAN

After business stops in France and Yugoslavia, Tony and Jamshid are met at Tehran's Mehrabad Airport by agent Jahangir. Tony checks into the Intercontinental Hotel, then is driven to his Elizabeth II Blvd. office for a business briefing. Assured that his projects are on schedule and within budget, Tony authorizes a five percent pay increase for his entire staff, then invites his two project managers for dinner at the cozy Chez Michel. Following dinner, Tony and Jamshid drive to their secure house on Shahrivar Street for a briefing on the status of Dan Hill. Jahangir and his agents report that Hill is still in casts in Arad Hospital and it is unknown how long he is to remain. He has not had any CIA nor SAVAK visitors. His only visitor has been his secretary, who brought him papers and books. Hill's anti Khomeini movement was over with the helicopter crash. His only phone conversations have been with Sammy in Las Vegas and Hal Brooks in Mexico City. According to Jahangir, Hill wants to keep his hospitalization a secret.

Tony interrupts the briefing. "Jahangir, was I mentioned in any of his conversations?"

"Yes, Sir. He told his secretary that if you called, she should tell you that he is in London and that you should avoid contact with the US Embassy."

"Did he say why?"

"Yes, Sir. He said Ambassador Helms is shaking things up there and re-bugging everything."

"Anything else?"

"Oh, yes. His secretary received a call from his wife in Chile. She told Mrs. Hill that her husband was out of the country on special assignment. That seems strange, doesn't it?"

"No, not for Hill. He always lies and keeps her in the dark. That's probably why she drinks."

"One other important thing, Sir. Mr. Brooks, who knows you were coming to Iran, told Hill you are in Mexico."

Tony lights a cigar, leans back and ponders at length before continuing. "Gentlemen, I do believe Mr. Brooks is trying to help me. It will be interesting to see Hill's reaction when I walk into his room tomorrow."

"You're going to the hospital?" asks Jahangir.

"Yes, of course. I want him to know he can't hide from us. I'll be interested in knowing who he contacts after I leave his room. By the way, I'll tell him I'm staying at the Intercontinental but I'll be sleeping here until I leave Iran. Good work, men! Thank you and good night."

Next morning, Tony is driven to Arad Hospital. Before entering, he buys a large bag of Rafsanjan's best pistachios from a bearded old vendor at the hospital entrance. Upon receiving the all-clear signal from Jahangir, Tony walks up to Hill's room. He finds Hill asleep, connected to an array of Rube Goldberg type pulleys, I.V. tubes and monitors. As he looks at the man he knows is planning to have him killed, Tony thinks: *"I'd like to smother the bastard right now, but I need him to get the others, so let's have some fun and torment the hell out of him."*

Instead of waiting for Hill to open his eyes, Tony writes a note, places it in the pistachio bag on Hill's bedside table and leaves the room unnoticed. At the hospital entrance, Tony buys another bag of pistachios from the old vendor, enters his waiting car and offers some to Jamshid and Jahangir as the car pulls away from the curb.

"Ah, Iran's finest pistachios," comments Jahangir.

"Yes," confirms Jamshid, "and your second purchase made the old man very happy."

"They were a great buy; but, you know something?" adds Tony, "Pay him to leave and replace him with one of our men."

Jamshid and Jahangir laugh, give thumbs-up, say something in Farsi and smile at their leader.

"OK, what's the joke?" asks Tony.

"The old pistachio man," replies Jamshid, "he is one of our men."

"Touché! Great move. I owe you one."

They enjoy a hearty laugh and drive to the Safe House.

One hour later a nurse awakens Hill for an injection, then leaves. Hill takes a drink of water and notices the bag. He opens the bag and reads the note: "Mr. Hill, please enjoy these fine pistachios and get well soon. The Committee."

In a panic, he immediately hits the bedside call button and summons the nurse.

"Who brought me this bag of pistachios?" He demands.

The blank look on the nurses face alerts Hill that she doesn't understand English.

He shouts, "English doctor! English doctor!" and waves her off.

Five minutes later the nurse returns with a doctor.

"Calm down, Mr. Hill. No one, other than the nurse, was seen entering or leaving your room all morning."

Hill calls his secretary. "Sarah," he commands abruptly, "Call the major hotels and find out if Anthony Berlotti or Carlo Perez are there. Then call Alamir and Hashemi and tell them to come here."

As the above call is monitored at the Safe House, Tony is advised that Alamir and Hashemi are Hill's men who were active in the anti-Khomeini movement.

Hill knows that either Tony Berlotti and Carlo Perez could be his ultimate nemesis. Both hate him and have good reasons to have him eliminated. He re-reads the note and wonders why it's signed "The Committee".

"It can't be my committee. Who? Why? I need to get out of here."

A half hour later he calls his secretary. "Sarah, what news do you have on Berlotti and Perez?"

"I'm sorry, Mr. Hill. Neither one is in Tehran."

"Call Mr. Brooks in Mexico and find out if he knows where Berlotti is located, then call Las Vegas and ask Sammy if he's seen or heard from Carlo lately. And did you contact Alamir and Hashemi?"

"Yes, Sir. They are on their way to the hospital. I will make the other calls right now. Good bye."

As Tony prepares to leave the Safe House for Bandar Abbas, Zahedan and Babolsar, radio silence is broken by a signal from the old pistachio vendor who alerts that Hashemi and Alamir have just entered the hospital.

Five minutes later, the two men enter Hill's room and the Montico bug picks up the conversation:

Hill shouts, "What the hell took you so long?" and points to the pistachio bag. "Look! Look!! Somebody is trying to kill me!"

"What? Who?" asks Alamir.

"They're pistachios, God damn it! Quick, get them out of here – very carefully. Have them analyzed for poison and explosives."

"Who brought them?" asks Hashemi.

"How the hell do I know? I was asleep. Now go! Get those damn things out of here! Go, damn it, Go!"

The note works beautifully, as planned. Hill's panic and hysterical paranoia is music to Tony's ears.

As they are about to leave Hill's room, Alamir adds an interesting twist to the conversation.

"There's an old pistachio vendor downstairs at the entrance. We will ask him if anyone purchased his pistachios this morning. If so he may give us a description of the buyer."

"Yes, do it! And bribe the old man to call you if that buyer returns," orders Hill.

The Safe House is now exploding with laughter as the SAVAK team celebrate their successful pistachio coup.

"Well," grins Tony with a rare smile, "Mr. Murphy is on our side for a change. There have to be a few breaks – and a few laughs – for us once in awhile."

CHAPTER 18

TONY HIRES DR. ASTI

SATURDAY, OCTOBER 19, 1974, NEW YORK

On Saturday, Tony and Jamshid arrive at JFK International Airport, lease a car and drive to the Montico electronic assembly shop on Long Island to pick up Dr. Monti's secret "Electronic Field Frequency Induction Coil".

"It's no secret," states Dr. Monti, "that the National Security Agency has been using a similar underwater device in their operation called Ivy Bells. Our device is superior due its electronic-field feature and tamper proof qualities. Ours will self destruct when tampering breaks the field. The only way the unit can be removed from a cable is by transmitting a pre-set electronic code to over-ride the self destruct mode, which then opens the unit from within."

Tony asks, "Is it paying off?"

"Yes. Misha is talking to an ex Mossad friend who told him money is no problem."

"That's good. Now walk us through its operation."

After his four hour demonstration, Dr. Monti looks at his watch. "Wow, look at the time. I'm in the mood for some good sea food. How about the Snapper Inn?"

"Frank, you read my mind. Let's go. And can you give me an update about Dr. Asti on the way? I feel responsible about what has happened to him - it's awful!"

Upon entering the Snapper Inn, Vincent, the maitre d' greets Dr. Monti. "Good evening, Dr. Monti. This way please. Your table is ready."

Jamshid assumes his usual back-up position - alone at a nearby table.

Tony immediately notices the table is set for a party of four.

"What's this, Frank. Who's joining us?"

"Must be a mistake. Come on—let's have a drink."

As Tony and Dr. Monti enjoy their cocktails, their discussion, as always, turns to strategies to trap Dan Hill, Carlo and Los Machos.

Tony then asks, "So, Frank, any luck on locating Dr. Asti?"

"Dr. Asti?"

"Yes, Frank, you remember, my poor physician and friend Dr. Asti."

Dr. Monti leans back in his chair, takes a sip of his Old Fashioned, then smiles. "Why don't you turn around and ask him yourself."

Tony turns and stares in disbelief. Standing behind him are Dr. Asti and Dr. Monti's son, Peter. Tony jumps up and hugs both men, "Holy mackerel! What a great surprise!"

As they are seated, Dr. Monti signals to Vincent for drinks, they all order sea food, then Tony pumps Dr. Asti for details regarding his unfortunate encounter with Los Machos. As Dr. Asti explains he is understandably full of anger, hostility and the desire for revenge. The fear of losing his family, his life and his license have prompted him to move out of state into a relative's summer home.

"I was so intimidated by those miserable bastards that I gave up my practice. I was innocent! I'd never perform an illegal abortion! But they have those damn photographs! The sons-of-bitches framed me! I'll never rest until I get even."

"Guy, I feel guilty as hell and sorrier than you can imagine. I'm afraid it was your association with me that got you framed and intimidated. I know the men who framed you. They are the same bastards that killed my Gloria, Nancy and Mary last year when they torched my home. I'll share the whole story with you, but not here." Tony glances around at the crowds of people. His meaning is obvious. "For now, let's enjoy our dinner. I can't tell you how relieved I am that you and your family are safe..."

Tony is thoughtful as the four men eat. Finally, he says, "Guy, if you'd like to get even, and I know you would, I have a unique plan to trap our mutual enemies that will also allow you to practice medicine in safety. If that interests you, come to my office tomorrow morning and we'll talk."

"Tony, I'll see you tomorrow morning."

Tony catches Dr. Monti's subtle nod, thinking, *"Yes, recruiting Guy should be a piece of cake. He'll be back in his field of work and getting his revenge..."*

OCTOBER 25, 1974, NEW YORK

Dr. Asti is early for his appointment, anxious to hear what Tony has to offer. Tony tells Dr. Asti why they have mutual enemies. Then he offers him an assignment. He owes this man for what happened.

"Your official, 'cover' position will be Medical Examiner for my engineering/construction business employees. Your duties are to establish, review and advise on corporate medical procedures and examine employees as required, under a three-year agreement. Sound OK to you?"

"That's good-but it isn't enough, Tony. I want revenge for what they did to me...and you!"

"That's just your 'cover' position, Guy. Your other, and primary, assignment will be to assist my A-Tec Corporation's Capture Team in pursuit and elimination of the assassins. Still interested?"

"Hand me that agreement!"

"You won't be sorry. We'll train you in clandestine operations, get you a passport with a new name. Dr. Monti will obtain a new medical license for you. You might want to grow a beard, change your style of dress etc. They won't find you. We'll give you and your family protection, too."

"I'm ready! When do I start?"

"Return to your family and wait until we provide you with all your new documents."

Early next morning, Tony meets George at Denny's Restaurant.

"So, Dad...were you surprised to see Dr. Asti?"

"I certainly was - and it's amazing how quickly Peter located him."

"I know. He told me how he and Judy did it. You think they'll get in trouble?"

"No way! Dr. Monti has a unique phone line protection system that can't be traced back to us."

"Cool! How does it work?"

"Eat your pancakes—they're getting cold."

"What...you don't know how it works?" George grins at his father.

"Lawyers don't need to know everything! Eat your pancakes."

"Ah ha -you don't know." It's the first time in a long time that Tony hears real laughter from his son.

"He told me," Tony grins at his son. "But to be honest, it was over my head. Now, shut up and eat your pancakes."

A few minutes later, after cleaning his plate, George flags the waitress, pays the check and father and son walk the two blocks to the campus. The grounds are covered with fallen leaves that look like a crazy quilt of colors. It's a brilliant day and both father and son feel exuberant and full of life. It is the first time since his personal tragedy that Tony feels that it is good to be alive.

"Perhaps time does heal, at least a little..."

"Okay, George. Now how about demonstrating your martial arts skills? Or have I been wasting my money?"

"I'm a good student, Dad, but no way, Dad, am I going to take you on. I'm afraid I'll hurt you."

"That'll be the day!" Tony grins at his son. "Come on...give it your best shot. Or are you chicken?"

"I love you, Dad and you know I'm not chicken." But seeing Tony's grin, he agrees. "Well, okay, if you insist. Now here comes your lesson."

They remove their jackets and square-off. Tony waits with open arms. George suddenly makes the first lightning head-on attack and both go crashing to the ground. As they take turns dropping each other, rolling over and over on the ground, scattering leaves in all directions, a group of students surround the pair and cheer them on. Most root for the George. A few root for the older man.

Moments later, George "gives".

The two men laugh, bear hug and begin to remove leaves out of their mouths, hair and clothes. The standing ovation is interrupted by the arrival of the campus security officer.

"OK...who started the fight?"

"Fight?...who was fighting?" responds Tony, raising his eyebrows and shrugging at the crowd.

"Then why are you guys all messed up?"

"This happens to be my son, Officer. And we like rolling around in the leaves in the fall."

The guard scratches his head. The crowd cheers again as Tony and George walk away.

"Whew," whispers Tony, "I thought that officer was gonna' find us guilty and write-up a citation."

"No, Dad. That would be practicing Napoleonic Law."

"Napoleonic Law? What the hell is that?"

"They don't teach that in engineering school. If you went to law school you'd know it means guilty until proven innocent. And that, Dad, is your legal lesson for the day."

"Touché. I'm proud of you, George. Keep up the good work. Another thing, let's think of what we'll call you when you become a female impersonator."

"I've been thinking about that. Since I'm George Gregory, how does 'Gi-Gi' sound?"

"Sounds like a French cream puff,...but, I like it...I guess!"

"I'm not gonna' need a face-lift...or 'stuff' like that...am I?"

"No way. You're a good lookin' kid. You have your mother's fine features and coloring. You'll need some help with the boobs - and a professional make-over from time to time. "

"Well, Dad, I know I'm going to feel ridiculous, but I'm looking forward to the challenge...especially if we can trap the assassins with my 'acting'."

"Yeah, my son - the sex kitten. You'll make one hell of a lure. They're gonna' pay for what they did to us, son. And, I'm sorry, George, but I must head back to New York. Then it's New Mexico, Arizona and Nevada. This operation is costing me an arm and a leg and I have to keep bringing it in - but I'll spend every cent I have if that 's what it takes. Keep up your good work. I'm proud of you!"

LATE 1974, MEXICO

Tony, pleased with his domestic projects, returns to Mexico City. He is met by his old friend and associate, Victor Moran, and briefed on the status of his two contracts in Mexico over a late dinner at their favorite restaurant, San Angel Inn. Then he is driven to his apartment.

Next morning during breakfast, Tony decides to review his diaries before calling Haldon Brooks. *"I need to look for clues that could link Brooks to the Conspiracy. He's been too helpful."*

He begins his review. Some notes are detailed; others just one or two word memory joggers.

Tony runs his yellow high-lighter through the following notes:

- ❑ Hoffa released from prison on December 23, '71 by Nixon. Quid pro quo?"
- ❑ Vesco takes off for Cuba w. $700 million in '72. Check Carlo/Vesco connection?
- ❑ Nixon resigns on Aug 9, '74. Ford grants him immunity from the law -
- ❑ In December '74, Director Colby turns over to Justice Dept. the Inspector General's report on Helms. Hill claims this seriously damaged counter-intelligence!
- ❑ Roselli in trouble with his people, especially Meyer Lansky, for skimming and double-cross. Hill tipped-off Giancana.
- ❑ Hill remains hospitalized in Tehran.
- ❑ Who is Hill's real employer? Is he a double-agent? Don't think he's CIA.
- ❑ How does Louis tie into the conspiracy? Is he Mossad? Have Misha check.
- ❑ Carlo in temporary hiding in Cuba after threat from Roselli.
- ❑ Los Machos shuttling between Bolivia, Cuba, Mexico and Vegas. Set them up for a sucker game at their hanger, then destroy it!
- ❑ Kruchenko incommunicado in Tucson. Check lockers at Marana!
- ❑ Dr. Asti eager for non medical action. Good.
- ❑ Hal Brooks just too friendly. Increase his tail!

Tony looks up from his diaries and notes, stretches, makes a cappuccino, lights a cigar, then reviews his financial position.

"Good thing my projects are turning a profit or this manhunt would ruin me. I've got to increase the cash flow to put more heat on the assassins. We could eliminate Hill and Sammy anytime, but need them to trap the others. It's OK, I can wait. Their time will come. Right now I've got to get a better handle on Hal Brooks." He makes another cappuccino and calls Brooks.

"Sorry, Mr. Berlotti," responds the secretary in perfect English, "Mr. and Mrs. Brooks are spending a few days at Lake Chapala. He told me to give you his number if you called."

She gives Tony the number, invites him to come to the office for a map of how to find Brooks on the lake, then suggests: "Or, if you're not tied-up, I can deliver the map to you later this evening somewhere."

"This sounds like it could be a come-on", thinks Tony, remembering that Dan Hill tried to nail him with a hooker in Iran. *"Brooks probably told her I'm a widower. Is this another set-up? I've got to find out, but not until we get ready for her. Damn, I didn't get a good look at her in Hal's office."*

"You know something? I don't even know your name."

"I'm sorry, I thought Mr. Brooks told you about me. Mrs. Brooks and I are cousins. I'm Lucia."

"Lucia...ah, what a pretty name. Are you married?"

"Yes...but my husband is in Guatemala on business."

"My, how convenient," thinks Tony before responding to her second opening.

"I'm tied up tonight. How about dinner tomorrow?"

"Fine."

"Good. I'll pick you up at your office tomorrow at 7 P.M. sharp, OK, Lucia?"

"I'll be waiting, Mr. Berlotti. Good day, Sir."

Tony alerts Jamshid and Rashid. They agree that Tony should take her to dinner at San Angel Inn. He is well known there, will occupy his favorite table and be covered by Jamshid and Rashid from separate nearby tables.

The next evening, Lucia is waiting at the front door of Brooks' building when he arrives in a taxi. She is alone and well dressed, but, much to his surprise, not the alluring bombshell Tony expected. Lucia has a pretty face but she's short, decidedly overweight and hardly the type who would attract the average man. *"Well, this is an interesting twist,"* thinks Tony. He greets her with a handshake, helps her into the taxi and instructs the driver to take them to San Angel Inn via the Anillo Periferico (the peripheral expressway). Jamshid follows in Tony's car. Rashid is already at San Angel Inn, reserving tables.

Upon entering the taxi, Lucia immediately engages Tony in conversation. "Hal...I mean Mr. Brooks told me..."

"That's OK, Lucia," interrupts Tony, "since Hal is a cousin by marriage, you don't need to be formal. And you can call me Tony."

"Thank you, Tony. He told me you're a widower...?" It was an unspoken question.

"I really don't like to talk about it, except to say that my wife and daughters died in a house fire."

"He didn't tell me. I'm so terribly sorry. I didn't mean to pry."

Her response piques Tony's curiosity. *"She really sounds honest. Or, is she a good liar.?"*

"No problem, Lucia. Now that you know about me...tell me about yourself."

Lucia doesn't hold back. She speaks non-stop all the way to San Angel Inn. Tony learns she's happily married to Alfredo, who sells heavy construction and mining equipment. She and Alfredo have been married eighteen years, have a son and a daughter who are honor students actively involved in sports and drama. Lucia learned English as an exchange student in Phoenix, Arizona and still corresponds with, what she calls, "my American family". In less than a half hour, Tony knows almost everything there is to know about Lucia.

With the taxi approaching the restaurant, Tony relaxes, thinking, *"She certainly never made anything that could be construed as a pass at me. I may be wrong. This girl could be for real."*

Dinner goes smoothly. Lucia does not ask Tony any personal questions nor push Alfredo's business on him. She has only good words to say about Hal Brooks and, during dessert, presents the Lake Chapala map.

Tony takes Lucia home to her apartment overlooking Parque America, by 10 P.M. He is pleased she does not invite him up for a nightcap, shakes her hand, promises to meet Alfredo and her children one day. He departs with one less suspicion to occupy his overburdened mind.

CHAPTER 19

TONY MEETS CARMEN

DECEMBER, 1974, MEXICO

Dr. Monti confirms that he has provided Dr. Asti with a new passport and that Asti is eager to start his dual assignments. While Tony and Hal Brooks are becoming friends, Tony is still cautious, wary of Hal's connections with Hill. They often schedule late lunches at Rincon Gaucho to review bridge strategy for games later in the evening. On December 14, during one of these luncheons, Hal extends an invitation.

"Tony, the Azteca Club is holding its yearly formal dinner dance next Saturday. If you will be in town, Alice and I would like you to come as our guest. Alice's good friend, Carmen, is visiting us and you would make it a great foursome. Later, we can have a marathon bridge game at our place."

Tony looks skeptical as he considers his schedule. "I've never dated, Hal, since Gloria died..."

"I understand Tony, but don't think of it as a date; just as making it a pleasant foursome. Let me tell you about Carmen. She's a knockout, divorced and from one of the most prestigious families in Mexico. She's well educated and wealthy; really loaded!"

"I don't know, Hal." Typically, Tony takes his time lighting a cigar while considering the invitation. *"Could this be another set-up? Damn, I'm so paranoid I can't look at anything, even an invitation to a holiday party, without considering the pitfalls. Well, I was wrong about his cousin, Lucia so I'll play along and see what happens. I need more to life..."*

"What the hell, Hal...it's that time of the year and I could use some socializing. Count me in."

"Great. I'll make the arrangements...and Tony, I guarantee, you won't be sorry."

Upon meeting Carmen, elegantly and expensively gowned, jeweled and coiffed, Tony, indeed, is not a bit sorry. She's the kind of woman he likes: tall, about five foot eleven, and full figured with a well defined waist, Carmen is the epitome of the classic Castilian beauty. Her smile is dazzling as she looks at Tony, extending her hand, and her laughing dark eyes are flirtatious but undeniably intelligent.

"Señor Berlotti, I've heard so much about you..."

Tony, impeccable in his tuxedo, bows low over Carmen's hand, kissing it lightly. Raising his head he catches a look of approval in Carmen's smile. At an imposing 6'-5" and 225 pounds, Tony looks like he just stepped out of an ad for *GENTLEMEN'S QUARTERLY*. As he steps back, Carmen tilts her head slightly to one side and voices her approval.

"How grand to look forward to dancing with a tall gentleman. I'm delighted to meet you, Señor Berlotti."

"Please, call me Tony. It will be my great pleasure to be your escort. May I call you Carmen?"

"Indeed, Tony."

Carmen and Tony seemingly have eyes only for each other and Hal Brooks gives his wife a conspiratorial wink as she squeezes his hand. Tony glances at the two and raises an eyebrow as he grins at them. It promises to be a wonderful evening.

All the stops are pulled out for this annual holiday affair and the party is a huge success. The food and service are superb and the music is classic "big band" with the occasional romantic bossanovas of Sergio Mendes, all conducive to intimate dancing. Mindful of his manners, Tony has a few dances throughout the evening with Alice, but finds Carmen more and more enticing and a beautiful dancer. He takes full advantage of the slow tunes to hold her as close as possible. Her curves mold themselves beautifully into Tony's body as he leads her about the floor. They are easily the most attractive and elegant couple on the floor.

Tony is just as impressed with Carmen's lively intelligence and subtle sense of humor as he is with her charm. *"She's certainly the right age if I judge correctly...like Alice, late forties or early fifties."*

For the first time since Gloria's death Tony finds himself intensely desiring a woman. Never one to throw caution to the winds, however, he tortures himself with unanswered questions about her motivation. *"Perhaps Hal is very subtle and using Carmen..."*

Close to midnight, Alice suggests that they return to their penthouse apartment for coffee and bridge.

"I must confess, folks, I'm wilting. My feet are protesting from all this dancing."

Tony is reluctant to give up the pleasure of holding Carmen in his arms, but feels there will be a greater opportunity to learn more about this intriguing lady in a private environment.

Later, while Alice and Hal are in the kitchen with the maid, Carmen makes a move that arouses Tony's suspicions.

"Tony, how would you like to spend the New Year holiday at my hacienda in Manzanillo?"

He does not look at Carmen but takes his time lighting a cigar. *"Looks like it's time for truth or consequences; her truth or my consequences."* As he looks at Carmen his eyes, heretofore warm and approving, are cool and watchful.

"I'm flattered Carmen, but, do you always ask strangers to your home on your first date?"

Carmen replies with a delightful laugh, then, "Why, Tony, you are so very proper! How refreshing! But I don't consider you a stranger at all. Hal has told me so much about you I feel I've known you for years. Be assured, propriety will be observed, Tony. Hal and Alice will be joining us."

Tony suppresses a sigh of relief. "I apologize, Carmen. I think it must be overwork. Manzanillo is one of my favorite places, especially Las Hadas. I'll be delighted to come. New Year's Eve is a bad time for me."

"I understand, Tony. I've had some times like that myself."

After coffee and assorted pastries, the four sit down for some lively bidding, smart defensive plays and stimulating, competitive bridge. Carmen is an excellent partner. After about an hour, Tony receives a silent electronic signal. He excuses himself and goes to the bathroom to receive the radio message from Dr. Monti.

"Hello, Frank...what's up?"

"Bad news, Tony," replies Dr. Monti. "They need you in Iran...like yesterday!"

"What's the problem?"

"That great Savak team of yours has learned that the original drilling records for your Zahedan copper project were falsified."

"Sons-a-bitches! They'll stop at nothing. I'll be out of here in 24 hours. Tell them to put a hold on the project. Then tell Jahangir to get my lawyer, Zangi, to start the paper work for a lawsuit against the drilling company. Damn! This is gonna' screw up the first great holiday since Gloria died."

"Sorry, Tony."

"Me, too, Frank." Tony's tone of voice changed from anger to regret. "I've been spending the evening with a friend of the Brooks', a really great gal, Carmen. I'll tell you about her later. But thanks for the call. Have Iran send me a cable informing me of the emergency. Good night, Frank."

Returning to the bridge game, time flies as Tony and Carmen learn more about each other. It turns out to be a marathon, with nobody noticing the time until the maid comes in about six and announces that breakfast is ready. "Breakfast," groans Tony. "We've been eating all night and I'm on a diet. How did it get to be morning already?"

It's obvious to Hal that Tony and Carmen are reluctant to call an end to the party. Their body language suggests a serious interest in advancing a relationship. Carmen grabs Tony's arm, however, and leads him into the dining room.

"Hey, big guy. A man like you needs to eat. Besides, it's not polite to refuse our host and hostess."

"Big guy! No one has called me that since Gloria." He grins, "You win!" Mentally cursing the situation in Iran, Tony willingly goes along with any plan that will prolong this pleasant encounter with Carmen. *"But this is why I can't be involved romantically with anyone!"*

After breakfast, Tony takes advantage of the ladies' absence to tell Hal why he must leave immediately for Iran.

"I'm sorry, Tony. I suspect Carmen will be, too. Anything I can do for you?"

"Thanks, Hal." *"This is the opening I've been waiting for; this should prove if Hal can be trusted."* "As a matter of fact, there is something. Don't advise Hill that I'm going to Iran."

"No problem, Tony. You got it."

The two men shake hands in agreement as the ladies return. They have changed from evening clothes into discrete gowns and peignoirs, ready for bed. Tony's immediate reaction, at the sight of Carmen, is physical and emotional. *"Jesus Christ, I want this woman! It's been so long and she's utterly desirable. And I don't just want a one-night stand. But what if this is a the set-up? How do I get out of here gracefully?"* As Tony struggles with his conflicting needs, his strong will power takes control. *"If this is meant to be, it will still be mine when the time is right."*

He walks over to Carmen as she looks at him expectantly, taking her hand in both of his. "I think we all need some sleep at this point. I know I do, much as I would like to stay longer. But, unfortunately I have a business meeting with my Mexican associate, Victor Moran, this morning. It's something I can't put off. If you don't mind, I'd like to have another cup of coffee with you and then I must go."

"I understand," replies Carmen, squeezing his hand.

Alice and Hal tactfully depart for their own room while Tony has a last cup of coffee with Carmen. He assures her of his desire to see her again, and often. Before leaving, he gives her his Mexican business card.

"Please call me, Carmen. Any excuse will do, even if it's just to say 'hello'."

Carmen retrieves her evening bag from the entry table, puts his card in it and returns, offering Tony her own business card. Tony tries to hide his astonishment as he reads, 'Carmen Vegas, Directora; Grupo Monterrey; Telefono (905) 584-9000.' The Monterrey Group is a small cartel of Mexico's richest citizens that controls much of the business and politics in Mexico.

"Well, I'll be damned! Brooks was certainly right about her. Certainly no financial motivation here for her to be involved in any intrigue against me."

While Tony debates whether or not he should kiss Carmen goodbye, she takes matters into her own hands. She hugs him close for a moment, then puts one hand on either side of his head and kisses him lightly on the mouth, then whispers, "Don't lose my card, Tony. You, too, may call anytime just to say 'hello'."

Still worried, Tony does not give her his apartment and Safe House numbers.

"I'm always on the go, Carmen, sometimes to very remote locations. And I often travel unexpectedly, just like this next trip. The office is the best place to get a message to me."

Carmen reassures Tony that she understands and does not question him, relieving Tony considerably. Before leaving he promises to call her as soon as possible, then impulsively takes her in his arms and gives her a kiss full of promise, whispering, "Buenas noches, Carmen, y dulce sueños." ("Goodnight, Carmen and sweet dreams.")

Tony flies to New York, picks up his Zahedan files and books his flight to Iran. Before leaving, he meets Dr. Monti for dinner and reveals some interesting facts about Carmen.

"Frank, meeting Carmen is the best thing that's happened to me since the fire. I really have a good feeling about her and, I must confess, feel I could be emotionally involved..."

"What did you find out about her?"

"Well, for starters, she's intelligent with a great sense of humor, elegant and tall with a shape to die-for. She's also a director in the Monterrey Group."

"Bingo! That means she has top level business and political connections there."

"Right! And, according to Hal, she's loaded."

"Of course, you can't be a part of the Monterrey Group without lots of money. What else?"

"Hal told me her father owned two silver mines, an underground sulfur mine, high rises in Acapulco and Mexico City and 5,000 acres of coastal land in Baja California. He was a powerful member of the Monterrey Group. And Hal's wife, Alice, told me that, as the only child of an adoring, protective and very rich father, Carmen was sent to the finest private schools in Mexico and the United States. She graduated as a business major from UCLA and then became a partner in her father's enterprises. As I mentioned, she is very sharp."

"Great, so far. Anything else?"

"Carmen told me her mother died at age thirty eight of silicosis (black lung). Her death was attributed to many years of exposure to dust and fumes from copper crushing plants, concentrators and smelters where her father worked in northern Mexico. She also told me her marriage to playboy Raul Vegas lasted less than one year. She divorced him after her father's private detective caught him cheating on her. After that, she devoted herself to business. Alice told me she has been distrustful of men and avoided any other relationships. When her father died of a heart attack, she was thirty-eight and the Monterrey Group unanimously accepted her as a director in his stead. She met Alice playing bridge over fifteen years ago and they have been best friends ever since."

"And what have you found out about Hal Brooks?"

"Hal grew up in Mexico while his father worked as a consultant to Pemex. He and Alice met at the American School as teenagers. They married soon after Hal graduated as a petroleum engineer. According to Carmen, Hal is a consultant to an international oil syndicate."

Surprised that so much information was revealed, Dr. Monti cautions Tony.

"I strongly suggest, Tony, that you continue to find out all you can about Carmen. Don't let your guard down, though. She may slip and provide some information you need..."

"Frank, you're more paranoid than me. But what if she's innocent? What if she is exactly who she seems? This is the first woman I've been attracted to since Gloria's death."

"Tony, I understand. You're lonely. You need, and deserve companionship, but, don't lose your head. Be cool. And you have to protect her, too. I know you remember what happened to Gloria and your girls. Guard your heart and cover your ass until you're sure you know the full truth."

"Don't worry, Frank, I will, even though my heart says 'go full steam ahead'!" There was a short pause, then Tony grinned like a schoolboy. "I think she likes me, Frank!"

"There are lots of women out there who would go for you, Tony."

All the way to Tehran, Tony, totally infatuated, can't help thinking about Carmen but wonders if she and Hal are part of the conspiracy. *"This whole scenario with Brooks is bizarre. He's gone out of his way to help me. He's told me the truth about Hill, yet he and Hill take orders from the same man and part of an organization that's out to kill me. But, then, I thought Brooks tried to set me up with Lucia. I was wrong. Now it's Carmen I have to worry about... Too bad I'll miss her New Year's invitation...but...first things first. Sooner or later I'll get to the truth about her...and Hal. Come on, Tony, you need to concentrate on this latest crises..."* he admonishes himself.

The news from his Savak Team about the Zahedan Project proves to be correct. With a tip by an inside source in the drilling company, Tony's Savak team correctly identified and exposed the falsified records and cover-up by the company's Managing Director and Chief Geologist. Tony begins a crash drilling program to determine the true ore grade and reserves, then implements legal action against the company. Frustrated and angry over this untimely and expensive turn of events, Tony calls his lifelong friend and confidante, Dr. Monti, to vent his pent up feelings.

"Hello, Frank. It's me, Tony. Yep, the bastards falsified the records! It'll be several months before I get accurate test results, but it doesn't look good. Regardless, Frank. the mothers' are gonna' pay for this!"

"Bad news, Tony, but you'll resolve it. Did Dan Hill's name come up in any of the records?"

"No, but I haven't ruled him out. The son-of-a-bitch is still in the hospital and doesn't know I'm in Iran. The conspirators' oil syndicate ordered him to locate Khomeini and have him eliminated."

"I'm not surprised. Khomeini would be bad news for everybody."

"Right, and we won't try to obstruct Hill's progress in that direction. Other than that, I'm stuck here for the holidays. And I really was looking forward to the holiday at Carmen's."

"Don't worry, Tony. You'll get your chance with her if it's meant to be. Good luck on your litigation. Ciao."

The press of business, preoccupation with the assassins, preparing for litigation and living in a non-Christian country conspire for Tony to lose track of time and the date until George calls on Christmas day.

"Merry Christmas, Dad. I'm with Uncle Frank, Peter and Judy. We all miss you, Dad."

At the sound of "Merry Christmas, Tony, with tears in his eyes, shakes his head.

"Great Scot, George, where did the time go? Merry Christmas, son !" He spends the next half hour talking with George and the group, then decides to call Carmen. After eight rings, Tony realizes he called her office. Frustrated, he throws her card on the desk, then lights a cigar. *"Damn, what's happening to me. I'm losing it! I forgot to get her home number and I forgot Christmas!"*

After blowing smoke in all directions, he bends over to tap his cigar in the ashtray and, voila, his frustration turns to a sigh of relief when he looks at Carmen's card. The card landed upside down and, clearly written on the back, is her home number. Tony looks at his watch again and estimates it's about midnight in Mexico. *"She told me not to lose her card. That shows interest. She invited me to her hacienda. That definitely shows interest. And she's given me her home number! I've got to call to let her know I really want to see her again."*

He relights his cigar and calls. A female answers on the sixth ring.

"Hola. Con quien habla?" (Hello. With whom am I speaking?")

The connection is poor and her voice sounds like it's coming from a submarine. Tony hesitates, then, *"It's her!"* "Hello, Carmen?"

"Yes, Tony, hello. You remembered. I'm so glad! Feliz Navidad." (Merry Christmas)

"Feliz Navidad, Carmen."

"Where are you, Tony? You sound so far away.."

"I am far away, in Tehran. But it feels like a million miles right now. Didn't Hal tell you?"

"No! We haven't spoken since the party."

"God, how I wish I could believe her completely." "I'm here on a business emergency, Carmen. Looks like I'll be stuck here for several weeks."

"Oh, Tony, what disappointing news." Carmen sounded truly regretful.

"I'm sorry, Carmen. I was looking forward to your invitation. May I have a rain-check?"

"Of course! If I'm not here, my office will tell you where to reach me. How do I reach you?"

Still paranoid that Carmen could be setting him up, Tony refrains from giving her his apartment and Safe House numbers. He explains that since he travels constantly, sometimes to remote sites, his Tehran office generally knows where to reach him. They each express their wish that they were back at the dinner dance and Hal's apartment, then Tony apologizes for calling so late.

"Tony, you can call me anytime!"

He promises to call her frequently, then ends the conversation with, "Buenas noches, Carmen, y dulce sueños." (Good night, Carmen, and sweet dreams.). Tony hears a little sniffle and a catch in Carmen's voice as she wishes Tony goodnight.

Tony spends the next two days being briefed on Dan Hill's activities. He learns that Hill was just released from Arad Hospital, is walking with a crutch and that before leaving the hospital, he instructed his men to tell the old pistachio vendor to report if anyone asks for him. He called Mr. Louis in Switzerland and was told that Louis left the country and his whereabouts are unknown. Apparently desperate to learn what happened to Louis, Hill called

Sammy. Sammy said he didn't hear anything about Louis, that Hoffa sounded disgusted with everyone, Giancana was annoyed with Roselli over the skimming allegations by Lansky and Trafficante warned that Hoffa and everybody else that they better keep their mouths shut to the Feds.

When dealing with the conspirators, Tony considers psychological warfare intriguing and a necessary tool in his arsenal. On the morning of New Year's Eve, he has the pistachio vendor call Hill's man, Alamir, advising that a man with a Spanish accent came to the hospital asking for Señor Hill. Anticipating a swift response, Tony, Jamshid and Jahangir sit in their car, a block from the U. S. Embassy, waiting for the call to Hill at the Semiramis Hotel. Their wait is short. The new Montico bug, placed in Hill's room several days ago, picks up the conversation.

"Hello, Mister Hill. This is Alamir."

"Yes, Alamir."

"The old pistachio man called. A man came to the hospital looking for you."

"Who? Did he leave a message? Did the old man give you a description?"

"No, Sir, no name. No message. Only that the man spoke with a Spanish accent, wanted to know where to find you and left in a taxi."

The long silence brings a smile to Tony's face. "Well, men, think he's worried?"

Jamshid gives a thumbs up. "Yes, Rais. He surely thinks it was Carlo Perez or one of the Machos."

Hill is heard cursing, then, as his paranoia mounts, he screams into the phone, "Go to the hospital and offer the old man money! Intimidate him! Make him talk! Whatever it takes! Find out who came to the hospital! Now, goddamn it!!"

"Sorry, Sir, we already checked. The old man is gone."

The cursing resumes and Tony lights a cigar, enjoying every second of Hill's anguish. " Ahhhh, now we know he's worried, men!"

Later, as always lately, Tony can't help thinking about Carmen; he hasn't been emotionally involved with a woman since Gloria. Determined to follow-up on what holds so much promise, Tony decides to call her at 11:30 P.M. Manzanillo time. A man answers the phone on the third ring.

"Buenas noches y feliz año nuevo!" (Good evening and Happy New Year!)

Tony immediately recognizes the voice. "Happy new year, Hal. This is Tony,"

"Greetings, Tony. Alice and I had a feeling you'd call. I assume you're still in Iran?"

"Yes, damn it! I wish I were there. I really feel bad about canceling Carmen's invitation. Is she upset about it?"

"No, just disappointed. Man, you made a hell of a hit with her. Hang on, Alice is with her on the balcony looking at a few premature fire works. I'll get her."

As Tony lights a cigar, he hears voices, laughter and the unmistakable sound of Guy Lombardo in the phone. His wait is short as soon an out of breath Carmen answers.

"Oh, my! Happy New Year, Tony. We wish you were here. Things are dull without you."

"Really? It sounds like you have plenty of company."

"It was just to be Alice, Hal, you and me. When I knew you couldn't come, I invited a few relatives and business associates to celebrate the New Year. How are you celebrating?"

"I'm not, that is, I didn't. It's already the morning of 1975 in Iran."

"Of course. You see, Tony, I don't think straight when I hear your voice."

"Do I take that as a good sign?"

"You should take it as a very good sign. I've only known you for a few hours and feel there's a void in my life without you. How I wish you were here."

"Oh, God!, I want to believe her. Is she telling the truth or is it part of the conspirator's master plan to get me?" Tony's silence alerts Carmen to a possible poor connection.

"Tony, are you still there?"

"Yes, Carmen. My dear, I feel the same about you. I promise to do something about it."

"Do I take that as a good sign?"

"Carmen, please consider it as a very good sign. I'll try to get away from here for a few days as soon as possible."

"Wonderful! I'll be waiting for your call. Oh, Hal wants to speak with you. Vaya con Dios, Tony." (Go with God).

Carmen passes the phone to Hal and rejoins Alice on the balcony.

"Tony, what's happening with Dan Hill?"

"He's finally out of the hospital and doesn't know I'm here. Thanks for not tipping him off that I came to Iran."

"Tony, I always keep my word. A strange thing happened a few days ago. I called Louis in Switzerland and was told he's gone. Disappeared! Do you know anything about that?"

Tony blows smoke into the mouthpiece, contemplating a reply. *"Very interesting. That confirms our bugged conversation between Hill and Switzerland. This guy really is being honest with me. Why?"*

"Yes, Hal. We know that Hill got the same story about Louis. Who are you reporting to now?"

"That's a good question, Tony. I have no other contact with the oil syndicate represented by Louis; but, I'm still a consultant to Pemex and they don't know of my Louis connection."

"I'll see what I can dig up on that situation and get back to you, Hal."

"Thanks, Tony and Happy New Year. Shall I get Carmen back?"

Tony hesitated, then, "No, thanks, Hal. Just tell her I'll be there soon."

JANUARY 2, 1975, IRAN

Tony's lawyer, Zangi, reports that the two men who falsified the drilling records have disappeared, mysteriously. Tony immediately summons his Savak men to the Safe House for a report. Jamshid, steely eyed and emotionless, asks Jahangir to report.

"Mister Berlotti, they did not disappear mysteriously. Unfortunately, their brakes failed on the icy mountain road near Damavand, almost 100 kilometers north east of Tehran. Their bodies will not be discovered until the snow melts. It's a pity."

Tony looks at Jamshid. Jamshid turns and looks at Jahangir. Jahangir looks at Tony and shrugs his shoulders.

Tony, with head bowed, "Yes, indeed, a pity."

Then he invites the team to dinner.

APRIL - MAY, 1975, IRAN

Four months later, satisfied that his law suit against the drilling company is progressing, for Iran at least, on schedule, and that Dan Hill remains preoccupied with the anti Khomeini movement but still paranoid over the Spanish speaking visitor, Tony decides to make time to visit Carmen in Manzanillo.

After three days of blissful solitude with Carmen, except for the occasional appearance of two maids, Tony is convinced she has no connection with the conspiracy. On the fourth morning, while he and Carmen are on the balcony having breakfast, a maid announces there is a call for Señor Berlotti.

"Hello, Tony. It's Hal."

"Hal, how did you know that I was here?"

"Carmen is so happy, Tony. She couldn't keep your visit secret. We knew you were coming. Are you getting better acquainted?"

"Yes, completely! She's everything you told me and more. But Hal, she's a very lonely lady."

"Yes, and she's lived alone so many years."

"I guess you have guessed, Hal? I'm really attracted to Carmen, perhaps fatally attracted..."

"Then do something about it. Alice and I have known her a long time. She's crazy about you."

"I don't know, Hal. There's a price on my head and I wouldn't want to expose her to danger."

"Tony, you've never told me who's trying to kill you. I may be in a position to help."

"Hmmmm. In a position to help kill me? Or what? He's been a loyal friend until now..."

"Hal, I appreciate your offer; but, since you and Hill are connected with Louis, I've got to withhold information that could jeopardize both of us. I hope you understand."

"Of course. It's your call, Tony. We know Louis disappeared, but don't know why or where he is. If I don't hear from him soon, I'll lose a healthy income from his source."

"What can you tell me about Louis?"

"Only that he has been the coordinator between a foreign oil syndicate and a bunch of investors in the Banque De Credit International. He hired me because of my association with Pemex, my fluency in Spanish and my connections, via Alice and her father, in Mexico's political machine."

"So...you provided insider information to Louis, right?"

"Yes, but that's all. And I strongly suspect, but can't prove it, that Louis provided Dan Hill with much of that information. I have never been privy to Hill's activities in Mexico."

"Have you met Louis?"

"Only once, when he hired me. He's short, overweight, gray haired and speaks with a Henry Kissinger type accent. How about you?"

"Yes, only once also - in Chile. And your description is accurate. He may be Swiss or Austrian."

"If you locate him, Tony, I'd appreciate your call. I'll do the same for you."

Tony promises to keep in touch with Hal, then redirects his attention to Carmen. "My dear, I hate doing this. You've made me very happy, happier than I've been for years, but, Carmen, all good things really do come to an end. I'm sorry, but I must return to Iran tomorrow."

Carmen's expression is full of disappointment and pain as she quickly turns her head aside to brush aside a tear, but she cannot suppress a quick sob. Tony picks her up, as gently as a baby, and carries her into her bedroom. Carmen's sobs are quickly replaced by words of entreaty.

"Don't leave me, Tony. I want you. I need you. I love you."

Tony holds her firmly in his arms and whispers, "And you know I feel the same about you." Crying with joy, she unties his robe as he gently disrobes Carmen. Her fingers lightly caress his muscular frame as they meld together.

"Oh, God, Carmen. It's been so long," he murmurs, surrendering to desire.

The sound of the maid's bell awakens them for lunch.

Kissing Tony, Carmen teases, "It may have been a long time but you still know all the right moves, my darling." Sitting on the edge of the bed, Carmen stretches her arms, full breasts taut and firm, then turns to Tony. "Tony, please take me with you?"

The question takes Tony by surprise. *"Oh, no! I can't expose her to the assassins or she could end up like Gloria."* "Carmen, I'm overjoyed that you want to be with me, but there are a number of reasons why you can't come."

"Tell me, Tony. Let's have no secrets between us, my love."

"Well, number one... I must leave tomorrow and you need a visa. Number two... I'm in the middle of a lawsuit there, plus two projects to oversee in remote areas which require my time sixteen or more hours a day. I'd only see you a few minutes a week. And number three... it wouldn't be safe,... for you."

"I could come after I get a visa...Seeing you only a few minutes a week is all I need... and I feel so safe and secure, - being near you. What's the real problem, Tony?"

"I can't tell her the truth... not yet. And I must be firm." Tony's demeanor changes from compassion to no-nonsense business. "You really have to trust me on this, my dear. I promise to tell you, some day, why you can't come. But, for now, Carmen, you can't come and that's final!"

Carmen accurately reads Tony. She puts her head on his shoulder. "Whatever you say, Tony."

BALANCE OF 1975

For Tony, the remainder of the year is up and down hill.

His relationship with Carmen blossoms into a serious love affair, and he becomes good friends with Hal Brooks, finally convinced that Brooks is not setting him up for the conspirators. He's satisfied that all his projects, except the Zahedan lawsuit, are on schedule and within budget. His Zahedan drilling lawsuit is fruitless; the drilling company is in Chapter 11, the money is gone and the proven low ore grades and reserves confirm that the copper project is not viable. The financial loss is hard on Tony as his cash expenditures mount. He is maintaining a large staff of people with travel expenses and costly surveillance in many divergent locations dedicated just to the elimination of the assassins.

Dan Hill remains occupied with the anti Khomeini movement and still convinced that the man with a Spanish accent is out to kill him. After numerous calls to Hal Brooks, he is informed that Tony shuttles between Mexico, Nevada, Arizona and New York and is still trying to locate Boris Kruchenko. From Hill's bugged conversations with his secretary, Tony learns that Hill's agents, Alamir and Hashemi, have located Tony's Iranian engineer, Farzan. They plan to befriend him in hopes he will lead them to his friend, Khomeini's son Ahmed, and ultimately to Khomeini. After careful consideration, Tony decides he will not try to interfere in Hill's anti-Khomeini movement.

Hill, still crippled and concerned over the loss of monthly income from Louis, travels to Canada and Switzerland in search of Louis. In a conversation with Sammy, Hill states that since Louis has disappeared, he needs to augment his income, even if it means working via Carlo's sources. Sammy advises that Carlo remains determined to eliminate Tony; that Hill is the man to deliver him for the kill and that Carlo agrees to keep Hill on the payroll as an incentive. Hill agrees but, still fearful that Carlo is out to get him, asks Brooks to call Sammy to find out for a certainty when and where Tony will be in Mexico. Hal Brooks proves he is not a player in the conspiracy as he agrees with Hill, but then advises Tony of the arrangement.

Several weeks before Christmas, Tony calls Carmen and invites her to New York for the holidays. "I want you to meet Dr. Monti, George and Peter. They are my remaining family."

"How wonderful. Give me all the details and I'll be there."

DECEMBER 22, 1975

Tony receives a call from Dr. Monti. "Tony, there's been a change in plans for Christmas."

"What change?"

"Never mind. Just fly to Manzanillo on Christmas eve. Carmen will have you picked up at the airport."

"What happened, Frank? I already have my flight booked to New York."

Tony and Dr. Monti have been friends for about fifty years and can never keep secrets from each other. "Well, I guess I must confess. Tony, that Carmen is one persuasive lady. She convinced me that Christmas in Manzanillo will be a lot better than in cold New York. She has already paid for George, Peter, Judy and me to fly there tomorrow. She wouldn't take no for an answer; said you'd understand. And, to tell you the truth, Tony, I agree with her. It's been miserably cold here."

Tony is happy to agree to the plan. On his flight to Mexico, Tony reviews his 1975 diary. The following entries are highlighted:

- ❑ June 5 to 15. Hill on vacation with wife in Chile.
- ❑ June 15. Pepe and Gabriel of Los Machos seen in Las Vegas looking for Roselli.
- ❑ June 18. Hill travels to Chicago.

- June 19. Sam Giancana assassinated in his Chicago home. Shot 6 times in the head by small caliber weapon. Inside job! Hill?
- June 20. George graduates. Peter and Judy graduate.
- June 21. Pepe and Gabriel travel to Detroit.
- June 24. Johnny Roselli testifies. Was he also in Chicago on June 19?
- July 30. Jimmy Hoffa disappears in Detroit.
- August 14. Clay Shaw died last year.
- August 25. Carlo still in Cuba with Manuel and Poncho.
- September 4. Carlo, Manuel and Poncho leave Cuba.
- September 10. Carlo, Manuel and Poncho seen in La Paz.
- September 22. Carlo, Manuel and Poncho seen in Panama.
- September 30. Carlo, Manuel and Poncho seen in Dominican Republic.
- October 11. Carlo, Manuel and Poncho seen in Las Vegas with Sammy, Pepe and Gabriel.
- " 17. Dr. Asti starts weapons training by Jamshid's men.
- November 3. Frank (Dr. Monti) working too hard.
- December 12. Jamshid and crew given 10% raise and two-week staggered home leaves.
- " 15. Hal Brooks not a conspirator.

Tony closes the diary, then orders a scotch and soda. Jamshid, sitting one seat behind Tony across the aisle, orders hot tea. Tony opens his briefcase, pulls out a Montico recorder and puts on headphones. As he takes a long swig, his mind races. *"Should I or shouldn't I hear this tape? Eavesdropping on a friend is wrong...but then, it was made before I knew Hal and Alice were friends."*

"Hal, what's wrong with Tony?" It's Alice's voice.

"Nothing, that I know of...Why?"

"Well... he seems serious about Carmen, but hasn't proposed to her."

"How do you know?'

"She would have told me. She tells me everything."

"I think he will in due time. He's been very busy lately. Has he been sleeping with her?"

"How would I know?"

"You said she tells you everything!"

"Well, she's a lady, Hal, and wouldn't discuss her sex life. But I know Carmen. He is," a chuckle from Alice, then, "That is,... they are,... that is,... sleeping together. I'm sure. She has a glow that could only come from a satisfying love affair."

Tony stops the tape, closes his eyes, smiles and falls into a deep sleep.

CHRISTMAS, 1975, MANZANILLO, MEXICO

On Christmas eve, Tony arrives at the Manzanillo airport on schedule and is happily surprised. Carmen leads a VIP reception committee followed by her ten house guests, complete with red carpet and mariachi band. As an embarrassed Tony stands speechless, Carmen hugs and kisses him, her guests applaud and the mariachis play louder.

After a few hours at Carmen's sprawling hacienda, Tony observes with pleasure that Carmen, Dr. Monti, George, Peter, Judy, Hal, Alice, Lucia, Alfredo and Ricardo and Isabel (Lucia and Alfredo's children) have already formed a mutual admiration society. He also learns, for the first time, that Hal and Alice have no children and that Alice had to have a hysterectomy after two near-death miscarriages.

After dinner, presents are exchanged around a large Christmas tree in the center of the circular, sky-lit atrium. Tony is embarrassed again as he receives most of the lavish gifts and, because this was an unexpected party, he came empty handed.

"I promise," he apologizes, "I'll make this up to you."

And he does, with great taste and generosity.

The next week passes happily but much too quickly and ends on a sad note, when farewells are exchanged. Carmen's TLC has been a healing balm for Tony and George is gratified as he hears his father laugh more often than he has for a couple of years. Carmen has complete acceptance by Tony's extended family.

As George tells Carmen, "I haven't seen my father so relaxed and happy for a very long time. Thank you, Carmen."

Carmen proclaims to everyone, "We will all do this again next year."

"Yes," adds Tony, "but next year is on me!"

CHAPTER 20
ENTER GI-GI

MARCH 6, NEW YORK

Tony spends the first week of the New Year with Dr. Monti. They agree on a plan to train George, Peter and Judy in surveillance techniques and the use of firearms. George will also obtain advanced martial arts training from Lin Komatsu. Thereafter, Peter and Judy will work at the Montico facility under the direct guidance of Dr. Monti and Misha. George, fluent in Spanish, will move to Mexico City and work, via Carmen's recommendation, with Licenciado (lawyer) Don Ricardo Pedrosa, an international finance attorney with the Monterrey Group. Tony and Dr. Monti also agree that training George as a female impersonator will begin after he completes one year of training under Licenciado Pedrosa and that his transformation will not be revealed to Hal Brooks and Carmen. Upon his return to Iran, Tony learns that Dan Hill is back in the hospital, suffering from a fall, re-injuring his broken leg and breaking his right arm. From his hospital bed, Hill continues his efforts to locate Khomeini. According to Jahangir, Hill, in a conversation with Sammy, promised to return to Las Vegas soon to set-up Tony for Carlo. Sammy stated that Carlo is still angry over being accused of skimming at the Desert Inn, that he will pay big money for information leading to Tony and his associates and is preparing to increase his drug trade. From Las Vegas, Mehdi reports that Sammy, Los Machos and Hank Palma have been frequent visitors to the MGM Grand, at Fronton's Jai Alai games, betting heavily on quinela's, exacta's and exacta boxing ("baseballing"). Their money never runs out and Hank is always seen trying to set-up one or two patsies for their card scam operation at McCarren Field.

MARCH 15, 1975, IRAN

From Tucson, Ali reports that early on March 15, 1976, Boris Kruchenko traveled from his Lake Patagonia cabin to Marana Field, placed money in locker #3 and returned to his condo in Tucson. The same afternoon, Gabriel of Los Machos, a man with an obviously phony limp, picked up the money and left a small bag of heroin on a purlin behind locker #4. The following day, Kruchenko picked up the heroin, drove to his cabin and returned to Tucson the next day.

Ali also reports that Kruchenko generally goes to the Tucson Bridge Center on Saturday nights and, on some afternoons, to a white house on Broadway, presumably to play bridge. Tony advises Ali to enroll in a beginners bridge class at the Center and attend Saturday night games as a bridge observer, but primarily to covertly photograph and obtain data on Kruchenko.

Weeks later, following Tony's advice, Ali reports that Kruchenko, a loner, is considered a fine bridge player, refuses to play with beginners and is registered under the name of Boris Gottlieb. He seldom plays with the same partner and always leaves alone. According to Ali, Boris does not like kibitzers sitting at his table, drinks a lot of black coffee and, except for the mandatory bidding, never engages anyone in conversation. On one occasion, when the director announced that Gaylor Kasle (one of the world's top master point holders) might come to play soon, everyone, except Boris, made a bid to partner with Kasle.

LATE JULY, 1976

Tony learns that Johnny Roselli's body was found in a 55 gallon drum full of holes in Dumbfounding Bay near Miami. He later learns, through a conversation between Hill and Sammy, that Roselli was probably set up by Carlo or Joe Aiuppa[15], who found out, from Sammy, that Roselli, contrary to instructions, was in Dallas on November 22, 1963. According to Hill, Aiuppa was not pleased that Roselli testified on June 24, 1975 and Sammy stated that Carlo went ballistic when he heard that Roselli went to the Dealey Plaza ambush against instructions.

---

[15] Aiuppa was running the Chicago mob at the time of Giancana's assassination.

MID SEPTEMBER, 1976, MEXICO CITY

Tony opens the International Labor Brokers at Avenida Rio Mixcoac #25, Despacho 10A in Mexico City. He hires Pedro Poot to oversee, under George's supervision, the hiring of construction personnel for certain of his overseas projects. George will also screen and select personnel as assets for Tony's A-Tec Corporation's "Capture Team". When Tony learns that his friend Nunzio Addabbo is now a construction consultant in Mexico, they agree to meet at Del Lago, where Addabbo provides Tony with a list of qualified engineers and people in other construction disciplines.

CHRISTMAS, 1976

The same family and friends gather at the same place for Christmas, but this time, Tony insists on paying all expenses. He also arranges for all of them to go to the Ixtapan De La Sal resort, a 2½ hour car drive SW of Mexico City, for their New Year's celebration, therapy, thermal baths, horseback riding and outstanding food. During their many moments alone together, Carmen asks Tony to marry her. Having run-out of plausible excuses, Tony realizes he must tell Carmen some of the truth.

"Carmen, I once told you that coming to Iran would be dangerous. Actually, being with me anywhere is a serious life-and-death business. Several years ago in Mexico City, I uncovered a monumental conspiracy that made me an immediate assassination target. There are people trying to have me killed. The deaths of my wife and daughters was no accident. Torching my husband and wife team in Bolivia was no accident and framing my doctor was no accident. These people are ruthless and will stop at nothing to draw me into their line of fire. Everyone with whom I am closely associated is at risk and, as my wife, you would be a prime target. I love you too much and will not allow that to happen. I can't lose you, my dear."

"I don't care, Tony. I have more money than we can ever use. I'll buy 'round the clock protection for us."

"I already have protection."

"We could get married, change our names and move."

"God, I'm sorry, Carmen. But, no, my dear, I'll never sleep until the assassins are dead."

"Tony, what did you uncover that's so dangerous?"

"Dearest, I promise to tell you as soon as I consider it safe. Meanwhile, please trust me."

"Does Hal know?"

Tony immediately becomes defensive.   "No. Why do you ask?"

"Only because he considers you a good friend and has connections. He might be able to help you."

"Good! When the time is right, I'll tell him, too. I love you, my darling, so please trust me."

EARLY 1977

The year begins favorably for Tony, although he is increasingly frustrated with his efforts to eliminate Carlo and Hill. Since they are his pipeline to the other assassins, he must get them first. He negotiates mining contracts in Nevada, California and Peru. In Mexico, delighting Alice Brooks, Tony awards a heavy equipment contract for stripping the overburden at the San Miguel copper mine, to Alfredo, Lucia's husband. Tony's confidence in Brooks is reinforced when on March 11, from Iran, Jahangir reports that Hill called Hal Brooks wanting to know if anyone has heard from Louis, if anyone has replaced Louis and if Brooks has heard from Tony, to which Brooks replied, "No, no, and no." When Hill asked Brooks how he's managing without Louis's income, Brooks responded, "Think I'll retire to Maine." Tony knows Hal and Alice will retire at Lake Chapala. In early June in Peru, Jamshid advises Tony that Carlo was seen in Columbia with Pablo Escobar, then flown to Panama by Manuel, where he was reported to have visited Manuel Noriega, and finally returned to Bolivia for meetings with Jose Martinez, his number one man. According to Jamshid, Mehdi reported from Vegas that Sammy, Hill, Hank and Los Machos are developing plans to increase their drug business. Carlo insists they need to find a new and novel way to export their products.

According to George, Peter called to say that his father, Dr. Monti, is working too hard, has frequent brief blackouts and won't see a doctor. Tony directs Dr. Asti to examine Frank and do whatever is best for him.   "Ground him. Hospitalize him if necessary. Don't take 'no' for an answer." Tony returns to New York in mid August. His first priority is the state of Dr. Monti's health.   Dr. Asti reports that Monti's blackouts are due to insufficient blood flow to the brain, which he calls apoplexy. Dr. Monti is ordered to stay away from his office, rest and undergo a series of tests. Misha, Peter and Judy do an outstanding job maintaining Montico's valuable business assets. With Dr. Monti's approval, they bring Josh, Misha's son, into their organization. Josh, a recent criminal justice law graduate, had plans to work for the FBI until Dr. Monti made him a more attractive offer.

In September, Carmen notifies Tony that, according to Licenciado Don Ricardo, George is an outstanding lawyer and has made many impressive contacts in the legal world.

Delighted with the news, Tony calls George. "Are you ready for your new job?"

George's positive, decisive personality comes through loud and clear. "Let's do it, Dad. I want the sons-a-bitches as bad as you! I'm ready for Gi-Gi."

"Good, George. But we have a small problem to resolve."

"What's that, Dad?"

"We need to create a credible cover story for your disappearance, especially for Don Ricardo, Carmen and her clan."

"You're right, Dad. I'll stay put until we come up with the cover."

One week later, George calls his father. "Dad, I have our cover."

"Well, don't keep me in suspense. Let's hear it."

"Tell everybody you have another legal case in Iran, that I'm going there to protect your legal interests and won't return until it's over. It'll work, Dad."

Tony hesitates, then, "By God, George, that will work! I'll set the wheels in motion."

One week later, all those who need to know are notified that George is on his way to Iran. George promises to keep in touch with Don Ricardo, then flies to New York to begin his transition to Gi-Gi and receive additional martial arts training from Lin Komatsu. By Thanksgiving, Dr. Monti states he feels good and ready for work. Dr. Asti agrees but insists that he only returns to "part-time work." Dr. Monti does not argue. He promises to spend less than 20 hours a week at the office and offers to play a major role in George's transformation to Gi-Gi.

"Turning George into Gi-Gi won't be work," he states. "Matter of fact, it'll be fun and relaxing." Tony agrees to the arrangement, travels to his new projects and returns to Mexico in mid December to spend the holidays with Carmen. Except for Jamshid and Rashid, who remain with Tony, all members of the Savak team are given a two week vacation. On December 20, Jahangir reports from Iran that Dan Hill, still crippled, plans to meet Sammy, Hank and Jose Martinez in Las Vegas on December 31st.

By years' end, Tony highlights the following notes in his 1977 diary:

- Gary Powers killed in chopper crash in California. Misha says Dan Hill knew Powers from U2 Black Lady of Espionage (code name) days.
- Elvis Presley died. Crowds went wild.
- George Bush out as CIA Director on January 20.
- Stansfield Turner new CIA Director effective March 9.
- Noriega accused of drug trafficking and buying tapes from members of army intelligence for dictator Omar Torrijos. He is exposed as a double agent and then dropped from CIA payroll by President Carter. Check his connection with Carlo, also Escobar.
- Dr. Asti's transition into Capture Team is smooth. He's determined to get even with Carlo, but Lin Komatsu says the doctor tries hard but is not good at martial arts. Jamshid says Asti is very good with firearms.
- Peter and Judy receiving martial arts lessons from Lin.
- There was a December 31st Las Vegas meeting with Hill, Sammy, Jose and Hank, but not covered by Jamshid's men.
- Frank (Dr. Monti) has George's new documents being prepared and has located a private female impersonator acting coach from a source on Bourbon Street. His stage name is "Miss Lola".
- Set up meeting with Zorro Plateado (Silver Fox).

JANUARY, 1978, NEW YORK

The year begins with George receiving intensive lessons in female impersonation six days a week. Upon Dr. Asti's recommendation, a skilled hypnotist is contracted to train George in self hypnosis. His acting lessons include general female behavior, voice projection, body movements, make-up, dress and the do's and don'ts around men. Dr. Asti places 6'-1" George on a strict diet to bring his weight down from 185 to 160 pounds. Dr. Monti arranges for a Saks Fifth Avenue dress designer to outfit George after his weight is down. Dr. Asti provides specially designed size 38 gel-packed bras, padded jock straps and detailed instructions on how to keep George's body smooth.

In late February, Misha advises Dr. Monti that an ex-Mossad friend, familiar with Misha's knowledge of South America, contacted him and offered a contract to locate two Nazi war criminals. As a young escapee of a German concentration camp in 1944, Misha has always been ready to offer his services in the name of justice, particularly against the Nazis. One of the criminals is Klaus Barbie, known as The Nazi Butcher of Lyons, reported to be in Bolivia. Presenting his case to Dr. Monti, Misha argues, "Since Carlo Perez and his hit team are Bolivian, I can serve a dual role by searching for both men under one contract." Dr. Monti approves. The second criminal is Josef Mengele, the Angel of Death, reported to be traveling between Paraguay and Brazil.

Misha states he will start in Bolivia, then travel to Paraguay. "I know," explains Misha, "that since WWII, Paraguay, under President Stroessner, has been a safe haven for criminals, especially Germans. Mengele should be there. My friend Simon will know."

Dr. Monti calls Tony to advise that Josh will assume his father's duties at Montico while Misha is on assignment. Tony offers to send one or two Savak agents as Misha's backup.

"No," states Dr. Monti. "Misha prefers to work alone."

"Not a good idea, Frank. Misha's Spanish is poor and what if he gets in trouble?"

"He's a pro. He knows the consequences."

Six weeks later, Misha reports to Dr. Monti that he contacted a man who showed him a photograph of Barbie sitting on concrete steps in La Paz, reading a newspaper. "The man," states Misha, "wants ten thousand dollars to tell me the exact location where the photo was taken. When he turned down my one thousand dollar offer, I told him I'd think about it. It does look like a Bolivian photo."

"Be careful, Misha, it could be a set up. Barbie should be pointed out in person, not in a photo."

"I know. I'll let him sweat a few days. Meanwhile I'm going to Paraguay for a Mengele lead."

"Look, Misha, you're Jewish and your Spanish is poor. On this mission that may be a handicap. Do you want Tony to send you some back-up?"

"Thank you, but no, Sir. I work better alone."

"Very well, but be very careful."

APRIL, 1978, NEW YORK

Tony's A-Tec Corporation New York office is fully staffed with Tony as President and CEO; Dr. Monti, Executive VP, Treasurer; George (Gi-Gi) VP, Secretary and Legal Council; Peter, part-time VP and Communications; Jamshid, VP, Chief of Security; Dr. Asti, VP, Corporate Medical Director. Judy, is VP in Computer Communications and there are nine Savak security agents. Peter, George's best friend, is also Montico's Operations Manager. Only the above, including Misha and Josh of Montico and Lin Komatsu are aware of George's new secret role as Gi-Gi.

During the last week in April, satisfied that George is ready to seek employment as a female impersonator, "Miss Lola" returns to his full time employment without the knowledge that the George he knew as a brunette will be posing as Tony's blonde secretary. Even Tony's good friend "Silver Fox", who knows George, is not aware of Gi-Gi's true identity.

Gi-Gi's first public appearance, as a blonde, is the morning of April 28th when she leaves Dr. Monti's apartment for a walk to the A-Tec office. She is whistled-at by a construction crew, honked-at by passing motorists and propositioned-by a high rise doorman. This immediate attention, as she continues to strut and show off her sensational endowments, does wonders for his/her ego. *"Oh, boy...this assignment is going to be challenging and...va, va vavoom...fun!"*. George is not only committed to revenge, but has the enthusiasm and bravado only found in an unencumbered young man.

Tony lays out his strategy to the Capture Team. "George, I mean 'Gi-Gi', will act as my personal secretary and travel with me on most business trips. He, I mean she,... Boy, I'm going to have to watch myself!... will be our primary lure in setting traps for the assassins."

"And don't forget Judy," adds Peter.

"Yes, Judy will be our back-up lure and appear at predetermined locations with Gi-Gi."

"We know," adds Dr. Monti, "that Los Machos are boozers and girl-crazy. We'll use that to our advantage."

During late afternoon the same day, Tony brings Gi-Gi to his engineering office and introduces him as his new private secretary. Gi-Gi receives approving looks from the men and a few dirty looks from jealous females. Her ego is further inflated, but she reasons, *"I can see I've got to spend very little time in this office or I'll be in trouble."* Tony is gratified that George's impersonation is so convincing.

Later, in their A-Tec office, Dr. Monti calls everyone to a meeting. "I have something I want all of you to hear." When they are gathered quietly around the conference table, he announces, "This is what your engineering staff said after you left this afternoon." He plays the tape.

The voices are clear but sometimes blocked by other voices and laughter. The only voice Tony recognizes is that of Barbara, his female blueprint machine operator, as she talks about Gi-Gi. "Can you believe the boss hiring that young blonde bimbo? I wonder what she did to get that job so fast without any of us knowing about it."

"Now, now, Barbara," a male voice is heard, "you better sheath those nails. She's probably a great secretary."

"How the hell would you know! Just because she's got great tits and wiggles her ass, doesn't mean she's a secretary!"

Another unidentified male voice is heard supporting the first. "Barbara is just jealous. We all know she's been trying to make Mr. Berlotti ever since his wife died."

And another male adds, "Give it up, Barbara. You're no match for Gi-Gi so how about going out with me?"

The next noise is an obvious slap in the face and Barbara's retort, "In your dreams, asshole!"

Dr. Monti stops the tape. "There's a lot more, but that gives you an idea of what faces you, Gi-Gi, in days to come. The guys are gonna' come on to you and girls will be jealous and catty."

"I tell you, " grins Peter, "if I didn't know better, I'd come on to him, er, her, like the others."

Gi-Gi makes a fist and feints a punch at Peter.

"Calm down, Peter," laughs Judy. "I'm your girl, remember?"

They all applaud Gi-Gi's success, then Tony adjourns the meeting.

MAY 1, 1978, CALIFORNIA

Dr. Monti calls Tony in California. "I'm worried, Tony. I haven't heard from Misha in days."

"God-damn-it, Frank, I was afraid of this. I wanted to provide his back up! Remember?"

"I know. I think we should wait a while before you do anything about it...OK?"

"OK, Frank - but let's not wait too long..."

MAY 2, 1978, LAS VEGAS

Mehdi reports that Manuel and Poncho of Los Machos checked into the Horseshoe Casino. Tony immediately dispatches Gi-Gi and Judy to his Capture Team's Vegas Safe House. They are to wait for his arrival.

The following evening, Tony, Jamshid, Mehdi, Gi-Gi and Judy meet.

"OK, team...here's what we do. When Mehdi's man advises that the Machos are in the casino, Gi-Gi and Judy go there, select an empty 21 table and start playing lousy blackjack. It will just be a matter of time before the girl-hungry Machos spot you and move in. One of our men wearing a pink shirt with black bow tie will come and stand behind them as an interested observer. That will identify the Machos. If they're not the Machos, move to another empty table. And don't worry. We'll be in disguise, watching from the sidelines."

Their meeting is interrupted by Mehdi's agent at 10 P.M. "The Machos are here!"

"OK, ladies," smiles Tony, "go get 'em!"

At 11 o'clock, Gi-Gi and Judy find an empty table and begin playing blackjack. As instructed, their play is amateurish. By 1 AM, several players have come and gone from their table, the agent with the pink shirt does not appear and the girls are down about five hundred dollars.

"Where the hell are they?" whispers Gi-Gi.

As Judy leans over to respond, Gi-Gi notices the male dealer taking a long look at Judy's boobs.

She stiffens and snarls, "Hey, you, keep your eyes on the cards. She's all mine!"

When the dealer smiles knowingly at Judy, Gi-Gi knows the dealer is thinking, "Damn lesbians!"

"Let's take a break, go downstairs and get something to eat," suggests Gi-Gi.

As they enter the restaurant, they notice two Latino looking individuals sitting alone in a booth. As Gi-Gi and Judy pass them to find seats, one of the men does a double take at Gi-Gi. The ladies find an empty booth, sit and wait for a waitress. As Judy orders coffee and English muffins, Gi-Gi notices that their man with the pink shirt and black bow tie has entered the room, stops in front of the two Latinos and pretends to be looking for someone.

"Bingo," whispers Gi-Gi. "That's them!"

By 2 AM, Gi-Gi and Judy are back at an empty blackjack table, buy some chips and begin play. Before the first deal is complete, the two Machos appear, sit next to the girls and pull out a fist full of chips. Poncho gives Manuel an approving nod, licks his lips and whispers in Spanish.

"Mira, Manuel." (Look, Manuel)

"Si...tenemos suerte." (Yes...we're in luck)

"Manuel, me gusta la rubia," (Manuel, I like the blonde)

"Y yo, Ponchito, me gusta la morena." (And me, Ponchito, I like the brunette)

Gi-Gi picks up the whispering, as Poncho brags, "Una puesta, Manuel. Voy a comer la rubia por desayuno." (A bet, Manuel. I'm gonna' eat the blonde for breakfast.).

As the Spanish whispering continues, Gi-Gi makes her first move. She turns to Poncho, tilts her head and gives him her rehearsed Mona Lisa smile, thinking, *"In your dreams! Just try, you Bolivian son-of-a-bitch, and I'll tear your fucking head off!"*

Gi-Gi and Judy's poor play is picked up by the Machos, giving them an opportunity to make their move. Poncho, sitting next to Gi-Gi, leans over and starts the conversation in broken English.

"Ladies, you must never take a heet with seventeen or more points. You must never split fives and tens. You must always double-down with eleven and you must to always split aces and eights...comprende?"

Gi-Gi takes a deep breath, leans back and gives Poncho an approving Marilyn Monroe smile.

"Oh, thank you, Sir. You are kind to help us. Are you from South America?"

"Yes," replies Poncho, "We from Sud America.   We never lose at this game. Why you ask?"

Gi-Gi shifts her position, crosses her legs, leans forward to give Poncho a better look at her pair of 38's, then whispers, "It was only a guess. I'm attracted to Latin men..."

With his ego salved, Poncho again whispers to Manuel that he'll have the blonde for breakfast.

The dealer clears his throat and interrupts this exchange by politely asking for bets. From across the room, Tony signals Judy to quit. When the dealer again asks for bets, Judy pulls in her chips and stands, announcing, "Sorry, gentlemen, we've lost too much, so we'll quit for tonight."

Gi-Gi looks at Poncho with a "sorry" look, shrugs her shoulders, picks up her chips, and stands next to Judy. "Well," she suggests, "There's still time to see more of Las Vegas."

Manuel and Poncho pick up their chips and make their move on the ladies. Manuel presses Judy's back with a sweaty palm as Poncho puts his arm tightly around Gi-Gi's waist, whispering, "Come, ladies, we show you the best of Vegas."

As the foursome walk to the exit, followed at a safe distance by Tony, Jamshid, Mehdi and another agent, Gi-Gi, at 6'-1" and a head taller than both men, asks, "Where are we going? We're looking for fun..."

"We going to a very private place," announces Poncho. "We weel dreenk pisco, dance and have lots of fun, make dee good time."

"Where's that?" asks Judy as they approach the exit.

"Never you mind," interrupts Manuel. "Joost come with us."

Judy, unaccustomed to dealing with male chauvinists, stops abruptly, places both hands on her hips and loses control. "I'm not going anywhere until you tell me where...and that's final!"

Manuel, unaccustomed to dealing with liberated women, reaches out and crudely squeezes one of Judy's breasts. "Vamanos" (let's go). He reaches for Judy's arm, but her well placed kick into his groin doubles him up on the floor, screaming in pain.

Judy's unexpected action immediately creates a circle of shocked onlookers. As Poncho kneels down to comfort Manuel, Gi-Gi is obviously considering giving him a martial arts lesson but Tony and Jamshid quickly pull Judy and Gi-Gi away from the crowd before the security guards arrive, leaving Mehdi and another agent there to observe the reaction.

Dazed and holding his groin, Manuel makes a supreme effort to get up, falls down again and screams at Poncho, "Concha su madre! Voy a matar la puta!" (Son-of-a-bitch! I'm gonna' kill the whore!).

"Ay chucha... se fueron!" (Oh fuck...they're gone!) announces Poncho as security arrives.

Forty-five minutes later at the Safe House, Judy apologizes for losing her cool. "I'm so sorry, Mr. Berlotti. I got scared, had all these preconceived ideas of what could happen and simply chickened out!"

Tony puts a comforting arm around her shoulder. "It's OK, Judy. You did good."

"Nothing serious would have happened, Judy," adds Gi-Gi, "I could immobilize both Bolivians with one hand tied behind my back!"

Tony puts his arm around his son. "I'm real proud of you, Gi-Gi. You exercised good judgment in restraining yourself. But don't ever forget - these guys are good with concealed knives. Now let's all get some sleep, head back to New York tomorrow and let this episode cool off."

JULY 1, 1978, LIMA, PERU

Tony meets his good friend and consultant, Nunzio Addabbo, in Lima to discuss the feasibility study for the 1,000 metric ton per day Pumire Sulfur Project in Palca, Chile, for International Labor Brokers of Mexico City. According to Addabbo, the project is not viable.

"There are too many negatives on this one," he explains. "The ore grade is minimal, there isn't enough water up there, it's a hostile environment, there's no railroad and it would cost a fortune to fix the roads and haul water to the area. Don't even think about it!"

"Well," states Tony with resignation, "That's another fifty grand down the tubes. With all the sulfur in the high Andes, there must be a good site somewhere."

"You're right, but what's needed is a better extraction process. Single batch autoclaves are slow and expensive. I'll keep you posted on developments. Now, let's drive up to Granja Azul and I'll treat you to Peru's best Chicken-in-the basket."

LATE JULY, 1978, MEXICO CITY

Three weeks later, after stops in Chile and Bolivia, Tony makes a surprise stop in Mexico City to visit Carmen. He is informed that she is in Baja California on business, expected to return in three days. *"Damn, I can't leave without seeing Carmen."* He decides to wait, calls Victor Moran for a project update, then calls Hal Brooks. "Hello, Hal. Tony here. Just arrived."

"Nice surprise, Tony! What's up?"

"Stopped here to unwind from my busy schedule, but, damn, Carmen is in Baja."

"I know. She'll be back in three days. How about joining Alice and me for dinner tomorrow, then some duplicate bridge?"

The next evening, during the start of the third round at the bridge club, Tony, the declarer, stops play momentarily, closes his eyes, raises his head and inhales deeply. The aroma of Shalimar is unmistakable. He knows. It's Carmen's favorite.

Tony looks across the table at 'dummy' Hal with arms crossed, unable to hide his grin, and asks, "What?"

Before Hal has a chance to reply, Carmen, who has been standing behind Tony for five minutes, gives him a hug and peck on the side of his neck.

Tony, never one to hold back his emotions, yells, "Carmen!"

He lays down his thirteen cards, rises quickly and embraces her with, "They all told me you were in Baja."

Tony and Hal's opponents, obviously die-hard duplicate players, don't appreciate this game delay. They call the director and complain. Hal apologizes, and Tony promises to speed up and play resumes after the director announces, "If there are no more interruptions there will be no penalty."

Later at the Brooks' apartment, Tony learns from Hal that Carmen left orders with her staff that she is to be notified anytime Tony calls or is known to be to Mexico.

"You know," states Tony, holding Carmen's hand, "you're what the doctor ordered."

"I'm so glad. Alice told me you'd be playing bridge with Hal tonight. The rest was easy."

Two days later during breakfast in Manzanillo, Carmen answers the phone. She holds the phone to her chest. "It's for you."

Tony immediately senses Carmen's disappointment. He whispers, "Tell them I'm not here."

"No, darling. It's Dr. Monti. He knows you're here and says it's important."

"Thanks, Carmen, I guess." Tony greets Dr. Monti, "Hello, Frank...something wrong?"

"Could be. We understand that Dan Hill's men located Khomeini in Paris, that the Shah is very sick and that his servants are packing many of his family's items. And listen to this, Tony. Hill just received a call from a man who identified himself as 'Rosy' who announced that he has replaced Louis and that the organization wants Khomeini dead."

Tony looks at Carmen, "It's important!" He then address Dr. Monti, "Frank, I'll be there tomorrow afternoon. Have Judy book Jamshid and me to Tehran in 72 hours. And thanks."

Tony's sudden change from relaxed and happy to tense and angry brings tears to Carmen's eyes. "What's wrong, Tony?"

Tony puts down his cappuccino, lights a cigar and leans back, counting off each reason on his fingers. "How about politics, religion, illness, finance, and murder?"

Carmen freezes. "It sounds too involved and dangerous. Don't go. I beg you, Tony, don't go."

"I'm sorry, my dear, but you know I am committed to finishing this."

"Tony, it's been five years since your wife and daughter were killed...do you really believe they are still after you. And, more importantly, that you can get to them?"

"Yes, Carmen, they are still after me. And I will get them; there's no other way to end this."

Four days later in his Tehran Safe House, Tony receives a briefing by Jamshid.

"Sorry, Rais (boss), but Jahangir can't be here. He's in the lobby of the Semiramis Hotel waiting for Hill to leave and go to The Foreign Trade Bank of Iran on Avenue Saadi. Two days ago, a large sum of money, we understand $50,000, was wired to Hill's account there by the man called 'Rosy'."

"Ah, ha! What else."

"Hill called Alamir and Hashemi this morning and told them to be at the bank at noon today to pick up 1,540,000 Rials; then go to Paris and eliminate Khomeini."

Tony raises his arm to signal 'wait' for a moment, then performs a mental calculation. "At the present rate of exchange, that's about twenty two thousand dollars. And Alamir and Hashemi will no doubt split it...Has Hill mentioned this to Carlo or Sammy?"

"No, Sir. As a matter of fact, Sammy told Hill last week that Carlo is annoyed with Hill for failing to set you up and that he may cut off Hill's drug traffic."

"As usual, Hill is playing both ends. Has he mentioned me?"

"Oh, yes, Sir. He keeps telling Sammy to tell Carlo he will deliver you as soon as he transfers to Las Vegas. That, of course, is just a stalling tactic. He doesn't know where you are."

"Good work, Jamshid...but be certain none of you get involved in Hill's Khomeini affair."

"We won't. In fact, we're all rooting for Hill to succeed on this one."

"By the way, where did engineer Farzan, the friend of Khomeini's son Ahmed, go after we shut down our Zahedan project?"

"He's now working on the Sar Cheshmeh copper project near Rafsanjan."

"Did Farzan help in locating Khomeini?"

"No, Sir. He's clean."

"Very good! Now, let's get out of here and see what we can do to trap Carlo."

MID OCTOBER, 1978, MEXICO CITY

After stops in Pakistan and Zaire, Tony returns to Mexico for one week of TLC as only Carmen can provide for this beleaguered man. As he tells her, Tony longs to be with her always and misses her constantly. During the third day, he receives a call from Dr. Monti.

"Tony, Mehdi reports from Vegas that Sammy has just received a call from Hill. It seems that Hill no longer trusts Hal Brooks. He wants Carlo to send one of the machos there to find out what Brooks is doing and with whom he's associating."

"Thanks, I'll warn Hal and have my men tail him. Anything else?"

"Yes," Frank chuckles, "Gi-Gi is agitating to see more action."

"Tell her I'm working on it. Remember, it's Carlo we want and he rarely makes an appearance."

"OK. Now, unfortunately, I have some bad news. I sent Josh to look for his father three weeks ago. Misha can't be found. I'm afraid he fell into a trap and got killed, either in Bolivia or Paraguay."

"I'm sorry but not surprised. Damn, he didn't want back up and knew the consequences."

"I told Josh to take as much time off as he pleases before returning to work. He took only four days and is back filling his father's shoes. He's very knowledgeable and a good kid."

"Give him my condolences, Frank. And tell him he won't be sorry he joined us."

Tony cradles the phone, lights a cigar and blows smoke rings. Carmen can read all the signs.

"Bad news," she sighs. "Right?"

Tony nods affirmatively and continues blowing rings. Carmen slides next to him, squeezes his hand, then places a large glass of freshly squeezed orange juice in his hand. "Drink! It's part of your therapy. Then let's get dressed and fly to Mexico City to see Hal."

Five hours later they are in the Brooks apartment. "Thanks for the tip, Tony. I'll watch my tail."

"Speaking of tail, Hal, I have already assigned an agent to tail you. We need to ID anybody sent to follow you. We may have the same enemy in Hill. Here's a photo of my agent."

"Thanks, Tony. You should know, however, that ever since Hill sent me Kruchenko's file, I've had my own protection, but I welcome double protection."

"Hal, have you ever heard of a man called Rosy?"

"No. Who's he?"

"He called Hill. Said he replaced Louis."

"Interesting. I must be out of the loop completely."

"Right. More reason to be concerned. Meanwhile, we have Hill under surveillance and will keep you in our loop."

NOVEMBER 20, 1978, NEW YORK

At 3 AM Jamshid receives an urgent call from Jahangir advising that Alamir just visited Hill at the Semiramis Hotel to report that Hashemi did not show up at the airport this morning. Alamir and Hashemi had tickets to Paris to carry out their Khomeini contract. Alamir told Hill he would not travel alone. When Hill told him to find a replacement, Alamir demanded another 770,000 Rials plus expenses to find and brief a suitable replacement. Hill became angered and offered Alamir a million Rials to find and kill Hashemi. Alamir agreed and will return later for his cash.

Jamshid, loyal, always protective and genuinely concerned for Tony's well being, decides to let the boss sleep. He reports Jahangir's call during breakfast.

"Oh, boy," grins Tony. "That got Hill's attention. Let's fuel the fire. Wait a few days, then have our 'old pistachio' agent deliver another bag to Hill, compliments of his Spanish speaking 'friend'."

DECEMBER, 1978, BAJA, CALIFORNIA AND SAN DIEGO, CALIFORNIA

Always conscious of having a price on his head, the pressure of worldwide business and hunting down conspirators take a heavy toll on Tony, physically and financially. During the second week of December, while in Baja California looking at one of Carmen's properties, Jamshid reports to Dr. Asti that the boss has been short of breath lately. Dr. Asti has Tony checked into Scripps Clinic in La Jolla, California for two days of comprehensive out-patient tests. The results are serious. Tony has high blood pressure (200/95), high cholesterol count (285) and a sacculated aneurysm of the aorta. He is advised to reduce his work load and rest.

Tony discusses his medical condition and options with Dr. Asti.

"Tony, your sacculated aneurysm is probably due to an old injury."

"Had plenty of those in my life. Now what?"

"I know they told you what to do, I have the reports. Slow down, eat properly, reduce your cappuccino intake and cut out the cigars. Take your medication and rest. Doctor's orders."

"Good luck!"

Before returning to Manzanillo for Christmas, Tony meets Silver Fox in Oceanside, California.

CHAPTER 21

1979 WAS A VERY BAD YEAR

JANUARY 11, 1979, NEW YORK

At Tony's A-Tec office, New York, Jamshid receives a call at 10 AM, listens, nods his head several times, then hangs-up. He looks at Tony and raises both arms in the air.

Tony notices Jamshid's concern. "What's happened, Jamshid?"

"Bad news, Rais. Jahangir told me that during the past week much of the Shah's personal property has been flown out of Tehran. Our inside man said the Shah is sick and everyone is worried that the Khomeini movement against him is stronger than expected. If the Shah leaves, it will be bad for Iranians, the United States and you. There is no one strong enough to replace the Shah."

"Well, I can't say that I'm surprised. Hill was right about this one and it does looks bad."

"Yes, Sir...but what can we do about it?"

"Nothing, I'm afraid, Jamshid. We'll have to let Hill and his organization deal with Khomeini. We are overextended now and we must concentrate on Carlo. We all deserve a better life..."

JANUARY 16, BAJA, CALIFORNIA

Jamshid's bad news is confirmed. News breaks out worldwide that the Shah of Iran and his family have fled to Egypt. Jahangir reports that Iran's religious leaders and Khomeini militants are already crying victory, but there is still no sign of Khomeini. On confirming the bad news, Tony returns to New York to plan his withdrawal from Iran. During the next two weeks, he reduces his Iranian staff to a skeleton force. He also learns that Dan Hill received a call from 'Rosy', who told him to intensify his activities against Khomeini. For many Iranians, the arrival of religious leader Khomeini on January 30th is their worst nightmare. Many businessmen arrange to leave the country and the U.S. Embassy is put on a state of alert. The arrival of Khomeini signals a return to the repressive ways of the past and many of the Shah's progressive achievements are destroyed. Hill offers Alamir another million Rials to have Khomeini assassinated. Alamir has not yet found Hashemi.

Mehdi reports from Vegas that, upon hearing the Khomeini news, Sammy and Hank called Carlo to determine how Khomeini's presence will affect their operation with Hill. Carlo told them to check with Jose Martinez. Jose stated that they are cutting off business with Hill.

A month later, with Iran in turmoil, Hill calls Sammy. "Hello, Sammy. Dan here. Listen, there was no deposit in my bank account this month. Know anything about that?"

There is a long silence as Sammy lights a cigar and frames a reply. *"I'll just tell him the truth!"* "Dan, we're cutting you off. If, and when, things cool down over there, we'll get back to you and talk."

Hill, generally sarcastic, articulate and under control, loses it. "What's all this ' we' shit! Since when are you involved in decisions? Who the fuck gave the order to stop my deposits?"

Hill's outburst does wonders for Sammy's sadistic streak and ego. *"Cry, you son-of-a-bitch, cry!"* "Dan, Dan, old pal. Why are you so angry?" he asks smoothly.

Hopelessly out of control, Hill snaps, "Listen, you fat, fucking slob, I have powerful worldwide connections - remember? Tell Carlo we're working on eliminating Khomeini. I need the money."

"Dealing with you now is too risky. Call me when Iran gets back to normal."

By mid March, Alamir reports to Hill that he has hired Hashemi's replacement, that they are planning a Khomeini ambush, but need another million Rials to hire two patsies. Hill, still outraged over his conversation with Sammy and probably low on funds, rejects Alamir's request. According to Jahangir, Alamir has not hired anyone and is making arrangements to move his family from Tehran to the port of Bandar Pahlavi on the Caspian Sea.

FRIDAY, APRIL 13, 1979, IRAN

The Capture Team's pistachio man, stationed at the Semiramis Hotel across the street from the U.S. Embassy, reports to Jahangir that Dan Hill just fainted in the hotel lobby, that he could not be revived and is being taken to the hospital by ambulance and that he is following by car. On hearing this news, Jamshid instructs Jahangir to access Hill's room for clues to his association with 'Rosy', the Khomeini affair and anything else he can dig up. One hour later from the hospital, 'Old Pistachio' calls Jahangir and two other agents in Hill's hotel room. Old Pistachio reports gleefully, "Hill is dead!"

In his New York A-Tec office, Tony's secure phone flashes. It's answered by Gi-Gi, who after listening, sets the receiver down next to Tony.

"Dad, it's Jahangir. I don't know if this is good or bad news. Dan Hill is dead."

Tony puts down his cappuccino, lights a cigar, then slams his hand on the desk.

"Much as I hate that bastard, it's bad news! It cuts my line of communication with his associates." He tells Jahangir, "Steal all the evidence you can from his room before the hotel is advised of his death. I'm not altogether surprised and have an idea of what happened."

The following day Tony learns that Hill was poisoned. Thankfully, Jahangir retrieved Hill's bank statements, a box of business cards, address books and a suitcase full of his diaries, calendar logs and photographs. Tony instructs Jahangir to leave Iran immediately with all of the stolen materials and report to Jamshid.

Hill's secretary, Sarah, is accustomed to long periods of silence from him. When she does not receive her biweekly pay check, she calls him at the Semiramis Hotel and receives the bad news. Suddenly unemployed, she calls Alamir. His phone is disconnected. She calls Hashemi. His phone is disconnected. She calls the bank and discovers Hill's account is closed. She checks the petty-cash box and counts what is left: 279,500 Rials. (Approximately $4,000 U.S.). She takes 30,000 Rials from the box, her two week salary, and decides to check on Hill's death. After the hospital tells her they have no idea of what happened to Hill's body, she sends a telex to Hill's wife, Rita. Rita's icy reply is that she is not surprised by his death, that his body, if found, is to remain in Iran and that she is relocating to a foreign country. Sarah, worried over Hill's death and the disappearance of Alamir and Hashemi, takes the remaining petty cash and leaves. Two weeks later, after Sarah's bugged phone remains silent, one of Jamshid's agents goes to Hill's office to check. The office is empty.

During dinner at Luigi's, with Dr. Monti, Gi-Gi, Peter and Judy, Tony postulates, "Well, it had to be Alamir, Hashemi or Khomeini's people who killed Hill."

Gi-Gi, the lawyer, always considering options, adds, "Let's not rule out Carlo and Rosy."

"No way, Gi-Gi baby. It's not Carlo because he needed Hill to get to me. And it's not Rosy because his organization wants Khomeini dead. Any more ideas?"

"OK, you made your point," concedes Gi-Gi, "But with Hill dead, our progress to trap Carlo has suddenly retrogressed. Now what?"

"Relax, Gi-Gi," soothes Dr. Monti, "We know you're looking for action. Be patient and we'll all get plenty of it."

Judy, still upset with herself for losing her cool in Las Vegas, shakes her head, "I'm sorry, Mr. Berlotti. I let you down that night. We would have seen plenty of action. It'll never happen again."

"Changing that subject," interrupts Peter, "Dr. Asti reported late today that four of your men on the Rio Plata job developed amoeba histolytica. He believes it was caused by eating contaminated river shrimp at your campsite mess-hall."

"Jesus Christ!" snaps Tony, "I don't want any more bad news! Let's stop and go eat." After a long silence he orders, "Have the field cook fired!"

APRIL 24, 1979, NEW YORK

Peter announces that he and Judy will marry on June 24, her birthday. Judy insists that the wedding be simple and private. Dr. Monti volunteers to make all the arrangements and tells Judy to forget the customary financial protocol, "This wedding is on me." When Tony invites Carmen to the wedding, she quickly responds that her wedding gift to Peter and Judy will be an all-expense paid two- week honeymoon at the fashionable Las Hadas resort in Manzanillo.

The wedding takes place as planned. Dr. Monti gives the bride away, Tony is best man and Carmen is matron of honor. As Tony looks longingly at the lovely Carmen, he wishes it were their wedding. Josh, Jamshid and two other agents are witnesses. When Carmen realizes that George is absent, she asks, "Tony, why couldn't George be here?"

Tony had anticipated her question. "Well, with all the turmoil in Iran, he's decided to move temporarily to Islamabad, Pakistan. He just couldn't get away." *"Damn it all—I hate lying to her."*

After weeks of examining Hill's bank statements, phone logs, photos and diaries, Dr. Monti, Peter, Judy and Jahangir cannot determine the true identity of Louis or Rosy. Hill's bank statements show he received money from three sources: Banque De Credit International, Permindex and Bank of America. Many of the transactions were certified checks and transferred into his accounts in Mexico, Chile and Iran.

His diaries and phone logs include the following highlighted names: Jack Ruby, Carousel Club; Lee Oswald, New Orleans; Sam Giancana, Chicago; Clay Shaw, CIA; Nicolae Malaxa, NY; Guy Bannister, FBI; Louie, OSS; Tom Hill, JBS (John Birch society); Ed Walker, JBS; Gary Powers, CIA; Jose Martinez, Bolivia; George de Mohrenschildt, Dallas; 2, Las Vegas; Lois Bernstein, NY; Brooks, Mexico; Bernie, Toronto; Jesus, D.C.; King, Dallas; King, Denver; Rusty, Santiago (Chile); Kruchenko, Mexico; Manuel, Mexico; Palma, Las Vegas and Katerina, Mexico.

His diaries also reveal he had a close relationship with Sam Giancana, showing he visited Sam in Mexico in 1967 and 1974 and was in Chicago on June 19, 1975, the day Giancana was killed. Strangely missing from Hill's effects are his passport and there is no mention of known associates Louis, Rosy, Hoffa, Roselli, Carlo, Ferrie, Lansky, Trafficante, Levinson and Marcello.

Also missing from his records is any mention of Tony Berlotti and Nunzio Addabbo.

Hill's photos are still being examined. Many are cropped to remove backgrounds, others show several unidentified males and females. Hill carried an international drivers license, showed his address as the Semiramis Hotel, Tehran, phone 825145, extension 19; a "in case of emergency" card to notify his wife, Rita Hill, at Hotel Miramar, Viña del Mar, Chile or Box 2288, Falls Church, Virginia 22048. Finally, there is a photo of Tony Berlotti smoking a cigar as he stands in front of an airplane.

Dr. Monti is convinced that Dan Hill, although he obviously had "inside" connections, was not on the CIA payroll.

Josh's father, Misha, is still missing, and Josh is following up connections for more clues to Hill's superiors.

AUGUST 1979, MEXICO

Late in the month, Gi-Gi accompanies Tony on a site visit to their Rio Plata project in Mexico.

Upon arrival, they are billeted in a three bedroom, campsite trailer with Warren Cox, the project manager. Tony and Gi-Gi spend the first day touring the mine site with Warren and Hans Hovland, site geologist. Later, Hans is invited to join them for a grilled chicken dinner. Following dinner the foursome decide to play party bridge. After the first rubber, while Gi-Gi is in the bath room, Warren suggests, "Boss, you can have my room while you're here."

"Why your room?"

"I have a king size bed. It'll be more comfortable for you and Gi-Gi."

"Warren, Warren," Tony smiles, "She's my secretary. I'm not sleeping with her."

Hans gives Warren a look of disbelief, obviously thinking, *"Jesus the boss must be losing it..."*

Tony sips his brandy, lights a cigar, then declares, "And you guys stay away from her."

Gi-Gi returns to the table and they resume the second rubber. Neither Warren nor Hans detect the impersonation.

The second day is spent touring the mill site. During their walk through, a tall good looking mill operator wearing a hard-hat, waves his flashlight at Gi-Gi, gives her a whistle and a lecherous look. Gi-Gi, who enjoys playing her role to the hilt, responds by tilting her head and giving him a suggestive smile before continuing the walk. Tony catches the exchange and warns Gi-Gi, "Don't get carried away with your new job. These men haven't seen a good looking woman for weeks. You're asking for trouble and I don't want you to blow your cover. Be cool."

After a grilled steak dinner, Gi-Gi says, "I'm going for a short walk before we play bridge."

As she walks past the mess hall, a voice from behind announces, "Hola, linda!" (Hi, beautiful).

Gi-Gi stops, turns around and just smiles. *"My, my, it's the mill operator. Don't even think about it, pal...I'm itching for a good fight."*

The only thing on the brave operator's mind is making a pass at Gi-Gi. He reaches out, grabs Gi-Gi's wrist and again announces, "Hola, linda!"

Gi-Gi's reaction is swift. The unfortunate mill operator suddenly finds himself on the ground, holding his groin in pain, as he watches the beautiful girl walk slowly away back to the double wide. Gi-Gi can hear him shouting, "Concha su madre!" (Sonofabitch).The following morning before breakfast, Warren receives word that some of his men witnessed Gi-Gi's performance and have decided it would be prudent to leave her alone.

Tony's comment at the breakfast table is, "Sorry I missed that. I hear you really creamed that guy." Privately he warns Gi-Gi again, "I told you not to ask for trouble."

FRIDAY, OCTOBER 19, 1979, NEW YORK

It's almost closing time at Tony's New York engineering office. Tony and Gi-Gi are in Tony's office preparing to leave for Phoenix, Arizona. They are unaware of what is taking place at the reception desk. Rhonda, the receptionist looks puzzled.

"You say you're Carmen and you want to surprise Mr. Berlotti?"

"Yes, is that a problem?" Carmen looks her most regal and elegant.

"I'm not sure. Does he know you?"

"Of course he knows me. Is he here?"

"Yes, but Mr. Berlotti and his secretary are getting ready to fly to Arizona."

As Rhonda picks up the phone to call Tony, Gi-Gi, totally oblivious of Carmen's presence, walks into the comptrollers' office for traveling cash. Rhonda sees him and points her out to Carmen.

"Oh, there goes Mr. Berlotti's secretary."

Carmen gets a good look at Gi-Gi and blinks. "She's going to Arizona with Mr. Berlotti?"

"Yes. She goes everywhere with him."

"Please tell Mr. Berlotti I'm here." Carmen's tone now is haughty and commanding.

After Rhonda calls and tells Tony that Carmen is at the front desk, there is a long silence.

"What's wrong?" asks Carmen.

"Nothing at all." Rhonda smiles. "Mr. Berlotti is coming."

Tony never expected this visit. Before his deliberately slow walk to reception, he ponders, *"Damn, I'm sorry I never mentioned Carmen to my staff."* His embarrassment mounts when he sees Rhonda introducing Gi-Gi to Carmen. *"Oh, God - I hope Gi-Gi doesn't blow his cover. I wonder what Rhonda told Carmen. Well, here goes nothing - or something."* As he approaches Carmen, he holds out his arms to her. "Carmen, what a grand surprise! Why didn't you tell me you were coming?"

Carmen looks at Gi-Gi, lifts her chin with a dazzling, proprietary smile and rushes into Tony's arms. Rhonda looks around the room and shrugs her shoulders at those watching this exchange.

Gi-Gi excuses herself, "Nice meeting you, Carmen. Sorry, but I'm leaving now for the weekend."

"How nice. Where are you going?"

Tony responds quickly as he sees Gi-Gi turning into another room, "She's going to meet her boyfriend in the Catskills." *"God, how I hate lying to her!"*

Carmen, deeply in love with Tony but a savvy lady, refrains from pressing Tony about Gi-Gi in front of Rhonda. She takes his arm and asks, "So, Tony, what are your plans for the weekend?"

It's quitting time, but no one is leaving. Some can be seen juggling papers, others walking from office to office, all hoping to see what happens next. They've never heard of Carmen and have assumed that Tony is having an affair with Gi-Gi. Tony looks at his watch, *"Good, it's quitting time. I wish they'd all leave."* When he realizes why no one is leaving, he puts his arm around Carmen and announces, loud enough to be heard around the room, "Carmen, my dear, I'm free, all weekend." *"There—that'll give them something to talk about!"* As he leads Carmen to his office, she gets some strange looks from those scrambling by her to the exit. Once in the office, Tony excuses himself. "Excuse me, sweetheart, while I go wash my face and hands. Be right back."

From the men's room, Tony calls Gi-Gi, who has been forced to use the ladies' room as part of her deception.

"Gi-Gi - come to our apartment. I've got to tell her the truth."

Gi-Gi leaves immediately and Tony returns to Carmen.

"So," smiles Carmen, pacing the floor. Her smile does not extend to her eyes. "You're free all weekend?"

"Yes, I've canceled my trip to Arizona."

"Tell me, dear, does your young blonde secretary know you canceled?"

"She knows! Rhonda told her about Gi-Gi." Tony lights a cigar and looks around for possible eavesdroppers. "Carmen, sit down. There's something you need to know about my secretary."

"No! I can handle the truth standing up!" Her obvious pain and anger are mounting.

"I love you, Carmen. You alone!   Come with me to my apartment and you'll meet my secretary."

"You can't be serious!"

"Trust me. Let's go."

Carmen looks depressed, but tries to put a good face on this painful development. "OK, my love. Surprise me."

Shortly thereafter, Carmen enters Tony's New York apartment for the first time. Her obvious agitation mounts when Tony leads her into the kitchen and she sees Gi-Gi drinking a beer.

Tony takes a long deep breath as he watches Carmen. *"The moment of truth. No more lying about this to Carmen."*

"Carmen - take a good long look at Gi-Gi."

"I am. Sooooo?"

"Sooooo, Carmen, my dear, what do you see?"

"All right! You asked! I see a big, tough looking, blonde female drinking beer from a bottle."

Gi-Gi can't stand it any longer. She pulls off her wig, unbuttons her blouse, pulls out her gel boobs, grins broadly at Carmen and gives a sigh of relief, "Ahhhhh, that feels better!"

Carmen stands motionless, in shock, until recognition finally registers. "My God! Tony - it's George - what is going on here?"

Tony explains why George is impersonating a female and that no one in his engineering office knows Gi-Gi's true identity. Carmen hugs Tony, tears in her eyes,

"Oh, Tony! I'm so sorry - and relieved. I was devastated and all I was thinking was how to kill both of you. Please forgive me."

Tony and George take turns hugging and consoling Carmen.

"Tony, darling, I'll never doubt you again. You know I love you, and trust you, completely."

With peace and tranquility restored, Tony looks at his watch and shouts, "Damn, we missed our flight to Arizona."

"After I get my act together again, let's go to dinner and then catch the midnight special to Phoenix. We'll take Carmen with us. We should make an interesting ménage et trois." laughs Gi-Gi.

OCTOBER 25, 1979

Montico receives a bid package from Cia. Minera Plata in Bolivia outlining the requirements for a crash program proposal for installation of a security system at their mining complex. With Dr. Monti away on a six week top-secret electronic installation in Pakistan, Peter decides he can provide the proposal and proceeds accordingly, backed-up by Judy and Josh.

NOVEMBER 4, 1979

November begins with bad news. Islamic revolutionaries under Ayatollah Khomeini seize the U.S. Embassy in Tehran, capturing over 50 diplomats while shouting "down with Satan!" Tony's business in Iran is over, as is Addabbo's and those of many other businessmen foreign to Iran.

Montico receives a telex on November 23 advising their proposal has made the short-list. They are further advised that a senior Montico representative is required to travel to Bolivia for a site visit within the next two weeks to be interviewed and meet local contractors.

Dr. Monti returns from Pakistan on November 25. He is delighted with Peter's proposal, has supreme confidence in his son's ability to handle the contract and authorizes him to travel to Bolivia.

During their regularly scheduled secure communication, Dr. Monti mentions to Tony how proud he is that Peter made the short-list in Bolivia. "That's great, Frank. Who's going with him?"

"He's going alone. Why?"

"Not a good idea, Frank. Peter's Spanish is bad. Bolivia is particularly dangerous. He doesn't know the area, and he's not streetwise as far as that part of the world is concerned."

"They said they have English speaking people who will meet him..."

"I don't care. Not good enough, Frank. I'll send someone to follow Peter around."

DECEMBER 3, 1979, BOLIVIA

Peter arrives in La Paz and is met at the airport by Jose, an English-speaking man who identifies himself as the person responsible for the bid package. Jose drives Peter to the Sheraton

Hotel and they check into separate rooms. They meet on the 15th floor for dinner, discuss the project and enjoy after dinner pisco sours. After two drinks, Peter complains of feeling dizzy.

"You're not accustomed to this high altitude," states Jose. "I'll order you a 'matte-de-coco'. That will make you feel better."

Peter does not argue. Jose flags a waiter for the drink. Unknown to Peter and Jose, one of Tony's agents observes and overhears this exchange from a nearby table. Moments later, Peter sips the drink, makes a funny face, states he doesn't like it and tells Jose he is going to bed.

Next morning, after an early breakfast, Jose and Peter leave La Paz by jeep. As they pass the Mina Salvadora mine area en route to the Plata site, over unpaved, dusty and dangerous hair-pin roads, Peter becomes lethargic and complains his head is spinning, unaware that he's undergoing the insidious onset of hypoxia. Jose stops the jeep, snaps an oxygen mask on Peter, then resumes driving. Two minutes later Jose announces they are passing through 4,800 meters (15,748 feet). Peter stays on oxygen until they descend to the Plata site at 4,100 meters (13,451 ft.). He gathers his senses and, still groggy and out of breath, asks, "Why aren't you on oxygen?"

"I was born in the high altitude Cochabamba. Mother nature provided me with large lungs. Also, I chew coco leaf and never get 'puna' (high altitude sickness)."

As Peter follows Jose towards a metal building, he is impressed with the surrounding skyline. He stops, takes a series of panoramic camera shots of the Andes Mountains, and enters the building with Jose. There he is led to a small room with a cot, blankets and dresser.

"OK, Peter, you can leave your personal belongings here, use the toilet across the hall, then come to our dining room at the end of the hall for some food and you'll meet our senior staff."

Peter, the New York city boy, is unaccustomed to roughing-it, especially at this oxygen-starved high altitude. Hoping to make a good first impression with the Bolivians, he rushes several times between the toilet and his room to be sure he's presentable and prepared for contract talks. Moments later he arrives dizzy and out of breath in the dining room.

As Peter focuses around the dining table, he sees four men already eating. Jose stands and asks Peter to sit next to him. Peter, still dizzy, complies and reaches for a piece of bread, hoping to reorganize his brain. Jose begins to introduce the staff.

"On your right, Peter, is Pepe." They shake hands.

"On Pepe's right is Gabriel." They shake.

"And across the table is Manuel." When Peter reaches across the table to shake hands, he does an obvious double-take and shakes his head in disbelief. *"Holy shit! It's Manuel...one of Carlo's men. These are the Machos. I've got to get a message to Dad and Uncle Tony! Fast!"*

Peter's reaction brings a smile to Manuel's face, as he refuses the hand shake. "What is wrong, Señor Peter? Like they say in your country - you see a ghost?"

Peter sits and fumbles with his soup spoon as he stalls for an answer. "Oh, no. No. Not at all. It's just that Manuel looks like an old classmate of mine."

"What is your friends name?" asks Manuel silkily.

Although Peter took two years of high school Spanish, with his lack of practice and no exposure to Spanish people, this sudden twist of events leave him hopelessly lost. He has trouble coming up with a name fast.

After shifting nervously in his chair, Peter invents a name. "Yes. Oh yes, his name is Juanito Lopez, a Mexican."

It's an obvious lie, but Peter's fate has been sealed since he entered Bolivia.

Manuel, leader of Los Machos, rises slowly, walks around the table, stands behind Peter and in his best English, asks, "Tell me, Peter Monti - who you are and how you know me?"

Peter, nervous, still dizzy and unaccustomed to dealing with crisis situations, comes unglued. He miserably attempts to convince Manuel he is being honest.

Manuel, unemotionally, calmly and deliberately, draws his weapon, places it against the back of Peter's head and orders, "Please stand, Señor Peter."

Peter complies and closes his eyes.

"Now, Señor Peter, empty all of your pockets."

Peter is panicking as he realizes he's in deep trouble. He begins to empty his pockets. *"God I hope this works..."* Peter is carrying one of Montico's mini DX transceivers. *"I better send a signal right now."* As he slowly removes items from his pockets with his right hand, his left hand reaches inside his left pants slit-pocket, activates the transceiver strapped to the inside of his thigh and depresses the 'distress' button. His right hand removes a pocket knife, whistle, comb, ball point pen, scientific calculator, miner's loop and, finally, his wallet, all placed in a line on the table.

"Is that all, Señor Peter?"

"Yes, that's all."

"Good. Now take off you clothes," orders Manuel.

"Take off my clothes? Why?"

Manuel sticks his weapon under Peter's chin, "I say take off all you clothes!"

"I'll catch cold," Peter responds feebly, clutching at straws.

Without warning, Manuel fires a shot through the ceiling. "Now!" he snarls.

Peter begins to remove his clothes.

Peter hesitates before removing his pants. *"I hope my signal was received."* As Peter drops his pants the transceiver is exposed. Jose, Carlo's communication and explosives expert, thinking it might be a bomb, rises slowly and motions everyone, "Don't move!"

Manuel asks, "Que pasa?" (What's the matter?")

Jose ignores Manuel and addresses Peter, "What is it?"

Scared, confused, cold and still dizzy, Peter responds honestly, "It's a radio. Why?"

Manuel rips the transceiver from Peter's leg and rotates the on button before Jose warns him not to touch the switches.

Manuel proudly announces, "Now, Señor Peter, let us see what we hear on dee leetle radio."

The radio remains silent as Manuel increases the volume control.

Although naked and cold, Peter has a brief moment of satisfaction. *"Gotcha' you sons-a-bitches!   It's already electronically destructed. You didn't know about the self destruct by-pass code!"*

"Why it not work?" asks Manuel.

"The battery is probably dead," lies Peter.

Jose glares at Manuel, calls him a 'tonto huevon' (asshole) and takes the unit away from him without an argument. He removes its small battery pack, tells Peter to get dressed and tells everyone he is going to check the battery. Manuel never argues with Jose.

By the time Peter is dressed, Jose returns and addresses Peter, "Your NiCad battery isn't dead. It has a standard 7.5 volt charge. Why isn't the radio working?"

With temporary relief that he is still alive and feeling better in warm clothes, Peter attempts a stalling tactic by offering other reasons why the radio won't work. Manuel doesn't accept the stall. He jams his weapon into Peter's chest, looks at Jose, and snarls, "El gringo concha su madre es un mentiroso!" (The sonofabitch foreigner is a liar!).

"Puede ser," (could be) responds Jose. He then looks at Peter, "Well, Peter, we will resolve this tonight when Carlo arrives."

Tony's agent following Peter, posing as an oxygen supplier, has been parked at the Minera Plata repair shop, across the road from the senior staff dining room, complaining of engine trouble. He heard all of the conversation in the dining room until Peter's transceiver crashed. With night-time approaching, Tony's agent requests and receives permission to remain over night in the employee's guest house, next door to the senior staff's unit containing the private dining room. Unknown to the agent, the dining room has an attached wing of bedrooms reserved for senior staff, one of which has been assigned to Peter.

In the dining room at 9 P.M., the agent, hoping to see Peter walk in, has been eating slowly. He drops a knife on the floor and, while picking it up, places a Montico bug under the table. As he finishes a cup of coffee and vanilla wafers, his delay is rewarded as Peter enters with Jose, followed by Pepe and Gabriel. Peter does not know the agent and the agent can not afford to expose his identity. The four sit at a private table, set for a party of six. Moments later, the door opens, Manuel leads Carlo into the room and Carlo sits at the head of the table without addressing Peter.

At 9:15, Tony's agent and the remaining four diners are asked to leave the room. The agent returns immediately to his guest house room and attempts to pick up the dining room conversation but without luck. The voices are not intelligible. Frustrated, the agent walks out hoping to eavesdrop from a dining room window. Again no luck. There is an armed guard standing at the entrance. The agent returns to his room for the night, with his receiver and earphones on, hoping to hear anything.

At 1 A.M. the agent awakens to Peter's voice, loud and clear in his earphones. "Hello, anybody that can hear me. This is Peter Monti at the Minera Plata mine. I'm Carlo Perez's hostage. Help." Peter keeps repeating the message until 2 A.M.; then silence.

The next morning at breakfast, the agent does not see Peter sitting with the others. Determined to find out what happened to

Peter, the agent makes a bold move. He approaches Carlo's table and asks, "Does anyone here know if there's any American in camp who can answer a question about American politics?"

Jose, the only one in the group who studied in the United states and mastered English, replies. "Why would anyone up here want to know anything about American politics?"

The agent is ready. "I simply want to know who is next in line to be Ambassador to Bolivia."

Carlo waves off the agent with, "There is no American here. Now go away."

The agent complies, walks to the repair shop to find, as he suspected, that his jeep is in good running order, then makes the long drive back to La Paz.

The next day, Tony's agent alerts him of the situation and warns him to expect the worst.

Tony calls Dr. Monti and braces him for possible bad news. "Frank, Peter is missing."

Two days later, Montico receives a crude telex from Cia. Minera Plata stating that Peter was last seen drunk, coming out of a whorehouse with a prostitute in the pueblo called Coroico. They left in a jeep and two days later both bodies were found with the jeep, burned to death in a deep quebrada (ravine). The first to read the telex at 7:30 A.M. is Judy, Peter's wife. She reads and rereads the telex several times before going into shock. When Dr. Monti arrives at 7:45, he finds Judy in a daze at her desk.

"Judy! Judy,...what's the matter? Are you all right?"

Judy remains in a daze, holding the telex, and looking at her father-in-law with glazed eyes, unable to respond. Dr. Monti sees the telex, reads it and falls to the floor on his hands and knees, moaning in pain. Josh arrives five minutes later and sees Dr. Monti and Judy holding each other on the floor and crying hysterically.

"What's happened?" asks Josh.

They ignore Josh and continue crying. Josh sees the telex on the floor, reads it and fights-off his impulse to join them on the floor and cry with them. Instead, he makes a quick call to Tony in Arizona and Dr. Asti in Mexico, advising them what has happened to Peter. He also suggests that Dr. Monti and Judy will probably require medical assistance. The following day, Tony, Gi-Gi, Jamshid and Dr. Asti are in New York giving moral and medical comfort to Dr. Monti and Judy.

Tony tries to help them, "It won't bring Peter back, but we'll get the truth, one way or other."

After a briefing with Tony's Bolivian agent, everyone agrees that there's no way Peter was drunk or with a prostitute.

Tony, devastated with the pain this conspiracy has caused to persons he holds dear, shouts, "That telex was a total fabricated lie and Peter's death was no accident. He was murdered by Carlo and Los Machos. We should have recognized this as another set-up and not allowed Peter to go..."

With Dr. Monti and Judy sedated and in mourning, Tony and Gi-Gi develop a strategy. They prepare a response to the Minera Plata telex, thanking them for the details of Peter's death and requesting that they arrange a Catholic burial, at Montico expense. They also request the location of the burial site so that next of kin can visit and pay their respects. The Minera Plata response is fast. They are "sorry that Peter died" and will comply with Montico's requests.

"Fine!" states Gi-Gi. "They're probably already planning an ambush for the ' next of kin'."

"Yes," cautions Tony, "It's unwise to play into the enemy's hand on his territory. We'll just stall and plan our own entrapment strategy. Meanwhile, we'll send two men to La Paz as decoy drug dealers. They'll spread big money around the Sheraton Hotel until word gets to Carlo and his crew that they're there to buy heroin - big time. I know these thugs now and how they operate. They'll take the bait."

DECEMBER 27, 1979

While Tony, Gi-Gi, Dr. Monti, Judy and Jamshid are spending the Christmas holidays with Carmen and the Brooks in Manzanillo, news breaks that Russia has seized control of Afghanistan.

"Very interesting," comments Tony. "Our man in Pakistan stated that Pakistani General Mohammad Mustaf predicted the take-over last year. He knew the Russians were building first class reinforced concrete kitchens and rest homes along newly built roads to be used by the invaders. Big mistake. Those new facilities will be sitting ducks for the Afghan guerrillas who know the territory and hide in hard to find caverns. Our position in Pakistan and the rest of the Middle East is now tentative. Damn it all! 1979 was a very bad year. All losses and no wins. Again!"

CHAPTER 22

DOUBLE- CROSS IN FLIGHT

EARLY JANUARY, 1980

Tony's Capture Team moves into action. Rashid and Jahangir are assigned to La Paz as drug dealers. Their strategy hits pay-dirt in May, when Manuel and Poncho meet Rashid, several times, in the lobby of the Sheraton Hotel in La Paz. Rashid proposes that the drug for money exchange be made in Las Vegas. With Carlo and Jose in the Dominican Republic, Manuel agrees to discuss the matter with their Las Vegas representative before making a firm exchange commitment.

MONDAY, JUNE 16, 1980, LAS VEGAS

Manuel and Poncho are met at McCarren Airport, Las Vegas, by Sammy and Hank. They are followed to Sammy's residence by Rashid and Mehdi. Jahangir remains in La Paz. The Montico bugs pick up the conversation.

"Well, boys," starts Sammy, "this is gonna' be a sweet deal - so let's not fuck it up!"

"Si, señores," adds Hank in his native tongue, "Hemos llegada a la penultima etapa." (Yes, men, we've arrived at the next to the last stage.)

"Speak English, god damn it!" snaps Sammy. "You know I don't understand that shit!"

"Don't be paranoid. We're not talking about you. They understand Spanish better, that's all."

"OK, OK, but what we need to do now is decide when, where and how to knock them off after we get their money. I have an idea."

"Eeets bad news for you, Sammy," interrupts Manuel, "Carlo say we no exchange in Vegas. He want exchange made in Mexico City."

"They won't buy it," snaps Sammy.

"Don Carlo is dee boss. He say exchange in Mexico City. Comprende?"

"Oh, I comprende (understand) all right, but it's a dumb ass idea! Vegas is my town. I can get away with murder here. I'll set it up!"

"Oiga, tonto! (Listen, jerk!) Don Carlo say Mexico City!" Comprende?"

The heated exchange continues for almost half an hour until Sammy finally concedes. "OK, we'll discuss the deal with them, here, in two days. But I guarantee, they won't buy it."

Tony's two Capture Team agents, posing as drug agents, are instructed to reject Mexico City.

"Instead," states Tony, "We'll make a counter proposal we know they'll reject, then make a final proposal to meet in Agua Prieta, just across the border from Douglas, Arizona."

"Why Agua Prieta?" Asks Gi-Gi.

"Because they know the town. But so do I!"

The meeting is held on schedule. Rashid rejects Mexico City. Sammy rejects Tucson. Rashid rejects Nogales but when he proposes Agua Prieta, Manuel, Sammy and Poncho go into a prolonged arm waving huddle. Their smiles give Rashid a sigh of relief.

"Agua Prieta be OK," states Manuel.

They agree that an initial half million dollar cash for drugs deal will be on July 12th. They will meet for lunch at the Cave restaurant (Poncho Villa's old hideout, formed by two caverns connected by a short tunnel). Then they will meet in Manuel's rented van, parked at the nearby airport near a Queen Air, for the exchange.

They shake hands on the start of a long relationship. The agents leave the meeting and drive to join Tony, Gi-Gi, Jamshid and another agent, who are already picking up the following exchange in their surveillance motor home:

"Well, boys," boasts Sammy, " we lucked out. I knew they'd reject Mexico City. Agua Prieta is very good."

"Yes," adds Manuel, "and we do dee same thing we planned for Mexico City."

"What's that? asks Hank.

"First we meet them to see what auto they drive. Then, when we eat, Jose weel wire their auto weeth explosives."

"Then what?" repeats Hank.

"After dee exchange - when we fly away from dee airport and they drive away in their auto, Jose weel blow them up via remote control from our avion (plane)," brags Manuel.

"What? And all that good heroin goes up with them?"

"You teenk we stupid?" glares Manuel.

"Explain it!" demands Sammy.

"Only 10% be dee good heroin. Dee rest be fake - bueno?" smiles Manuel.

"Bueno my ass!" shouts Sammy. "What if they spot check the shit before we get our dough?"

"Then," adds the stone faced Poncho, "we keel them and fly away."

"Sounds good to me," says Hank, rubbing his hands.

"What the fuck would you know," snarls Sammy. "Anything sounds good to you as long as you get your 10%. You're only in this because you know Spanish. You always..."

"Bueno, amigos," interrupts Manuel, raising his arms, "nothing more to discuss. We all in this together. We all make dinero (money). OK, Sammy, call dee ladies and we celebrate."

Armed with their enemies' plan, but disappointed that Carlo will not be in Agua Prieta, the Capture Team develops appropriate counter measures, but are always mindful that Carlo is still their primary target.

JULY 12, 1980, PONCHO VILLA'S CAVE RESTAURANT, AGUA PRIETA, SONORA, MEXICO

Hank is seated at a large table, waiting for the others to arrive. Manuel and Poncho are waiting at the front door when Rashid and Mehdi arrive. Manuel suggests that Rashid and Mehdi should drive him to the airport. Rashid agrees and points out his car. Inside, meanwhile, Hank has already focused his eyes on a tall, shapely redhead, seated alone across the dimly lit room. Tony and Jamshid, in disguise, are seated at a table behind the redhead and a Capture Team agent is seated alone near the exit. Hank keeps trying to get the redhead's attention before the others arrive. It's obvious he's already planning to make his move on her. The others arrive before Hank makes contact. They all order margueritas before lunch and Hank immediately steers the conversation to ethnic backgrounds. "So, tell me," he asks, "what's your nationality?"

"We," lies Rashid, "are Armenians. And you?"

"I'm American. Manuel and Poncho are Cubans," lies Hank.

"Never mind who we are," scowls Manuel, "I very hungry."

Throughout lunch, Hank is unsuccessful in making eye contact with the redhead. One hour later, Manuel asks for the check and announces, "Bueno, amigos - vamanos." (OK, friends, let's go.)

Hank remains seated, claiming, "You don't need me to complete this transaction. I'll see you in Vegas at the Horseshoe."

With the foursome safely gone, Hank makes his move. He orders two jumbo margueritas and carries them to the redhead's table. When he arrives, he receives a demure smile.

"Nice...very nice. Nothing I like better than a big, sexy redhead." "Hello, I'm Hank and I see you're alone. Here, have a real marguerita." He sits across the table without asking permission.

The redhead accepts the drink and smiles, "Hello, Hank. I'm Gi-Gi. Thanks for the drink, but I think you should know I'm waiting for a male friend."

"Too bad. You've been here a long time. Did he stand you up?"

"I hope not." Gi-Gi shrugs her shoulders. "But why would you care?"

"I would never stand you up. You're very attractive and sexy, baby."

"Well...thank you, Hank."

Hank has trouble controlling himself. He begins to feel the start of an erection as he watches Gi-Gi move provocatively while she adjusts her short skirt, her shirt taut across her 38D silicon pads.

"Gi-Gi, do you ever travel alone?"

"Well, yes, I do occasionally. Why?"

"Do you ever travel to Las Vegas?"

"Oh, indeed I do, Hank. I love Vegas. It's so exciting. Why? Are you from Vegas?"

"Yeah. Here's my card. Be sure to call me next time you're in town, baby. I'll show you around."

Hank reaches across the width of the table with his card in hand.

Gi-Gi makes sure her breasts rub his hand as she reaches for his card. "Thank you, Hank. I'm really looking forward to seeing you there. And soon, I hope."

Hank takes her hand, squeezes it, throws her a kiss, and thinking, *"Oh, yeah. She's available - and for me!"*

Mission accomplished, he stands, bows, excuses himself and leaves in a hurry to the airport.

Tony looks at Jamshid, winks and whispers, "Gi-Gi hooked him."

The drug transaction at the airport proceeds as planned.

"Let's see the merchandise," demands Rashid.

Poncho hands Mehdi a bag of heroin. Mehdi samples it and, without emotion, announces, "Now another bag, please."

After sampling the second bag, Mehdi announces, "This is good. Very good."

"Now," motions Manuel, "let me see dee money."

Rashid opens his briefcase, exposing the money. "I guarantee - it's all here."

Manuel examines the briefcase, does not detect anything unusual, spot checks the money, closes the case, then nods his head in agreement.

"It be a good deal to start. We make bigger business in future, si?"

"Si, señor," agrees Rashid as they all shake hands. The exchanges made, Manuel and Poncho walk to the twin engine Queen Air, where Jose is already seated. Rashid and Mehdi get into their vehicle and wait for the aircraft to take off.

After a short engine 'run-up' at the end of the runway, the Queen Air lifts off, making a climbing turn to the left. The aircraft, expertly piloted by Manuel, levels off at 2000 feet on a long downwind leg, then doubles back over the runway. The noise level in the Queen air is high but the following Montico bug transmission is loud and clear:

"Bueno, Jose," announces Manuel, "Estamos a dos mil pies sobre la pista." (OK, Manuel, we're at 2000 feet over the runway.) Manuel dips the right wing.

Jose, in the right seat, holds a remote unit. He looks down, sees their target vehicle, depresses the explode button and proudly declares, "Adios, amigos!"

The vehicle is seen driving slowly away from the field. Jose depresses the explode button again and again. Nothing happens.

"Jose," shouts Manuel, "Que pasa?" (What's wrong?)

Jose curses as he continues to aim and press the button.

Rashid, meanwhile, looks up at the aircraft, smiles at Mehdi and states, "Now."

Mehdi aims his remote at the Queen Air and depresses the burn button.

Manuel does a steep 360 degree turn over the runway, shouting, "Push dee button! - bush dee damn button!"

The vehicle with Rashid and Mehdi does not explode. As the aircraft levels off, then begins a climb away from the field, Poncho announces from a rear seat, "Manuel, que pasa con el avion? Hay un olor malo." (What's wrong with the plane? There's a bad smell.)

"Si," concurs Jose, "algo quemando, atras mi asiento." (Yes, something burning, behind my seat)

"Nada mas que la maleta aqui." states Poncho. (Nothing but the briefcase here.)

Poncho picks up the briefcase and screams, "Chucha!" (fuck)

"Que pasa, Poncho?"

"Me quemo los dedos!" (I burned my fingers)

Manuel reaches under his seat, then hands Poncho a pair of leather gloves, shouting,

"Abra la maleta!" (open the briefcase.)

Poncho opens the case, looks at the smoke emerging from within, then looks down at the moving vehicle and shouts, "Putamadres!" (mother-fuckers).

Rashid and Mehdi watch the Queen Air. It makes two more circles over the field, then climbs and heads south.

"It all went well up there," states Mehdi.

"Yes, Dr. Monti's burn units never fail. Let's go meet the boss."

They drive to Douglas, Arizona and rendezvous on the street in front of the smelter with Tony, Gi-Gi and Jamshid. After congratulating themselves for pulling off the double/double-cross, Rashid asks, "Where's Dr. Asti? Wasn't he supposed to be in the restaurant?"

"He didn't show up and I'm concerned," replies Tony.

"And what about Hank?" asks Gi-Gi, "Did he show up at the airport after he left me?"

"No, Sir. We waited half an hour, then left," answers Rashid.

The next morning, at the Capture Team's Tucson Safe House, Dr. Monti calls Tony.

"Tony, Dr. Asti is on his way to Las Vegas to meet you. He was involved in a car accident yesterday and couldn't make the trip to Agua Prieta."

"Is he OK?"

"He smacked his head on the steering wheel, broke a tooth and had to see a dentist."

"Thank God it wasn't serious. We have had too many 'accidents' in this dirty business. I'm flying up to Vegas tonight. By the way, is Judy still in a deep depression over Peter's death?"

"She's getting over it. She wants to be more involved in going after the assassins."

Tony is thoughtful, then, "It may be her best therapy, Frank. Tell her to be patient. She'll get her chance."

Meanwhile in Las Vegas, Sammy's phone rings at 9 A.M. He picks up on the sixth ring.

"Yeah?"

"Sammy, it's me. We gotta' talk - right away!"

"Christ, Hank! Can't it wait? I just got to bed."

"No! This is about yesterday and it can't wait."

"Holy shit! Don't tell me those dumb-ass Machos fucked-up!"

"Come to my place and I'll explain."

"No. You come here and I'll fix breakfast. My old lady is gone again - selfish bitch!"

Forty minutes later, Hank explains, "Well, the Machos got away with the money. But the Armenians' car didn't blow up. I saw them driving away from the airport after the plane was out of sight."

"Shit, I had a feeling something would go wrong."

"Carlo will surely get pissed over this."

"Why the hell should he - they got their money."

"Yeah, but the Armenians will make trouble when they find out they've been had."

"That's the Machos problem. Now get on the horn and get our cut - I'm going back to bed,"

JULY 24, 1980, LAS VEGAS

Sammy, Hank, Manuel and Poncho meet for breakfast at the Horseshoe Casino, then drive to their McCarren field hanger. The Capture Team's surveillance motor home, parked in the general aviation lot, picks up the assassins' conversations.

"OK, amigos. Let's get down to business," begins Sammy.

"What business," waves Manuel, "We make no business. Dee Armenians - how you say - dey double-crossid us. Dey burn up all dee money."

"What the fuck do you mean - burned the money? Is this some kind of joke or are you clowns tryin' to rip us off?"

"No yoke, Sammy. Dee Armenians must have time delay device or something to burn dinero (money). I tell you, Sammy - all dee dinero is quemado (burned) pooof!"

"I can't fucking believe this! You bastards are trying to screw me!" screams Sammy. "You guys are worst than the Keystone cops! Now what do we do?"

Manuel lights a cigarette, pours himself a pisco and announces, "Don Carlo say find and keel dee Armenians."

"Oh, sure," snaps Sammy, "keeel dee Armenians! "We got set up, 'muchachos' (boys) and I guarantee that son-of-a- bitch, Tony Berlotti, was behind it."

"How - and when - do we get Berlotti?" asks Hank.

"With Dan Hill gone," replies Sammy, "it won't be easy. He's a smart bastard and knows more about us than we do about him. Now I'm getting really worried."

"No worry," interrupts Poncho, "we weel find and keel heem."

This exchange continues until Manuel announces that Carlo wants to set a trap for Tony.

They agree to meet next week to discuss ideas, then adjourn as Hank says, "Come on, gang, let's get some rest. I have four broads lined-up tonight."

Meanwhile at Tony's Las Vegas Safe House, Dr. Asti explains why he was unable to come to Agua Prieta, then, "I'm glad you're all safe. What happened?"

"It was a piece of cake," boasts Gi-Gi. "I was in the restaurant when they arrived. Then, while I made sure Hank got a good look at me during lunch, agent Ahmed was outside watching Jose set his explosive device under our car. When Jose left for the airport, Ahmed removed the explosive."

"Then what?"

"When they finished lunch and left, Hank stayed, and then came to my table with two huge margueritas. I encouraged him, of course." Gi-Gi gave a broad wink.

"Yes," interrupts Tony, "and you gave an Academy Award performance. It's a wonder he didn't jump you on the table."

"I loooove my job!" smiles Gi-Gi in her best Jayne Mansfield imitation.

"And what happened at the airport?" asks Dr. Asti.

"Well," begins Rashid, "we made a smooth exchange - our money for their heroin. After we accepted their fake heroin, Manuel quickly examined our briefcase and counterfeit money. He found nothing wrong and we both agreed to the deal. Before I gave them the briefcase, I armed Dr. Monti's burn unit. We hit the burn switch after they were airborne."

"You know," grins Gi-Gi, "this would make a good movie."

"It sure would make a good movie!. How I wish I had been there to witness it," Dr. Asti rubs his hands gleefully.

"With Dan Hill gone, Hank may be our next link to Carlo," states Tony.

He then turns to his son and squeezes his shoulder.

"Gi-Gi - get ready for your next seduction assignment."

"I'm ready, Dad!"

CHAPTER 23

GI-GI STRIKES

When the Capture Team confirms that Los Machos will meet Sammy and Hank at Sammy's residence on August 30, Tony prepares Gi-Gi for action.

SATURDAY, AUGUST 28, 1980

Gi-Gi calls Hank, using her most seductive voice. "Hello, Hank?"

"Yes. Who's this?"

"This is Gi-Gi, the tall redhead. Remember me from Agua Prieta?"

"Of course. I couldn't forget you, baby. Where are you?"

"I'm in New York, but I'll be in Vegas tomorrow - at the Jockey Club." Gi-Gi's voice is intimate, suggestive, "And, Hank, I'll be traveling alone. Would you like to see me?"

"Absolutely!"

"Marvelous. Can you meet me in the bar-lounge, at, let's say - 7 P.M.?"

"You got it, baby. I'll be there."

The next day, dressed in an expensive designer silk suit, Hank struts into the lounge at the Jockey Club at 6:30 P.M., looks around, selects a quiet corner table and orders a double marguerita. At 7:30, as Hank finishes his second double, Gi-Gi makes a dramatic, deliberately slow entrance, then stops to get the maitre-d's attention. She looks stunning and available in her slinky hot pink pants suit.

Hank, bon vivant and self proclaimed ladies-man, stands as she approaches his table, commenting, "Ah, Gi-Gi, baby, you look great." Then, looking up at her, "Oh, yeah, and I do like tall girls."

"Nice to see you, too, Hank. My, oh my," looking him over provocatively from head to toe, "you look pretty terrific yourself."

Gi-Gi extends her hand to Hank's for his kiss. He keeps visually devouring Gi-Gi, seemingly hypnotized by her unique size and beauty, with the intoxicating scent of wild roses engulfing her.

Hank takes a long, deep breath. "Ahhh, Gi-Gi, you smell delicious - good enough to eat."

Gi-Gi raises a knowing eyebrow at that. "Thank you, Hank. Let's sit down, shall we?"

Still mesmerized as he offers a chair, "Sorry, I was just thinking...things."

"What kind of things, Hank?" *As if I didn't know what kind of things..."*

Still in a trance, he stumbles for words, "You know - just together things."

"Nice, fun things, I hope. For now, honey, I'll have what you're having."

"Ahhhh, my kind of lady!"

As he orders two double margueritas, Gi-Gi makes sure she is positioned so he gets a good look at her voluptuous twin 38's. As Hank continues to plan ahead to an exciting evening, he orders another double for himself and Gi-Gi continues to masterfully massage and inflate his ego.

"I'm so glad we met, honey. You're a real classy guy." *"Come on, Hank...make a move!"*

Gi-Gi notices the two waiters standing near the bar, leering lecherously at her, whispering their obvious approval.

"Guess I'm doing good. Wish Dad could see this."

When a waiter brings the drinks, Hank offers a toast, "Here's to a big night."

Gi-Gi clicks his glass, her voice is suggestive, low and throaty, "And Hank, here's getting to know you better." *"Dream on, Hankie, baby. One false move and I'll tear your fucking arms off."*

Hank's body action is easy to read as he looks at her, obviously undergoing a dress rehearsal for 'things' planned. *"He's hooked!"* knows Gi-Gi, *" All I do now is reel-in the line!"*

About an hour later, after two more drinks, their intimate tête-à-tête is interrupted by a loud crash from a nearby table. It's Gi-Gi's signal. As the waiters rush to that table to clean up the spilled drink and glass, Gi-Gi pushes her chair back, "Excuse me, Hank. I need to powder my nose."

As Gi-Gi walks away to the ladies room, Hank decides he, too, needs to make a pit stop and walks out to the men's room.

Hank returns to the table, finishes his drink and orders another.

When Gi-Gi returns, she sits next to Hank, leans over, blows gently and provocatively into his ear, whispering, "All better now?"

Hank loses control. He suddenly reaches out and cups one of Gi-Gi's soft, beautifully contoured 'silicone' breasts, drooling, "Nice, - very nice," thoroughly enjoying his first free feel.

Gi-Gi pulls back quickly, "Please, Hank...not yet...not here."

"Come on, baby, let's go," he continues groping and taking his second feel.

"Hank, people are watching," removing his hand. *"Try again you son-of-a-bitch. Three strikes and you're out."*

Never one to accept rejection, Hank confidently attempts 'strike three'. He suddenly receives a devastating slap across the face, sending him and the drinks crashing to the floor.

Gi-Gi's smile is enigmatic. *"Aaaaah...that felt good. Wish Dad were here."* She rises calmly, collects her things and walks quietly out.

The two Capture Team agents who have been sitting nearby since 7 P.M. and had spilled the drink earlier, grin and applaud silently. The waiters scramble to Hank's table trying to figure out what happened. On the floor, dazed, drunk and bleeding profusely from the nose, Hank reaches for a napkin and tries to stop the bleeding. When the waiters help him up and on a chair, he looks around, still dazed. Gi-Gi is gone. He curses in Spanish, then, nose still bleeding, announces, "I need a drink!"

Half an hour later, Hank staggers out of the Jockey Club. He drives home erratically, followed by the two agents. Then he runs into his garage door before it is fully retracted, parks his car half-way into the garage and enters his townhouse, waving both arms in the air, cursing in English and Spanish.

The next afternoon, when Hank does not arrive at Sammy's house for their meeting and they can't reach him at home, Sammy and Los Machos drive to the Horseshoe Casino, his usual hang-out. Assured he isn't there, they drive to Hank's townhouse.

When they arrive, Hank's garage door is still open and the damage conspicuous.

"Drunk again," declares Sammy, as they enter the garage.

The door to the laundry room is open, they walk in and see a bloody napkin with a Jockey Club logo on it on the washing machine. Sammy calls out, "Hank, are you here?" No response.

Poncho shouts, "Hola, Enrique, contestame, viejo." (hello, Hank, answer me, ol' boy). Nothing. They immediately begin a cautious walk-through.

"There he is," whispers Sammy, spotting Hank on the couch.

Hank is face down with one hand extended towards the telephone. Manuel examines Hank, looks up, raises both arms and states, "Muerto." (dead). Then, in English for Sammy's sake, "He dead."

"Holly shit! Quick, you guys - help me find his diaries." orders Sammy.

Poncho, puzzled, looks at Manuel, "No intiendo. Que dijo el gordo?" (I don't understand. What did the fat one say?)

Annoyed with their inability to communicate in English, Sammy waves them off, shouting, "Assholes!", then begins a search. Moments later, when Manuel realizes what Sammy wants, the two Bolivians assist. After three hours of rummaging through Hank's townhouse, they find no diaries, no notes.. The only item that catches Sammy's eye is a large framed photo of a girl in Hank's bedroom. The photo is marked: "I love you, Hank. You're my guy!" signed: "Louise".

Sammy's only comment, "I didn't know he had a girl friend."

Frustrated, they give up. Using sign language, English and a few Spanish words, Sammy tells the Machos to move the car into the garage, fix the door, get rid of the body and lock the doors.

In their surveillance motor home, the Capture Team agents give two thumbs up as they look at Hank's diaries, then hear more loud cursing from the Montico bugs.

Sammy's final words before leaving are, "First Dan Hill, now Hank. I bet that son-of-a-bitch Tony Berlotti was behind this!"

Obviously concerned that he may be next, Sammy goes home and arranges a trip to Bolivia.

When Tony learns that Sammy has scheduled a trip to Bolivia for the second week in September, he sends Rashid, who speaks good Spanish, to La Paz to join Jahangir. Gi-Gi returns to New York and receives a warm welcome from everyone at A-Tec.

"Well, Gi-Gi," praises Judy, "we heard you gave a brilliant performance at the Jockey Club. I'm still praying for a piece of the action."

"Don't worry, Judy," comforts Tony, "you'll get your chance."

"What I want to know is," asks Dr. Monti, "how did Hank die?"

Turning to Jamshid, Tony asks, "What did you find out?"

"I'm very sorry," replies Jamshid, ruefully rubbing his chin, "when Gi-Gi and Hank were in the rest rooms and the waiters were cleaning the mess at his table, Reza dropped a pill in Hank's drink."

"You weren't supposed to kill him," shouts Tony, jumping up. "He was a good line of communication with Carlo and the Machos. Send Reza back to Iran!"

"I already fired him, Rais. Again, I'm terribly sorry. It will never happen again."

Still angry, Tony pounds the table, "Goddamnit - I pay you guys big bucks to follow instructions and I don't like fuck-ups! - Sorry, Judy." Judy simply nods.

"Come on, Dad," interrupts Gi-Gi, "It wasn't Jamshid's fault."

Tony lights a cigar, calms down, then asks Judy to make him a cappuccino.

Dr. Monti waves a diary in the air, "Hank's diaries are mostly in Spanish. The last entry scribbled in here before he died was, "Get Gi-Gi - bitch!!!"

SEPTEMBER 27, 1980

Jamshid receives the report from Rashid and meets Tony for a briefing at noon over a box lunch. "OK, Jamshid, let's have it," grumbles Tony, still annoyed.

"Sammy met all week with Carlo, Jose, Gabriel and Pepe. When Sammy stated you were the one that set-up Hank, Carlo offered him twenty five thousand dollars for information leading to your location. Sammy accepted."

"What else?"

"Jose, the real brains in that group, said their primary concern is to destroy your conspiracy photo."

"They don't know it, but the negative was destroyed when the bastards torched my house. I'm guarding the print with my life."

"Did Jose say anything else?" Asks Dr. Monti.

"He said they are sending Gabriel to Las Vegas with Sammy in a couple of days to replace Hank. They will send Gabriel because he knows enough English to communicate with Sammy. According to Jahangir, Gabriel, like Hank, is a good hit-man and card shark. Remember, he was the one who fired the first shots when Oswald left the sixth floor. But, he's another womanizer and drinker."

"That's good news," states Gi-Gi rubbing her hands.

"Is that all?" asks Tony.

"No Sir," continues Jamshid, "Carlo also said you are not to be killed. "Killing Tony Berlotti," he said, "Is my job!"

"OK, Gi-Gi," states Tony, "let's prepare you for the next assignment. And, by the way – killing Carlo is my job – and it will be my extreme pleasure!"

CHAPTER 24

THE DOUBLE WHAMMY

SEPTEMBER 29, 1980, LAS VEGAS

Sammy and Gabriel arrive in Las Vegas. According to Mehdi, Sammy's wife moved out of the house and in with her sister in North Las Vegas when Sammy allowed Gabriel into the house.

In a taped conversation, Sammy tells Gabriel, "Bitch! She looked for any excuse to leave!"

"I weel move to dee Horseshoe, mañana, (tomorrow)" states Gabriel.

"Do whatever you want. Right now, I need to find Berlotti."

Tony, meanwhile, following Dr. Asti's "You need to rest" order, flies to Manzanillo for some of "Carmen's TLC".

"What am I going to do with you?" asks Carmen. "You can't go on like this!"

"My dear Carmen, I'm on a mission. I can't rest until I get closure. It wouldn't be fair to you. You know how I feel about putting you in danger."

Carmen has learned that changing Tony's mind is futile. She offers financial support, legal connections and promises to stand by him - "forever."

Tony enjoys a full week of uninterrupted happiness with Carmen. Before his arrival at Carmen's hacienda, Carmen, Dr. Monti, Gi-Gi et al agreed to maintain complete telephone and radio silence with Tony, except for real emergencies.

DECEMBER 5, 1980

Sammy, alone in his house, calls a private detective friend. "Hello, Fritz?"

"Hello, Sammy. What's up?"

"You speak Spanish, don't you?" he asks rhetorically. "I need to locate a man in Mexico. He was last seen in Chihuahua. Come to my place and I'll explain the set-up. I'll give you five grand up front and five grand after you locate the son-of-a-bitch."

SATURDAY, DECEMBER 6, 1980, MARANA AIR PARK,
ARIZONA

Tony, Gi-Gi, Jamshid and Ali are attending the scheduled
'Solar Challenger' flight and also to monitor their 'bugs'. While
Tony is examining the Challenger's solar panels, along with other
visitors, Nunzio Addabbo, with his mother in the right seat, touches
down in his Skyhawk aircraft, taxies and ties-down. He and his
mother, also there for the occasion, walk into the Challenger's
hanger.

Tony, at 6'-5", 230 pounds, is easy to spot. He is now engaged
in conversation with the Solar Challenger's petite pilot, Janice
Brown. Jamshid and Ali are elsewhere checking the 'bugs'.

Nunzio stands silently behind Tony for a few seconds, then
whispers, "Hola, Antonio. Que tal?" (Hello, Tony. What's up?).

Voice recognition is one of Tony's gifts, especially easy when
he hears an old friend. He turns,

"Nunzio! We keep meeting in the strangest places."

They bear hug, then Nunzio introduces his mother to Tony and
Tony introduces Gi-Gi to Mrs. Addabbo and Nunzio. "Meet Gi-Gi
Gondolier - my secretary."

Nunzio has known George for many years, but is totally
unaware he's Gi-Gi. He looks at Gi-Gi, then at Tony, with a look
that only these two old buddies understand.

As Tony and Nunzio walk together around the small solar
panel aircraft, Tony whispers, "Meet me at Scordato's (restaurant)
tonight at seven."

Nunzio nods his agreement. As they continue their walk-
around, it's announced that due to excessive cloud cover, the
Challenger will not fly today. Tony and Gi-Gi say goodbye and
walk away to the parking lot, followed by Jamshid and Ali. Nunzio
and Mrs. Addabbo return to their plane and fly down to Nogales
International Airport for coffee and hot rolls. Mrs. Addabbo, at age
79, loves to fly. Except for take-offs, landings and radio control, she
does most of the flying.

Nunzio walks into Scordato's at 7P.M. Tony is already seated
and alone.

"So, Tony," asks Nunzio, after they order drinks, "Where's your secretary?"

Tony smiles, "Hey, Nunz, I know what you're thinking - and it's not what you think. She's a terrific legal secretary; also a pilot. I take her everywhere. It's all business - really."

"Hey, Tony, I'm your buddy, remember? How about the two guys that followed you to your car?"

"Employees. One is my Tucson coordinator; the other just a driver."

"So tell me, Tony, what are you doing now?"

"Good news. I recently made a deal to purchase some used milling equipment in Cananea for an outfit in Chihuahua. We have a team in Santiago (Chile) bidding on copper and sulfur projects, another team in Mexico City doing detail engineering for a waterfront property in Baja California, an exploration crew in Peru, developing a special leaching process in Nevada and plenty of business development in New York. You want a job? You know I'd love to have you on our team."

"No, I'm happy where I am, Tony - but thanks anyway. I'm V.P. of Mountain States Engineers in Tucson with projects in Pakistan and Peru. I'm also trying to get Ed Frohling, President of Mountain States, to let me open an office in Chile."

"I heard of Frohling, but never met him. But, say, I hope you do go to Chile. I'm there a lot and we could spend more time together."

During their dinner of scampi, they discuss their projects, flying and bridge, until Nunzio finally feels Tony is ready to be asked, "Tony, you once told me you have a photo you want me to see that will make history. What's that all about?"

"You're right - I do. And I'll show it to you, soon. Deal?"

Nunzio knows Tony well enough to know that pressing him for details won't work. "Sure, Tony, a deal. But you sure have roused my curiosity."

DECEMBER 16, 1980

Fritz, Sammy's private investigator, disguised as a prospector, finally locates Tony, not in Chihuahua as expected, but in Cananea, just south of Naco, Arizona.

Fritz finds Tony in the field along with a crew of men who are salvaging used equipment for a gold project near Chihuahua.

Identifying himself as a prospector, he tells Tony he is the owner of a small high grade copper mine near the town of Nacozzari in the Province of Sonora.

"I heard you're the man to see about developing new projects."

"I am if they're viable. Tell me about your mine, Fritz."

Fritz did not do his homework. His amateurish description of the underground mine, failure to answer Tony's technical questions properly plus his inability to communicate in Spanish immediately peg him as an impostor.

After Fritz completes his pitch, Tony lights a cigar, then walks slowly around in a circle, thinking, *"This guy doesn't know his ass from the hole in the ground he wants me to see. He's surely trying to set me up for Carlo. That's exactly what we figured."*

He stops, looks at Fritz and shakes his hand. "Sounds like it might be a good deal, Fritz. I'm interested in taking a look."

Tony agrees to meet Fritz at the mine shaft on January 15, 1981. When they shake hands, again, Tony notices that Fritz keeps looking at his hard hat. The front of Tony's white hard hat has the name "Jefe" printed in large black letters.

"Bet Fritz thinks "Jefe " is my nick-name." (Jefe is Spanish for Boss). "See you, Fritz."

Before taking Carmen to the charming lake district in southern Chile for a Christmas vacation, Tony arranges to have his Capture Team set up a decoy surveying tent near Fritz's designated mine shaft. Rashid and Ali drive to the shaft near Nacozzari, via the Agua Prieta immigration check point, and set-up their tent and surveillance gear on January 4, 1981.

JANUARY 4, 1981, NEW YORK

Tony and Jamshid walk into the conference room at the A-tec office. Tony is smoking a cigar, looks happy and carries a large photo file. They receive a welcoming applause from Dr. Monti, Gi-Gi, Judy, Josh and two Capture Team agents.

Tony thanks them, sits, pulls out some photos and proudly announces. "Look! We caught a dozen of these large bass beauties at the lake. And I feel great!"

He passes his vacation photos around the room and receives enthusiastic accolades until the phone interrupts the gathering.

Judy answers. "For you, Mr. Berlotti. It's Mehdi in Vegas."

"Welcome back, Mr. Berlotti. We just learned that Sammy hired a hit-man, named Luke, for ten thousand dollars. He is scheduled to travel to the mine shaft with Fritz and ambush you on January 15th. They agreed to three thousand up front; the balance after he hits you."

"Anything else, Mehdi?"

"Yes, Sir. But only that he told Sammy 'it will be a piece of cake'."

Tony thanks Mehdi, hangs up, gathers his vacation photos, relights his cigar and looks at Gi-Gi.

"OK, Gi-Gi, you irresistible seductress. Let's get you ready for combat."

Armed with the knowledge that Gabriel is a gambler and womanizer, the Capture Team develops a plan to have Gi-Gi lure him into a trap. Tony, Gi-Gi and Jamshid fly to Las Vegas.

JANUARY 9, 1981, LAS VEGAS

At 10 PM, in the Horseshoe Casino, Gabriel is playing alone at his favorite 21 table, looking around for a stray girl. He's in luck. After he's been properly identified by two Capture Team agents, Gi-Gi, now a stunning brunette, elegantly dressed in a loose but clinging white chiffon pants suit, walks to his table and takes a seat one chair away from Gabriel. She opens her purse, pulls out a large roll of twenties, buys chips and begins to play.

Gabriel watches her closely, obviously waiting for the right moment to make his move. Gi-Gi deliberately plays poorly. Fifteen minutes later she stops, orders a diet cola, lights a cigarette, then resumes amateurish play. After losing most of her chips, Gi-Gi asks the dealer, "What does a girl have to do around here to win?"

Gabriel's seizes this opportunity to make a move. He gives the dealer a "don't you answer" signal, moves quickly to the chair next to Gi-Gi, taps her gently on the shoulder.

"Sorry to bother you, lady, but you not playing dee cards right."

Gi-Gi looks at him, "I don't know you!" and snaps her head away with her "hard-to-get" look.

Gabriel, like all the Machos, doesn't like rejection.

"Oh, I very sorry. Me name eez Gabriel and I expert card player. I help you."

Gi-Gi lays her cards on the table, then turns slowly to Gabriel, "Hello, Gabriel. Sorry I was rude. I thought you were making a pass at me. By the way, my name is Greta."

The Capture Team agents, watching from two different locations, signal each other with, "He's hooked."

Gabriel, pleased, so far, looks at Greta with a wolfish grin.

"You nice, Greta. Very nice. But like I say - you play bad cards."

"Well, Gabriel – how nice that you're an expert. And are you Spanish?"

"Yes, I Spanish from Sud America. You speeek Espanish?"

"Oh, no," lies Greta. "I know a few words - like bienvenidos and amigo, but that's all."

They continue this exchange until the dealer, after receiving a "get-with-it" signal from the pit boss, politely announces, "Place your bets, please."

Gabriel ignores the dealer and explains to Greta, "You must to always spleeet aces and eights. Never spleeet fives and tens. Remember to always double down weeth eleven and never take a heeet when you got seventeen or more puntos (points)...comprende?".(understand?)

"Goodness," declares Greta, placing a bet, "I'll never remember all that."

"I can teach you all dee ways to weeen."

Greta leans over, close enough for Gabriel to inhale the lingering fragrance of Magie Noir, whispering seductively, "I would love to have you teach me how to play good blackjack."

Gabriel is a textbook case of how men get hooked on the packaging of a woman, exotic perfumes and all. He is no longer interested in playing at the Horseshoe. His obvious thoughts, as he folds his cards, are playing with Greta. He tips the dealer with five twenty dollar chips, cashes-in and turns to Greta.

"Come, Greta - we go to dee Jockey Club for a dreeenk and I teach you good card play een my private room."

Greta stiffens at the suggestion, thinking, *"It's too soon after my episode there with Hank. There's no way I'm going to the Jockey Club. In fact - I'm not going anywhere with you tonight!"*

Gabriel stands and waits. Greta cashes-in, then delivers her well prepared response.

"Oh, Gabriel, you're so verrrry kind - but I'm sorry, I must leave this evening with my uncle. He's taking me to Mexico. We're going to see a gold mine he's buying, then spend a few days at his ranch near Hermosillo."

"What time you leave?"

"Oh," looking at her watch, "Very soon. My uncle's driver is coming for me. But, Gabriel, perhaps you would like to meet me in Mexico?"

"What weeeel your uncle say?"

"Oh, don't worry. I'll tell him you're a land developer. Then after we leave the mine, we'll go to his ranch. He has a nice guest house on the property. I could arrange for you to stay there. We could spend real time together...It's very private," she adds seductively. "Would you like that?"

At this point, mesmerized, Gabriel would be willing to travel to the ends of the earth to be with Greta. He rubs his hands. "How I get there?"

Greta provides verbal instructions, then pulls detailed location maps of the mine and ranch out of her travel tote. Her final instructions are, "Oh, and Gabriel, be sure to wear construction clothes and a white hard hat." She reaches in her tote again and pulls out a self stick decal with the large black letters: "JEFE".

"Here, stick this on the front of your hard hat before you come and no one will bother you."

He smiles as he accepts the decal, "I see I weeel be dee Boss."

"Yes and you will be received with respect. No one will bother you on the property."

"Bueno, (good). I weel breeeng Pisco, new cards and we make good time in Sonora - si?"

"Yes, si, I'll be looking forward to your visit." She gives her agents across the room a signal, "Oh, Gabriel, here comes my uncle's driver. I must leave you now."

Mehdi, in disguise, escorts Greta out of the casino. Gabriel, proud of his progress, receives a thumbs-up from the dealer, then walks downstairs to the restaurant.

The next day at Tony's Las Vegas Safe House, Jamshid announces that Sammy told Fritz and Luke to keep their plan secret.

"It's obvious," states Jamshid, "that Sammy doesn't want Gabriel to know his plan for fear that Gabriel would tell Carlo."

That evening, Jamshid reports that Sammy and Gabriel met all day and discussed various methods to trap Tony.

"Not once," states Jamshid, "did Gabriel tell Sammy of his plan to meet Greta in Mexico. He's probably afraid that Sammy would tell Carlo he's fooling around on the side instead of concentrating on Tony."

Tony lights a cigar, "Very interesting scenario. I do believe the double whammy is on."

JANUARY 15, 1981, MEXICO

From inside their survey tent, Rashid and Ali observe the arrival of prospector Fritz and hit-man Luke. Luke takes a position behind a broken-down drill rig, waiting for his target: the man wearing a white hard hat with the name JEFE in black letters across the front. Fritz spots the survey tent in the distance and begins to approach it. Rashid and Ali make a quick exit and take new positions at a safe distance behind the tent, leaving only food, whiskey, bedding, surveying instruments and a radio tuned loudly to a local music station.

As the minutes tick by, Fritz remains in the tent, obviously enjoying the music, food and drink.

At 10:30 A.M., a car approaches the area and stops about 50 yards away from the mine shaft. The driver is alone. He opens the trunk, puts on a white hard hat and walks around the car a few times, obviously waiting for someone. He then walks to the shaft area.

With loud mariachi music blaring in the tent, Fritz does not hear the car arrive.

From behind the old drill rig, Luke, peering through his rifle's telescope, has zeroed-in on the man. The stranger is wearing a white hard hat, but Luke has yet to see the name "JEFE". When the stranger gets within ten yards of the shaft, Luke takes a deep breath as "JEFE", his target, becomes clear in his sight. At 20 yards from his target, Luke requires only one shot. The shot over-rides the loud mariachi music, bringing Fritz rushing out of the tent to the shaft.

He looks at the body as Luke stands over it, gloating, "Piece of cake!"

"Jesus Christ!!" screams Fritz, "This is the wrong man!! This isn't Berlotti!!"

"Well, shit, Fritz! I never heard the name Berlotti. My assignment was to hit the man with "JEFE" on his hard hat - and his says " JEFE"!"

"Let's get out of here fast. But first, let's find out who you killed."

Through binoculars, Rashid and Ali watch the pair open the dead man's wallet for I.D. Fritz is seen scratching his head, obviously saying, "His name is Gabriel Torre." He seems unaware that Gabriel had any connection to Sammy. They leave the body and scramble from the scene.

Rashid and Ali quickly pack their gear, torch Gabriel's car, leave the body and drive away before anyone is aware of the shooting. They return to their Tucson Safe House, via Agua Prieta and Douglas, for a brief rest. Then they fly to Las Vegas.

Next morning, Sammy is having breakfast in the Horseshoe restaurant, smoking his cigar between bites, waiting for the good news. Mehdi, in disguise, is having breakfast in the booth behind him. Fritz and Luke arrive at 10:30 A.M., spot Sammy and walk to his table. Sammy, rubs his hands, blows smoke in the air, then reaches to shake hands with Fritz. Fritz keeps his hands in his pockets and looks down, shaking his head in denial.

Sammy, realizing that something went wrong with his plan, immediately flies into a rage, "OK," Waving a knife under Fritz's chin, "Don't fuckin' tell me you mothers' blew the deal!"

"Lower your voice and put the knife down," snaps Luke, "I hit my target as contracted. And, Sammy, I want my money - today!"

Still in a rage, Sammy snarls between clenched teeth, "Keep your mouth shut, Luke. You get nothin' until I know what happened! Nothin'! What happened, Fritz?"

"Luke hit the wrong man, simple as that. He was told to hit the guy wearing a white hard hat with the name "JEFE" in front. He did it as planned - except it wasn't Tony Berlotti."

"I don't fucking believe this! Who was it?"

Fritz pulls out an I.D. card and hands it to Sammy. "This is the guy."

Sammy looks at the I.D. and goes into shock. He sits and recovers slowly after he pops a nitro pill under his tongue.

"What's with you?" asks Fritz, "You knew him?"

"Sort of," lies Sammy, struggling for control.

"Sammy, I don't care what your problem is, if you knew him or not. " snarls Luke, "I want my money. And I want it today!"

Still shocked, Sammy lights another cigar, then waves his arms, totally unable to cope with this latest turn of events. "Oh, what the hell - let's go to my place for the dough. You mothers better not be rippin' me off!"

In their surveillance motor home at McCarren field in Las Vegas, Tony, Greta(George) and Jamshid are being briefed by Rashid and Ali.

"Very good work, everyone," praises Tony. "That's one more down and six to go."

"Dad," asks George, "How do you suppose Sammy will explain Gabriel's death to Carlo?"

"Oh, he'll probably make up some cock-and-bull story to save his hide. He'll never tell Carlo the truth or he's a dead man."

Rashid stands, looks at George and applauds.

"You were a very convincing lady when you conned Gabriel in the Horseshoe. When this is over, you should get a job in Hollywood. You're good, really good!"

"That's my boy," brags Tony. "Come on, let's take in a show. Then we'll get ready for our next assignment."

"I tell you, Dad," concludes George as they walk out, "I really love this work. It's such sweet revenge."

George has a dangerous look in his eyes that suddenly worries Tony. He knows that this kind of revenge; setting up men, no matter how vile, to be killed, can be brutally hardening to a young man like George.

He tells himself, *"It's heady stuff, all this intrigue, danger and killing. When this is all over, when Gloria and the girls, Peter and my other team are avenged, and there is no longer a price on all our heads, I've got to encourage George to get back into the practice of international law, get married and have a family."*

CHAPTER 25

ADDABBO SAVES TONY

LATE JANUARY 1981, MEXICO

Tony, Jamshid and Rashid are back in Mexico shuttling between Chihuahua and Cananea; Greta aka George, is in New York with Dr. Monti and Judy, maintaining contact with all Capture Team members; Mehdi, in Las Vegas is busy tracking Sammy's activities; Ali, in Tucson, continues tailing Boris Kruchenko; Jahangir, in Bolivia, provides weekly updates on Carlo and Jose; and Dr. Asti continues to provide medical service to Tony's international employees.

When Carmen learns that Tony is back in Mexico, she arranges to meet him for a weekend reunion, with Hal and Alice at their new home at Lake Chapala.

During this visit, Hal informs Tony, "I haven't heard a word recently from anyone in the Oil Syndicate. I guess they achieved their goals and cut me out of the loop."

"And how about the other money suppliers?" asks Tony. "Any news from them?"

"Nothing, Tony. Absolutely nothing."

"Any idea where Lansky, Trafficante and the rest are? And what about Boris Kruchenko?"

"No idea. I never had contact with any of them. Luckily, I'm still a consultant to Pemex. As to Kruchenko, I only know that Dan Hill told me he's a KGB agent who needs to be monitored. I gave you his dossier."

"Yes, and I'm sure it's phony. We've had Kruchenko under surveillance for some time. He's dealing in drugs with Los Machos, but no way involved in spying. I don't think he's KGB, Hal."

Carmen, once again, begs Tony to retire and enjoy a peaceful, stress-free life with her. Painfully, Tony again reminds Carmen he's on a mission; that he can't rest until there is finality.

Three months later from Las Vegas, Mehdi reports that Sammy lied to Carlo about Gabriel's unfortunate death. Sammy said, "Gabriel went to Disneyland and never returned."

"I no surprised," states Carlo, "What eez more important, where eez Tony Berlotti?"

When Sammy confirms that Tony is still in Mexico, Carlo sends Manuel and Pepe to locate him.

"Remember," orders Carlo in Spanish, "Don't kill him - he's mine!"

Two weeks later, after shuttling between Cananea and Chihuahua, they learn that Tony has gone to a new project in the United States. They spend a weekend in Las Vegas with Sammy before returning, frustrated, to Bolivia. While in Vegas, Manuel maneuvers himself into a favorable position by convincing Sammy that he should replace Gabriel. Sammy agrees and decides to convey the message to Jose.

"Jose," he tells Manuel, "will agree. And Carlo always agrees with Jose."

Sammy is right and Manuel gets his wish. In mid June, Carlo sends Manuel to Las Vegas to locate Tony, coordinate narco deals and set-up high rollers.

According to Jahangir, shortly after Manuel left La Paz, Carlo, Jose, Pepe and Poncho fled to Cuba to avoid capture by the Elite Bolivian Rangers. They fled because some of Carlo's drug runners were trapped by the Rangers. The Rangers are the same group that trapped and shot Che Guevara at La Higuera, Bolivia on October 9, 1967. Before fleeing, Jose told Carlo they need to develop a new and unique way to smuggle their heroin out of Bolivia.

When George, again as Gi-Gi the blonde secretary, learns that Carlo is in Cuba, she volunteers to go there as a professional free-lance Spanish-English interpreter to Cuba's business groups.

"I'll spread the word that my side-line is drugs. That should draw Carlo to us."

Tony's immediate reaction, "No damn way!! Don't worry, they'll return to Bolivia and Vegas."

TUESDAY, OCTOBER 22, 1981, TUCSON, ARIZONA.

Mrs. Gerald (Betty) Ford and Sammy Davies Jr., are hosting a testimonial dinner honoring Senator Barry Goldwater. Guests are there by invitation only.

During dinner, Nunzio Addabbo, seated at Table 66, receives a tap on the shoulder. The voice from behind is unmistakable.

"Nunzio, we've got to stop meeting like this."

"Tony[16], what a surprise! Let's play catch up after the ceremonies and I'll introduce you to Barry."

After dinner, speeches and entertainment, Addabbo, who knows and has communicated with Senator Goldwater (K7UGA), via short-wave radio voice, Morse code and the mail, introduces Tony to Barry. Barry, with a painful back problem, sits as the three amateur radio operators enjoy a brief discussion about their rigs, stations and antennas. As Tony and Nunzio leave, allowing others in line to talk with Barry, he extends an invitation.

"Nunz, bring Tony to visit me and my station - anytime."

Later, at the Tucson International Airport's General Aviation Pilot Lounge, Tony again makes a promise. "Nunzio, I'm getting close to showing you that conspiracy photo. Hang tight. Ciao."

After checking weather, Jepp Charts and pre-flighting his aircraft, Tony, along with Jamshid, takes off without filing a telephoned flight plan to Las Vegas. He's made this flight many times and has memorized the courses and radio frequencies. He actually files IFR from his plane.

With Carlo and his hit-team hiding in Cuba, drug trafficking through Sammy is seriously curtailed. Sammy and Manuel intensify their card scam operation at the McCarren field hanger. In early October, Manuel advises Sammy he is flying their Queen Air to Mexico City.

"I must locate Kruchenko. We lose contact weeth heem. I theek he in La Capital (the capital)."

On October 15, the Capture Team learns that Sammy instructed Manuel to meet him at noon on October 20 in the General Aviation lounge at McCarren Field. Mehdi and another agent drive there in their surveillance vehicle.

In the lounge, disguised, Mehdi hears the following: "Why you here?" Manuel asks Sammy. "You never meet me here."

Sammy, pacing, chewing and smoking his fat cigar, waves his hands in the air in disgust. "Manuel, mi amigo, we are out of business."

"What you mean - out of business?"

"You'll soon find out. Follow me."

---

[16] The odds of two old friends meeting so frequently, in most unusual places, are astronomical, as are other bizarre coincidences, but it's partly a function of mutual interests and mutual businesses.

The pair quickly walk to their hanger. From their vehicle, the agents monitor the following: Manuel walks in, looks around, sees everything is totally destroyed, including the magnificent Persian silk carpets that have been shredded to smithereens. He screams, "Who do this to us?"

"Who do you think?"

Manuel walks around, cursing in Spanish, kicking and spitting at broken pieces of furniture and busted electronic equipment, then throws things in the air, shouting, "I weel keel Berlotti!!!"

"Good - but come. There's more..." Sammy leads Manuel to the bedroom, also totally destroyed, and points to an empty corner.

Manuel takes one look and turns to Sammy, "Ay chucha - el dinero." (oh, fuck - the money).

"Yeah, the bastards stole the safe. We are fucking broke, man!"

"Not to worry," consoles Manuel, "I get more money from Carlo and we start new."

"No! They've got our number. This operation is over. What we gotta' do is eliminate Berlotti."

Satisfied with results, Mehdi and his agent drive back to their Safe House.

SUNDAY, NOVEMBER 14, 1982

Addabbo, on a business development trip for Mountain States Engineers has gone to the Chicote Grande Mine in Bolivia. Always looking for new and unusual places to visit, he is taken to see Che Guevara's burial site at an approximate elevation of 2,850 meters (9350 feet), near the town of Vallegrande. The guide provides many details of how the Elite Rangers captured and assassinated Guevara. Tony will learn, from Addabbo, that a man called Carlo tipped off the rangers of Guevara's location. At this time, Addabbo has no idea that Tony is after Carlo Perez, that Perez is after Tony, or that Perez and Jose Martinez organized the Kennedy ambush at Dealey Plaza.

The year of 1983 is yet another busy one. Tony is negotiating contracts with several foreign mine owners but having little success in trapping Carlo and is very frustrated. The Capture Team learns that Kruchenko is a loner, that he does not appear to be a drug addict, has managed to avoid contact with Manuel by shuttling between Tucson, Patagonia, Arizona and Las Vegas and no longer visits Marana Air Park. Jahangir reports that Jose Martinez, Carlo's number one man, is seeking novel ways to export heroin from Bolivia. Sammy and Manuel, short on cash, operate on a reduced budget, running drugs with Sammy's local contacts. Tony does not delude himself, however, that there is no longer a price on his head or that anyone close to him is not at risk. The vendetta has changed character but is just as intense. In mid-1983, Tony agrees to finance the Guallatiri sulfur project in northern Chile, but only if the mine owner can provide clear title and confirmed reserves, grades and proven technology. After months of expensive research, field trips, design reviews and advice from his friend Addabbo, he terminates negotiations due to logistics and the proposed slow single-stage autoclave smelting process.

Between business trips, Tony manages brief stops in Manzanillo and Mexico City for quality time, rest and relaxation with Carmen. Dr. Asti cautions Tony to slow down on his demanding work schedule.

Dr. Monti repeats his constant warning. "Damn it, Tony! Listen to Dr. Asti. Your work will kill you before we get the assassins - or they get you."

As always, Tony tries hard to heed their advice, but within weeks is again back to a sixteen hour daily schedule. The first quarter of 1984 draws worldwide attention to proposed new and expanding mining projects in Chile. Blessed with many undeveloped high grade sulfur deposits in the Andes Mountains, coupled with the largest and most productive copper mines in the world and given that, at this time, Chile has the most stable economy in South America, Tony studies the markets. With sulfur prices at $140 per ton and operating costs at approximately $85 per ton, he returns to Chile. By the third quarter of 1984, Nunzio Addabbo is transferred to Chile to establish and manage a new business development and engineering subsidiary for Mountain States Engineers. After two months in a hotel, he and his wife rent a three-bedroom apartment in the Providencia section.

JANUARY, 1985, SANTIAGO, CHILE

On a hot afternoon in early January, Addabbo, after a photo I.D. check, briefcase and body search, is cleared to the second floor in the Parallel Exchange Office at Bandera 75 in downtown Santiago, to legally exchange dollars for pesos. As he counts his money, he hears an unmistakable voice from the hall doorway, "Hola, viejo!" (Hello ol' man).

Tony and Nunzio greet each other warmly. Jorge Perez, the official money exchanger behind the desk, greets Tony, stating, "I didn't know you two were friends."

Completing their transactions, Tony and Nunzio go to the Hotel Carrera for a drink and discuss their new projects, bridge, flying, radio and Chile's southern lake district. As happens with good friends, they can pick up where they left off even after long separations. When Tony mentions he wants to develop high-grade sulfur mines, if he can design a continuous refining system, Nunzio advises he is already working with a German chemist on a continuous batch reactor and a pilot plant design. Intrigued with the idea, Tony offers to finance the pilot plant.

"Unfortunately, Tony, we're already committed to a turn-key project with a Chilean company and finance negotiations are already underway."

An hour later, they exchange business cards and promise to stay in close contact.

SUNDAY, MARCH 3, 1985

Tony arrives at Nunzio's apartment on Avenida Ricardo Lyon to play rubber bridge. His first time partner is Alex Steiner, M.D., a good friend of the Addabbos. Alex is Austrian, an internist, divorced, a great raconteur and fine bridge player who just happens to like to eat 'chicken-in-the-basket'. He and Tony quickly establish an easy rapport. Before play starts, Tony complains he has a headache. Alex goes down to his car, returns with the classic black bag and hands Tony a pill.

"Here, take this. Then let's play cards!"

After a late lunch and more bridge, a strange phenomenon happens. Dogs are howling on the side street. Within seconds, more dogs are heard. The foursome go to the window and see six dogs running around in a circle, continuing to howl. Seconds later, the building begins to vibrate. Having already experienced earthquakes, all four immediately assume precautionary positions.

When the dogs stop howling, Dr. Steiner, under a doorway, shouts into the eerie silence, "Here it comes!"

The earthquake slams the country with devastating force, causing the building to undergo severe oscillations. Oil paintings, shelved nick-knacks and lamps crash to the floor. Pieces of furniture slide to new positions and the kitchen sounds like a rifle range as things fall out of cupboards and the refrigerator. The violent tremor and loud rumbling diminish, but do not stop. The after-shocks are frequent and some are intense. At 11 P.M., while there is still rumbling, they assess the damage, clean up the mess and call it a night. The next morning, they learn that the quake's epicenter was near the city of Viña Del Mar and registered 8.4 on the Richter scale, with after shocks as high as 6.0.

FRIDAY, MAY 3 1985, SANTIAGO, CHILE

Two months later, Addabbo and Dr. Steiner are having lunch at the Pizza Nostra restaurant, planning a surprise birthday party for Addabbo's wife, Teri. They are seated in a curved booth with their backs to the entrance. Halfway through lunch, barely audible over the clattering of dishes, music and adjoining conversation, from behind them Addabbo hears the gravelly voice of a woman mention the name, "El señor Berlotti."

Addabbo writes a note and hands it to Dr. Steiner. "Listen to the woman behind us, but don't turn around."

For the next half hour, they hear the woman giving instructions to a man she addresses as Oscar.

"The order to kill Antonio Berlotti," she states in Spanish, "comes from Don Carlo."

As the instructions continue, Oscar's only words are, "Si Señora, si Señora."

Addabbo and Dr. Steiner take turns going to the men's room, hoping, as they return to their seats, to identify the two conspirators. Both are total strangers. Dr. Steiner, however, makes a couple of significant observations, writes a note and passes it to Addabbo.

"She's about fifty-five and has had a face lift. He's about forty and has a scar under his chin." When the conspirators leave, Dr. Steiner whispers, "Nunzio, I cannot imagine why anyone would want to kill Tony. I think we should notify the police."

Addabbo hesitates before answering. *"I'm certain Tony is involved in a dangerous clandestine operation - but how, who, why? Tipping off the police could create problems for him."* "No, Alex. I've known Tony a long time. I'll notify him first to hear what he wants to do about it."

Alex agrees and they leave the restaurant. Addabbo knows that Tony is up north in the port city of Arica, taking sulfur samples from the remote undeveloped New York 126 mine, negotiating with local officials and contractors to obtain trucking and railroad rates. He calls Tony at 10 P.M. and provides the details of what he has heard: when, where and how he's to be hit in an ambush by Oscar. The news obviously comes as no surprise to Tony.

"Nunzio, old buddy, thanks for the timely tip. I'm really glad you didn't report it to the police. It would just complicate things..."

"Does it have anything to do with the conspiracy photo you promised to show me?"

"Absolutely! I've been on their hit list for years. Look, this is really big-time, but I've gotta' settle the matter on my own - I trust you, Nunz, but I can't trust many others, even people who should be able to help me. Understand?"

"Don't worry, I'll never talk. And don't worry about Alex. I'll talk to him and know he'll cooperate."

"Man, Nunzio! I owe you a big one! I'll make it up to you."

"Forget it. Is there anything you want me to do here before you return to Santiago?"

"No. And don't look for me at Pudahuel Airport next Thursday. I won't be landing there. See you at the birthday party next Friday. So long. And thanks again, Nunzio."

The next day, Addabbo drives to Pudahuel, then backtracks 6 ½ kilometers (4 miles) along the road Tony always takes back to his office to the planned ambush site. Although he does not slow down, he sees nothing unusual. He repeats the drive on Wednesday, May eighth. Now at the ambush site is a ten-ton dump truck on the side of the road. Next to it is a small burial sign, a cross and some fresh flowers.

As Addabbo drives by, he tells himself, *"It's part of the set-up."* He wonders, for the hundredth time, *"Why do they want Tony dead? Could any photo be that important?"* He has no answers.

FRIDAY, MAY 10, 1985, SANTIAGO, CHILE

The birthday party for Teri Addabbo at their apartment is winding down. Addabbo looks at his watch, *"Damn, 10 o'clock and no Tony. Did something go wrong? Was there another ambush?"*

At 10:30, the major-domo at the downstairs front desk rings the Addabbo apartment and announces, "Por fin... es el Señor

Berlotti...con una mujer." (at last...it's Mr. Berlotti...with a woman). Two minutes later Tony enters. "Surprise! Here's Carmen." Then, "Sorry, Nunzio, Carmen's plane had a late arrival. I could use a big drink, pal. And sooner is better than later."

With most of the guests gone at 11:30, Nunzio leads Tony to the balcony. "Tony, what the hell's going on? What happened yesterday?"

"When I didn't land at Pudahuel yesterday, they didn't show at the ambush site. Oh, and their dump truck will never run again."

"Tony, obviously this is really serious business. Perhaps you need government protection?"

"They can't - or wouldn't help me, Nunz. I know why I'm on a hit list and who's calling the shots, but it wouldn't be fair, or safe, to involve you in my problem. Nunzio, you saved my life and I'll never forget that. I owe you. I promise you'll understand everything when I show you that conspiracy photo, and a whole lot more, that will make history."

"Sounds like it has the making of an action packed book and movie."

"It absolutely is. And when this is over, you've got exclusive rights to write the story. Deal?"

"Sounds terrific! It's a deal." They shake hands, then Addabbo turns the conversation to Carmen, "So, Tony, when are you going to marry Carmen? She's obviously crazy about you."

"I wish it could be right now, Nunz. I'm totally committed to her, too. But, as my wife, her life would be in jeopardy. I can't – I won't – do that to another woman I love. And you know Carmen. She would want me to slow down. I'm on a mission, Nunz. I can't rest until I have avenged the deaths of Gloria, the girls, Dr. Monti's son, Peter, and another husband and wife I involved. No one close to me is safe, perhaps even you and Teri."

The party ends. Instead of returning home, Tony and Carmen remain overnight with the Addabbos. One week later, Carmen returns to Mexico. Tony, back in Arica, learns that the sulfur grade in the New York 126 mine is only 30%, instead of the owner's purported 50%. He nixes the project and assigns two men to explore more sulfur mines in northern Chile and returns to Santiago.

Before returning to New York, Tony stops at Addabbo's office. "Nunzio, if you or Dr. Steiner ever run into the woman with the gravelly voice, or this guy called Oscar, I'd appreciate a call."

After a business stop in Lima, Peru, Tony arrives in New York looking tired and, seemingly, in a foul mood. George, as the secretary Gi-Gi, and Judy meet him at JFK.

"Welcome home, Dad." George hugs his father but then looks at him critically. "Are you OK?"

"Yeah, I'm OK. But that was really a close call in Santiago. Addabbo saved my ass."

Judy grabs Tony's briefcase, "You don't look good, Mr. Berlotti."

"You, too, Judy? I said I'm OK! Let's get back to the office. I have a lot to do..."

Tony tries to dismiss their worries, but his smile is tight and unconvincing.

Two hours later, at the A-Tec office, Tony is greeted by Dr. Monti and Dr. Asti.

Immediately after greeting Tony, Dr. Monti, his oldest and closest friend, grabs Tony's sleeve and orders, "Now, don't argue with me! Go to your bedroom and let Dr. Asti examine you. Now!"

"Now, Dad! You're going to kill yourself. The assassins won't have to!" orders George

Fifteen minutes later, Dr. Asti gives Tony the bad news. "Your blood pressure is 220 over 120. That puts you in stroke range. Now, fearless leader, here's what we're going to do..."

One hour later, outnumbered and realizing it would be futile to reject their arguments and instructions, Tony raises his arms in surrender. "OK, guys...you win... this round."

CHAPTER 26

GEORGE and JUDY FAIL

During Tony's month long rest and recovery with Carmen in Manzanillo, Dr. Monti directs all A-Tec activities. He sends George, Josh and a Savak agent to Switzerland in hopes of identifying and locating Louis or Rosy through George's banking contacts. Two weeks later, having spent thirty thousand dollars on travel, hotels and bribes, they return with no clues.

"All dead-ends," complains George. "The Swiss know how to protect their best clients."

"Yes," confirms Dr. Monti, "but look at this list of assassinated, died or disappeared players in this conspiracy. Then tell me what you think."

The following names are highlighted: JFK-November 1963, Oswald-November 1963, Banister-June 1964, Ruby- January 1967, Ferrie-February 1967, Bronfman-1971, Malaxa-1972, Shaw-August 1974, Giancana-June 1975, Hoffa-July 1975, Roselli- July 1976, de Mohrenschildt- March 1977[17], Dan Hill-April 1979, Hank-August 1980, Gabriel-January 1981, Lansky-1983, Louis-?, King- ?, Rosy-?

"It's pretty obvious," reasons George, "that many in the conspiracy, now mostly all gone, accomplished their goal. The remaining then disassociated themselves from Sammy, Carlo and Los Machos, but we now have plenty of conspiracy evidence, especially Dad's photo."

"And," adds Judy, "we've traced the money flow to the assassins."

"Boris Kruchenko is still a mystery player in this conspiracy," observes George.

"All my sources," adds Josh, "tell me he isn't KGB. But he knows something about this conspiracy and we need to find out what that is."

"Sammy is still our best shot at trapping Carlo and Los Machos. When Tony returns," concludes Dr. Monti, " we need to concentrate on Sammy and Kruchenko."

---

[17] Oswald's friend, who committed suicide.

"There's just one more thing," pleads Judy. "Please include me in George's next set-up."

They all recognize that Judy, in her intense grief, seeks revenge for Peter's murder."

JULY 8, 1985, NEW YORK

Tony returns to New York with Dr. Asti. The first order of business at the A-Tec office is a meeting to discuss Tony's health.

"I have good news and bad news," reports Dr. Asti. "The good news is we have Tony's pressure stabilized at 160 over 80 with 'Diutensen', his cholesterol is down to 200 with 'Lopid' and he's sleeping better with 'Unisom'."

"What's the bad news?" asks George.

"The sacculated aneurysm of his aorta is serious and, you know Tony, he refuses surgery."

"What else?" asks Dr. Monti.

"His recurring angina pectoris attacks and associated dyspnea requires that his nitro pills are always immediately available. If he passes out...pop one under his tongue."

"That's it, Dad," declares George, slamming the table. "You're going to the hospital!"

"Over my dead body," snaps Tony. "I'm OK and nobody is gonna' cut me until I'm ready!"

Everyone in this room knows that Tony won't back down until he gets even with the assassins."

Dr. Monti, in poor health himself, neutralizes the father-son dispute with a proposal. "Let's get to the subject we're all passionate about. I think we should train George and Judy in drug trafficking, send them to Las Vegas, as dealers, and have them lure the assassins into Capture Team traps."

Tony, ignoring Dr. Asti's good health tips, lights a cigar, orders a cappuccino and thinks about the proposal. He gets up slowly, blows smoke towards the ceiling, walks to Dr. Monti, kisses the top of his balding head and announces, "Let's do it."

SEPTEMBER 19, 1985 LAS VEGAS

After seven weeks of intensive training in narcotics operations, George and Judy are met at McCarren field by Mehdi and driven to their Safe House. George, now known as Berta, has a new hairdo, smaller bust-line, and flashy clothes. Judy, also in disguise, is now Hilda.

"Remember, Judy," cautions George. "We're a couple of tough, street smart broads now."

"I won't forget. I can do anything to avenge Peter's death."

Three nights later, as George and Judy, aka Berta and Hilda, watch the late TV news, the phone rings. "They're here," alerts Mehdi, "playing 21 at the Tropicana. Rashid, in disguise, is sitting at their table."

Half an hour later, Berta and Hilda enter the casino and walk around until they spot Rashid. Manuel and Sammy are seated side by side, with Rashid next to Sammy. When the girls approach the table, Rashid picks up his chips and leaves, making room for Berta. Hilda stands behind Berta. Their presence does not go unnoticed, as Sammy elbows Manuel, whispering, "Wow."

Berta opens her purse, pulls out a roll of $100 bills, buys chips, makes a $500 bet, wins, then lets the money ride. Sammy and Manuel watch with intense interest. The hostess arrives. When Hilda orders two Pisco Sours, Manuel again elbows Sammy.

The puzzled looking hostess asks, "Did you say pissscow sours?"

"No! I said, peeeesco sours. That's spelled Pisco."

"Is this a joke, or what?"

Hilda glares at the hostess, "Do I look and sound like I'm joking? Hurry it up! We're thirsty."

The hostess writes down the name and walks away in a huff. Sammy winks at Manuel, then seizes the opportunity to open a dialogue with the ladies.

He turns to Berta. "You girls are out of luck. They don't have Pisco in this place."

"Oh, really?" snaps Berta, sarcastically, "How would you know?"

"My friend here, Manuel, tried to get it last week. They have to special-order it. How do you know about Pisco sours?"

"We travel on business a lot - mostly South America. Satisfied?"

"What kind of business?"

"Are you writing a book or what? You ask too many questions."

"Just trying to be friendly, that's all." Sammy shrugs his shoulders in innocence.

"Well," glares Berta. "We didn't come here to make friends."

"We're here on business," adds Hilda, but Berta scowls at her.

Then Berta deliberately leans forward, allowing her gold neck chain to swing out. The move allows Sammy and Manuel to get a good look at the pair of gold razor blade charms hanging from the chain. Manuel's double take delights Hilda, and she gives Berta a pinch in the shoulder.

Sammy places his cigar in the ashtray, turns slowly to Berta, reaches over to finger the blades, whispering, "My, my, big Mama...I know what business you're in."

"Really, now. What?" smiles Berta, splitting a pair of eights.

Sammy doubles-down with eleven and continues, "We both know what business. Tell me, are you buying or selling?"

"We don't do business with small time operators, whatever your name. Go take a hike!"

"Nobody tells me to take a hike in this town. I'm a big man in Vegas. Let's go somewhere and talk. By the way, my name is Sammy. What's yours?"

Berta ignores Sammy, signals the dealer for a hit, then turns to Hilda, "Think we should signal for our back-up?"

"Not yet, Berta. We did come to shop. Maybe we should at least talk to Mister Sammy."

Manuel finally enters the conversation, addressing Hilda, "Very smart young lady."

"These two jerks don't look big-time to me," Berta's voice is barroom husky. "We don't make deals, Hilda, unless we know the principals involved. You know that!"

Sammy, annoyed, lights his cigar, foolishly takes a hit on seventeen, then turns to Berta, snarling, "We are the principals, you big broad. We make the deals and we got the best stuff you can find!"

Berta waves off the offensive smoke, splits a pair of aces and whispers, "Sammy, everybody has a boss. Who's yours? And, how do we know you guys aren't narcs?"

"That be easy," interrupts Manuel. "You peek dee time and dee place."

"Anything that easy sucks!" replies Hilda. "I don't trust these clowns, Berta!"

"Look, Berta," insists Sammy, "you're talkin' to the horse's mouth. Another thing, how do we know you're not setting us up?"

Berta tips the dealer, then glares. "Sammy, give us a break and get lost."

The waitress returns smiling at Hilda. "Good news - the bartender ordered the Pisco. May I bring you a different drink for now?"

"Forget it. We'll be in South America before the Pisco gets here. Come on, Berta, let's get out of this dump."

"Wait, Lady," bellows Manuel, "I get all dee Pisco you want."

"Never mind the Pisco," snaps Sammy. He then addresses Berta. "As I said, how do we know you're not setting us up?" He reaches over, pulls the gold chain out of Berta's sweater again and fingers the gold blades.

Berta turns abruptly away from Sammy and gives a discreet signal to Mehdi and Rashid, who have been watching from a nearby wall. Seconds later, as planned, Mehdi arrives, smiling.

"My, my, Berta," Mehdi is looking at Sammy, "What a surprise. You find a new supplier?"

Berta stiffens, glaring at Mehdi, "Don't come near me you sonofabitch or I'll call my back-up!"

"Hey, what's wrong?" asks Mehdi.

"You bastards," whispers Berta, "You unloaded inferior stuff on us. Now get lost!"

"Look, Berta, we can work it out."

"No! You're history. Get out of here!"

Sammy comes to Berta's aid. He rises slowly, blows a smoke signal at Manuel and jams his index finger into Mehdi's chest, snarling, "You heard the lady. Get lost, sucker!"

Manuel moves quickly alongside Mehdi, switch blade at the ready in his pocket, as two security guards approach. "What's the problem here?" asks one.

"It's OK, sir," motions Berta, "he's leaving."

Sammy doesn't hold back, claiming, "This bum was bothering the ladies!"

The tall senior guard turns to the dealer, "Is that true, Elmer?"

"Sort of... they've all been arguing."

"OK, that's it. You," pointing at Mehdi, "follow my partner out of the casino. And the rest of you follow me - you're out of here too."

They all leave without an argument. Once outside, Sammy suggests, "Why don't we go somewhere and talk?"

"Yes," adds Manuel, "and I breeng dee Pisco."

Berta nods slightly. "Not tonight. We need to make some calls."

"When?" asks Sammy.

"We need to think about it," interrupts Hilda.

The two men continue to press for agreement to meet until Berta feels the two men are safely hooked. She agrees to meet them in two days at the Horseshoe Casino. Berta and Hilda flag a cab, drive around the block, doubling back to the Tropicana, meet Mehdi and Rashid, then return to their Safe House and report their progress to Tony.

SEPTEMBER 24, 1985, HORSESHOE CASINO, LAS VEGAS

Negotiations are underway in a private room with Berta insisting, "We're not going to be ripped off, Sammy. This will only be a $5000 cash introductory transaction, contingent on sampling and approval of your heroin – agreed?"

"We told you. We have the best stuff in town."

"Good - then we won't have any problems. Now, who's your supplier and where's your source?"

"Get real, Berta!" snaps Sammy. "You don't need to know."

"OK," interrupts Hilda, looking at Berta, "let's go." They walk out in a huff, ignoring Manuel's plea to continue talks.

During their next meeting with the ladies, Sammy and Manuel, low on cash and desperate to close a deal, reluctantly reveal their source is from Bolivia.

"Unfortunately," explains Sammy, "we may have a problem meeting your deadline due to export problems."

Hilda raises her arms in disgust, "See, Berta, I told you these guys are small time. Let's go."

"Wait," pleads Sammy, "we can work it out. Let me make some calls."

"Si," adds Manuel, forgetting his English, "necesitamos tiempo." (Yes, we need time).

Berta now makes a crucial mistake. She automatically responds to Manuel in Spanish,

"Bueno, Manuel. Estamos de acuerdo." (Very well, Manuel, we're in agreement.)

"What did she say," asks Sammy, with a surprised look.

"She say they agree."

Sammy shakes hands with the ladies, promising, "Don't worry, ladies, we'll work it out."

Berta's mistake does not go un-noticed by Manuel. After Berta and Hilda leave, he points a finger at Sammy, "That Berta lady...she speeek perfecto Spanish. I no like."

"So, what's the big deal? A lot of people speak Spanish. They go to South America a lot."

"We must to be careful. I no trust them. They luke vary familiar."

"Stop worrying, Manuel. You'll get an ulcer, or give me one! Come on. I want a steak."

SEPTEMBER 27, 1985, NEW YORK

Tony, Dr. Monti, George, Judy, Josh, Dr. Asti, Jamshid, Rashid and two agents are seated around a conference table at the A-Tec office. Tony opens the meeting.

"Good news, team. Jahangir reports that Carlo and Jose made some big pay-offs and are back making plans to find a novel way to export their heroin. That leads me to my entrapment plan."

"Good," George groans in frustration. "We've been dragging this thing out long enough."

Tony lights a cigar, smiles and continues, "Yes, we all deserve to 'get a life' as they say. Gang, I recently spent considerable time in Chile, looking at sulfur deposits. Carlo wants a novel way to export heroin. I have the way."

"Let me understand, Tony. You're going to trap them up in Chile?" asks Dr. Asti.

"Yes. Let me explain. We're going to set up a small, single-batch autoclave sulfur refining process at La Nueva Esperanza mine near the town of Ascotan. Then we get word to Carlo, via Sammy and Manuel, that we can run their heroin through our product."

"Great idea, Dad!" agrees George. " I know that area. There's a large archeological site nearby and also a rail line that runs down to the port of Antofagasta."

"How are you going to prepare and conceal the heroin," asks Dr. Asti.

"Novel is what they want. Novel is what they'll get. We'll fill metal cigar tubes with their stuff, insulate the tubes, then cast them individually into large sulfur bricks. We can cast dozens of bricks daily from a single autoclave."

"Sir," interrupts Jamshid, "it'll never pass customs."

"I know. But Frank and I have that problem worked out. We produce fake documents showing that our product has already cleared customs in the U.S. We show these documents and our bricks to Sammy and Manuel, then get Carlo and his hit-team to inspect our Ascotan operation. When they visit us, to see how we conceal the product...we ambush the bastards! It will finally be over, finished!"

"What if Carlo doesn't come to Ascotan?" asks Judy.

"This is a very big deal. Something I'm sure he wants to witness. I'm gambling they all come," states Tony.

"I agree," adds George, "When do we start?"

"A used autoclave is on the way and I've already mobilized a small Chilean crew to assemble the plant. We can make refined sulfur in 90 days. I'll outline the details tomorrow."

Dr. Monti hands out communications instructions. "Remember," he warns, "destroy these instructions after you've memorized them."

They adjourn and meet later for dinner at Luigi's.

Armed with their plan, George and Judy return to Las Vegas as Berta and Hilda. They meet Sammy and Manuel at the Horseshoe Casino and advise they are scheduling a business trip to South America.

"We have friends down there," boasts Berta, "who can solve the export problem."

"Yes," adds Hilda, "but only if your stuff is top grade!"

"Like I keep telling you," brags Sammy, "we have the best stuff you can buy."

Manuel, the experienced pilot and trigger-happy Macho of the group, keeps looking at Judy. "You never tell me and Sammy you name."

"You never asked. I'm Hilda."

"You luke vary familiar."

"Never mind trying to get friendly. We're only interested in doing business with you."

Berta doesn't like the direction of the conversation and breaks up the meeting. "Bye, boys. See you in a couple of months."

A week later, George, Judy and Rashid meet Tony and Jahangir at the Hotel Carrera in Santiago, Chile. They travel to Ascotan and their La Nueva Esperanza sulfur mine, check construction progress, obtain R.R. and ocean freight rates and plan their next meeting with Sammy and Manuel. During this period, Dr. Monti contracts the production of twenty-four steel molds for casting their sulfur bricks. Josh, through contacts of his deceased father, purchases the high-grade heroin they require for casting in the bricks.

NOON, DECEMBER 15, 1985, LAS VEGAS

Mehdi and another agent are in their surveillance motor home, parked near Sammy's residence, monitoring Sammy's phone calls.

"Hello, amigo Manuel. The girls just called. They're back from South America."

"Yeah?"

"Yes, they want to meet us tonight."

"OK."

"My old lady is still at her sister's house, so I told 'em to come to my place."

"OK."

"Hey, amigo, you're pretty quiet. You got a problem?"

"Like I tell you before, we must to be careful with dee ladies. They luke familiar."

"Manuel, Manuel! You worry too much. Remember, they'll be on my territory. If they give us trouble, we'll waste 'em!"

"OK."

At 9 P.M. Berta and Hilda arrive in a taxi driven by one of Mehdi's agents. Sammy welcomes the two ladies and notices that the taxi remains in the driveway.

"So tell me Berta," opens Sammy, "how was your trip and what's new?"

"We had an exhausting trip but return with good news."

"How good?"

"We witnessed a truly unique sulfur refining operation in Chile."

"How unique?"

"This you'll like. The refinery is a cover for smuggling heroin out of the country."

"How they do it?" asks Manuel, mixing four Pisco sours.

"They encapsulate the heroin in sulfur bricks, haul them by rail to the port of Antofagasta and load them on ships for several destinations."

"It's a slick operation," adds Hilda, "and we've already arranged a small shipment to arrive in February."

"Where's that operation and why do we have to wait until February?"

"We won't tell you its location until we have a sealed deal. I'm sure you and your associates will want to see the operation. The earliest delivery is February. That's because the mine is at very high altitude, cold, windy and operations are only conducted during the summer months of December through March."[18]

Manuel stares at the ladies, hands them the drinks, then offers a simple toast, "Salud."

Sammy lights a cigar and blows smoke at Berta.

"Sammy, I don't like smoke in my face!" demands Berta.

"And, Berta, I don't like your proposition. Why the hell do you want to deal with us if you already have a source?"

"Two reasons, Sammy. First, the operation can't obtain enough high quality heroin and second, we were looking for an alternate source to take up the slack in declining deliveries from Peru. Your Bolivian source would be ideal. We're talking big time, Sammy. You'd be damn fool to turn it down."

Sammy gulps his drink, then declares, "Ladies, we'll think about it."

"See, Berta," snaps Hilda, "I told you we're dealing with small fries. They need to check with their bosses. Let's get the hell out of here!"

"No," yells Manuel, "Tenemos que hablar." (We need to talk)

"Olvidalo," (forget it) replies Berta, smoothly. "Su socio es un tonto! Vamanos Hilda." (your partner is a fool. Let's go).

As the ladies storm out of the house into the waiting taxi, Sammy's phone rings.

One hour later, at their Safe House, after George and Judy relayed their encounter to Dr. Monti in New York, Mehdi arrives with both arms in the air.

"What?" asks George.

"Not good. As you were leaving, Sammy got a call from Jose. He said all deals are off because he, Carlo and the others were back in Cuba."

"Anything else?"

---

[18] Summer in South America is, of course, the opposite months of summer in North America.

"Yes, and this is very bad. Manuel told Sammy he knew you couldn't be trusted. He said he remembers now that it was Hilda who kicked him in the groin at the Horseshoe back in May, 1978." "That is bad," agrees George.

The next day, George and Judy are back in New York. Tony stops all operations at La Nueva Esperanza and dispatches Dr. Asti to Tucson, to assist Ali in tailing Boris Kruchenko.

Dr. Monti advises that the brick molds are ready at his plant. Josh advises he has the heroin safely stored.

"Now," states Tony, "we need to shift gears."

CHAPTER 27

SETTING-UP CARLO

DECEMBER 21, 1985, NEW YORK

After a business trip to Nevada and California, Tony returns to New York and immediately meets with his Capture Team. "As I said a few days ago, team, we need to shift gears."

"I've been thinking about that, Dad. Let me go to Cuba to find and set-up Carlo."

"No way, George. They have you pegged. You'd never leave alive. I have a better idea."

"Whatever it is, I'm ready."

"How would you like to spend some time in Bolivia as Roberto Ugarte?"

"You mean terminate my female impersonations?"

"That's what I mean. Aren't you tired of wearing boobs, wigs and dresses?"

"Yeah - I'm not really a drag queen at heart. But the action was worth it in this case."

"And you know you loved it!" grins Judy, raising her eyebrows.

"You were good, George," this from Dr. Monti. "You even fooled Zorro Plateado." (Silver Fox).

"George, you're going to Chile first. Buy some typical Chilean clothes, then have business cards printed showing you as Roberto Ugarte, Socio, Cia. Minera Azufres, Isluga, Chile. Include Rashid's Santiago phone number."

"Remember," cautions Dr. Monti, " that you're George Berlotti with a legal U.S.A. passport until you clear immigration and customs in Chile. Then you immediately become Roberto Ugarte. Your Chilean passport will be ready in two weeks."

"Stay at the Hotel Carrera in Santiago and be sure to visit Nunzio Addabbo. Tell him I'll be there in early February to check out new mines and maybe visit our place in the Southern Lake District."

"Okay, no problem there, but what do I tell Mr. Addabbo if he asks why I'm in Chile?"

"He knows you're a lawyer. Tell him you're there getting foreign experience, specifically to obtain tax details for Decree Law 600. He'll understand."

"Does Mr. Addabbo know anything about our covert operation?" asks Judy.

"Nunzio," reports Tony, " is unaware of our operation. But he knows I'm on to something big. A few years ago I told him I'd show him a photo I took that will make history. Then, after he saved my life last May, I told him I'll make it up to him. I've known Nunzio a long time. Even if he knew, he wouldn't talk."

"What about his friend, Dr. Steiner?" asks George.

"No need to worry about him. Nunzio said he bought our story that the planned hit on me was a case of mistaken identity by a disgruntled import-export operative."

"While you're on vacation, Tony," interjects Dr. Monti, "we'll set up our small sulfur smelting operation in my shop and test its brick casting capability. We'll use 99.5% granulated Canadian sulfur."

"Remember, George," pointing a finger at his son, "Don't enter Bolivia with anything that looks or smells like Uncle Sam. I think a gaucho type moustache might be a good idea. Carry only your fake Chilean passport at all times in Bolivia. As Señor Ugarte, you're in La Paz making it known that you're looking to sell 99.5% refined sulfur at $80 per ton. That's $35 below world market prices."

"When those numbers reach Carlo or Jose, you can be sure they'll contact you," adds Dr. Monti.

"Yes. You can be sure Sammy and Manuel have already told them about our smuggling deal. Understanding their mentality, I'm betting that what they'll try to do is cut Berta and Hilda out of the loop and make a deal with you, George."

Dr. Monti hands George a large folder labeled: "Recursos De Azufre En Chile" (sulfur resources in Chile) and "La Mineria Del Azufre En Chile" (the sulfur mines in Chile). "Here's your crash program on sulfur operations in Chile. Understand these reports completely before entering Bolivia."

"And, team, I've agreed to follow Dr. Asti's orders and will leave for Mexico in three days. Carmen and Hal Brooks will meet me in Mexico City, then we'll play it by ear. You know how to reach me."

MID JANUARY, 1986, NEW YORK

At the Montico plant in New York, Tony and Dr. Monti supervise the casting of twenty-four sulfur-heroin bricks. The bright yellow bricks are packaged, banded, labeled and carry authentic-looking shipping and customs documents. Before two Capture Team agents deliver them to Mehdi in Las Vegas, the package is roughed-up, giving it the customary overseas "handled" look.

George arrives in Santiago, Chile, the last week in January, checks into the Hotel Carrera and calls Nunzio Addabbo. Emilio Rossi, Addabbo's office manager, advises that Addabbo is north in Potrerillos, meeting with Codelco engineers, reviewing detail design drawings for the new 4,000 ton per day El Hueso Gold Refinery Project for the Chilean government. George decides to wait for Addabbo before buying Chilean clothes.

Two days later, Addabbo returns to his Providencia apartment in Santiago and is surprised to find George sitting in the living room with Mrs. Addabbo. George stays for dinner, explains why he's in Chile and advises that his father will come to Santiago next month. When the Addabbos invite George to stay at their apartment, George lies, "I'd sure like to, but I've got to fly down to Concepcion to meet some lawyers, then meet a girl that went to school with me at Nido de Aguilas." (Eagles nest).

A week later, George, now aka Roberto Ugarte, is met in La Paz by Rashid and settles-in at the Sheraton Hotel. Santiago, Chile is a relatively quiet city during the month of February. Most people are on vacation at busy Pacific beaches in and near Viña del Mar or the serene Southern Lake District. Tony arrives the first week in February, checks into the Hotel Carrera and calls Addabbo.

"Nunzio, I'm at the Carrera but I'm leaving in the morning for Arica to check out some hot sulfur deposits. Be back in about ten days. How about getting together with Dr. Steiner to play some bridge?"

"Welcome back, viejo (old man). Sure, bridge is certainly do-able. Let me know if you need any help up north. By the way, George is a fine young man. We enjoyed his company. See ya'."

Tony returns to Santiago on schedule, dines with the Addabbos and Dr. Steiner, they play bridge until midnight and the attempted ambush on Tony last May is never mentioned.

Before Tony leaves for his next stop, Bolivia, he and Nunzio meet at the Pizza Nostra Restaurant for lunch. Nunzio points out where he and Dr. Steiner were seated when they heard the plan to ambush Tony. "I've been back here a dozen times since last May, and never saw Oscar or the woman with the gravely voice. Tony, can't you tell me the real reason why you're a target?"

"Nunz, I have that photo - and it exposes some big-time conspirators and assassins. They're after me and my photo. I'm after them because they're the bastards that killed Gloria and my girls, Dr. Monti's son Peter and another young team working for me. So it's become a double manhunt. I'm getting close to settling the matter and will give you all the details. I promise!"

"You know you can trust me, Tony. If I have details, I may be able to help you."

"Of course I trust you, Nunz, and not only because you saved my life. But, as it is with Carmen, your involvement would put you and Teri in danger. You may be under scrutiny already because you associate with me. I don't want anything to happen to you or your family."

After lunch, Tony flies to Bolivia, and Nunzio returns to his gold project office. In late 1986, Addabbo plans a business trip to Peru and discovers his passport is missing. He reports the loss to the U.S. Consulate Office in Santiago and cannot state if it was lost or stolen. A new passport is issued on December 2, 1986.

"There's no way I lost that passport," thinks Addabbo, then, reflecting upon Tony's recent words. *"Somebody stole it. I wonder if it could have anything to do with my association with Tony?"*

1987

The New Year does not bode well, beginning as it does with bad news. Dr. Monti suffers a heart attack and Dr. Asti orders him to a four-hour maximum workday. He continues to warn Tony that he must slow down as well. Judy remains in New York, full time, shuttling between A-Tec and Montico offices. George, still in Bolivia, discovers that Carlo and Los Machos, except for Jose, are back in Cuba after avoiding a police raid. Jose is near the Cerro Patalani area, near the Chilean border, establishing a base camp.

George and Rashid believe the base camp is the start of a sulfur operation, providing a short haul to the port of Iquique. It is not clear how they propose to operate.

In a radio contact with his father, George reports, "Dad, these people don't know anything about the sulfur processing business."

A week later, Tony contacts George. "Here's the plan. Print some business cards for Rashid and spread them around to local mining suppliers in La Paz and Oruro. His new name is Ramsey Rushard, Design Consultant, Sulfur Projects. That may eventually lure Jose to us."

"Dad, Rashid doesn't know anything about sulfur refining."

"He soon will. I'm sending one of my stand-by engineers from our La Nueva Esperanza plant to give him a crash program on the subject. I'm also sending you some sulfur plant details I obtained from Mr. Addabbo."

In Tucson, Dr. Asti and Ali continue tailing Boris Kruchenko. With Tony shuttling between Chile, Peru, Mexico and the U.S.A., they report to Dr. Monti that Boris made several trips, in disguise, to Marana Air Park but never entered a building.

"We don't know why he went or who he was looking for," reports Dr. Asti. "We did learn, from Dan Hill's logs, that Air America and Southern Air Transport were CIA covers, using Marana to retrofit some of their aircraft."

"How does Kruchenko spend his time?" asks Dr. Monti.

"He travels often between his Patagonia cabin, Las Vegas and his condo on Skyline Drive. When he's in Tucson, he plays at the Bridge Center on Saturday nights. He has no male or female friends, his demeanor, for whatever reason, reflects acute paranoia and he always has plenty of cash on hand. We plan to break into his cabin next time he's in Vegas."

NOVEMBER, 1987

With Kruchenko in Las Vegas, Dr. Asti and Ali make a midnight entry into Kruchenko's small Patagonia cabin. They make a remarkable discovery. On a nightstand, in a silver frame, is a photo of Kruchenko and Lee Harvey Oswald side-by-side on a sidewalk in front of a bus.

Holding the frame carefully with rubber gloves, a closer examination of the photo shows Oswald carrying a briefcase and Kruchenko carrying what appears to be a pouch. Clearly visible under a magnifying glass, the advertising on the bus establishes the scene to be Mexico City. As they prepare to examine other items and rooms, a dog's bark freezes them in the dark room. Fearing that someone may be in the area watching the cabin, they decide to stand by quietly until it appears safe to leave. One hour later, they exit the cabin, walk one mile to their car and return to Tucson, asking each other: "Why does Kruchenko have that photo? Why was Kruchenko with Oswald? Who took the photo? Was Kruchenko Oswald's friend while Oswald was in Russia? What was Kruchenko's interest in Oswald in Mexico City?"

"Tony," observes Dr. Asti, "will certainly want answers to these puzzling questions."

Ali remains silent, then comments, "I believe someone was watching the cabin tonight."

The next day, when Tony is apprized of the break-in, Dr. Asti and Ali are instructed to stay away from the cabin, but to alert Mehdi and then follow Kruchenko the next time he goes to Las Vegas.

"Also," instructs Tony, "I.D. his Tucson bridge partners. We may get clues from them."

Rashid and Jahangir remain in La Paz for the holidays. Judy and Josh monitor A-Tec and Montico operations in New York and maintain daily communications with Tony and Dr. Monti. Tony, Carmen and Dr. Monti spend the holidays with Hal and Alice Brooks at Lake Chapala, Mexico. George travels to Chile, hoping to surprise the Addabbos and spend Christmas with them. He learns that shortly after the El Hueso gold project was completed, Addabbo closed the Santiago office and returned to the U.S due to his wife's failing health. George spends Christmas alone at the Miramar Hotel in Viña del Mar, Chile and returns to Bolivia before the new year. Mehdi reports that Sammy and Manuel are on their way to Cuba to meet Carlo. Dr. Asti spends the holidays with his family in the south. Ali, with two additional Capture Team agents, continues tailing Boris Kruchenko.

MAY, 1988

A significant event takes place. Jose, in desperate need of a professional to organize the Patalani sulfur project, learns that consultant Ramsey Rushard (Rashid) is available and interviews him at the Sheraton Hotel in La Paz.

One week later, George reports to Tony that Rashid conned his way into Carlo's organization. Jose hired Rashid as their adviser who would assemble a team of engineers to produce working drawings for a 100-ton per day sulfur refinery.

"That's music to my ears," states Tony. "Have Rashid put our Chilean sulfur engineer on the payroll with instructions to design a flaw in the process. When production fails, blame it on sabotage. Under no circumstances is that refinery to cast sulfur bricks."

"We'll do that! And Dad, you were right. They are planning to use our heroin brick idea."

LATE SEPTEMBER, 1988

Jose's Patalani base camp and detail engineering for the refinery are completed in late September. Construction of the refinery, under the direction of Rashid and Tony's Chilean sulfur engineer, begins. In mid October, George advises that Carlo is back in Bolivia, pleased with Jose's progress and, to satisfy local police authorities, has started to retrofit his Oruro plant to resemble a new sulfur refining operation.

Tony's sulfur engineer, worried that design flaws can always be corrected, breathes a sigh of relief when he discovers, after a series of his own on-site tests, that the average grade of the ore body to be mined is only 18% sulfur. Documents presented by Jose for process design are based on an old feasibility report showing a grade of 60%. George reports this significant finding to Tony.

"Dad, Jose doesn't know it yet, but his mine is worthless."

"That's great news! I want to see a conclusion to this problem before I'm dead or dead broke! What's their target date for start-up?"

"In five months. They're shooting for mid March."

Tony and Carmen spend the 1988 Christmas week at Tony's cabin in Chile's southern lake district, then fly to Carmen's condo at her Baja, California resort for the New Year, where they are joined by Hal and Alice Brooks. Tony and Carmen are accepted by everyone as man and wife, certainly as soul mates. The love they share is obvious to all and everyone feels that Tony is a better man, and a healthier one, because of Carmen's complete devotion to him. Reining him in is still impossible, although the toll of his activities on his health is evident to all. The vendetta for each side has escalated rather than diminished with time. For Tony, especially, it is time for closure and a life of normalcy.

February 1989

Carlo and Jose, after several trips to Cuba and Panama, begin to stockpile heroin in a small, 24 hour guarded, metal shed at the Patalani sulfur plant, nearing completion. Mehdi reports from Las Vegas that Carlo is in weekly contact with Sammy and Manuel for information regarding Tony's location. With Dan Hill dead, Sammy and Manuel have no clues where to begin another search. Sammy tells Carlo, "We need to wait for him to make the next move. Then we'll set him up for you."

Dr. Asti reports from Tucson that Boris Kruchenko recently started playing afternoon bridge at a small white house on Broadway and continues Saturday night bridge at the Center when he's in town. Kruchenko has not been to Las Vegas in over six months. His activities there are still a mystery.

Jose's Patalani refinery starts up on schedule. After 72 hours of around the clock failed batches, Rashid, well aware of the problem, orders an assay of the stockpiled sulfur. Jose rejects the test, stating, "Listen, Ramsey, the grade of this sulfur is 60%. There must be a problem with your process."

"Sorry, Jose. With all the slag coming out of these batches, the grade of your sulfur is very low."

Two days and four assays later, Jose painfully realizes his ore body is worthless. He advises Carlo of the disaster, orders a plant shutdown and dismisses all personnel except a skeleton force to guard the heroin. Tony's Chilean sulfur engineer estimates the total cost expended to date at Patalani is almost three quarters of a million dollars.

Jose returns to Oruro and meets Carlo. Rashid returns to La Paz and meets with George. Jahangir remains in Oruro and Tony's Chilean Sulfur Engineer returns to Chile.

MAY, 1989

Tony reviews a feasibility report for mining the Taltalina ore body, a high grade Chilean sulfur deposit in the Plato de Sopa area near the Argentine border due east of the port town of Taltal. Pleased with reported reserves and grades between 50% to 70%,

Tony decides to consult with his old friend, Nunzio Addabbo. He learns that Addabbo is in the Dominican Republic trouble-shooting Rosario's Transition Gold Project.

Tony and Nunzio meet at the Hotel Embajador in Santo Domingo on Sunday, June 4. Tony explains his plan to develop Taltalina if Addabbo can provide a continuous refining process. His stay is short when Addabbo advises, "Tony, I've been there. Reserves are massive but grades are only 20% to 50%. There's no water in the area. You'd have a monumental logistics problem and sulfur prices are down now. Don't fall for that optimistic report. Taltalina is a loser. Forget it."

"I've already sent my Chilean sulfur engineer to the area. I hope to hell you're wrong."

"I'll bet you a thousand dollars I'm right."

Tony lights a fresh Dominican cigar, then smiles, "Dinner is on me."

Two months later, Tony's engineer reports that the Taltalina sulfur mine is not worth developing at this time. Tony sends Addabbo a short FAX: "Sure glad I didn't bet on Taltalina."

In the fall, frustrated with his lack of success in trapping Carlo, Tony begins to devote most of his time and money directly with his Capture Team. With Carlo and Los Machos back in Bolivia and Jose's failure at Patalani, Tony gambles that Carlo is ready to meet anyone able to safely export his stockpiled heroin. Luring Carlo and Los Machos to the La Nueva Esperanza sulfur plant for an ambush is now top priority. Tony mobilizes his Chilean sulfur team, stockpiles some high-grade sulfur and restarts the refinery in a stand-by mode. In late October, Mehdi advises that Carlo called Manuel with instructions to contact the two ladies who claimed to have smuggling contacts in Chile.

When Manuel convinces Carlo that the two ladies can't be trusted and that they have disappeared, Carlo orders Manuel back to Bolivia, then asks Jose to rehire Ramsey Rushard (Rashid). Two days later in the Sheraton restaurant, Carlo and Jose instruct Rashid to return to Chile and search for a sulfur plant that is known to be exporting sulfur-heroin bricks.

Rashid acts disturbed at the instruction. "That's a very dangerous assignment."

"Yes, it is," states Jose. "Here is $10,000 for the danger...and Carlo promises another $10,000 when you find the operation."

"Don't worry," promises Carlo, "if anybody bother you - we keel them."

George, now a master impersonator, is seated nearby monitoring them as a priest. Before retiring that night, he calls Tony.

Jamshid answers. "George, your father is sleeping. He had chest pains."

George brings Jamshid up to date, then asks for Judy.

"Judy, take care of Dad and don't tell him what's going on. We can handle it."

"I know how much you love your dad, but, George, I can't do it. I'll have to tell him in the morning."

The next day, pain free and pleased with the news, Tony alerts Mehdi in Las Vegas.

"Get those bricks ready for Sammy. We're ready to move."

Tony contacts George. "The hooks are in. Now make yourself available as Roberto Ugarte and under no circumstances is the location of La Nueva Esperanza to be revealed."

"The timing is perfect. Jose has already started asking around for Señor Ugarte. He probably hopes I may be involved with the smuggling operation at Isluga. Hang tight, Dad! We're zeroing in."

"I know, but let's not look anxious. Let's tease them awhile."

FRIDAY, NOVEMBER 17, 1989

Tony's hard-to-get strategy pays off. On Friday November 17th, with Jose in the Sheraton lobby, George arranges to have his shoes shined on the street corner. The hotel doorman sees him and runs into the hotel. Jahangir, in disguise in the lobby, sees Jose paying the doorman. Seconds later, Jose approaches George.

"Disculpame (excuse me), Señor Roberto Ungarge?"

(The following exchange is translated from Spanish to English.)

"Yes, what can I do for you?"

"I have your business card. I see you're a partner in the Isluga sulfur mine."

"Yes, but we have other operations as well. Why do you ask?"

"My partner and I are interested in sulfur. If you're free, we would like to invite you to dinner tonight and talk business. We could make you very rich."

"What's your name and who's your partner?"

"Sorry. I'm Jose Martinez." Jose pauses, then lights a cigar. "My partner is Don Carlo."

"Very good," thinks George, *"now here's more juicy bait."* "I definitely want to meet with you, but, unfortunately, I'm leaving immediately for Chile for an important meeting with two American ladies also in the sulfur business. I will return in about ten days."

At the mention of "two American ladies", George notes the surprised look on Jose's face.

Jose seeks reassurance that George will return and again promises to make him rich.

Three days later, Tony and Jamshid arrive in Calama, Chile and meet George and Rashid, who just arrived from La Nueva Esperanza and Ascotan.

"Great work, George. They took the bait. But you're not meeting with Carlo and Jose. It may be a trap."

"I think we should send Rashid back to Bolivia," suggests Jamshid. "He can advise them he located the smuggling operation and knows that Señor Ugarte is here cutting a deal with two American women. That will really get their attention."

"I agree," states Tony. "Meanwhile, we'll go up to Ascotan and plan the ambush at La Nueva Esperanza."

DECEMBER 4, 1989

Rashid arrives in La Paz. Manuel, after stops in Mexico and Panama, arrives in La Paz the next day.

DECEMBER 6, 1989, LAS VEGAS

With instructions from Tony, Mehdi calls Sammy.

"Hello, Sammy?"

"Yeah...who's this?"

"My name is Jimmy Arguidas. I was asked to contact you about a sulfur deal."

Sammy's response is delayed. "Who told you to call me?"

"A couple of business associates. I think you know them. Berta and Hilda. They asked me to apologize for not getting back to you sooner. They're in Chile closing a big deal, but sent something important for you."

'Really? Like what?"

"A large crate with sulfur bricks."

"Where'd you get them?"

"They were shipped from the Chilean port of Antofagasta to Los Angeles. I cleared them through customs two days ago."

"Where are you and where are the bricks?"

"I'm at the Horseshoe Casino. The bricks are in the back of my van."

"I'll be right over. Let's meet downstairs in front of the men's room. How do I recognize you?"

"I'm 5'-9", 160 pounds, wearing a red and white ski jacket with black pants and I'm smoking a cigar."

"Hey, you're my kind of guy. I'm 5'-6", 230 pounds and I'll be smokin' a long Havana."

One hour later, Sammy, carrying a gift-wrapped package, walks into the Horseshoe accompanied by a 6'-0", 250 pound unsavory looking tough-guy, also smoking a cigar.

They immediately recognize each other and shake hands. Then Mehdi coldly scrutinizes the big man.

"Who's he?"

"He's my sulfur expert," lies Sammy. "Here," handing Mehdi the package, "enjoy these fine Cuban cigars."

Mehdi accepts the package and motions for them to follow him. They walk to the parking garage to Mehdi's van. Parked and waiting in another van, three spaces away, is Mehdi's back-up agent. Before Mehdi opens the door, the unidentified strong-arm carefully frisks him.

"Sorry, Jimmy," apologizes Sammy, "you know the routine."

Mehdi nods, opens the door, exposing the official looking crate, then hands Sammy the official looking documents.

"Here. These shipping papers are for you."

Sammy examines the documents, checks them with the crate and nods, "Looks OK, so far. Now let's get to the good part."

Mehdi cuts open the crate, pulls out a sulfur brick and hands it to Sammy.

"Here, compliments of Berta and Hilda."

Sammy holds the bright yellow brick in one hand, smells it, then blows cigar smoke at Mehdi.

"Well, Jimmy, and how do I get to my prize?"

Mehdi takes the brick away from Sammy, grabs a lug wrench and whacks the middle of the brick. The brick falls apart easily and out pops the insulated cigar tube. He carefully removes the insulation, opens the tube and hands it to Sammy. "Here, man. Taste it."

Sammy looks in the tube, smiles and hands it back to Mehdi. "You first, Jimmy."

Mehdi complies and hands it to the burly thug. "We hope your stuff is as pure as this!"

He takes several tastes, then nods his approval.

"OK, Jimmy, let's do another."

They select three more bricks at random and continue the procedure.

"OK," states Sammy, turning to his back-up, "give Jimmy the envelope."

"What's this?" asks Mehdi.

"Just a token of our appreciation."

"The ladies said - 'no charge'. It was their pleasure. They hope to see you soon."

"Take it anyway and tell 'em thanks. I'm ready to do business."

Sammy, pleased with this development, tells his back-up to guard the bricks while he goes for his car at another section of the garage. Ten minutes later, they transfer the bricks to Sammy's car, bid Mehdi farewell and drive to Sammy's house, followed by Mehdi's back-up agent. Mehdi drives to their Safe House, transfers to the surveillance motor home, then drives and parks one block from Sammy's residence where his back-up joins him. Eavesdropping on Sammy is now routine.

According to Mehdi's back-up, the second man already transferred the bricks to his car and is inside having a drink with Sammy. After several drinks, Sammy explains why his wife is gone, how this operation is going to make plenty of tax free money, why he hates the Lakers, why he loves Las Vegas and how much he hates a guy named Tony Berlotti.

One hour later, the second man states, "It's a long drive back, Sammy. Gotta' go."

"OK, Izzy. Tell the boys in Los Angeles I'll be in touch soon."

When Izzy departs, Sammy is immediately on the phone to Bolivia. According to Mehdi, Sammy has difficulty communicating with Carlo and usually calls Jose, who has a good command of English. On the fifth ring, Sammy hears, "Hola, quien es?" (hello, who is it?)

Sammy recognizes Jose's voice. "Hello, Jose. Sammy here."

"Hello, Sammy. How are things in Las Vegas?"

"Good. The two American women shipped me a crate of those sulfur bricks without a customs problem. We can do business with them, but I'm really pissed!"

"What happened?"

"Carlo pulled Manuel out of here without talking to me. Before leaving, Manuel said Carlo and you are gonna' meet those two American broads to make a sulfur deal. "

"So...what's wrong with that? What's your problem?"

"I'm the one who made the first contact with those broads and nobody is gonna' cut me out!"

"Don't worry, Sammy, we won't cut you out. You're our U.S. contact. We need you."

"I don't care. I don't trust Carlo and I'm comin' to Bolivia for that deal."

"He won't like it! And you know Carlo."

"That's the problem. I do know him. Do me a favor, Jose, and don't tell him I'm coming."

"Well..."

"Come on, Jose, you owe me - remember?"

"OK. I'll act surprised when you arrive."

"Good. Just give me a 72 hour notice before that meeting."

DECEMBER 8, 1989, LA PAZ

At the Sheraton Hotel, Rashid meets Jose and advises that he located the smuggling operation. One hour later, Jose introduces Rashid to Carlo and Manuel.

Carlo does not shake hands with Rashid. Instead, he smiles and hands him a cigar.

"So, Señor Rushard...Tell me about dee operation."

Ex Savak agent Rashid, like CIA contract agents, has mastered the art of lying when expedient.

"An old prospector friend told me how to find it. It is near the town of Ascotan," whispers Rashid. " I went there posing as an agent for a drug syndicate, was searched, then interrogated by two men. They believed my story and then showed me the sulfur plant. While there I noticed they were negotiating a contract with two American ladies. Then..."

"Who were the ladies?" interrupts Jose.

"I don't know, except one was very tall and the other quite small."

"Dey show you how dey smuggle?" asks Carlo.

"No. They told me to come back in three days."

"Muy bien," (very good) smiles Carlo. " Manuel and you fly to dee plant via helicopter and meet dee smuggle chief."

"What should I tell him?"

Carlo lights a cigar, then rubs his chin. "Tell heem Manuel must to be satisfied with dee operation before I agree to come to make deal."

"The refinery is at high altitude. There is a helicopter pad, but can Manuel find it?"

"Manuel," assures Jose, "is an experienced pilot with many flying hours over and around the Andes Mountains. And he knows how to avoid radar detection along the Chilean border."

The next day, Jahangir alerts Jamshid.

"Tell Mr. Berlotti that Rashid and Manuel will arrive in two days by helicopter for a plant inspection."

That night, Dr. Asti arrives in Ascotan, is picked up by George and driven to La Nueva Esperanza. Tony, meanwhile, supervises the casting, curing and stock-piling of 48 sulfur-heroin bricks, clean-up of the area, the hiding of all weapons and readying the facility for Manuel's inspection.

The next morning, before he leaves for Calama with George, Tony leaves team instructions:

"Dr. Asti stays as Señor Greco, the smuggling chief. Jamshid stays as Señor Cardonian, the operations manager and the rest of you are plant operators. Also, Rasihd is not to leave the area with Manuel. Dr. Asti will spike Rashid's drink to immobilize him. Then he will explain Rashid has suffered a heart attack or stroke and must be driven immediately to the hospital in Chuquicamata or Calama. Dr. Asti will tell Manuel that Rashid could not survive the helicopter ride back to Bolivia."

"One more thing," states George, "Dr. Asti will tell Manuel that the two American ladies are in Santiago and will return with money on the second of January. Now that Carlo and Jose know that the women arranged that shipment to Sammy, they'll surely want to meet them. And remember, Manuel doesn't trust them, so he'll want to eye-ball them again. You can bet they'll come on January second.

"Yes," concludes Tony, "And that's when we ambush the assassins. And pray to God, everyone, that it will be the end of this nightmare! We all need to live without a price on our heads. I no longer know what it is to live without a gun under my pillow, wondering what will come next."

MONDAY, DECEMBER 11, 1989, CHILE

Manuel straps Rashid in the turbo helicopter and takes-off for Ascotan, Chile.

As Manuel skillfully maneuvers the large aircraft between mountain peaks and through some severe up and down drafts, Rashid appears very disoriented. Upon landing at noon, Manuel gives him 10 minutes of pure oxygen before they exit the helicopter.

Dr. Asti and Jamshid, both in disguise, greet them at the landing pad. As they walk to the lunch room, Dr. Asti notices and comments on Rashid's irregular walk. "Señor Rushard, are you OK?"

"Just dizzy. I'll feel better after I have something to eat and drink."

The lunch room tables are stacked with packages of assorted wafers and bottled water. Rashid opens a package and gives a sigh of relief after eating six wafers. Dr. Asti opens a bottle of water and hands it to him.

"Here - drink some water, then eat more wafers."

Jamshid then raises a large chalk board showing a flow diagram of the sulfur operation. He explains, in great detail, how the sulfur is mined, crushed, pulverized, smelted and cast into bricks. Manuel is not impressed.

"Never mind all dee details. I come to see and test dee final breeks."

"Very well," states Dr. Asti, "Mr. Cardonian will escort you to the shipping platform. Mr. Rushard doesn't look good. I'll stay here with him."

Manuel agrees and leaves with Jamshid. The refinery (see Plate 4AB) is an open air facility at 4450 meters (14,600 feet), exposed to the cold winds of the Andes and occasional blowing dry snow. There is the lingering odor of harmful SO_2 gas (sulfur dioxide).

The shipping platform contains three pallets of crated and banded sulfur bricks, ready to be loaded for shipping. Ahead of the platform, arriving on a slow moving conveyor belt, are a dozen bright yellow bricks. Jamshid stops the belt at the platform, then hands Manuel a sledge hammer.

"Here, Manuel. Break one open."

Manuel hands the hammer back. "You break it."

Jamshid picks up a brick, cracks it open with one blow and watches the surprised expression on Manuel's face when the insulated tube falls on the ground.

Jamshid carefully unwraps the tube, opens it, then hands it to Manuel.

"Here's your prize, amigo. All our bricks are the same."

Manuel is impressed. He breaks open and samples the contents of the next six bricks, whispering, "Te amo", (I love you) with each sampling.

Jamshid then walks to the pallets. "Manuel, do you want me to open these?"

"No - no. I see enough. Vamanos. (let's go)."

During their walk back to the lunch room, Jamshid prepares Manuel for the bad news.

"I hope your Señor Rushard is OK."

When Jamshid and Manuel walk into the lunch room, Rashid is covered with a blanket, unconscious on a stretcher, ready to be moved. Dr. Asti's planned panic act gets Manuel's attention.

"Que paso?" (what happened?)

Dr. Asti ignores the question and directs two men to move Rashid to a 4 X 4, shouting:

"This man can't go back with you. He'd never survive the helicopter ride. He appears to have had a stroke. We need to transport him to the Chuquicamata hospital immediately."

Manuel, seemingly unconcerned, shrugs his shoulders. "OK. I go back alone and return weet Don Carlo on January two. He make all dee negotiations."

Dr. Asti puts his arm around Manuel's shoulder, "Thank you, Manuel. It will be our pleasure to meet and do business with Don Carlo. Come, friend, I'll walk you to your helicopter."

Twenty minutes later, the helicopter is airborne, headed north. Jamshid calls Tony in Calama.

"Rais, (boss), everything went according to plan. They will return on January second."

"Very good. Esperanza is on!" - "Esperanza" (hope) is their code word for the ambush.

CHAPTER 28

AMBUSH IN THE ANDES

DECEMBER 13, 1989, LA PAZ, BOLIVIA

Jahangir calls Jamshid. Their conversation, in Farsi, is translated as follows:

"Manuel arrived last night and met with Carlo and Jose. He told them our system of smuggling is excellent, that the two American women will be in La Nueva Esperanza on January second. Then, why Rashid couldn't return with him, that he stopped in Patalani to check the security of their heroin, and then stopped in Oruro to fill his oxygen bottles."

"Anything else?"

"Yes. Here's the most important thing. Be careful. They will be heavily armed when they arrive there on January second. "

Tony's only reaction to the warning, "So will we - the surprise will be on them!"

Two days later, Tony receives word from Mehdi that Jose called Sammy regarding the January second meeting in La Nueva Esperanza and that Sammy will arrive La Paz on December thirty.

During this recent and rapid turn of events, Tony is unaware that Nunzio Addabbo is also in Chile managing construction of the concentrate filtering, storage and ship loading facilities in Coloso for the one billion dollar Escondida copper project. He believes Addabbo is still in the Dominican Republic. Addabbo assumes that Tony is in New York.

DECEMBER 18, ANTOFAGASTA, CHILE

At the Addabbo's apartment in Antofagasta, ten miles north of Coloso, Mrs. Addabbo receives a call from her friend Amelia Rojas, M.D., in Santiago. They have been friends since 1984, after meeting at a U.S. Embassy party in Santiago. Dr. Rojas, an internist, has an interesting hobby. She has been researching the mummifying process of buried cadavers in the Atacama Desert. Mrs. Addabbo has been on several field trips with Dr. Rojas and on this day is invited for a two day site visit on December twenty-seventh to a high elevation burial site near Ascotan.

"Oh, I'd love to, but, Amelia, I'm sorry. Nunz has already booked our Christmas week at Lago Ranco (Lake Ranco). We'll be back in Antofagsata the afternoon of December thirty first."

"No problem," states Amelia. "How about if I pick you up the afternoon of January first?"

"I know Nunz is going back to Coloso on the first, so I'm sure I can make it. I'll call you tonight if there's a problem. Thanks, Amelia! What an interesting way to start the new year!"

DECEMBER 29, 1989

At the La Nueva Esperanza sulfur operation, Tony gives final instructions to his Capture Team, concluding with: "Remember, Jamshid fires first. After that, show no mercy and take no prisoners."

JANUARY 1, 1990

As planned, Dr. Rojas arrives in her fully equipped jeep at two PM to pick up Teri Addabbo. They leave immediately for the high Atacama, the most arid desert in the world. They spend the first night in Calama, leave early the next morning, making rest stops in Chiuchiu and San Pedro. Eventually, they stop at a small shanty just south of Ascotan to ask for directions to the burial site. An old toothless Indian, wearing an alpaca poncho, comes out of the shack and gives the ladies a friendly smile. After he enjoys a cold bottle of fresh water offered by Amelia, he points northeast.

"Mas o menos quince kilometros." (15 kilometers, more or less).

A half hour later, unfamiliar with this new area, with no visible landmarks for navigation and no signs of a burial site, they stop when the jeep begins to lose power.

"The jeep seems to be undergoing oxygen starvation," says Dr. Rojas. "And I think we're lost."

"I need oxygen, too. I feel ready to pass out." replies Teri. "But, look!" waving at a small puff of smoke on the horizon. "We're not lost!"

Dr. Rojas opens her black medical bag, then squeezes twenty drops of Coramina into a small cup of water.

"Here drink this, Teri. I'll have some, too. Then I'll give us both some pure oxygen," she says as she reaches for the oxygen tank.

Both women are greatly relieved that there's life on the horizon. With the jeep moving at a snail's pace, they head towards the smoke.

"That looks like some kind of mining operation," reasons Teri, familiar with such operations as a result of visiting so many sites with Nunzio.

"Yes, and it must be sulfur."

The Jeep quits at about half a kilometer from the mining operation. Teri opens her husband's pocket altimeter. It reads 4435 meters (14,550 feet). They pick up their small oxygen bottles and begin walking to the mine area.

"Well," observes Teri, "the smoke was no mirage. There must be life here."

There is life indeed. As they walk past a large stockpile of sulfur, two armed men wearing white hard hats appear and quickly handcuff them.

"What's going on here?" shouts the indignant doctor.

The men do not reply as the ladies are led into a corrugated metal shed. Teri's fear and apprehension turn to a surprised cry of relief when she sees Tony Berlotti sitting at the head of a long table, backed up by two armed guards.

"My God, Tony! Is that really you?"

Tony is equally surprised to see the two unexpected visitors.

"Teri Addabbo! What the hell are you doing up here? And who's your friend?"

"First take off these stupid damn handcuffs, Tony. Let us sit down. And give us some water, right away, please."

Tony removes the cuffs.

"Sorry about this, Teri. What are you doing up here and who's your friend?"

"Meet my dear friend, Amelia Rojas. Amelia is a physician from Santiago."

Tony shakes Amelia's hand.

"A pleasure, Dr. Rojas. But why are you two up here in this God-forsaken part of the world?"

"I do research on DNA and the mummifying process. We came here looking for a burial site and got lost."

"So," complains a very frustrated and tired Teri, "Why is everybody armed? Why were we handcuffed? And why are all of you wearing white hard hats?"

"This is a temporary sulfur refinery. I set it up for a special occasion."

"Looks like a military operation to me," snaps a doubtful and irritable Teri. "What gives, Tony?"

"Relax, Teri. Here, have some vanilla wafers. I'll explain later." Tony is distracted and also impatient. *"We certainly don't need this extra complication here today. Damn it all anyway!"*

"Does Nunz know about this?"

"I said later, Teri." Tony's voice is stern. "Right now we're..."

The door opens and George rushes into the lunch room.

"I hear the helicopter!" He then does a double-take. "Mrs. Addabbo? What are you doing here?"

"Later, goddamnit!" shouts Tony. "Jamshid, escort Dr. Rojas to the generator shed. Arm her and explain how she should defend herself."

Dr. Rojas is too confused to protest or ask questions. She follows Jamshid.

"Here, Teri," handing her an automatic hand gun, "Nunz said you know how to handle a gun. You stay in here and shoot anybody not wearing a white hard hat. I'll explain later, but that planned hit on me in May 1985 by a bunch of conspirators is still on and, now, it's pay-off time."

"I can't believe this!" Teri's big blue eyes are even larger with fear and she is trembling.

"Believe it! Now! Do as I say, Teri. Your life depends on it." Tony is stern. "Calm down and be careful, for God's sake!"

Tony leaves the lunchroom. As the helicopter is seen approaching the area from the northeast, he directs his men to assume the previously orchestrated ambush positions. The helicopter circles twice around the plant area, then lands on the cross of a large white landing pad at 12:30 P.M. Rashid is waiting at the pad to greet them. Poncho, the first man to exit the chopper, frisks him before the others exit. Rashid is relieved he's "clean", but does not feel secure being unarmed. He shakes hands with Carlo, Pepe and Sammy. He does not fail to note that Sammy is pale and out of breath. Manuel finally exits, puts his arm around Rashid.

"We glad to see you feel better," he comments, looking carefully at Rashid.

"Thank you. I just had a mini stroke," lies Rashid.

He and Manuel lead the group away from the helicopter towards the sulfur stockpile. (Plate 4AB). Rashid notices they are all wearing large bulky parkas, obviously concealing their weapons. He does not question why Jose did not join the group.

"Never mind dee pile of azufre (sulfur)" growls Carlo. "Take me to dee boss."

"Yes, Sir, Don Carlo, " replies Rashid.

They continue walking until Jamshid, on the crushing platform, shouts, "Hola, Manuel. Sorry about this. I'll be down as soon as I get the crushers running."

Jamshid's shotgun is concealed. As the group approaches the two autoclave platforms, Manuel looks up and spots Dr. Asti adjusting a valve.

"Hola, Señor Greco. Don Carlo here to meet you."

"I'll be right down and will meet you at the shipping platform to show Carlo the bricks and meet the two American ladies."

Before the group begins a brisk walk towards the shipping platform, Carlo and Manuel take a long look at Dr. Asti. As they approach the conveyor belt between the autoclaves and casting, Sammy, miserably out of shape, huffing and puffing, stops and raises his arms. He is obviously suffering 'puna' (high altitude sickness in the Andes).

"Holy shit! This place stinks." Then, with panic in his voice, "I can't breathe."

"Doen complain," shouts Carlo, "you insist to be here!"

Stopped at the conveyor belt, Carlo and Manuel keep looking at the autoclave platform.

When they see Dr. Asti move behind a reactor, Manuel whispers, "Concha su madre! Es el Doctor Asti!" (Sonofabitch-It's Dr. Asti). Carlo orders Manuel to the chopper for hand grenades.

The group remains silent as Carlo calls for a huddle, ordering Rashid to step aside. Rashid, unarmed and vulnerable, realizes this may be his only chance to survive the ambush. He begins a very slow walk along the conveyor belt towards George and an agent in the casting area. Other than Rashid, Tony and his men are heavily armed and are monitoring their walkie-talkies.

Rashid breaks the silence, whispering, "Get ready!"

Jamshid keeps an eye on Rashid, waiting for him to get out of the line of fire. When Rashid sees that Manuel started the helicopter and is now coming with grenades, he sprints to the casting area, but is immediately spotted by Sammy, who shouts, "Ramsey!"

Within seconds, Carlo, Poncho, Pepe and Sammy rip open their parkas and draw their semi-automatic weapons. They ignore Rashid because they know he's unarmed. When they turn towards the autoclaves, looking for Dr. Asti, Jamshid initiates the ambush. In the open crossfire, with no place to take cover, the assassins immediately spread-out and return gunfire as they run.

(See Plate 4AB for the firing sequence and attempted escape directions).

Carlo runs for the helicopter, firing in Jamshid's direction. Poncho races towards the dorm for cover, also firing at Jamshid. He is quickly cut down. Pepe sprints in the direction of a bulldozer and forklift. On the run, he also fires towards Jamshid and is eliminated by Hash, the agent with Dr. Asti. Sammy makes a run towards the shipping platform, where Tony and two agents wait, ready to fire. He stumbles, drops his weapon, runs again, then falls to the ground and lays motionless, face down. Manuel, running towards Carlo, fires at Jamshid. He is taken by surprise when he is fired upon by Mrs. Addabbo from the lunch room. Still on the run, he fires into the lunch room, then once again at Jamshid. When he sees Carlo go down from Jamshid's shotgun blast, he drops his weapon, removes his heavy parka and sprints to the helicopter. At this altitude the average person would not run far without gasping for breath. Born in Cochabamba, mother nature provided Manuel with oversized lungs. That, coupled with being an experienced mountain climber, gives Manuel a decided edge in escaping. With Carlo face up and motionless, Jamshid climbs down cautiously from the crushing platform, hoping to stop Manuel. Unfortunately he gets off only one round before the helicopter is air-born and out of range.

On the ground, below the crushers, Jamshid shouts, "All clear!"

The Capture Team quickly assembles over Carlo's body.

"The bastard is dead!" Dr. Asti proclaims.

Missing, forgotten for the moment, are Teri Addabbo and Dr. Rojas.

"Damn," shouts Tony, "the ladies are missing. Quick, - check the lunch room and generator shed. No - wait! I'll go first."

Tony, who left his hard hat at the shipping platform, approaches the lunch room, not knowing if Mrs. Addabbo is dead, wounded or waiting to fire at the first person she sees without a white hard hat. He shouts, "Teri...don't shoot! It's me, Tony."

Getting no response, he kicks-in the door, stands to the side and peeks in, with gun at the ready. He can't believe his eyes. Teri is sitting at a table, trembling, eyes glazed and eating vanilla wafers.

"Teri, - it's all over. Are you OK?"

She looks at Tony in a robotic trance, "Is this all you've got to eat? I'm hungry!", then faints.

Tony picks her up, yells for Dr. Asti and carries her to the dorm.

"Check her while I go to the generator shed for Dr. Rojas."

With the shed door open, Tony shouts, "Dr. Rojas, don't shoot. It's Tony Berlotti."

Dr. Rojas, hiding behind the noisy generator, does not hear Tony. George comes to his father's side and hands him his hard hat. "Here, Dad, put this on before you go in there."

Tony enters slowly, stops at the generator and gives a sigh of relief, thinking, *"This is a streak of luck."* He shuts-down the generator, waits for the noise to subside, then shouts, "Dr. Rojas, don't shoot - it's Tony Berlotti."

Shaking, grimy with grease and still holding a gun, Dr. Rojas walks around the generator to Tony, hands him the weapon and cries, "My God, what's happening? Where's Teri?"

"I'm glad you're Okay. Teri is all right. I'll take you to her."

They enter the room and see Teri covered with a blanket. Dr. Asti is holding an oxygen mask over her face.

"Let me examine her," states Dr. Rojas.

"She'll be okay," states Dr. Asti. "She's in shock and suffering from hypoxia."

Dr. Rojas pushes him aside, "I said 'let me examine her'. I'm her friend and a medical doctor!"

Dr. Asti moves a bit reluctantly, "So am I."

"Sorry, I didn't have time to introduce you earlier," smiles Tony. "Dr. Rojas, meet Dr. Asti."

A few minutes later, Teri responds to sights and sounds. Dr. Rojas tells her to sit up and eat some wafers.

"Now," announces Tony, "let's examine the bodies."

"I'll stay with Teri," insists Dr. Rojas.

Teri gets up, regains her equilibrium and declares herself ready to follow Tony. "I want to see these assassins!"

The first body examined by both doctors is Carlo, dead of chest wounds. "He suffered before dying," concludes Dr. Asti.

"I agree," concurs Dr. Rojas.

"I certainly hope so," Tony gives two thumbs-up but there are tears in his eyes as he remembers Gloria and his daughters. "There is some grim satisfaction in retribution."

The examinations go on. Poncho's face is shattered. He died instantly. Pepe, shot in the back, bled to death. The last body to be examined is Sammy's. Both doctors agree he was not shot, but died of a heart attack.

Tony then asks, "Rashid, what made you start running?"

"I knew you didn't hear him, but Carlo told Manuel to go for hand grenades. When he started back from the helicopter, I figured he would start throwing them at us, so I ran - praying that Jamshid would start the ambush."

"Manuel dropped his weapon and parka before fleeing," observes Jamshid, flinching and squeezing his left biceps.

"What's wrong?" asks Dr. Asti.

"It's nothing. Carlo got lucky. One of his shots grazed my arm."

Dr. Asti walks Jamshid to the dorm and dresses his wound. Meanwhile, Tony, George and the others find Manuel's parka, weapon and six grenades.

"Too bad he got away," states George.

"Don't worry," assures Tony, "we'll get the sonofabitch - and Jose too!"

A frustrated Dr. Rojas stands with her arms akimbo, "Will someone tell me what's going on?"

"It's OK, Amelia," whispers Teri, "I'll tell you later."

"Well, Teri, I wouldn't have predicted this ending to our field trip. We never found the burial site but here are four dead bodies."

"Don't worry, " motions George, "I know where the site is and will point it out before we leave."

"That's it, gang. It's getting late," announces Tony. "Let's pack up and head down the hill to Calama, eat, and then get a good night's sleep."

"What about the four bodies?" asks Teri.

"These are four lucky men," comments Tony, sarcastically. "Upon death, they all wished to be cremated and our sulfur reactors just happen to be ready to receive them. Now let's go and don't ask any more questions!" At this, Teri turns ashen. "Besides, Teri, you don't look good."

A half hour later, Jamshid and Dr. Asti lead the three vehicle convoy away from La Nueva Esperanza, followed by Dr. Rojas and Teri in the jeep, followed by Tony and George. Rashid and the others remain to take care of the bodies.

After several stops to check on Mrs. Addabbo's condition, the convoy arrives at the Hotel at 7 P.M. After checking into three rooms, Dr. Rojas immediately examines Teri, and medicates her, deciding she needs some sleep. At nine, when Tony calls everyone to dinner, Teri suddenly appears.

"You were all going to eat without me?"

Dr. Rojas is nonplussed. "I thought you'd sleep until morning."

"What's wrong with her?" asks George.

"She's hypoglycemic. An abnormally low glucose level in her blood," the doctor explains. "She needs more carbohydrates to bring it up to normal."

As George thanks Dr. Rojas, Tony gets a nod of agreement from Dr. Asti.

The next morning after breakfast, George and Dr. Asti return to La Nueva Esperanza to assist in dismantling the refinery. Tony, Jamshid, Dr. Rojas and Teri, feeling better, convoy approximately 217 kilometers (135 miles) to Addabbo's apartment in Antofagasta.

At 1:30 P.M., Nunzio Addabbo is in his Coloso field office reading a FAX when the phone rings. He picks up on the second ring.

"Hello."

"Nunz, it's me. Can you come home? It's very important."

He hesitates, thinking, *"What's wrong? Her voice isn't normal... she wasn't due back until tomorrow."* "I'll be right there!"

A half hour later, Teri meets Nunz at the door. He immediately notices her glazed eyes and holds her close. "What's wrong? Your body is shaking like it's attached to a jack-hammer."

"Come to the living room."

"Right away. Just let me clean up a bit."

As he walks to the bathroom, he passes the kitchen, then dining room. He notices the table is set for a party of four, that the maid is gone and the stereo is unusually loud with Nat King Cole singing in Spanish. In the bathroom, the stereo makes the voices in the living room undistinguishable.

He rushes his ablutions thinking, *"Why is the maid gone if we have guests? What went wrong on the field trip and who's in there?"*

Refreshed Nunzio enters the living room and does a double-double-take.

"Tony! Jamshid! What a surprise. I had no idea you were in Chile."

"And until yesterday, I thought you were still in the Dominican Republic."

The two old-timers bear hug, then Tony hands Nunzio a pisco sour.

"Are we celebrating something, Tony?"

"Yes, we're celebrating, Nunz. We made history yesterday and, believe it or not, Teri and Dr. Rojas were unexpected witnesses."

"Witnesses to what?"

"Come on, let's eat and we'll explain."

"So, why is the maid gone?" Nunz looks at Teri

"Nunz, you know she's learning English. And this, she can't hear."

Lunch begins with Teri explaining how she and Dr. Rojas arrived in Ascotan, got lost, then captured - by Tony. Tony then unbuttons his shirt pocket and pulls out a plastic zip-lock type bag containing a photo.

"Nunzio, I made you a promise a long time ago, remember?"

"Yes. Is this is the photo you promised to show me?"

"Right. I took it on Sunday September 29, 1963 in Mexico City. Here - take a good look."

Nunzio looks, shrugs his shoulders, then walks into the bedroom, returns with a miners loop and takes another look. He rubs his eyes and looks again.

"Wowww - Jack Ruby with Dan Hill at one table... Oswald with someone I don't recognize at the rear table. I knew you were involved in something big, but Tony, this is dynamite!"

"You bet! It blows the whole Kennedy assassination theory all to hell. Show it to Teri."

Teri borrows the loop and looks. "Yes, it's them all right. And, my God, the man sitting with Oswald is one of the men killed yesterday at Ascotan! The one you called 'Carlo' !"

"You and Amelia were involved in the shooting?" asks Nunz in disbelief.

"Only by accident. But, Nunz, the one that shot at me got away."

"Yes," confirms Tony, "his name is Manuel. Unfortunately, he got a good look at Teri. Nunz, I'm damn sorry about this, but I'm afraid she will become another one of his targets. You see..."

"Tony told me," interrupts Teri, "That the hit team expected to meet two women drug dealers and that Manuel guy probably thinks I'm one of them."

Nunz is thoughtful, then, "Well, that's it. Teri, you can't stay in Chile if you're on some killer's hit list. I'm sending you right home."

"And ASAP!" agrees Tony. "I feel terrible, Nunz. This is why I've been so secretive about this."

The conversation and lunch continues until the phone rings at three thirty. Mr. Addabbo's security engineer calls to remind him of the underwater blast at four.

"Sorry, Tony, but I've got to leave right away. By the way, you look like hell. Why don't you and Jamshid stay here overnight? We'll go to the yacht club for dinner and talk about this."

Jamshid looks at Tony, "Mr. Addabbo is right. We should stay."

During dinner, Tony inquires, "Where's Dr. Rojas? Can she be trusted?"

"She's already back in Santiago. And trust me, Tony," assures Teri, "she won't talk."

"Tony," questions Nunzio, "why the hell didn't you notify the authorities about this?"

"You must be crazy, Nunz! Dan Hill was originally represented as a CIA agent. I haven't been able to trust anyone but my team. The government couldn't protect me. Hell, they couldn't protect Kennedy! And the Secret Service, F.B.I. and C.I.A. would have interfered with my operation. And they would be on my ass till I die. I would have lost control when they took over. It wouldn't have worked."

"What will you do now?"

"Probably leave the country. Hey, this congrio (sea eel) is great." It was time to change the subject.

JANUARY 11, 1990

Teri Addabbo is on a plane to the U.S. With her is Rashid, whom Tony is sending as her bodyguard. A few days later, at the Addabbo residence, Rashid installs a Montico security system.

CHAPTER 29

SAVED BY A DOG

JANUARY 12, 1990. ANTOFAGASTA,

Tony and Jamshid arrive at the port of Coloso, are cleared and escorted to Nunzio Addabbo's office by a security guard. After a half hour tour of the project, Nunzio hands Tony his apartment keys. "Here, make yourself comfortable. I'll be home around seven, get cleaned up and we'll go back to the yacht club for some more of that great congrio."

At the apartment after dinner, Tony hands Nunzio a briefcase. "I said I owe you a big one for saving my life, Nunz. In here are some tapes, diaries, phone logs, notes, telexes and milestones George and I started on the conspiracy. I'm giving you carte blanche to write the story and will give you more data next time I come to Chile. Meanwhile, get a handle on all of this. And be careful. Like I told you, there are still two assassins out there and the story isn't complete until they're eliminated. And no one involved is safe."

Nunzio opens the briefcase. "Thanks, Tony. I won't let you down. There's just one thing."

"What's that, Nunz?"

"I'm running 800 men on a seven day, around the clock project. Writing will be slow."

"No problem. Set your own pace. If you have any questions you know how to reach me. Oh, Jamshid set-up the Montico security system this afternoon. He'll check you out in a minute, but first, here's a souvenir from our ambush."

Nunz looks at the object Tony hands him. "It's a hand grenade."

"Yes. It came from Manuel's parka. It's safe. Jamshid de-armed it."

"Thanks, I'll treasure this. So, what are your immediate plans?"

"Back up the hill to see that the refinery is dismantled and moved out of the area. I lost my ass on this one. But know something, Nunz? It was worth it. Then it's back to New York to concentrate on trapping Manuel and Jose and trying to recoup some of my losses."

"Surely Carmen knows what's going on?"

"Yes, I finally had to tell her. She worries, of course, and wants me to give up the chase. But that isn't gonna' happen."

"She may be right, Tony. With Carlo gone the others may disappear."

"I won't let them live to talk about what they did. Manuel is a cold-blooded murderer. He's the one who killed Peter Monti, framed Dr. Asti and torched my house with my family in it. And remember, he's the one who may have I.D'd your wife during the ambush. He may come back."

"And Jose?"

"Jose? He's the smartest of the lot. He planned the Grassy Knoll surprise and escape at Dealy Plaza. He had my Chilean team torched in Bolivia and told Manuel how to destroy my home, Gloria and my little girls. There's no way they can hide from me!"

"I understand, Tony. I can't fault you. And don't worry. This material will be in a safe place."

SUNDAY AFTERNOON, FEBRUARY 11, 1990, COLOSO, CHILE

Nunzio Addabbo is standing on a high stockpile of very large boulders outside the perimeter fence of the plant where he is working. The boulders will be placed as site protection against heavy seas. He is scanning the shoreline for a convenient area to launch an underwater effluent pipeline. The sea is choppy with a strong wind blowing in from the west and standing on the smooth rock is difficult. As he scans, contemplating the possibilities, he hears a dog barking from behind. He knows it's not one of his three trained police dogs as they are always on a leash with a security guard.

"It must be one of the stray dogs that hang around here looking for handouts...but he can't be barking at me - I feed them - they all know me."

The bark suddenly turns to a growl and Addabbo turns quickly for a look. It is one of the stray dogs and he is not growling at Addabbo; he is charging a rifleman standing in front of a pick-up and taking aim to fire at Addabbo.

Upon seeing the gunman, Addabbo's reaction is spontaneous. He turns quickly to avoid the shot, slips on the smooth rock and tumbles to the hard ground below, hitting his head and back on the way down. Dazed, bleeding and unable to stand, he tries to crawl between the rock openings to avoid any further attempts on his life. Under him, he feels the two-way radio that fell out of his hand. He calls his safety engineer for immediate medical assistance. Within seconds hears the plant siren, a second gun shot and engine ignition, followed by the sound of the departing pick-up.

Fading in and out of consciousness, Addabbo assumes that the gunman is gone. The sound of the approaching ambulance is reassuring. The safety engineer and 'practicante' (hospital intern) lift him into the ambulance and ride in the rear with him to the Antofagasta Hospital, where he is examined by a traumatologist, x-rayed, sedated and attached to I.V. tubes.

According to the safety engineer, Addabbo kept repeating, all the way to the hospital, "Era una caida muy fuerte." ("It was a very hard fall.") No one asks what made him fall.

Four days, many x-rays and scans later, the diagnosis is concussion, compressed vertebrae of the neck and spine, cracked ribs, pinched left sciatic nerve, several bruises and lacerations.

That night at 8 P.M., Max Dollman, Project Office Manager, is in Addabbo's room and takes a call from Mrs. Addabbo in the U.S. He advises her that Nunzio will be OK.. Later that night, Rashid, Mrs. Addabbo's bodyguard, advises Dr. Monti, in New York, of Addabbo's accident.

Nunzio's condition does not improve. On February 21st, Laddy Richardson, Project Administrative Manager, sends a FAX to corporate headquarters in California advising that Addabbo is being transferred at seven that night, by aircraft, to a waiting ambulance in Santiago, then to the Clinica Las Condes (hospital). Charlie Hanna, Project Director, accompanies Addabbo to Santiago. During the flight, Addabbo decides that his close friend, Charlie, should know that he was shot at, but only if he swears to keep it secret. Charlie agrees to remain silent.

After listening to the details, he says, "Nunz, you're lucky to be alive. Do you know who it was? Why did he want to kill you?"

"I don't know who it was, Charlie. All I can do is guess it has something to do with a conspiracy."

"You think it's part of a conspiracy?"

"Yes. I'll give you some more details when I know more myself. Charlie, that dog saved my life."

"You said you believe the second shot was to kill the dog? The accident report doesn't include a dead dog at the scene."

"The gunman and dog weren't near the rock pile. They were on the access road at least seventy-five yards behind me. Maybe he missed the dog."

Charlie is satisfied with the explanation, they shake hands and Nunzio falls asleep.

The next afternoon, Nunzio awakens and sees a stranger sitting next to his bed.

"Who are you?" Nunzio is immediately alert and wary.

"Hello, Mr. Addabbo. Mr. Berlotti sent me. I'm Vakil, one of his men from the refinery we just dismantled. Mr. Berlotti says he is concerned about you, and wants me to go to your job to ask questions about your accident."

Although Addabbo is still sedated, the presence of this stranger alarms him and gives him an adrenalin rush. He questions the stranger's identity. "OK, Vakil, but I need to know who was with you at the refinery?"

He correctly names every member of Tony's Capture Team.

"Thank you, Vakil. There's one thing Mr. Berlotti doesn't know, but may suspect. My fall was no accident."

Addabbo gives him the details and concludes with, "That stray dog charging the gunman caused him to miss me. The second shot probably killed the dog."

"Thank you. We will go to Coloso and investigate."

"Good. If you encounter any problem getting on site, ask for Charlie Hanna." Nunzio scribbles a message on a piece of paper. "Here's a note to give him if necessary."

MARCH 1, 1990

After seven more days of treatment in the second hospital, Addabbo's doctors agree their hydro-facility is inadequate for his needs. He is flown to California for physical therapy.

Two days later, Addabbo calls Tony. "Christ, Tony! Associating with you is life threatening!"

"Now you know why I didn't want you involved. I heard what happened. How the hell are you?"

"I hurt all over, but I'll be OK."

"I'm really relieved, Nunz. Did you get a good look at who was shooting at you?"

"It happened too fast for an I.D. I have no clue."

"I have a gut feeling it was Manuel. Remember, he exchanged shots with Teri. He may have recognized her and added you to his hit list. After all, they framed my personal physician. Dan Hill probably provided Carlo and los Machos with photos and other data on everyone involved a long time ago. So, what are they doing for you?"

"They tell me I need four weeks of intensive hydrotherapy, ultrasound and manipulation before I can return to Chile. And Vakil? How did he make out?"

"Rotten luck. He had a gall bladder attack the day after he saw you and has been laid-up. He's going to Coloso in a couple of days."

"Be sure to have him look for signs of a dead dog. I tell you, Tony, that dog saved my life."

"We will. Meanwhile, Rashid will stay with you and Teri until you can travel again. Then he's off to Bolivia."

MARCH 31, 1990

Nunzio responds well to therapy and is cleared to return to Chile. Tony and Nunzio agree Mrs. Addabbo will be safer in Chile than alone in the U.S. They arm their home with two Montico security systems and fly back to Santiago. Two days later, Addabbo arrives in Coloso to a cheering staff. After a tour of the project he begins to read a stack of mail, Faxes, memos and blueprints. An hour or so later he opens a letter marked PERSONAL and CONFIDENTIAL.

"Nunzio, Vakil found the dog and buried him. You were right. You were saved by a dog. Tony."

CHAPTER 30

TRACKING KRUCHENKO TO BAJA

MID 1990

With no new contracts and running low on funds, Tony decides to dramatically down-size his engineering and construction operations, allowing him to concentrate on the elimination of Manuel and Jose, the final two assassins. He knows he will never have a life until they are gone.

Feeling vindicated for the frame-up perpetrated against him with Carlo's death, Dr. Asti decides to return to full-time medicine. With Dr. Monti's help, he assumes a new identity with new licenses, undergoes minor plastic surgery and joins his family in a southwestern state.

Before leaving, Dr. Asti advises Dr. Monti to retire, warning, "Look, Frank, you're playing Russian-roulette with your life if you continue on such a fast pace. If you don't slow down, your weak heart, the emphysema or the side effects of the prednisone will kill you."

Dr. Monti accepts the warning. He scales-down his operation and decides to assist Tony full-time in Capture Team activities. He leaves Josh to manage Montico. Judy's grieving is finally over when she meets David, a fine young man who is a missionary. Greatly relieved by the vindication of Peter's murder with Carlo's death, she plans to join David in Africa after they marry in August. George, however, rejects Tony's attempt to force him into a full time law practice.

"Don't even think about it, Dad! I'm with you until we eliminate Manuel and Jose, period! After that, I'll renew my association with lawyer friends in Mexico. And on another subject, Dad, you don't look good at all. Dr. Asti told you the sacculated aneurism of your aorta could rupture any time and your blood pressure is still too high. Slow down and spend more time with Carmen."

Tony takes George's advice; but, with Manuel and Jose constantly on his mind, spends only one week with Carmen. He returns to New York and calls a meeting of the Capture Team.

"I've been thinking about Manuel and ways to trap him. We know there's a link between Manuel and Boris Kruchenko, so let's pursue him through Kruchenko."

"I'm ready for action," agrees George.

"Good. We'll get you ready for your next impersonation."

"Dad, not another female, please. I've just gotten back to my fighting weight!"

"No. This time I want you to grow a beard, let your hair grow and start wearing grubby clothes. You're gonna' be a ne'er-do-well Puerto Rican hippy car mechanic with a passion for duplicate bridge."

"Bridge I know. Cars I don't."

"All you have to worry about is bridge. Jamshid and the others will take care of the cars."

"Sounds like I'm going to meet Boris Kruchenko at a bridge table."

"You read my mind, son."

"Hollywood, here I come."

Tony gives George a playful jab. "Now George, don't get a fat head. This won't be Hollywood, where stunt men do your dirty tricks. No one will stand-in for you on this assignment."

"I'm in good shape, Dad. Been working out and can be ready in less than a month. What's my new name?"

"How do you like Felipe Duran? Your new I.D.'s will be ready in two days."

"You better brush up on your bridge," states Dr. Monti. "Kruchenko is a good player but rarely has the same partner. He plays strong opening two clubs, weak twos, Jacoby transfers, splinters, unusual no trump, Michaels que, Stayman, Blackwood, limit raises, negative doubles and an occasional psych. Except for bidding, he doesn't talk during or after a hand and drinks a lot of coffee. In short, he's weird."

"Here's the way I see the set-up," begins Tony. "You've got to befriend this guy, so you'll start by making yourself a regular at the Saturday night games. Ali will point him out to you but let him sign-up first. If he plays north- south, you sign up east-west and vice versa. The first night you play opposite him, introduce yourself and avoid conversation. Just let him see you play good bridge."

"Since he doesn't have a steady partner, there will come a night," adds Dr. Monti, "when you will be paired with him. That's when Ali will cut his car's ignition cable."

Tony sips his cappuccino, then lights a cigar.

"Later, while he's trying to start his car, Ali will tell you where and how to fix the cable. Finally, out comes Felipe, the good Samaritan. Explain you're a car mechanic and can get his car started. Don't accept money. Just say how much you enjoyed playing with him. Let him make the next move."

At this point, Dr. Monti announces, "I'm hungry! Let's talk over the details at Luigi's. I want some of his special gnocchi Piedmontese."

A month later, Tony checks out George as Felipe but puts a hold on George's trip to Tucson. "You're hair isn't long enough."

By mid September, George's hair is shoulder length. Appropriately attired now as a "hippie", he flies to Tucson and is met at the airport by Ali and another agent. Ali presents George with a beat-up 1970 V W van. George has always had good cars.

"This is my transportation?"

"Yes, George," confirms Ali, "It's your father's instructions."

"Thank you very much. Does it run?"

The Iranians don't pick up George's sarcasm.

"Oh, yes, sir," states the agent seriously. "We had it tuned up yesterday. Since you are a car mechanic it must be in excellent running order."

They drive to Denny's for brunch, then to Tony's Safe House and look at photos of Kruchenko. After lunch they drive to Patagonia and, from a distance, observe Kruchenko's cabin, which is surrounded by a new chain link fence.

"When did he install that fence?" asks George.

"It had to be during the past week."

SATURDAY, SEPTEMBER 15

The following morning, they drive to Kruchenko's condo on Sunrise and Ali points out his car. George rubs his hands in anticipation. "Very good. Maybe he'll play bridge tonight."

"You can bet on it," assures Ali.

George arrives at the bridge center in his smooth running but battered old van at six-thirty. He parks at the far end of the parking lot assuring that Kruchenko will have to park closer to the main door. He sees Ali already parked nearby in his motor home and calls him by radio.

"Ali, I don't see his car."

"It's early. Don't worry, he'll come. Keep low or pretend to be doing something to your van."

Ten minutes later, Kruchenko arrives and signs-in to play north-south. George enters right behind him and notices that the Russian signed-in as Boris Gottlieb. George requests an east-west seat, then told he is partnered with Mildred. He pays the entry fee, asking, "Where's Mildred?"

The sign-up lady points, "Table number one. The lady with the white hair."

"Damn. I would get an old lady. They never play the new conventions."

George sits and introduces himself to Mildred and the north-south pair. The boards are already made. George, noticing that Mildred, a well groomed lady, doesn't have a convention card, asks, "Mildred, what conventions do you play?"

"Oh, just standard old Goren."

"That's good," smiles George. "I can adjust to old Goren." *"I knew it! Why me, O' Lord?"*

Mildred looks at George's convention card and smiles, "My, Felipe, you certainly play a lot of conventions. But let's stick with old Goren. It rarely lets me down."

George notices his lady opponent, sitting north, is smiling at her husband in the south chair. *"Did I do something wrong, or what? Anyway, I'm glad this is a Mitchell movement. We'll be moving to play against Kruchenko."*

When the director announces, "Start round one," George crosses his fingers under he table. *"I wonder if she ever played with old Charlie Goren?"*

Round one ends with a smile on George's face as he politely escorts Mildred to table two. *"Wow, I'm never going to badmouth little old ladies who play Goren again. Mildred plays offense and defense like a pro. She made an overtrick on a difficult contract, set the opponents with a hold-up play on what should have been a lay-down and responded correctly to all my signals!"*

As he offers Mildred a seat at table two, she remarks, "Felipe, you play well. Where did you learn bridge?"

"Thank you, Mildred. I learned in San Juan. I'm Puerto Rican." George sees that they will play against Kruchenko in round four.

Rounds two and three don't disappoint George. He and Mildred agree they may have two tops and at least a tie for top. Before moving, Mildred whispers. "Felipe, the next round may be more difficult. That Boris fellow is an excellent player, but I've never seen his young partner."

George seats Mildred and notices Kruchenko is tapping his fingers on the table while glaring at his female partner. George introduces himself and Mildred.

Without looking up, Kruchenko takes a deep breath, "My name is Boris."

Kruchenko's partner tilts her head and smiles suggestively at George, "And I'm Mitsy."

George immediately offers to bring everyone coffee.

"Black," states Kruchenko.

"Thank you, Felipe," replies Mildred. "Cream and sugar in mine."

Mildred thanks George for the coffee but Kruchenko merely nods at him. Before play begins, George reads the Russian's convention card, then turns to Mitsy.

"Do you play everything shown on Boris's card?"

"I try."

Play begins with Kruchenko correctly putting Mitsy in a small heart slam. Unfortunately she loses transportation to the dummy and butchers the lay-down contract that everyone else makes. George gives Mildred a subtle grimace and shrug of the shoulders as they see Boris chafing with utter frustration.

The only conversation is Mitsy's, "Sorry, partner."

The last board belongs to George. After he makes a difficult contract, Kruchenko looks at him and nods his approval. George returns the nod with a smile.

"Aha, progress!."

George and Mildred continue making overtricks and setting contracts. When the last round ends, Kruchenko has a brief conversation with the director and leaves without waiting for the scoring. Mitsy is met at the front door by a leather jacketed biker-type. She gives George an inviting smile before leaving. Mildred thanks George for his fine playing, retires briefly to the ladies' room and leaves before the scoring is complete. George, knowing Ali will follow Kruchenko, waits for the scores.

George is delighted. He and Mildred are first east-west. Boris and Mitsy are next to bottom north-south. He runs out to give Mildred the good news as she enters her old white Chevy.

"Mildred - wait. We came in first."

"Yes," she replies calmly, "I knew we would. That's why I left."

"Guess you've been playing a long time?"

"Lord, yes! I've been a Life Master for over thirty years."

George returns to the bridge room to pick up his score sheet. The director has been looking for him. "You and Mildred did very well. I hope you'll continue to play here. And, by the way, if you want to play next Saturday, I have a good partner for you."

"Who?"

"Boris Gottlieb, the Russian you played against at table four. He likes the way you play. He would like you for his partner next week if you're available. I'm sure you would rather play with Mildred but she plays here very seldom as she directs her own games."

"Sure," agrees George nonchalantly, controlling his enthusiasm. "I'll play with him."

Later, George calls Tony with the progress report and advises that Ali is following Kruchenko to the Patagonia cabin.

"Good work, George. Next Saturday will be 'ignition night'. It will also be our opportunity to get into his cabin and find out his connection with the conspirators. Meanwhile, we'll keep him and the Marana hangers under 24-hour surveillance. "

The days pass without action. Kruchenko remains in his cabin. He has not had any visitors or been to Marana since Manual left Las Vegas. On Thursday, Ali reports that Kruchenko has loaded his car with a stack of shipping boxes.

"That's a signal for us to act fast," states Tony. "I'm coming to Tucson."

Forty-eight hours later, George and Ali meet Tony and Jamshid at Tucson International Airport.

"You were right, Dad. We need to act. Boris arrived at his Skyline condo last night with a lot of shipping boxes and two large rolls of wrapping paper."

"Ok. Let's go to our Safe House and discuss tonight's action."

When they get to George's van, Tony laughs.

"Who the hell is driving this old wreck?"

"Sure," responds George. " Like you don't know this is my old wreck!"

"You gotta be kidding. Ali, you didn't really need to get him such beat up transportation. Does it run?"

"Oh, yes, Sir. We had it tuned up for George. It runs good."

"Well," observes Tony, "it's certainly in keeping with your disguise. Let's go."

En route to their Safe House, Tony pats the dashboard. "Man, she purrs like a Mustang."

SATURDAY, SEPTEMBER 22, 1990, TUCSON

During breakfast, Tony lays out their plan.

"While George plays bridge tonight, Ali will disable Kruchenko's ignition system. Jamshid and I, meanwhile, will be disguised as locksmiths, get into his condo and look around for clues to his connection to the conspirators. George, you'll be wired and know what to do after bridge."

The meeting is interrupted by a radio message from one of Ali's agents.

"I'm following Mr. Kruchenko. He's driving up to the Kitt Peak Observatory."

"That's a break for us," declares Tony. "Let's go, Jamshid. We can access his condo now!"

One hour later, Tony and Jamshid, wearing rubber gloves, are in the condo. The hall contains the shipping cartons and paper rolls. The living room contains eight cardboard boxes, 18" x 18" by 12", already packed and labeled: "Hold for B. Kruchenko, c/o United Van Lines, Nogales, AZ 85621."

The room also contains four empty cartons, three cases of vodka and two full boxes of $50 and $100 tokens from various Las Vegas and Reno casinos.

"Unbelievable," thinks Tony, *"He's got a fortune here."*

They move around quietly, taking photos, looking in closets, drawers and cabinets. Tony finds nothing unusual until he opens a closet in one of the bedrooms. It contains four photo albums. The albums are neatly arranged and labeled in chronological order, in Russian. Fortunately, Jamshid grew up in Northeast Iran in the town of Eshqabad, on the USSR border, and is fluent in Russian.

The photos in the first three albums show Kruchenko growing up, between the ages of two and eight in baggy pants; at age ten playing bridge with his mother, father and sister; at 15 playing hockey with his buddies; in a wrestling match at age 16; shooting skeet with his father at 17; in a military uniform at 18; and several photos of his pretty 18 year old cousin Katerina.

The last album is a bonanza.

"Bingo," whispers Tony.

One photo shows Kruchenko with Dan Hill but no revealing background. The next shows Kruchenko, Hill and Carlo.

"Could Kruchenko have been involved in drug trafficking with Hill and Carlo? Is he an addict? And I wonder who took that one?" Tony shakes his head at the next photo. *"Kruchenko with Oswald, both carrying briefcases! And the background is certainly Mexico. Did Oswald meet Kruchenko in Russia? But who took the photo?"*

The next photo is equally interesting and revealing.

"Oswald and Carlo, in Mexico and Oswald is carrying the same briefcase. Did Kruchenko take the photo?"

The next photo is easily recognizable.

"Ah ha! Here's a copy of the photo I took for Dan Hill, showing Carlo and Oswald at one table, Hill and Ruby in front of them and Victor standing next to the copper sculpture."

The last photo in the album shows Kruchenko standing between two casino security guards.

"This one I don't get. What casino could it be and who took the photo?"

When Tony leaves the bedroom, Jamshid escorts him to the bathroom.

"The medicine cabinet," whispers Jamshid.

Tony looks in and starts enumerating.

"Lenoxin, Lasix, Prednisone, Fiorinal, Codeine, Valium, Potassium and I wonder what the aspirin is for! Looks like he may have a heart and liver problem."

"Well, we know he likes vodka."

"Yes, but we still don't know how he is involved in the conspiracy. Let's keep looking."

They can't find a passport, insurance policy, weapon, computer, bank book, foreign newspaper or political propaganda. Except for the boxes, the rooms are clean and orderly, unlike Kruchenko's Patagonia cabin. Of particular interest is the large bookcase, stocked with an enviable collection of bridge books and stacks of classical music cassettes.

"Looks like his life revolves around bridge, classical music and drugs," observes Jamshid.

"The guy's a split-personality. And I need to know what's in those boxes."

Their search stops when Ali signals that Kruchenko is leaving Kitt Peak.

Before leaving, Tony lowers the volume and plays the two messages on Kruchenko's answering machine.

"Hello, Mr. Curtis. It's 3 P.m. Wednesday September 19 and this is Chuck at First Interstate. Please call me as soon as possible. Thank you."

"Hola, Boris. I going to Baja after Jose make new papers. I be there in November. Adios."

Tony picks up the Spanish accent and whispers, "That has to be Manuel."

He saves the messages, keys his mike and waits for the all clear signal before they exit the condo.

When Tony and Jamshid arrive at the Safe House, George is reviewing bridge conventions.

"George, I'm glad you're brushing up," observes Tony. "Kruchenko is really into bridge. He's also into drugs, classical music, and casino tokens. More importantly, he definitely knew Hill, Oswald and Carlo."

"I'm ready for him. By the way, I checked with ACBL in Memphis. They have no record on him."

"The bank calls him Mr. Curtis. We'll have to check that."

Ali receives a call from his agent.

"Kruchenko is now headed up to Mt. Lemon in the Catalina Mountains. He seemed to be in a trance at Kitt Peak. He chain smoked ten cigarettes, just walked around alone, never talked to anyone and his driving is normal."

"Don't lose him," orders Jamshid.

"We need to open those boxes going to Nogales. Any ideas?"

"Yes," suggests George, "we could hi-jack the United Van truck."

"Not bad. But let's toss around another idea. I took a photo of each box and estimated its weight. We can duplicate the boxes. Then, at a convenient area between Tucson and Nogales, Jamshid and I will stop the van, posing as DEA agents in an unmarked car.

I'll order the driver to the front of the van for interrogation. Ali will then arrive in a panel van with the boxes and his two black lab drug sniffers. I tell the driver we're searching for drugs and he can go if his van is clean. Meanwhile, Ali and Jamshid will transfer the boxes. We'll do it all in less than five minutes."

"What if the driver isn't alone?" asks George.

"Odds are, he'll be alone. Drivers generally pick-up helpers at loading and unloading points only. If he has a helper, we'll interrogate them both in front of the van."

"And," continues George, "what if the highway patrol comes along?"

"We can cover that scenario. You'll be parked in your beat up VW, one mile behind us, with a help sticker on your antenna. If you see the police coming, call and we'll move on while you stall them."

George smiles, points his index finger at Tony and continues playing the devil's advocate.

"What if the cops approach from your end and cross over before they get to me?"

"We can cover that, too. We'll be parked in an area that can't be crossed between us. Ali will pick several possible areas tomorrow."

Jamshid makes an interesting observation. "Manuel called stating he will be in Baja California in November, but Kruchenko is shipping his boxes to Nogales."

"True, but he could have packed the boxes before Manuel's call. He may re-route his shipment to San Ysidro, California. Getting into Mexico from there would be easy."

"I have an idea," continues Jamshid. "Why don't we print some brochures, offering moving services, directly into Mexico, at insured and greatly reduced rates. We would guarantee our bid 50% below anyone else."

Tony lights a fresh cigar, then gives Jamshid a thumbs-up. "I like that idea. Let's do it."

"Great!" agrees George, "I'll get the brochures printed. We'll call ourselves Worldwide Movers or something like that, then spread them around his condo complex and on his windshield."

The meeting is interrupted by Ali's agent.

"Kruchenko is now driving down the Mt. Lemon road. He just wandered around up there, looking down on Tucson, like he was saying goodbye to the area. I don't know where he's headed now."

"Good! Don't lose him," orders Jamshid.

A half hour later, as the meeting continues, Ali's agent calls again.

"He drove to the Pinnacle Peak restaurant, made a u-turn, then drove to the Piccadilly Cafeteria. He's eating fried chicken."

"What are you eating?" asks Jamshid.

"Nothing. I'm back outside, waiting."

"Stay with him."

George looks at his watch and shouts towards the kitchen. "Speaking of fried chicken, I'm hungry and it's getting late. What are we having for dinner tonight?"

The Iranian's voice from the kitchen shouts.

"Ju-jay kabob and berenj, in five minutes."

"Well, that sounds interesting - I think! What is it?"

"You'll enjoy it," assures Jamshid, "It's chicken kabob and rice."

A half hour later, as George prepares to leave for the bridge center, Ali's agent reports,

"Kruchenko just left the Piccadilly. He's headed for the bridge club."

George leaves in his VW. Tony and Jamshid follow by car, with Ali and another agent following in the surveillance motor home.

George walks into the center at 6:45 and notices Kruchenko already seated north, drinking coffee. At the sign-up table, he notices he is already paired with Boris and is listed as Felipe Duran. His fee has been paid.

"Oh, oh! We didn't discuss this. Do I offer to pay or will he consider it an insult?"

As he approaches Kruchenko's table, he decides. *"I'll take the polite route and offer to pay."*

George greets Kruchenko with a firm handshake, sits and begins to pull out his wallet.

"No no, Felipe," whispers Kruchenko, motioning him to re-pocket the wallet. "I ask director to seat you with me tonight, so I pay."

George turns on the charm with his Spanish accent.

"Thank you, Sir. You are very generous. I hope I don't disappoint you. But I do promise to play better than your lady partner last week."

"Ahhhh, I tell director I never play with her again. Show me you convention card."

George notices Kruchenko smile for the first time. Their cards are identical.

"I theenk," states Kruchenko, "Mr. Goren say, 'play bridge weeth any partner, even a stranger'-correct?"

"Yes, Sir. That eez what Mr. Goren say."

"That mean we have ideal partnership. I like how you play last week. I no like play weeth beginners."

Ali advised George that competition at the Tucson Bridge Center is at a high level. Many of its members are national and international champions. Some play for blood and some would rather play bridge than eat. The atmosphere is rarely congenial.

Before play begins, George offers to refill Kruchenko's cup.

"Thank you, yes. Black and no sugar."

"Making progress. Now I need to play good bridge."

George and Kruchenko crushed their opponents on round one.

George bows his head at Kruchenko.

"What a great way to start. He's good; really good!"

The stoical Russian nods, but remains silent.

Round two begins with George bidding and making a gutsy slam. George looks for a congratulation or smile. He reads the Russian's head tilt as, "Not bad."

George ends round two with a brilliant 'coup en passant' end-play that brings the first sign of emotion from Kruchenko. The Russian smiles, gets up and walks to the coffee machines.

"Jesus Christ, this guy is really weird. Here I am knocking myself out, playing like a pro, taking top boards and the son-of-a-bitch doesn't even say thanks."

They continue acing their opponents as Tony monitors every bid from the surveillance motor home. Ali, meanwhile, has already cut Kruchenko's car cables. When round seven ends, Kruchenko stands and surprises George.

"Felipe, may I breeng you a cup of coffee?"

"Yes, Sir. Thank you very much, Sir." *"I guess that's his way of saying thanks."*

When Kruchenko returns with the coffee, he again surprises George.

"Your 'coup en passant' in round two, you played like professional. You are new in Tucson?"

"Now this is real progress." George's Spanish accent is natural for him and convincing. "Thank you, Sir. But I not

professional. I be playing cards since little boy. I car mechanic, coming from New Mexico last month."

Kruchenko nods and play continues. At 10:30, the director declares them run-away North-South winners.

George continues his polite charm.

"Thank you, Sir. It was my privilege to play with a professional."

Kruchenko lights a cigarette.

"Thank you," and departs.

"Damn. I thought I was getting through to him."

George waits about five minutes, then starts a slow walk to his van. As he approaches the Russian's car, Kruchenko is sitting behind the wheel waving his arms in the air, obviously disgusted. George continues walking, until he hears, "Felipe! Felipe, wait!"

George stops and acts surprised as Kruchenko runs out of his car.

"Felipe, I no can start car. You say you are car mechanic, yes?"

"Yes, Sir. I feex all cars." *"I can fix yours in sixty seconds, blindfolded."*

George's performance is masterful. After twenty minutes of making the job look difficult, George rubs his hands and asks Kruchenko to start the engine.

"Bravo, Felipe! You good mechanic. How much I owe for feexing car?"

"Oh, no, thank you, Sir. It be my pleasure. I only hope you play weeth me next week."

"Sorry, Felipe. I leaving Tucson, maybe next week."

"I sorry too. Where you go?"

"Baja, California."

"That very interesting because if I no find work here, I going to San Diego look for job. Where you be in Baja?"

There is a long silence.

"Not sure. Maybe Tecate; maybe Rosarita. Why you ask?"

"I would like play bridge weeth you again. If I move to San Diego maybe we meet in Tijuana?"

Another long pause.

"Better we meet in San Diego. How I find you?"

George pulls out a scrap of paper and writes down the name of the San Diego Bridge Club.

"Here, Sir. Please call me when you be located in Baja and leave a message for me."

Kruchenko pockets the note, nods and drives away.

George walks to the motor home.

"We heard it all," states Tony. "He's going to Baja to meet Manuel. By the way, you played great. Now let's get back to the Safe House and plan our next move."

Ali's agent follows Kruchenko to the Skyline condo.

SUNDAY, SEPTEMBER 23, 1990

At three in the morning, Tony and Jamshid arrive at Kruchenko's Patagonia cabin. George remains in Tucson to arrange printing of the moving company brochures, while Ali and his agent monitor the condo. There is no electric power to Kruchenko's cabin. A small shed houses a silent five thousand watt generator and old hand pump for water. Another small shed is the out-house. Tony and Jamshid put on rubber gloves, draw their weapons and knock on the door. Getting no response, they set Montico alarms around the house, then enter the cabin, being careful to avoid booby-traps and battery alarms. Tony shines his flashlight around.

"Good grief! This place looks like it was hit by a tornado! What a mess! It's out of character for the Kruchenko in Tucson. His condo is immaculate."

"Yes. And look at this," whispers Jamshid "It's a photo of Kruchenko with Oswald in Mexico."

Tony picks up the 5 X 7 picture, removes the photo from the frame and looks at its back.

"Well I'll be damned. It's signed by his cousin Katerina. We saw her picture in Kruchenko's condo. And look here - it has a Russian Embassy stamp below her name. I'll bet she took those pictures in Mexico City."

"I agree, but how did Kruchenko get involved in the conspiracy?"

"I definitely remember reading the name 'Kate' in Hill's diaries. Hill must have known her."

"Yes. And he probably set up Kruchenko to meet Oswald, but why?"

"We need to re-read Hill's diaries for more clues."

"I've been a Savak agent many years and know KGB agents. Kruchenko is not KGB."

"I agree, but we need to know how and why he got involved in the conspiracy. Hill may have set him up as a patsy. He may still be associated with Manuel and Jose. Was Katerina involved? And what has me really puzzled is his split personality."

Jamshid examines the picture. "Why do you suppose he keeps this photo in plain view?"

"Good question. I'm not clairvoyant nor a psychiatrist, but he may well be on a powerful guilt trip over Oswald's death. He may be the one who introduced Oswald to Carlo and Los Machos."

"If that's true," observes Jamshid, "why haven't they killed him too?"

"Good question! There must be a good reason why they allowed him to live this long. We may find that answer after he relocates."

"Shhhhhh," whispers Jamshid. "I hear something."

With flashlights off and weapons ready, they listen to a scratching sound that intensifies as they move slowly to the back door.

"No alarm - so it can't be anyone near the door," whispers Jamshid.

Suddenly the scratching turns to a loud metal crash, then more scratching.

"No problem, Jamshid. A cat or dog just knocked over Kruchenko's garbage can. Might even be a mountain lion."

Jamshid moves the curtain slowly and peeks outside towards the sheds.

"Ah, just enough moonlight tonight. You're right. It's a big dog eating garbage."

"Good. Let's continue looking for clues."

A medicine cabinet in the kitchen area provides another surprise. "Oh, my! Look, Rais, (boss). A sack of heroin, hypodermic needles, razors and two sticks of opium."

"Very interesting, indeed. None of these appeared in his condo."

"Yes, Sir. And from the dust on the shelf, these items haven't been used in a long time."

"I've seen enough tonight, Jamshid. Let's go."

Jamshid remotely disarms the outside alarms, then whispers, "That big dog is still out there. Shall I kill it?"

"No. He'll probably run away when we open the door. Kill it only if it tries to attack us. Be sure to use your silencer."

Tony's prediction is correct. The dog runs, then barks from the woods as they drive away.

They arrive in Tucson at 6 A.M., have a Denny's breakfast, drive to their Old Spanish Trail Safe House and sleep until noon.

George arrives, out of breath, for their 1 P.M. business lunch.

"I'll have those moving company brochures tomorrow. I'm hungry. What's for lunch?"

The familiar Iranian voice from the kitchen announces, "Ju-jay kabob and barenj."

"Chicken and rice again? We just had that." George scowls.

"What," grumbles Tony, "you'd rather go out for Mc-nuggets?"

"No. I like Persian food. But every once in a while I'd like a juicy cheeseburger or foot-long Coney Island hot dog."

"Now George, eating junk food is an insidious form of suicide. Cholesterol and fat are killers. Enjoy your kabob, stay healthy and let's talk strategy."

"Look who's talking! The doctor keeps telling you to cut out the cigars and so much cappuccino."

George ends up eating two portions, then complains when there is no more. Ali reports that Kruchenko is still in the condo, obviously packing. Jamshid reports that while Tony was sleeping, he talked with Dr. Monti in New York and learned that Hill's diaries included several entries showing a connection between Kruchenko, Manuel, Katerina and a Rosita.

"Damn," complains Tony, "now we have two women involved?"

"Speaking of women, Dad. Carmen called while you were asleep. I told her you're OK and will get back to her. She said Haldon Brooks officially retired. He and Alice now live at Lake Chapala."

While Ali and another agent maintain a vigil at Kruchenko's condo, Tony, George and Jamshid drive to Old Tucson for an afternoon of entertainment. At ten that night, Ali calls the Safe House from his Skyline post.

"Kruchenko didn't leave his condo all day, his lights have been off more than half an hour and it appears he's staying for the night."

At six the following morning, Ali calls the Safe House.

"Jamshid, we are following Kruchenko heading south on I-19. We just passed the Twin Buttes open pit copper mine. He must be going to Nogales."

"Don't lose him."

Ali calls again at seven.

"He's having breakfast in Tubac. Don't worry, I won't lose him."

Jamshid awakens Tony.

"It's five after seven. Kruchenko is in Tubac, headed for Nogales."

"Let's go," shouts Tony.

"What about your breakfast?"

"Never mind. We'll make a quick stop at Dunkin' Donuts."

At eight., Ali advises, "Kruchenko is walking aimlessly around downtown Nogales, chain-smoking. Now he's entering Denny's again for more breakfast."

"Good. Enjoy your coffee, Ali, and don't lose him."

A half hour later Ali reports again.

"Good news. He's headed for his Patagonia cabin."

Tony and Jamshid park in a secluded area near the cabin and meet Ali.

"What's he doing?" whispers Tony.

"He has been loading personal items in the car and burning papers and other unidentifiable things in the fifty gallon drum next to the out-house."

Two hours later, after burning more items in the fifty gallon drum, loading suitcases, a portable radio and miscellaneous small boxes into his car, Kruchenko exits. He leaves the door open, ignores the fire, gets into his car, lights a cigarette and drives away, obviously abandoning the cabin forever.

Ali and another agent follow him. Tony and Jamshid quickly hand-pump enough water to put out the fire, then enter the cabin. Except for the old worn-out furniture, the cabin has been stripped clean, including the items in the medicine cabinet.

"Look," notes Tony, "the photo on his night stand is gone as well as the albums."

"I wonder if he took them or burned them?"

They return to the garbage drum, dump it on the ground and begin their examination.

"Here's that 5" X 7" metal picture frame from his night stand," observes Jamshid.

"Yes. I see he burned a lot of photos and papers. This is one strange guy but I still believe he's trying to remove old memories and guilt feelings over Oswald."

"The question is," asks Jamshid, "why does he want to meet Manuel?"

"He's changing his move from Nogales to Baja, so he must have a very good reason. And the other question is: are the two women involved? Come on. Let's go."

Two hours later, Tony and Jamshid meet George at the Safe House for a progress report.

"Everything's on schedule, Dad. I distributed the moving brochures after lunch. Kruchenko stopped at the First Interstate Bank for money, had lunch at Kentucky Fried Chicken, arrived at his condo about three and unloaded his car. And, for the good news - he picked up and read my brochure on his door. Ali and his agent are there monitoring him."

"What name did you call us?"

"Tri-State Movers, specializing in across-the-border moves."

At about eight the next morning, the Safe House phone rings.

"Hello," answers Jamshid.

"Good mornink. Are you Tri State Mover?"

"Yes, Sir. May I help you?"

"Can you come make estimate for move to California?"

Across the breakfast table, Jamshid gives Tony and George a "he's hooked" thumbs-up. The Russian provides his address and asks Jamshid to be there before noon.

Jamshid and Ali arrive at ten. They notice that Kruchenko is alert, shows no signs of drug use and knows exactly what he wants.

"All items, box and suitcase to be number, insure and transport to San Ysidro, California."

Jamshid looks around the rooms, then guarantees to underbid all others by 50%.

"How you can guarantee such big discount?"

"You are in luck, Sir. You don't have a big shipment, we already have a pre-paid load going to San Diego for the Navy and there is plenty of room in our van for your effects. Please call us back when you have the other bids."

The hook works. That afternoon Kruchenko calls.

"Dee low bid be eight hundred and eighty dollars. "

"That is a very good bid," smiles Jamshid, as he winks at George. "But we always keep our word. We will deliver your load to San Ysidro for four hundred and forty dollars. How will you pay for the shipment?"

"Cash when items arrive California. How soon you can pick up?"

"First we need to return to your home, pack and number the items. We can pick up your load on Thursday October fourth. That is when we have the Navy shipment scheduled."

There is a very long silence.

"Oh, oh," whispers Jamshid to George, "now he's thinking about it."

After what seems like minutes, Jamshid hears, "That be OK."

Tony's plan to delay the move gives George another opportunity to play bridge with Kruchenko, befriend him and report his projected move to San Diego.

Three days later, when Jamshid and Ali return to pack and itemize Kruchenko's effects, the Russian will not allow them to open and re-pack any boxes.

"No problem," states Jamshid, "except we can't insure breakage in the boxes you packed." Kruchenko nods his agreement.

George is not disappointed. At six twenty, on Saturday October twenty-ninth, he sits alone at a corner bridge table, acting depressed. Kruchenko arrives, sees him and walks over, looking surprised.

"Hello, Felipe. I glad I come early with hope to find you. Something is wrong. You tell me?"

"I come to say good bye, amigo. I must go to San Diego to find job."

"Okay. We play together tonight."

"No, Sir. I sorry but no can play. I only have enough money for travel."

"Never mind. I pay for bridge. Later, we go and talk."

George's 'wire' transmits a clear and loud signal in Tony's surveillance vehicle.

"That's my boy," boasts Tony to the others. "Trouble is - he'll expect rave reviews and an Academy Award for this performance."

George continues his masterful performance as a poor Puerto Rican car mechanic with a passion for bridge. Tonight, however, he deliberately plays bridge that is not up to his usual standards to convey his concern for his future.

When play ends, Kruchenko puts his arm around George's shoulder.

"Come, Felipe. We go to Dunkin' Donuts and talk."

Fifteen minutes later, sitting at the counter, enjoying their coffee and donuts, Kruchenko is exceptionally talkative.

"I go live in Mexico in few days, but not sure if it be Rosarita or Tecate. I have friend in Tecate and cousin in Rosarita who live with friend. Sometime I stay with them."

"Well, sir, I'm..."

"Please," interrupts Kruchenko. "Call me Boris."

"Thank you, Boris. You do me great honor." *"Ah—real progress."* "I happy for you. Maybe we play again some day."

"First I go San Ysidro to arrange move of boxes. Call me when you come San Diego."

"How I find you?"

"I be at Motel Six for one, maybe two week."

"What if you be gone?"

"Then I be in Rosarita house where I stay until November. Then I make decision to stay or move to Tecate. Here, I show how you find me."

Kruchenko draws a map of the house location on his napkin, then continues, "Easy to find house. If I not there, leave message with my cousin Katerina on where you be in San Diego."

Tony, parked nearby, monitoring every word, snaps his fingers

"Ah ha, Jamshid. Katerina is in Rosarita, but who's her friend?"

"It may be Manuel..."

"Could be. Here's what I want you to do. Tell Kruchenko that in addition to your low price, you guarantee moving his effects from San Ysidro to Rosarita for only two hundred dollars. I'll come along, in disguise, as your border crossing negotiator and arrange the 'mordida'."

"Mordidia? What's that?"

"It's a bribe. The amount will depend on how much stuff there is and the mood of the inspector. I'll have at least five hundred dollars in twenties on hand for the pay-off."

Kruchenko orders more coffee and donuts.

"Eat, Felipe and be not so sad."

"Thank you, Boris. I very pleased you have family in Mexico. How Katerina decide live there?"

"She live with good friend, Rosita. Rosita is fine Cuban lady who have house in Rosarita."

"So nice for you cousin. How she meet Rosita?'

"They meet in Mexico City, many year go at embassy."

"Good. I have idea. They play bridge?"

"Yes, but I no like play with them. They not serious players and make too much talk at table."

In the car, Tony nods at Jamshid.

"Well, we know Manuel isn't there. Maybe he's in Tecate."

George declines another coffee and continues to follow his script.

"You think I find job in San Diego?"

"Good mechanic like you have no problem. If not, I help you. We must continue bridge."

"That's it. I've asked enough questions." "Thank you, Boris. You very kind. I promise visit you."

Kruchenko leaves a one dollar tip and as he follows George to the parking lot, he jams money into George's shirt pocket.

"Shhhh. This help you move."

"Thank you, amigo. I pay you back soon."

Back in the car, Tony rubs his hands.

"This has been a very productive night. Let's get back to the Safe House and meet George."

The next days flow according to plan. Jamshid and Ali move Kruchenko's effects to San Ysidro. George drives through San Diego and rents a furnished apartment in Chula Vista, between San Diego and San Ysidro. Pleased with the move to San Ysidro, Kruchenko agrees to have Jamshid handle the move to Rosarita. Before traveling to San Ysidro, Tony calls Dr. Monti.

"Frank, here are two first names for you to check out. Katerina at the Russian Embassy and Rosita at the Cuban Embassy. I may have their last names in a few days."

"Good, we're making progress. But from what you told me, Kruchenko can't possibly be a drug addict. According to Jahangir, Jose warned Manuel about meeting the Russian."

Tony arrives in time to negotiate the border crossing for three hundred dollars. Kruchenko, impressed, leads Tony and Jamshid to Rosarita.

Rosarita is a pleasant Pacific coast village about 14 road miles south of Tijuana.

As they follow Kruchenko into an up-scale looking development, Tony observes, "Looks like the two ladies live the good life."

"It appears so. Look! He's pulling into that driveway."

They stop in front of a large modern ranch house. Kruchenko motions Tony and Jamshid to follow him to the front door. Kruchenko rings the bell four times with no response.

"Someone must be home," states Jamshid. "I hear music."

Kruchenko pounds the door, sending reverberations through the house.

He yells, "Katerina, Rosita."

"The pounding got their attention," comments Tony as the door opens.

Katerina is first out and hugs her cousin Boris. When Rosita exits, she looks around the area, then hugs Boris. She speaks in Spanish.

"Hola, Boris, donde esta Manuel?" (Hello, Boris, where's Manuel?")

Tony does not fail to notice the hostility in Rosita's tone of voice. Boris introduces the two movers and invites them into the kitchen for a cold drink before his effects are unloaded. Both ladies are middle aged, well groomed and overweight. After Kruchenko praises his movers for the easy move, Tony and Jamshid are instructed to unload all boxes in one of the bedrooms.

Tony notes that this is a very clean, well furnished, three bedroom house with large covered patio. As he walks through the hall with boxes, he stops and notices the photos and certificates arranged neatly on the wall. Three frames catch his eye. One a photo of Rosita sitting on Manuel's lap. The second, a certificate to Rosita by the Consul de Cuba and the third, a letter to Katerina from the Russian Embassy. Tony moves slowly to the bedroom.

"A lot of things are beginning to add up.."

As Tony and Jamshid continue unloading, Kruchenko and the two ladies remain at the kitchen table in conversation. Tony hears Kruchenko switching between Russian and Spanish.

"That's strange. He thinks George is Puerto Rican and never spoke Spanish with him."

On one pass to the bedroom, Tony hears Kruchenko asking Rosita if she needs money. Rosita tells him she could use two hundred dollars because the landlord raised the rent when the lease was renewed and they are now behind in their payments. Kruchenko pulls out a roll of bills.

"Here, take this four hundred dollars and don't worry any more about the rent."

While Jamshid walks through the hall as a distraction, Tony continues to eavesdrop. Rosita and Katerina take turns warning Boris to keep Manuel away from them because he is so evil.

"I hate what he did to you," shouts Katerina.

"It's all my fault," cries Rosita.

Tony stiffens when he hears Kruchenko.

"Katerina, Rosita - don't worry, I am all cured now. I have been cured for a long time and Manuel does not know it. I have come to get him."

Kruchenko rises and Tony quickly carries the last box into the bedroom.

"That was very good and fast move," observes Kruchenko.

He pulls out a large roll of twenties and begins to count.

Tony interrupts. "Would you like us to open and get rid of the boxes?"

"No. That not necessary."

"It's all part of the fee, Sir."

"Thank you, no. Here is money and sixty dollar tip for good job."

"Damn! I should have opened the boxes without permission and played dumb if he complained."

They say good bye to the ladies, shake Kruchenko's hand and leave.

An hour later, as Tony and Jamshid sit in their truck waiting to check through immigration and customs, they exchange thoughts about Kruchenko's involvement in the conspiracy.

"The plot thickens," states Tony. "The Russian is back to get Manuel. But why?"

"Yes, and why are Rosita and Katerina so angry with Manuel. We saw Rosita sitting on Manuel's lap in that picture. They must have been good friends at some time."

"I figure Manuel must have done something to Kruchenko and now it's pay-back time."

"That will certainly make our job easier."

"I agree, but now Katerina and Rosita have entered the equation. We need to check them as well as Kruchenko's ties to the conspirators."

"It's strange that the Russian has been unemployed for years but always has plenty of money in the bank. We know he's not KGB and we know he hasn't been into drugs for a long time."

"I think I've already got that figured. Those casino tokens I saw in his condo are his income. But how did he get so many?"

A half hour later, they clear customs, drive off I-805 at Chula Vista, check into La Quinta Inn, then drive to George's apartment.

After George is briefed at length on how to approach Kruchenko and the ladies, he drives his father and Jamshid across town to Jake's South Bay Restaurant for a seafood dinner.

On their return drive to Tucson, Tony keeps pondering their next move.

"Kruchenko has been playing a very effective dual personality game. Finding out why will be George's next job."

CHAPTER 31

GEORGE MEETS KRUCHENKO'S LADIES

Back in Tucson, Tony instructs Ali and two agents to drive their surveillance motor home to Chula Vista and back-up George. With Kruchenko gone, Tony closes the Safe House. He and Jamshid return to New York and brief Dr. Monti, Judy and Josh on latest developments.

OCTOBER 15, 1990, MONDAY MORNING, BAJA, CALIFORNIA

George, Ali and two agents park their motor home at the border crossing parking lot on the south side of San Ysidro. One agent remains in the vehicle while the others walk separately across the border, take separate taxis to downtown Tijuana and meet in Denny's for breakfast. At ten, George hires a taxi for the day and drives to Rosita's house. He is followed by Ali and his agent, in another all-day taxi, who park approximately 100 yards from Rosita's house. George, pumped-up, ready to greet Kruchenko, takes a deep breath, then rings the doorbell.

"If he isn't home, I'm ready for Rosita or Katerina."

The door opens and George freezes. A shapely, lovely young lady looks him over.

"Buenos dias." (good morning)

As the nanoseconds flash through his brain, George forgets he's a poor Puerto Rican hippy, thinking *"Wow! What a cool chick. Was Dad pulling my leg? This can't be Rosita or Katerina."*

He quickly remembers his mission. "Buenos dias, Señorita. El Señor Boris, por favor."

"Que es su nombre?" (What's your name?)

"Felipe Duran."

"Ahhh, Felipe," extending her hand, "Bien venido."

George is well trained. He can play the ruthless street wise gang leader or consummate Latin Don Juan. He never misses a golden opportunity to play the right part. He quickly clicks his heels, bows and kisses her hand, thinking, *"Who is she? Could she be Kruchenko's daughter?"*

Impressed, she holds his hand, leading him directly into the kitchen without identifying herself.

Gorge recognizes the two ladies sitting at the table from their photos, and the kitchen is exactly as described by Tony. Katerina is preparing a bowl of fruit compote, Rosita is peeling onions. Both are oblivious to their surroundings until the young lady makes an announcement.

"Sopresa—sopresa!" (surprise-surprise).

The young lady keeps Katerina and Rosita in limbo momentarily, then curtsies and announces, "El Señor Felipe Duran!"

The ladies shout in unison, "Por fin, por fin." (At last–at last) and George suddenly finds himself being embraced by three women.[19]

"I like this, but what have I done to deserve all this affection? And who's the young chick?"

"This is Katerina, my mother. This is Rosita, our friend, and I am Rimma."

"Nice to meet you, but why are you all so happy to see me?" asks George.

"Because," states Katerina, "we have not seen Boris so happy for a long time. It has been many years of drugs and depression. He's now better and tell us you bring great joy in his life by being a kind friend and good bridge player. He thinks you are a very nice young man. And honest!"

"I am honored and look forward to be his bridge partner. By the way, where is Boris?"

"He is taking a walk on the beach," replies Rosita. "He said he wants to think about the future."

"I can take you to him," offers Rimma.

"No," interrupts Katerina. "Boris wants to be alone this morning. He said he has a big problem to solve and wants to make plans."

"He has been very kind and helped me. I want help him," insists George.

"No," continues Katerina, "he said he must do this alone."

Rimma raises her arms, "Wait! Uncle Boris told me what he wants to do and it is very dangerous. Maybe Felipe can help him."

---

[19] From this point forward, it should be understood that the conversations between George, the three ladies and Boris are all in Spanish.

"Boris will make that decision. Please stay, Felipe. Boris will return for lunch."

"We know he wants to get Manuel, but why, where, when?" I need to find out." "Thank you, ladies I would like to stay. I must see my friend."

"Good. We will have a nice lunch."

Rimma takes George's hand and leads him into the large covered patio. He is greeted in Spanish by a beautifully colored parrot.

"Hola! Hola!" (hello) screeches the parrot.

George walks to the bird, whispering, "Loro loco, loro loco." (crazy parrot)

"Felipe, that wasn't nice. He's a smart bird and likes you or he wouldn't have said hello."

"I like him, too. He's beautiful. *(And so are you!)* Why did you bring me out here, Rimma?"

"To speak with you alone. I'm worried about my Uncle Boris. You said you would help him."

"Boris is your uncle?"

"No. He is my mother's cousin. After my father died, he helped my mother and me for many years. Now it's our turn to help him."

George reaches out and places a hand on Rimma's shoulder.

Thinking of his mother, George is sincerely sympathetic. "I'm sorry your father died." Then, looking at the parrot, George asks, "What will your uncle do that's so dangerous?"

Rimma closes her eyes. "He's going to make Manuel pay for what he did to him and to us."

George ignores the parrot and focuses on the lovely Rimma.

("God, she's beautiful! Stay focused, George!") "Who is Manuel. What did he do that's so bad?"

With her eyes still shut, Rimma shakes her head.

"Oh, Felipe, Rosita is right. Uncle Boris must decide if he needs your help. We all hate Manuel. He's a real bastard; an evil man without a conscience!"

The tense silence is broken by the parrot practicing his new words. "Loro loco. Loro loco."

"See what you've done, Felipe?" laughs Rimma. "If he knew what it meant, he'd develop a complex. Tell him something nice."

"Okay." George looks the parrot in the eye. "Simpatica Rimma." ("Appealing Rimma")

"Thank you, Felipe. I'm flattered."

George looks at the parrot, waiting The parrot looks at George and tilts its head.

"Loro loco; loro loco."

Rimma stamps her foot, but smiles. "That wasn't fair! You gave the bird a tongue twister."

"Yes, but he's a smart bird to remember 'loro loco'."

Rimma shakes her finger at George, then whispers something to the parrot.

George walks away slowly, in thought. *"I think she likes me. I have a feeling I can get plenty of information from her on what Kruchenko plans to do. Where was she when Dad and Jamshid were here? Wonder how much she knows about the conspiracy... Wow! She's got a great shape, too. Keep your mind on the job, George."*

The parrot suddenly shouts, "Hola. Hola," signifying the entrance of Rosita, waving her arms.

"Good news. Boris is walking down the street toward home."

George gives a thumbs up, nodding in approval and smiling. Almost simultaneously, he receives a silent electronic signal from Ali, confirming Kruchenko's arrival.

"Quick, Felipe," whispers Rimma, pulling him behind the swinging patio door. "Hide here and surprise Uncle Boris."

She then joins her mother and Rosita in the kitchen. George hears the front door open. Kruchenko walks into the kitchen and asks, "Why is there a taxi in the driveway?"

"How was your walk, Uncle Boris?"

"Very relaxing. Why is there a taxi out front?"

"We have a surprise for you, Boris," announces Katerina.

"Who would come to see me in taxi?"

"Who would you like it to be," asks Rosita.

"It would be nice to see my new friend, Felipe. But he's in Tucson. Besides, he can't afford a taxi. There aren't too many other people I would want to see here."

"Good thing we rehearsed this scenario," thinks George. *"I hope he buys my inheritance story."*

Rimma grabs Kruchenko's hand.

"Uncle Boris, come - I have a surprise."

She leads him, followed by Katerina and Rosita, into the patio. The parrot is first to speak, "Loro loco. Loro loco."

Kruchenko points at the bird and doubles over with laughter.

"My dear cousin," smiles Katerina, "this is the first time I've seen you happy in many years."

"Yes," agrees Rimma, "and I know who's responsible for making the bird say those words."

George seizes the opportunity to surprise Boris. He remains behind the door and mimics the parrot, "Loro loco! Loro loco!"

Kruchenko looks at the 'crazy bird', amazed. "That bird is a good ventriloquist too. He doesn't move his lips!"

George tries to mimic the bird again, but can't control his laughter.

Kruchenko turns and looks towards the door, "Who's there?"

George swings the door and makes a grand entrance, raising arms and fingers in victory.

"My friend Boris. I hoped to find you to say, 'I am rich'!"

"Ah, my good friend, Felipe! I'm happy you are here."

He shakes George's hand and smiles as he and George are surrounded by the three ladies.

Delighted by this happy occasion, Katerina announces, "This calls for a celebration. We'll have a light lunch now, but tonight I'll prepare a special dinner."

"No, no, no," interrupts Kruchenko. "Tonight we all will go out for a special feast. Tell me, Felipe, do you like seafood?"

"Ah, yes. Good seafood is my favorite food. I grew up on it in Puerto Rico."

"Where are you taking us, Uncle Boris? asks Rimma.

"Tonight we'll go to La Costa Restaurant for the best seafood in Baja."

"Oh, no! Dad and I have been there. Will they remember me? No, not in this hippie get-up."

"Lunch in ten minutes," announces Rosita.

Following a pleasant lunch on the patio, Kruchenko invites George outside for a walk along the beach. The Russian expresses his pleasure at seeing George and how much he will enjoy playing bridge again. He then asks the question George has been waiting for.

"At Rosita's you said you're rich now. What did you mean? How did it happen?""

"Ah, Boris, I'm so relieved. Two days after I moved into an apartment in Chula Vista, I received word from a cousin in Miami that I will inherit twenty five thousand dollars from the estate of my late Aunt Felicia. I didn't even know she was gone, but I was very fond of her."

"I'm happy for you. But why did you move to Chula Vista and not San Diego?"

"Two reasons. First, Chula Vista is a lot cheaper than San Diego and I was very broke, remember? And, second, it would be closer to you so we can play bridge. I want to become as good as you. Wouldn't you like to play more? We made a pretty good team."

"Yes, a very good team. But I can't play until I finish a very important project."

"Look, Boris, you helped me in my time of need. Please allow me help you now."

"No, Felipe. I'm sorry. This is something I must do alone."

Both men are thoughtful as they continue walking along the beach.

"Sure," reasons George, "You're going after Manuel but how do I make you talk? Perhaps my best shot is to get Rimma on my side and use her as my conduit. That should be easy. I think she likes me and I really want to be with her. It's one of the few good things that have happened."

The following two weeks move according to Tony's plan. George advises Kruchenko he must go to Miami to settle his aunt's estate. Before leaving Rosarita, he succeeds in bugging Rosita's house and phone. Meanwhile, Ali learns that Rimma lives there full time, has a degree in nursing and works part-time for a doctor in Tijuana. Kruchenko walks along the beach every morning, evidently pondering his course of action. Rosita works part time in real estate and Katerina tends the house full time.

TUESDAY, OCTOBER 30, 1990

Ali and his agent, in separate taxis, follow Kruchenko towards Tecate. They lose him temporarily when he turns on a winding narrow dirt road in the La Puerta area.

Fortunately the car's dust cloud signals the path and Kruchenko's destination: a one story terra cotta colored ranch house with Spanish tile roof. Ali parks in front of a house about 400 yards behind Kruchenko. Ali's agent continues and parks about 300 yards in front of the Russian. The nearest house to Kruchenko is about 400 yards.

Kruchenko remains in his car and honks four times. He then exits the car, looks around and then walks around the house, stopping at the front door. When there is no response to his knock, he returns to his car, makes a slow u-turn and drives away. He is followed to Rosarita by Ali's agent. Ali remains, photographs the house from all sides and returns to Chula Vista to brief George. Ali's agent remains in Tijuana for the night.

Next morning, George calls his father in New York. Judy answers the phone.

"Hi George, I should say 'hippy Felipe'. How are things on your end?"

"I'm making progress. And Judy, you won't believe it but this girl Rimma is a knockout and I think she likes me. I'm..."

"Cool it, George. Stay focused. Ah, here comes Dr. Monti. He wants to talk with you."

"Hello, Uncle Frank. Good news. Ali followed Kruchenko to a ranch house in La Puerta, near Tecate. We think that's where he plans to meet Manuel. Katerina and Rosita are really nice ladies. They seem to hate Manuel passionately. I can't believe they were directly involved in the conspiracy. And Rimma, wow! I'm going to befriend her as much as possible as my conduit to Kruchenko. So, how are you and where's Dad?"

"I'm OK, George, but your Dad suffered a myocardial infarction yesterday. He's resting and Dr. Asti will be here this afternoon. Meanwhile, keep up the good work. By the way, I approve using Rimma as your pipeline to Kruchenko. I take it, George, that you like her?"

A long pause. "Yes, it's a very tempting situation but I'm keeping it strictly business. I really wouldn't want her to be hurt, Uncle Frank."

The following afternoon, George receives a surprise call.

"Dad, I thought you were in bed."

"Bed is for sissies! You're all making a big deal out of a little chest pain. I feel better already. And Carmen is arriving tonight and you know she'll take care of me. Now, George, don't lose your head over that cute chick, Rimma! Be careful. She may be setting you up."

"Dad, if I'm any judge of character at all, Rimma is incapable of deception. Besides, paranoia leads to stress, and stress you don't need! Don't worry. I'm taking lots of cold showers! I'm cool and I think I'm in control. As I told uncle Frank, it isn't easy, but I'm keeping it strictly business."

"Good! Keep it that way, George. Now here's the latest. We got word this morning from La Paz that Manuel may not be coming to Mexico as planned. Apparently he got caught in a wind shear flying out of Patalani and totaled the chopper. The hell of it is, there was no sign of his body at the crash site. The reports are mixed. Some say he walked away from the crash. Others say he was found dead and buried nearby. And yet another story is that he was kidnapped and being held for ransom due to his ties with Carlo. I guess the word isn't out that Carlo is already dead."

"Well, Dad, on this end we have to decide on how to handle Kruchenko. He wants to play serious bridge with me, but not until he settles his problem with Manuel."

"I know. I understand he thinks you're in Miami settling your 'aunt's' estate. So come to New York instead and we'll talk over our strategies."

Two weeks later, George returns to Chula Vista ready to implement Tony's plan. Ali reports that Kruchenko has been making daily trips to La Puerta, taking his daily walks along the beach and dining frequently with his three ladies at La Costa. There have been no signs of Manuel.

NOVEMBER 15, 1990

In the afternoon, George arrives in Rosarita and knocks on Rosita's door.

"Felipe, how nice to see you. Come in."

"Rimma! I didn't expect to find you home. I thought you would be working today."

"I had a little fever last night and decided to rest today. Now I'm glad I stayed home. Uncle Boris is gone but we expect him soon." Rimma's face is shining with happiness.

It's all George can do to restrain himself from taking her in his arms, but he resists.

An hour later, Kruchenko arrives and is delighted to see George. George explains the ease in settling his aunt's estate. In spite of his good fortune, he's still looking for a mechanic's job in Chula Vista or San Diego as he is not going to waste money. And he again assures Boris of how much he will enjoy playing bridge again with him.

At 5 P.M. according to plan, George receives an electronic signal, alerting the arrival of Ali.

Rimma answers the doorbell and signs the receipt for a telegram for Boris. She thanks Ali and hurries into the living room.

"Uncle Boris. A telegram for you."

Kruchenko eyes the official looking envelope, then thinks *"Manuel? Jose?"*

The telegram is in Spanish and translates to read: "I have business in Cuba. Will leave in July for Mexico City, then Tijuana to meet you. Regards, Manuel."

Kruchenko does not seem pleased as he pockets the telegram.

"What is it Uncle Boris?"

"Personal and not important."

George knows that Kruchenko doesn't like the delay in Manuel's arrival. *"That's what we figured"* "I'm glad the telegram isn't important, Boris. Since I have had some good fortune, thanks to my aunt, tonight we'll celebrate. I invite all of you to be my guests at La Costa for a big seafood dinner."

"Felipe," states Rosita, "you're a fine and generous young man. Instead of driving back to Chula Vista after dinner, plan to stay with us tonight. We have a comfortable rollout bed in the patio."

"Please, Felipe" begs Rimma, "say you'll stay."

Her flirtatious look does not go unnoticed by her mother, who nudges Rosita.

George looks at Kruchenko, then Rosita, Katerina and finally Rimma. *"Oh boy! She's going to make it really difficult for me. But I'll learn more here than in Chula Vista..."*

"I insist you stay," orders Kruchenko.

George smiles, reaches in his pocket and pulls out a twenty dollar token from Caesar's Palace.

He rubs and kisses the token, waving it in the air. "This is my lucky charm. This is my lucky day!"

"Why are you kissing a casino token?" asks Kruchenko.

George closes his eyes, *"Ah, Dad, you're a genius. The bait is working."*

He flashes the token for all to see. "This token brought me luck. I inherited the money from my aunt and now I have a new family."

"How did you win the token?" questions Kruchenko.

"It's very long story, but I'll explain if you have time...?"

"Oh, please tell," beg the ladies as Kruchenko nods.

"One day I lost four hundred dollars at the crap table in Las Vegas, except for this token. I took it to Big Wheel to make one final bet. The odds were one hundred to one. I closed my eyes. When I opened them - Chihuahua! I won two thousand dollars! I quit and promised myself to never gamble again. Yes, my dear friends, this is my lucky token."

Kruchenko smiles, shakes George's hand, then, "Keep your token in safe place, George. Tomorrow we talk real business."

CHAPTER 32

KRUCHENKO'S SECRET

NOVEMBER, 16, 1990

After a superb dinner, fine wines and a slow moonlit drive back from La Costa, with Rimma holding his hand, George agonizes over his relationship with the lovely girl. *"Man, what a dilemma. I think I'm in love, I know she likes me, but is very proper. And I have to keep my distance."*

After a midnight toast, Kruchenko offers George a pair of pajamas, then Katerina announces that Rimma will sleep with her tonight.

"Good thing," sighs George. *"My testosterone level is already pushing the envelope."*

The next morning, after breakfast, Kruchenko invites George for a walk along the beach. Ali, dressed as a tourist, carrying a metal detector and binoculars, follows them at a safe distance. Ali's agent is in La Puerta, watching for signs of Manuel. After walking south about one mile, Kruchenko stops and looks at George.

"Felipe, I know you're a good card player. And you love it. How would you like to never again work as car mechanic and make plenty of money playing cards?"

"Playing cards? Oh, I like the idea but how is that possible? What must I do?"

"Come. I'll show you."

A sudden burst of lightning and thunder cause them to hurry before it rains. A heavy rain starts as soon as they enter the house. Kruchenko picks up a note on the kitchen table.

"Katerina and Rosita have gone to Tijuana shopping and Rimma is working at the doctor's office. Good! Finally, we're alone. Come into my bedroom."

"Jesus Christ! Don't tell me he's gay."

They walk into the bedroom and Kruchenko closes the door.

"Oh, oh! I was hoping he wouldn't do that."

Kruchenko pulls down the window shade.

"I swear, if he makes one pass at me, I'll knock the sonofabitch into next week!"

The Russian walks to the closet and pulls out a foot locker.

"This should be interesting..." As Kruchenko sets the four digit code on the lock, George sends an alert signal to Ali. *"If I send Ali my distress signal, he'll bust in here with guns blazing."*

Kruchenko opens the locker, George looks-in and does a double-take.

"Wow—I knew you had plenty of casino tokens, but not a trunk full!" "My friend Boris, these are casino tokens!"

"Yes, Felipe. And I have plenty more! Now I share my secret with you."

"Secret?"

"I am a blackjack expert. For many years, I kept winning in Las Vegas until one pit boss recognized me. He called security, they took me to the manager, they took my picture and told me I'm no longer welcome in Las Vegas. Felipe, I can teach you to win."

"I would like that. But is what you do legal?"

"Yes. Absolutely! I never cheat the casinos or they would have me killed."

"How long does it take to learn your system?"

"You must work with me eight hours every day, five days a week, for at least six months. In our free time, we will play serious bridge and get some exercise. Good?"

"It sounds good. But I'll only do it with one condition."

"What condition is that?"

"Rosita said you have a big problem to solve and Rimma says what you plan is dangerous. I want to help you, my friend."

"I must decide what I should do. We'll talk about it later. How soon you can start as my student?"

"I have no job and must wait until the estate is final before I get the money."

"No need for us to wait. I have plenty money and will finance you until you start to win in Vegas. Then you pay me back."

George pulls out his Caesar's token and kisses it.

"This is my lucky charm."

"Good. First, George, we need to make a trip to Las Vegas to exchange tokens for cash."

As Kruchenko closes his locker, George rubs the token.

"And I thought he was gay. Sorry about that, Boris!"

A few minutes later, Katerina and Rosita return. George helps them unload a trunk full of groceries, then asks, "Katerina, did you visit Rimma at the clinic this morning?"

"Yes. She said she'll be home early today."

Rosita looks at George and raises her eyebrows suggestively.

"She thinks you're very simpatico, George."

"The feeling is mutual, Rosita. I'm sorry, but I can't be here this afternoon to see her."

"Yes," interrupts Kruchenko, "Felipe will go home to pack. Tomorrow we will fly to Las Vegas."

Katerina rushes out of the room. She returns five minutes later. "I called Rimma. She'll be home in one hour to lunch with us."

George agrees to stay, wondering, *"What could Rimma have on her mind?"*

Immediately following dessert, Rimma invites George for a walk on the beach. They walk north towards the bull ring.

"Felipe, I must talk with you about Uncle Boris before you go to Vegas."

"It must be important, Rimma."

"Yes, and you must never tell Uncle Boris I told you. Many years ago, my mother was working in the Russian Embassy and Rosita was with the Cuban Embassy in Mexico City. They met and have been good friends ever since. At the time, Rosita was dating Manuel."

"So, why is Boris going after Manuel?"

"According to my mother, a man named Daniel Hill told Manuel to get Rosita to arrange a meeting between Lee Harvey Oswald and a Russian diplomat."

George acts surprised. "Oswald? You mean the one who shot President Kennedy?"

"Yes. Manuel knew that Rosita and Mother were good friends. He also knew that Uncle Boris had just entered Mexico and was looking for a job. Manuel made up the story that he was working undercover for the Mexican authorities and needed to set up Oswald, a suspected spy, for a sting operation, by having him meet someone he believed to be a Russian diplomat. Manuel would introduce Oswald to the diplomat and the diplomat would introduce Oswald to a man named Carlo."

"And Boris agreed?"

"No! My mother told Uncle Boris not to get involved."

"So, I don't understand. What happened?"

"That's when Manuel started to take advantage of Uncle Boris's vulnerability. He was a poor man from Russia, after all. He wined and dined him, promised a ten thousand dollar fee plus continued profitable undercover work. Then he introduced Uncle Boris to drugs and supplied him until he was hooked."

"Now I understand. Hooked on drugs, Boris agreed to introduce Oswald to Carlo. Oswald got shot by Jack Ruby. Now Boris feels guilty for Oswald's murder and wants to kill Manuel-correct?"

"Yes, that's certainly part of it, plus the drugs. After that, we lost contact with Uncle Boris. Then Manuel and a man named Jose would come here about once a year to give us money from my uncle. They said he was still working undercover. Manuel came one day and told Rosita that Uncle Boris was killed during a drug raid in Columbia. He has not been here in over five years."

"Did your uncle talk to you about that?"

"Yes, he told us they were using him for drug deals in Mexico, Las Vegas and Tucson until he got cured. I believe he cured himself. Then he decided to pretend he was still under Manuel's influence and shuttled between Tucson and Las Vegas for several years, gambling and running drugs for Manuel and Jose. We don't know much about Jose, except that he's very intelligent. Rosita knows Manuel very well and says he's a killer. We hate him."

"Don't worry, Rimma. I'll help Boris get Manuel. You're all my family now."

"It's beginning to add up and confirms Dad's theory."

"Please, Felipe. You must promise. You must keep all this secret."

He puts his arm tightly around her shoulders.

"Nothing will happen to Uncle Boris. I promise, Rimma."

"Why are you going to Las Vegas?"

"Boris said he has business there, but it's not with Manuel. He asked me to go to help."

Rimma stops and leans her head on George's shoulder.

"You're a very special person to all of us. I don't want anything to happen to you. Be careful."

Again, George has to restrain himself from taking this girl in his arms as they walk back to the house. He bids farewell to the ladies, agrees to meet Kruchenko at the airport the next morning and returns to his apartment. Ali and his agent remain to monitor the house in La Puerta for signs of Manuel. That night, George calls his father and briefs him on Kruchenko's secret.

"That figures. It's pretty much what we thought." states Tony. "It explains the photos we saw of him with the casino guards and with Manuel and Oswald. So, he, too, was a patsy! They used everyone they could for their own dirty tricks. Jamshid and I are coming to Vegas. We'll meet Mehdi and two other agents in my Safe House in twenty four hours. Good luck, son. I love you."

THURSDAY, NOVEMBER 22, 1990, LAS VEGAS, NEVADA

Kruchenko and George take a taxi from McCarren field to the Tropicana Casino.

"When and where you will exchange tokens for cash?" asks George.

"We will wait for the weekend when it will be busy. It's not smart to exchange them all in one place. We exchange some here, some at Caesar's Palace, more at Circus Circus and Palace Station. Then we hit the downtown casinos. For the next two days I'll show you around the casinos. We will act like other tourists and watch some blackjack tables, visit Hoover Dam, see some shows, eat good food and relax. During weekend we exchange tokens and go home with twenty-four thousand dollars."

"Sounds like a good plan..."

From the parking lot, after lunch, George calls the Safe House by radio. The agent on duty advises that Tony and others will arrive in the morning. George tells the agent he and Kruchenko are at the Tropicana, provides their room numbers, their general plans and returns to his room for the night.

Kruchenko and George stick to their simple game plan and return to San Diego Sunday night, resulting in Tony's trip to Las Vegas to be expensive and a waste of time. George, in his beat up van, drives Kruchenko back to the international border into Tijuana, then returns to his apartment.

Tony and his entourage remain in the Safe House waiting for George's call. They all agree that Kruchenko is free of drugs, smokes excessively, enjoys his vodka and treats George as a son. As they lounge in the living room waiting for George's call, Tony lights a fresh cigar and asks for a cappuccino refill.

"I tell you, my George is doing a masterful job. He really has the Russian believing he's a poor hippy, bridge playing, car mechanic from Puerto Rico."

"Yes, Rais," agrees Jamshid, "and his Spanish accent is so convincing."

"It'll be interesting to see Kruchenko's reaction when he learns the truth about George."

At midnight, a phone call from George interrupts the conversation.

"Hello, Dad. Kruchenko is coming to my place tomorrow to start me on his card system. And I have some good news for you. Don't transfer any more money to my account. He insists on paying all, I mean all, my expenses."

"Well, George, that's good news because this operation is breaking me - and fast."

"Hang tight, Dad. I think we're getting close to the end. Relax and do something about your aneurysm."

"I will. After we get Manuel and Jose."

"Look here, Dad. It'll be months before Manuel comes to Mexico. In the meantime, Kruchenko will be at my place, and with me constantly. So, please Dad, take a break and relax with Carmen."

THURSDAY, DECEMBER 6, 1990, NEW YORK

Rashid has just arrived from Bolivia. He is being briefed by Tony, Dr. Monti and Jamshid in Tony's office.

"Rashid, we're sending you and Jahangir two more agents, providing you with new identity documents and an impressive mining portfolio. Dr. Monti and Judy will work on your disguise."

"How I wish I could have killed Manuel at Ascotan. But, as you know, I wasn't armed. The next time we meet I will kill him!"

"Tracking him down will be difficult and dangerous," warns Dr. Monti.

"If he shows up in Mexico," advises Tony, "we're confident Kruchenko will lead us to him."

Judy returns to the conference table with Tony's fresh cappuccino. "Send me to Bolivia with Rashid. I want a piece of Manuel for what he did to Peter!"

Tony lights a fresh cigar and looks at Judy, preparing his reply. Dr. Monti, the consummate diplomat, intercedes.

"Judy, you're too valuable here in our communications network. We couldn't get along without you."

"I promise you, Judy," assures Rashid, "When I kill Manuel, one of the bullets will be yours."

Tony takes George's advice and makes arrangements to be with Carmen for Christmas. Before leaving for Mexico he advises Dr. Monti that he and Jamshid will travel to Chile for the first anniversary of the Ascotan ambush.

TUESDAY, DECEMBER 18, 1990

In his field office, Coloso, Chile, Nunzio Addabbo receives a FAX from Tony.

"Nunzio, I'll be in Hotel Carrera on the second of January Have considerable data for you."

Addabbo's port facility project loads the first ship with copper concentrate on December 28, signaling the end of his contract. He removes all evidence of the Montico security system and bugs from his apartment and attends a typical Chilean 'despedida' (farewell dinner).

The next day he and his wife fly to Santiago. They visit friends, take a two day rest in Viña Del Mar and meet Tony, Carmen and Jamshid on January second. Carmen's arrival with Tony is a pleasant surprise. Tony provides Nunzio additional data for the exposé and reluctantly cancels his visit to last year's ambush site when Nunzio warns him about the serious health risk at high altitudes for anyone with a heart problem. Carmen is pleased with the warning.

"I try to keep him healthy, Nunzio, but it is difficult to keep him reined in"

During one of Tony's briefing sessions, Nunzio asks about the cost of the effort.

"Have you kept a record or estimated how much you've spent on Capture Team activities?"

"Several million dollars more than I had in the bank. Carmen insisted on financing our efforts until the last two assassins are eliminated. Then, by God, I'll change my identity, marry Carmen, settle down and have some fun. I need a normal life!"

"I certainly agree with that. Have you decided where you'll settle?"

"We have several prime locations in mind. But you can be certain it won't be the U.S."

"Why's that, Tony? I know you're a loyal American."

"When this story breaks, Nunz, every Tom, Dick and Harry will be looking for me. I'd never get any peace from the reporters, paparazzi and government agents on my ass. There will be no end of questions. When you finish the book about this, and it's published, you may be harassed, too."

"What about George and Frank? (Dr. Monti)"

"They'll also change identities and relocate. Jamshid will always know how to reach us."

They remain with the Addabbo's and enjoy sight-seeing, dining and playing bridge. On January fourth, Tony insists on dining at La Pizza Nostra, where, on May 3, 1985, Nunzio and Dr. Steiner overheard the planned hit on him. Tony, Carmen and Jamshid leave Chile on January fifth and return to Mexico City. Tony and Jamshid return to New York on January fifteenth.

Before leaving Chile, Nunzio returns the weapons and Montico surveillance gear to Shahen, Tony's Santiago agent, who reports that, since the ambush, there has been no activity at the La Nueva Esperanza sulfur mine and no signs of Manuel or Jose.

THURSDAY, JANUARY 17, 1991, NEW YORK

At Tony's A-Tec office, Judy receives a radio alert from Rashid in Bolivia. She rotates the protected roof-top split-paraboloid antenna to an azimuth of 170 degrees, obtaining maximum signal strength and listens to the coded message.

Fifteen minutes later she interrupts a meeting between Tony and Dr. Monti.

"Mr. Berlotti, Rashid reports that Jahangir learned the location of Manuel's crashed helicopter and that they are on their way to the crash site. They will be reporting back in two days."

"Let's hope," says Dr. Monti, "that they find Manuel's body!"

Tony finishes his cappuccino and lights a fresh cigar.

"I'll give you odds, Frank, that the bastard is still alive."

Judy, always well mannered in the presence of Tony and Dr. Monti, flies into a rage.

"I hope they find the miserable son-of-a-bitch in a thousand pieces!"

"Good girl," praises Tony. "Vent that frustration. And, Judy, another cappuccino, please?"

Meanwhile, in Chula Vista, California, Kruchenko is bunked at George's apartment, teaching his protégé the fine points of making money at blackjack.

"You're learning fast," states Kruchenko. "You have natural card sense and are good with the odds."

George remains polite and respectful, always agreeing with the Russian and never showing any disappointment when Kruchenko refuses to answer questions about Manuel.

Every Tuesday and Saturday, Kruchenko tells George he has private business in Tijuana and insists on traveling there alone. George always bids him a safe trip and alerts Ali that the Russian is coming.

Kruchenko's business is never in Tijuana. He always drives directly to the La Puerta house hoping to find Manuel. Before returning to Chula Vista, he stops to visit Katerina, Rosita and Rimma, bringing food and money. Rimma invariably begs him for news of Felipe.

"Uncle Boris, I like Felipe so much. Please bring him on your next visit."

Two days later, Judy receives Rashid's report on Manuel. She paces the floor in an angry mood, makes a cappuccino for Tony and enters his office.

"Here! You'd better drink this before I hand you Rashid's message."

Dr. Monti looks at Judy, then gives Tony a nod, "You were right. Manuel's alive."

The report is as follows.

"We found traces of heroin in the aft section of the wreckage, indicating that Manuel, and possibly Jose, removed the heroin supply from Patalani. There was no personal clothing and it appears it was a minimum impact crash, reinforcing the argument that Manuel is alive. Jahangir is on his way to Patalani to confirm the heroin removal. We suspect the heroin is now at their Oruro operation which has been retrofitted to resemble a sulfur refinery. More info in two days."

Tony puffs cigar smoke at the report and cracks his knuckles.

"Don't worry, Judy. We'll get the miserable son-of-a-bitch."

"I think," states Dr. Monti, "we'd better advise Silver Fox that Manuel is alive."

Three days later, Rashid confirms.

"All heroin at Patalani was removed. Also, Jahangir cracked his left ulna when his jeep fell off the jack while he was changing a tire. He'll be OK."

Tony calls Addabbo on March fifteenth.

"Hello, Nunzio. How's everything going?"

"Not so good, Tony. Teri has suddenly gotten weak and lost her appetite. Preliminary tests show she's anemic. There are more tests scheduled for next week. Meanwhile, the book is on the back burner."

"I'm sorry about Teri, Nunz. But don't worry, viejo (old man). You don't have a timetable. Keep me posted and let me know if there's anything I can do."

By mid June, Kruchenko congratulates George.

"Felipe, you're ready. You play the system better than me and are ready for Las Vegas. First, how about we spend a few days in Rosarita?"

The idea of spending some time with Rimma certainly appeals to George. Before packing and leaving Chula Vista, Kruchenko surprises George with a last minute instruction.

"Felipe, now you must cut your hair, shave off the beard and wear tourist clothes. You must not look like a hippy in Las Vegas. Hippies stand out in a crowd. You must look and act like any other regular tourist."

George is delighted. *"I gotta' hand it to him—this Russian thinks of everything."*

He complies with Kruchenko's order and twenty four hours later, looking like a 'normal person', gets a thumbs up and another surprise from the now very friendly Russian.

"Very good! And, Felipe, Rimma will like you more this way."

"Are you sure?"

"Very sure. She tell me you handsome and smart and want to know you better."

"Thank you, Boris. Shall we go?"

En route to Rosarita, Kruchenko reveals the practical-joker side of his personality by betting which of the ladies would be first to identify George.

"I think Rosita will be first."

"I think," guesses George, "Rimma will be first."

They arrive and ring Rosita's doorbell at 9 P.M. Rosita barely opens the chained door and sees only George, as Kruchenko is hiding on the side of the house. She looks him over.

"Yes, Sir. What can I do for you?"

"I'm looking for Rimma, please?"

"Rimma? Does Rimma know you?"

"Yes."

"What's your name?"

George puts his index finger to his lips "Shhhh, Rosita. Don't you recognize me? I am Felipe!"

Rosita puts her hands on hips and shakes her head in disbelief as she takes a closer look.

She knows she's been fooled when Kruchenko appears behind George.

"Wait," she grins with a whisper, "I'll get Rimma."

"I was wrong," whispers Kruchenko, hiding again.

Rimma appears. "Yes? You asked to see me?"

"Yes" George is trying desperately to manage the right accent. *"I can't speak with Felipe's accent or she'll recognize it and I can't speak good English or it'll blow my cover."*

Rimma continues looking at George. "I don't know you. What do you want?"

He gives her his George Berlotti smile and whispers, "Loro loco."

Hearing "Crazy parrot" makes her scream with joy. She unchains the door and bear hugs Felipe, kissing him on the cheek as Kruchenko appears, smiling.

"We both lose, Felipe. Rimma didn't recognize you either."

And neither does Katerina. When George appears in the kitchen, Katerina is drying dishes. She looks at George, then asks Kruchenko.

"Who is your friend, Boris?"

As time passes, the ladies agree that the relationship between Rimma and George is serious. "Your daughter," concludes Rosita, "is falling in love with Felipe."

"I know. I like him very much but we know so little about him, just that Boris says he a good person. I'd certainly like to know something about his family."

George, meanwhile, is passionately dedicated to completing his father's mission as quickly as possible but is struggling with his stressful moral dilemma.

"Rimma is the first woman I could commit to for a lifetime. I'm crazy about her. But I can't let my feelings for her interfere with nailing the last two assassins. I can't tell her the truth...not yet."

Before leaving for Las Vegas, George promises to take Rimma to Disneyland for a short vacation before the end of the year. Katerina's objection to Rimma traveling alone with George is unanimously overruled. George, still completely dedicated to the family mission, promises Katerina that Rimma will have her own room.

With Kruchenko's blackjack system, strict money management and proper targeting of casinos, George is now solvent, no longer a financial drain on his father. George is proving to be a master of the game, his winnings averaging four to five thousand dollars per night. Kruchenko, in disguise and always in George's view, provides the signal to leave the table or casino. Unknown to Kruchenko, two of Tony's agents are always nearby in radio contact with George.

JULY 4, 1991

Except for George's good news, 1991 does not go smoothly. On the fourth, Dr. Monti suffers another heart attack, followed at the end of July with Tony having another heart attack. Early in September, Addabbo reports that his wife, Teri, has had bone marrow tests while hospitalized in nine different hospitals from UCSF in Northern California to Scripts Clinic in the South. The test results are the same. She is suffering from severe myelodysplastic syndrome and requires frequent blood transfusions. Finally, in late September, Ali develops a case of amoebic dysentery from eating contaminated shrimp.

NOVEMBER 15, 1991

Still waiting for news regarding the appearance of Manuel and/or Jose, Tony and Dr. Monti agree to visit Carmen at her Manzanilla hacienda. Hal and Alice Brooks join Carmen, Tony and Dr. Monti for the Christmas week and enjoy many rounds of bridge and private dining. They all travel to the Brooks' lake house at Lake Chapala for the New Year celebration.

Keeping his promise, George takes Rimma to Disneyland December twentieth for eight days. Katerina is pleased to hear they have separate rooms, but the chemistry between them is not conducive to a platonic relationship and George fights desperately to remain in control of the situation.

"You don't love me?" asks Rimma.

"I do love you, Rimma. Honest! But, besides getting on my feet financially, I need time for something very important. I can't explain so please believe me."

Gracefully, Rimma doesn't pressure George. "It's Okay, Felipe. I can wait."

Her patience endears her even more to George.

CHAPTER 33

SEVEN DOWN - TWO TO GO

JANUARY 1992

The year does not start well for Tony and his Capture Team. On the seventh, Dr. Monti, his life long and most trusted friend, suffers another heart attack and dies. Feeling guilty for allowing Dr. Monti to devote full time on Capture Team activities, Tony becomes depressed. Judy, who loved Dr. Monti like a father, promises Tony she will not abandon him until the last two assassins are eliminated. Dr. Asti, a consummate diagnostician and Tony's physician for many years, orders him to spend some time with Carmen, rest, address his aneurism, stop smoking, reduce his cappuccino intake and start on a new depression medication. Tony refuses medication, promises he'll visit Carmen, will take care of the aneurism after the last two assassins are eliminated.

"But I'll never give up my fine cigars and cappuccino!"

Josh, per Dr. Monti's will, begins the liquidation of all Montico assets. When that is complete he will devote full time working with Tony, Judy and security agents at A-Tec in New York.

As Tony prepares to leave to see Carmen on January eighteenth, Nunzio Addabbo calls him with additional bad news.

"Tony, I hate to add to your stress, but I know you would want to know...Teri died yesterday."

There is a silence, then, "Nunzio, I'm so sorry. Christ, I'm losing all my friends. What can I do?"

"Nothing, Tony. And don't cancel your trip to visit Carmen. I'll call you when I get a chance."

With no signs of Manuel and Jose, no activity at the Oruro heroin plant and Kruchenko no longer a threat to George, Tony remains in Manzanillo with Carmen until the first week in June. He arrives in New York no longer depressed, looking fit and rested. His mind-set now is that of an angry God preparing to engage the devil in battle. Judy is first victim of his wrath when he discovers the cappuccino machine and large cigar humidor are missing.

"Judy! I don't care what Dr. Asti told you - don't ever get rid of our cappuccino machine and my humidor again!"

Judy looks desolate.

"I'm sorry, Mr. Berlotti, I didn't get rid of them. I simply hid them."

"I don't care! If I don't have a cappuccino and fresh Churchills and Macanudos (cigars) on my desk within fifteen minutes, I'll,...I'll..." *"Do what? I' could never fire her."*

"Please, Mr. Berlotti, don't blame Dr. Asti. It was my idea. I did it for you."

"Thank you, Judy." Chagrined at his display of bad temper, Tony looks at his watch and grins. "Now you have fourteen minutes."

Ten minutes later, with Jamshid and Josh at his desk, Tony leans back in his high-back executive chair, raises both arms in the air and takes a long deep breath as the aroma of fresh cappuccino permeates his office. Judy appears with Tony's favorite drink, followed by an agent carrying the portable humidor. Tony clips the end off a Macanudo, lights it, then raises the cappuccino in a toast.

"Ahhhh - now this is living. I'd die without these."

"Sir," cautions Josh, "those could kill you, too."

"Is this another conspiracy? Or what? Any more enemies I don't need!"

Jamshid gives Josh a "Don't press the issue" nod.

The phone interrupts them.

"Mr. Berlotti," signals Judy, "it's Dr. Asti."

"Tony. How was your long vacation? Have you changed your mind about my suggestions?"

"Great vacation. Now I'm ready to go full throttle for the last two assassins."

"Look, Tony, with the major conspirators gone, Manuel and Jose are probably in a financial bind and no longer a threat to you. Let it go and start enjoying life again. Your body can't take running full throttle in the fast lane much longer."

"Guy, Guy. You worry too much.

"I have good reasons to worry: your high blood pressure, high cholesterol, sacculated aneurysm, emphysema, dyspnea and, yes, acute tunnel vision. I'm your friend and I shouldn't worry?"

"Guy, you're forgetting something. These sons-of-bitches killed my wife and daughters, they murdered Peter Monti, killed my husband and wife team. And remember, they framed you. They have me set up for assassination, tried to assassinate my pal Addabbo, made patsies of Kruchenko, Oswald and Ruby, assassinated our President and ruined my life. And I should let go?"

There is a long silence. "Okay, Tony. You win. What can I do to help?"

"Thanks, Guy. You're a fine doctor and good friend. I'll call if we need you."

George continues netting an average of sixty thousand dollars a month in Vegas. He and Kruchenko visit the ladies in Rosarita every Monday, always bringing a car load of food and gifts. On one of the visits, George surprises Rimma with a new Tycos sphygmomanometer for her clinic and a companion for her "loro loco". On another occasion, Kruchenko promises to move the ladies into a new house after he settles with Manuel. He drives to the La Puerta house at least once a week and never discusses Manuel with George.

JULY, 1992

During the last week in July, Rashid reports to Jamshid that, based on several conversations with one of the 'friendly' Oruro plant guards, Jose came to the plant in disguise and spent three days there working secretly on electronic equipment. According to the guard, the decoy sulfur refinery is not operating due to lack of funds and Jose is evading local police. He left the facility with several bags of heroin. The guard stated that probably Jose and Manuel are either in Panama, Cuba or the Dominican Republic.

AUGUST, 1992

Tony and Nunzio have several conversations regarding the Capture Team and conspiracy. "Nunzio, I'm going to Bolivia soon to supervise a concentrated search for Manuel and Jose and set some traps. Then I'm headed for Chile. I told George to keep you informed on his progress with Kruchenko. Meanwhile, your progress on the book looks good."

"Now, Tony. Please listen to me. You're not 30 years old any more, you've got serious medical problems and high altitudes should not be on your itinerary."

"You been talkin' to Guy, right?"

"Of course. He gave me your medical record. I'm supposed to know everything about you, remember?"

"Okay, I'll take it easy. Meanwhile, I told George to keep you informed on his progress with Kruchenko. I'll FAX you or use the 600 ohm line from Chile. I may need some new contacts."

"I'll Federal Express you my latest list of important names in Chile, including their home numbers. You may find you need legal, medical, mining, military, investigative and other government help. I'll also throw in some good bridge players and who to contact at the aero club."

"Thanks, Nunz. But forget the aero club. Guy grounded me. I can't pass a flight physical."

"I know, but if you want to fly in Chile, call my aero club buddy. Good luck, viejo."

WEDNESDAY, OCTOBER 14, 1992

Nunzio Addabbo receives a call from George.

"Mr. Addabbo, I haven't heard from Dad in four days. Do you know anything?"

"No, George. But I feel sure he's still in Chile. When we talked last week he said he was going to visit Dr. Rojas and present her with a new GPS system so she won't get lost any more on her field trips in the high desert. But I know you're worried. Where are you?"

"I'm in Vegas with Kruchenko, still winning at the tables. Dad usually calls me three or four times a week and I'm afraid he may have suffered another attack and is keeping it from us."

"I don't think so, George. Jamshid would notify you." Then trying to change the subject, "By the way, I know you're winning about four grand a day, but what's you're biggest loss?"

"Believe it or not, my worst day has been break-even."

"Good boy! So tell me, what's your disguise today?"

"I'm a rich Poncho Villa type miner from San Luis Potosi. Next week I'll be an Italian from Naples."

"What's going on with Kruchenko?"

"He continues to make at least one trip a week to La Puerta in search of Manuel. We play afternoon bridge twice a week. He never mentions Manuel, he still chain smokes and always has a couple of vodkas with his meals. He's a loner but really a nice guy."

"Are you splitting your winnings with him?"

"He won't have it. All he wanted was reimbursement for setting me up and I did that the first week of play. Now I pay all our expenses and still bank fifteen grand a week."

"That's great! He sounds like a good guy. What about your love life. Still seeing Rimma?"

"Absolutely! I'm really serious about her. She has all the qualities I like in a woman. And she tells me everything."

"What has she told you about Kruchenko?"

"He's definitely planning to kill Manuel."

"George, a bit of advice. Limit your association with him to bridge and blackjack. Don't even think about becoming an accomplice to murder."

"Now you sound like my father."

"That's right. You're all he has left so don't screw things up. Let him call the shots."

" I'm cool, Mr. Addabbo. I'm still focused and I'm still a lawyer."

"Good. I know you know your way around, George. Just keep it that way and don't worry about Tony. I'm sure he's fine."

DECEMBER 20, 1992

Tony decides to relax and spend Christmas with Carmen in Manzanillo. He arrives at her hacienda to a pleasant surprise. Four hours earlier, Rashid had sent the following FAX:

"Manuel and Jose are in the Dominican Republic. Manuel rented a home in the Puerto Plata area where he is still recuperating from his helicopter crash. According to the Oruro plant guard, they plan to return to Bolivia in February to activate the plant. We're ready at this end."

JANUARY 4, 1993, NEW YORK

Tony returns to his New York office to be briefed on his engineering projects. Judy is still depressed over Dr. Monti's death. He had treated her like the daughter he never had. And she still wants to be vindicated for the murder of Peter, her husband. She seals her allegiance to the Capture Team by giving Tony her new year's resolution.

"Mr. Berlotti, I've decided to delay my marriage to David until we get justice. I'll be here for you twenty-four hours a day."

On February fourth, as Tony prepares to return to Bolivia, Addabbo receives a call from him.

"Nunzio, I just got word there's a Chilean company looking to finance a Bioniq project. I was told you have data on that. Is it true? And what's Bioniq?"

"What company?"

"Lican Ray Mining Corp."

"Tony, amigo mio (my friend), do a fast one-eighty and don't look back."

"Problems?"

"Big time. Lican Ray is a paper company. No assets, no technology, no organization - zip -nada (nothing). It's a one man operation and the inventor of Bioniq is a German chemist who happens to be a friend of mine. He won't deal with Lican Ray."

"Okay. But what's Bioniq?"

"Bioniq is the registered trademark for a natural bio-organic, high-energy mineral plant food, under Chilean patent. I prepared a feasibility study for the inventor a few years ago and can send you a copy. The capital cost at that time was around five to five and a half million dollars."

"Good rate of return?"

"I think it was around seven million a year with a capital payback in two."

"I'm on my way to Bolivia but will stop and visit George in Vegas first, then I'll come to your place in a couple of days for that study and bring you up to date on things. Okay?"

"Sure. I'll look forward to seeing you. And remind George not to get trapped between Kruchenko and Manuel."

"He told me you lectured him on that subject. George may appear impulsive and unconventional at times, but he's still very focused on our mission and never forgets he's a lawyer."

"That's good. I guess I just can't help feeling a bit fatherly toward him. You know how that goes, once a father, always a father. I'll have more manuscript pages for your review when you get here."

FEBRUARY 8, 1993

Tony meets Nunzio in California. They discuss the Bioniq project, Nunzio gives Tony an introduction letter, photo and home number of the German chemist and Tony briefs Nunzio on latest developments and Capture Team plans. Nunzio gives Tony a worried look.

"Tony, you better slow down. You look like hell! How many pounds have you lost?"

"You sound like Dr. Asti. Look, I'm down to 200, my fighting weight. There's no way I'm gonna' slow down until I get Manuel and Jose! Nunz, you of all people know how we Italians are... "

Nunzio has known Tony since 1953 and accepts the fact that you can't argue with an angry pit-bull on attack. And he knows he would feel the same way.

Manuel and Jose do not arrive in Oruro as expected. According to Rashid, the Oruro plant guard figures they're probably in Panama or Columbia working out a heroin deal. Also, the guard is sure that local police need to be bribed before operations can resume at Jose's Oruro operation. Frustrated, Tony returns to Las Vegas to prepare Kruchenko for Manuel. When the Russian departs for his usual solo trip to La Puerta, Tony meets his son.

"George, we've somehow got to maneuver you into a position where Kruchenko considers it necessary to have your help to get to Manuel."

"He doesn't want me involved and I can't tip my hand that I know Manuel."

Tony, George and Jamshid agree that George needs to use Rimma.

"Here's the plan," states Tony. "When Manuel goes to the La Puerta house, Ali will notify George. George notifies Rimma that Manuel is there and not alone."

"Hold it." Interrupts George. "How do I convince her I know Manuel is there and how does she explain to her uncle that he's there?"

"Patience, George. Let me finish. Tell her that on one occasion you were concerned about Kruchenko's safety and followed him to the La Puerta house and saw him knocking on the door. Then tell her you saw Manuel in Tijuana last week when you were buying groceries and recognized him from the photo of him with Rosita."

Jamshid expands on Tony's argument. "You must convince Rimma she needs to lie to her Uncle. She must tell him that Manuel called saying he is in La Puerta and needs to meet with him - Kruchenko - as soon as possible."

Tony picks up after Jamshid. "It should be easy to convince her that she needs to persuade her uncle it's too dangerous to go alone; that he needs you as back-up."

"What's our plan," asks George, "if Manuel stops first at the Rosarita house?"

"You've got to convince Rimma to have her mother and Rosita lie as well, for Kruchenko's sake. They should tell Manuel that they haven't heard from Boris in over two years. If he doesn't leave immediately, they should tell him that Rosita is now dating a police officer who stops by every day and it wouldn't be prudent for him to be seen there. When he leaves, they should call Rimma immediately."

"I know Rimma. She'll do it because she loves her Uncle and trusts me!" George reluctantly assures Tony and Jamshid. "If Kruchenko balks at my going with him I'll insist he can't go alone."

"Not a good idea, George. He may immobilize you and go, then we'd probably lose communications. If he balks, simply follow him. Agreed?"

"Agreed."

Two weeks later, George calls Tony in New York.

"Dad, the ladies agreed, but you know something? I feel guilty as hell about lying to Rimma."

"That's to your credit, George, but don't worry. You'll get your chance to tell her the truth. And when you do, she'll understand. Meanwhile, 'Felipe', stay focused."

APRIL 2, 1993

Nunzio receives a call from George.

"Mr. Addabbo, for the record, and I know you would want to know, Dad has had another heart attack. He refused angioplasty, refuses to have me go to New York to manage his day-to-day activities and he's increased his security force. He's more paranoid all the time and it isn't helping his health."

"George, I'm sorry about the news. Unfortunately, we both know his paranoia is justified. There still are the two assassins out there who are out to kill him, perhaps the rest of us, too."

"Dr. Asti tells me Dad won't follow his medical advice. You're his buddy. Maybe he'll listen to you. He desperately needs to slow down."

"George, I've known your father more than forty years. He'll agree with me - and then do his own thing as always. I'll try, but his best medicine right now is quality time with Carmen. Anything new with Kruchenko?"

"Only that he's frustrated and more and more agitated by Manuel's silence."

"I guess there's nothing you can do to hurry the situation. It's a waiting game. Keep me posted, George. And try not to worry about your father. He's one tough guy."

MAY 6, 1993, 11 PM, TROPICANA CASINO, LAS VEGAS

George, about two thousand dollars ahead at his second blackjack table, receives a "move now" nod from Kruchenko. He picks up his chips, moves to an empty blackjack table, then makes a serious mistake. He addresses the Latino dealer in Spanish. The dealer smiles and nods.

"Welcome back. I recognize your voice. You were here last week, right? And you were a big winner."

"Sorry, but you're mistaken. I wasn't here last week. Now deal - I'll play two hands."

The dealer complies and George immediately goes into a losing mode. Kruchenko's signal indicates that the dealer has alerted the pit boss. After losing five hundred dollars, George complains that the cards are "cold", picks up his chips, tips the dealer and walks away. Kruchenko and George believe he was photographed. Blackjack at the Tropicana is no longer an option and they decide to return to Rosarita for a few days. As George continues to win in Las Vegas he gives Rimma five hundred dollars a week for household expenses to be shared with Rosita and Katerina. Rosita gives George a key to the house.

"Felipe, you are like family. Nuestra casa es su casa." ("Our house is your house.")

During an afternoon drive south to Ensenada, Rimma, now very much in love with George, repeats all she knows about Kruchenko's involvement with Manuel, Dan Hill, Oswald, Carlo and Jose.

"Please," begs Rimma, "you must keep all this our secret."

"Rimma, my lips are sealed."

"They made Uncle Boris a patsy and junkie. Now, to get even, he's going to kill Manuel."

"Rimma, I'm going to help your Uncle. I can't tell you why, when or how but, please, just trust me."

"How could I not trust the man I love?"

"Thank you for trusting me. I will need your help, Rimma."

"I'll do whatever you ask."

"When this is all over, Rimma, I will have much to tell you, things that will surprise you, but for now, I just have to ask you to trust me completely."

MAY 15, 1993

Rashid reports that Manuel's cousin, from Cochabamba, visited the Oruro guard, advising he was to alert the local police that Jose and Manuel are expected soon with cash. Kruchenko, frustrated that Manuel has not appeared, decides to return to his abandoned Patagonia cabin, hoping to find Manuel. According to Ali, who followed him, the cabin remains empty and there are no signs that Manuel has been there. Since Kruchenko's condo phone was disconnected, Manuel would assume that the Russian received his message and had moved out.

In New York, Judy and Josh continue maintaining daily communications with Tony and other members of the Capture Team. Tony, feeling guilty that Carmen continues to finance his covert operation, decides to liquidate his engineering and management offices to repay Carmen and hire more agents for his Capture Team to pursue the remaining two assassins. Carmen not only refuses Tony's payback, but automatically increases her monthly deposit to his account by ten thousand dollars.

"My love, I want this nightmare over. I know you'll never rest or have any peace of mind until it's finished. I'll do anything to speed up the search for these killers. I want to have a chance to really live with you while there's still some time for us. You know I'll do anything I can to help you finish this..."

"I can never repay you, my dear. But, I promise you, when this is finally over, I'll give it all up. We'll be married and live 'happily ever after' – for whatever time there is left for us. God willing... "

CHAPTER 34

SETTING UP MANUEL

JUNE 2, 1993, MANZANILLO, MEXICO, CARMEN'S HACIENDA

Tony, still recuperating from his heart attack, receives word from Rashid that Jose and Manuel have returned to Oruro, made a police payoff and started to re-energize the retrofitted sulfur/heroin plant. Rashid's news is Tony's best medicine. Sensing imminent closure to an almost thirty year nightmare, his mood changes immediately from lethargic to euphoric.

"Carmen, you'll soon have your wish. We have the last two assassins in sight. I'm going to New York to set-up Manuel, then on to Bolivia."

"Take me with you. I really want to see them die so I can believe this is finally over."

"Not a chance. It's too dangerous. But start packing your bags, darling, for a long vacation."

The next afternoon, Tony arrives at his New York office with Jamshid. He alerts Ali to return to Tucson and directs him to send the following telegram from Kruchenko to Manuel:

"My friend, Manuel, I have large cash buyer with easy air access. Leaving Arizona soon and will wait in La Puerta to meet you."

Tony alerts George that Kruchenko also will receive a fake telegram from Manuel, to be delivered by Ali's agent to the Rosarita house. Before flying to Bolivia, Tony calls Addabbo.

"Nunzio, I'm off to Bolivia. We're zeroing-in on Manuel and Jose. I hope to get Kruchenko and Manuel together at La Puerta soon."

"Manuel is the sonofabitch that shot me off the rock pile in Coloso. What can I do to help you?"

"Just keep recording the facts as we give 'em to you. When we meet again we'll celebrate."

JUNE 8, 1993

Addabbo receives Tony's coded message.

"Manuel received Kruchenko's telegram and is flying to Mexico. Jose runs operations in Oruro. I'll call you from Tucson or San Diego."

When Tony calls from San Diego, Addabbo has a question.

"Do you have any agents watching the Patagonia cabin?"

"Yes, two. Manuel may go there first, thinking Kruchenko is still hooked. If he does, the agents will bury the bastard."

"Manuel and Jose may wonder how Kruchenko found out about the Oruro operation and suspect a double cross from him. Did Kruchenko know they had a heroin operation there? And how do you keep Manuel from killing Kruchenko?"

"We don't know if Kruchenko knows about the Oruro plant. That's why I'll have men protecting him from Manuel and Jose. According to George, Rimma told him Kruchenko never trusted Manuel and that Jose has always been the real brains of the hit-team."

"When will Kruchenko receive Manuel's telegram?"

"Day after tomorrow. That's when we're sure Rimma will be home."

"I'll be in New York in a couple of weeks for my fiftieth high school reunion and will be staying with my cousin Phily Monti, in Islip. You have the number. I recently completed Plate 1AB showing the 'hit-team' organization for your review and just started Plate 2AB of Dealey Plaza. So long."

JUNE 10. 1993, 8 PM

The official looking telegram from Manuel to Kruchenko is delivered to the Rosarita house. Rimma is unaware of the lure but sure to find Kruchenko in his hotel room. She calls him at eight the next morning.

"Uncle Boris. A telegram was delivered for you here last night."

"Read it for me, Rimma."

She opens the envelope.

"It's in Spanish and it's from Manuel. 'Dear Boris, sorry for the long delay. I will travel to Mexico soon and will come directly to La Puerta.   Come and we will talk business.   Your friend, Manuel'."

"Thank you, Rimma.   And don't tell Felipe about the telegram. I will see you soon."

"Yes, Uncle Boris."

That night after a long blackjack session at Caesar's Palace, George notices that Kruchenko is not at his usual position. Thinking Boris might be in the men's room, he plays several more hands. A half hour later, George cashes-in and looks for the Russian.

"It's not like him to disappear while I'm playing. Maybe he got sick."

When Kruchenko does not appear in the nearest men's room, bar and restaurant, George goes to Kruchenko's room.

"Good thing we exchanged pass keys."

Kruchenko and his suitcases are gone.   George rushes to his room and receives a phone message to call Rimma. After a long delay in getting connected with Rosartita, Rimma answers the phone.

"Hello."

"Hello, Rimma, it's Felipe."

"Oh, Felipe, I wasn't supposed to tell you this, but Uncle Boris received a telegram from Manuel who wants to meet him in La Puerta. I'm afraid for my uncle and had to let you know. I'm sorry."

"That explains it. Boris is gone. He must be on his way there. I'll leave right away."

George catches the first morning flight to San Diego, drives to his apartment in Chula Vista, apprizes Tony of the situation, picks-up his weapons and drives to Rosarita. Two of Tony's agents park in sight of Rosita's house. Ali and another agent are in La Puerta, parked in view of Manuel's house. Although George has a house key, he elects to ring the doorbell, with weapon at the ready.

The chained door opens slightly. "Who is it?" asks Rimma, nervously.

"Felipe. Is everything OK?" His nod and smile signal 'all clear'.

When the door opens, George finds himself being embraced by the three ladies.

"Thank God you're here," whispers Rosita.

"Where's Boris?" asks George.

"Cousin Boris came and is already gone."

"Did he tell you where he's going?"

"No," explains Rimma. "He went to his room, changed clothes and left immediately with a suitcase. He also took his guns, because they're missing. We know he's gone out to kill Manuel."

"Yes," adds Rosita, "He's no match for Manuel. Manuel is a professional killer."

"Where does he expect to find Manuel?" asks George.

"No idea," replies a weeping Katerina.

Realizing the ladies are totally innocent in the conspiracy and not aware of Manuel's La Puerta house, George decides to tell the truth.

"Sit down, ladies. You need to hear this information and then follow my instructions."

George reveals his true identity, explains the basics of the conspiracy and why the Capture Team is after Manuel and Jose. The ladies sit wide eyed, mouths agape, momentarily stunned at what they are hearing.

"Felipe, I mean George," Rosita spreads her hands wide. "We had no idea."

Rimma hugs George.

"I had a really good feeling about you when we first met. You are here to save Uncle Boris. I do believe in destiny."

"What can we do?" asks Katerina.

George explains the role each must play if Boris or Manuel calls or arrives at the house. He provides Rimma with a mini Montico hand held transceiver and briefs her on its coded operation.

"Remember," concludes George, "we will have one or two of our agents nearby at all times, so don't panic or expose them." He hands the ladies a photo of Ali and the other agents. "These are our men who will always be in your area to protect you."

George spends a few moments on the patio alone with Rimma, assuring her of his love, then leaves for La Puerta to meet Ali, and hoping to find Kruchenko.

After three days of around the clock monitoring of the La Puerta house and Patagonia cabin, each wired to provide entry signals, but with no signs of Kruchenko and Manuel, George receives word from Tony.

"Manuel and Jose have just left Oruro without notice. I'm on my way to San Diego."

JUNE 15, 1993, CHULA VISTA, CALIFORNIA. GEORGE'S APARTMENT

Tony and Jamshid arrive at noon for a business lunch with George and Ali.

"We figure," begins Tony, "that Kruchenko may be in the La Puerta house waiting to kill Manuel. Here's our plan. You're going there in a real estate car driven by Ali. If Kruchenko answers the doorbell, you should look utterly shocked to see him. Explain you are looking for a rental to be closer to him and Rimma. If Manuel appears, Ali will eliminate him."

10 AM JUNE 17, 1993

George, in disguise, and Ali, arrive at the La Puerta house in a station wagon marked "Propriedades Gonzalez" (Gonzalez Properties) and park in the driveway. Two agents are parked at a safe distance but in view of the house. They ring the doorbell for two minutes, then pound hard on the front and rear doors. When no one responds to the knocks, Ali picks the lock and, with drawn weapon, enters the house followed by George. A search confirms that the house is not occupied.

It is well furnished with convincing photographic evidence that this is one of Manuel's hideouts. George sees a photo of Manuel and Rosita in earlier days, another of Manuel with Kruchenko, one showing Carlo in what looks like a Bolivian Ranger uniform, a photo of Dan Hill with Carlo, one with Hill and Sammy Shickarian, another of Katerina with Kruchenko and several with Jose, Carlo and the other Los Machos assassins. George photographs everything.

The only phone in the house is in the kitchen. On the wall above the phone is a list of the area codes and phones numbers of Carlo and Jose. The names of Dan Hill and Hank Palma are crossed off the list, indicating that Manuel and/or Jose may have been in the house recently.

"Bingo," whispers George, "Now we'll get some action." He quickly zooms-in and photographs the list.

The pantry is dusty but well stocked with canned foods, two cases of Bolivian Pisco, (grape brandy), two sawed-off shotguns, two 357 magnums and a modified AK-47, all loaded. Forty five minutes later, they bug the telephone, re-arm the house and depart.

At a strategy meeting the following day, Tony announces the next move.

"Finding those phone numbers was like finding oil and may open a few doors. I'll start calling them, representing myself as the attorney for the Carlo Perez estate, looking for his only beneficiaries-Manuel, Poncho, Gabriel, Pepe and Jose."

"How," asks legal eagle George, "will you explain how you know Carlo is dead and how you located the beneficiaries?"

"I'll say that Carlo contacted me at least once a year. In the event that I haven't seen or heard from him in three years, I should, according to the terms of his will, assume he is dead and contact the beneficiaries in his will."

"That's good, Dad. I'll draw up a will in Spanish for you to read to them if they ask."

JUNE 20, 1993, NEW YORK, TONY'S A-TEC OFFICE

Judy puts through the first call to Manuel's number in Bolivia. The lady that answers the phone explains she is the maid, that Manuel has gone to Mexico via the Dominican Republic, but she doesn't have a forwarding address, only a phone number.

The call to the Dominican Republic is answered by a man claiming to be the caretaker. He states that Manuel came for a few days rest, then left for Puerto Rico to seek medical treatment for the leg he injured in a helicopter crash.

After Judy advises Tony that the Puerto Rican phone number listed for Carlo, Jose and Manuel has been disconnected, she calls Mexico City. When a lady answers the phone, Judy transfers the call to Tony. Speaking in perfect Castilian Spanish, Tony introduces himself as Carlo's attorney. She, too, states she is the maid, Manuel is still in Puerto Rico and that she is preparing the apartment for his arrival soon. Tony promises to pay the maid a thousand dollar "finders fee" if she locates Manuel. All she is able to provide are the disconnected number in Puerto Rico and the La Puerta number.

Twenty four hours later, hoping that Manuel is still getting medical treatment in Puerto Rico, Tony and Jamshid arrive in San Juan and begin a systematic search of medical facilities for him.

After two sixteen hour days visiting or calling the major hospitals and physical therapy facilities in and around San Juan, Manuel cannot be located. Reasoning that if Manuel is still in

Puerto Rico and receiving private treatment, making it almost impossible to locate him, Tony and Jamshid return to New York on June twenty-third.

The next morning, Josh reports that Jahangir, in Oruro, has not seen Jose and Manuel, that the friendly Oruro guard claims he has not been paid in over two months and may walk away from the plant. Tony instructs Jamshid to have Rashid pay the guard double his regular salary to stay on the job and report all activities.

Judy reports that George has not seen or heard from Kruchenko and there are still no signs of Manuel or Jose.

FRIDAY, JUNE 25, 1993, LONG ISLAND

Nunzio Addabbo is attending his fiftieth high school reunion dinner at Porky and Glen's Restaurant on Long Island. At approximately ten, a waiter advises Nunzio that Mr. Berlotti is seated in the next room. Later, after bidding farewell to old classmates, Nunzio joins Tony and Jamshid at a corner table. Tony briefs Nunzio on latest developments and provides additional conspiracy notes. Nunzio outlines the status of the manuscript and hands Tony two computer disks of the first one hundred and fifty pages.

"Please understand, Tony, that this is just the first draft. The re-write, after your input, will correct spelling, punctuation, grammar and other changes you consider necessary. And I hope to polish the writing so that it's a real grabber, a very personal story of legitimate revenge."

"The only thing that bothers me now is the title, WE DELIVER. It sounds like a pizza commercial."

"You know, you're absolutely right," laughs Nunz. "The title and book jacket must hook the reader. What about *THE CONSPIRATORS ARE DEAD?*"

"That might work. But we can make that one of our last decisions."

The conversation is interrupted when Philip Monti arrives at the table.

Nunzio greets Philip with a thumbs up.

"Tony, Jamshid, meet my first cousin Phily Monti. I'm staying at his house in Islip. If you can squeeze it into your schedule, you're invited to graduation ceremonies in Islip Terrace tomorrow."

"Thanks for the invite," states Tony, "but I'm leaving for San Diego in the morning."

Since Philip isn't privy to any conspiracy details, Nunzio switches the conversation to baseball standings. Moments later, they shake hands and depart Porky and Glen's.

JUNE 26, 1993, NEW YORK, TONY'S A-TECH OFFICES

Next morning, before flying to San Diego, Tony meets with Judy and Josh at his office.

Judy is waiting with a smile.

"Good news, Mr. Berlotti. Janhagir reports that Jose has reappeared at the Oruro plant, paid the guards and stockpiled several tons of sulfur ore in the plant."

"Anything on Manuel?"

"Nothing. But Jahangir has taps on the plant phones, plus the guard we are paying allowed Jahangir to take interior photos of the plant while Jose was away."

"Did George call last night?"

"Yes. He said that when they last followed Kruchenko to La Puerta, our tailing agent stopped at the bottom of the dirt road to Manuel's house, waited momentarily, then continued up the road to the house. When he got there, Kruchenko's car was not in the carport."

"That agent," grumbles Jamshid, "will be replaced for failing to keep the Russian in sight!"

Tony lights a cigar, asks for a cappuccino and thinks as he begins packing his briefcase. *"Did Kruchenko already meet Manuel, kill him and run? Or did they meet and Manuel killed Kruchenko? If they met - where did they meet? If they haven't met, where is the Russian? His last notice was that Manuel was on his way to Mexico to meet him."*

Tony closes his briefcase with a snap and locks it.

"Come on, Jamshid. Let's go to the Patagonia cabin."

Twenty four hours later, Tony, Jamshid and another agent case the abandoned Patagonia cabin and determine that no one has entered since their last visit. They return to Tucson, fly to San Diego and meet George in Chula Vista. That night Tony calls Rashid in La Paz.

"We're preparing a telegram for you to deliver to Jose. It will identify us as lawyers for Carlo's estate, in search of five beneficiaries named, including Jose. We will ask his assistance in locating the other four and arrange a meeting to settle the large estate. Since Jose and Manuel are the only two remaining beneficiaries, coupled with the fact that they appear to be in a financial bind, our telegram should get a positive response."

JUNE 28, 1993

The next morning, feeling tired and guilty for failing to be with Carmen more often, Tony flies to Manzanillo to stay until word is received on Jose, Manuel or Kruchenko. Carmen is pleasantly surprised by Tony's visit, but deeply saddened by his looks. She wastes no time in contacting Hal Brooks.

"Hal, Tony looks exhausted and has lost a lot of weight. He needs to take his mind off work and relax. Why don't you and Alice fly down for a few days of bridge and recreation. Maybe he'll listen to you."

"Of course, Carmen. We'll be packed and on our way in a couple of hours."

George, meanwhile, remains in the Rosarita house with Rimma, Katarina and Rosita. Two agents remain parked near the house, while Ali and two other agents maintain surveillance of the La Puerta house.

SUNDAY, JULY 4, 1993, MANZANILLO

While relaxing at Carmen's hacienda, Tony receives a call from Judy in New York.

"Mr. Berlotti, Jose received our telegram. Rashid reports that Jose then contacted Manuel in Puerto Rico regarding Carlo's estate, but Manuel didn't buy it, explaining it could be a trap."

"Manuel has always been a suspicious bastard. But I clue you - he'll fall into our trap! What else did Rashid say?"

"Manuel is flying soon to Mexico City to meet Kruchenko for an important deal."

Jamshid, Tony's loyal and fearless bodyguard, known for his control and cool composure, surprises his boss with a temper flare-up.

"Rais, let me go to Mexico City. I want the honor and pleasure of killing him. It was my fault he escaped by helicopter at the La Esperanza sulfur mine ambush."

"Thanks, Jamshid.   Your constant loyalty continues to overwhelm me.   But I have a better idea.   We'll all kill the little Bolivian son-of-a-bitch!"

There are no longer any secrets between Tony, Carmen and the Brooks.   Carmen insists on offering additional money to increase the Capture Team staff. Hal promises to contact Mexican friends who can provide police protection.   Tony rejects the generous offers.

"Thanks, but we have enough money, manpower, firepower and technology now to end this nightmare soon. Then Carmen and I will fly into the wild blue yonder and enjoy a real life!"

The next day, Tony and Jamshid return to George's apartment in Chula Vista to organize Manuel's trap.   Two agents are dispatched to Mexico City to locate Manuel's apartment. Two agents return to the Patagonia cabin, Ali and two agents remain in La Puerta and George with two agents remains with the ladies in Rosarita. Tony and Jamshid remain at George's apartment.

Feeling re-energized, Tony decides to try to pass a third-class flight medical denied by Dr. Asti.   Given his present physical condition, he fails again. Now into his seventies, with over 6,000 hours of pilot-in-command, he decides it's time to let George, with 1,500 hours, sit in the left seat and take title to his aircraft at Montgomery Field, San Diego.

JULY 10, 1993

Tony receives a call from Rashid.

"Mr. Berlotti, I have good news and bad news."

"What's the bad news?"

"Jose installed a new security system at the Oruro plant. It will be some time before we figure how to by-pass it."

"That's no problem for you and Jahangir, but be very careful. What's the good news?"

"Jose called Manuel in Puerto Rico regarding Kruchenko and we have that number. Manuel told Jose he is leaving immediately to meet the Russian in La Puerta for a business deal."

"Now that's very good news. We may soon get two for the price of one! Keep Jose under a tight watch."

JULY 15, 1993, MEXICO CITY

The telegram is delivered to a maid in Manuel's apartment. She states that Manuel has not yet arrived but expected soon. When asked if Mr. Kruchenko has arrived or called, she doesn't recognize the name and claims no one has been there in many months. The agents are directed to watch the apartment until further notice.

Tony's assessment of Kruchenko's sudden disappearance can mean only one thing.

"He's hiding somewhere and plans to ambush Manuel on his own. But where can he be?"

CHAPTER 35

SUICIDE IN LA PUERTA

JULY 16, 1993, TIJUANA, MEXICO

Tony and Jamshid walk across the border into Tijuana and take a taxi into downtown.

They meet Rosita at La Costa restaurant for lunch, then drive to her house in Rosarita in her car, where George, Rimma and Katarina are waiting. Two agents are parked nearby in their surveillance motor home. George reports that there have been no phone calls, no activity at the La Puerta house and no arrivals at Manuel's Mexico City apartment. Given the recent developments, Tony requests that the Rosarita house be the command center. Rosita and Katerina agree without hesitation.

It is agreed that Tony will sleep in George's bed on the patio, George and Jamshid will rotate a night watch, taking Kruchenko's bed for rest. Rimma will answer all telephone calls and the two agents will rotate a night watch from the surveillance motor home in view of the house. Before retiring, Tony receives a call from Judy.

"Mr. Berlotti, Carmen called here because she didn't know where to reach you. She said she has sold the controlling shares in her silver operations and deposited five hundred thousand dollars in your Capture Team account - should you need it."

Tony, sudden tears in his eyes, shakes his head. "I can't believe the generosity of this woman. Thanks, Judy. I'll call her first thing in the morning."

The evening passes quietly without incident. George is asleep when the phone rings as Tony, Rosita, Katarina and Rimma are having breakfast. Rimma picks up the phone, speaking softly.

"Buenos dias."

The male voice sounds familiar. "Hola. Rosita?"

"No, soy Rimma. Manuel?" (No, I'm Rimma. Manuel?)

"Si. Que tal, linda?" (Yes. What's up, pretty one?")

Tony motions Rimma to keep talking.

Rimma acknowledges Tony's signal and continues.

"Que sopresa. Donde estas, Manuel?"(What a surprise. Where are you, Manuel?)

Manuel hesitates, "Estoy en la Distrita Federal." (I'm in Mexico City.)

Rimma asks if he expects to come to Rosarita for a visit soon. He hesitates again, stating yes, but first needs to speak with Boris.

Expecting this question, Rimma tells Manuel that Boris is due any moment and asks for his number so Boris can return his call.

As Tony smiles at the Montico phone decoder and gives Rimma a thumbs-up, Manuel tells her he will call back later and hangs up.

"He's at his La Puerta number! Quick, Rimma! Wake up George and give him the news. I'll have another cappuccino; then we're on our way. You ladies stay here with my two agents."

As George drinks a tall milk, Ali calls from La Puerta, confirming that the call came from the house. Then the unexpected happens as the Montico recorder picks up a call to the La Puerta house.

"Hello, Manuel?"

"Yes, Boris. Where are you, my friend?"

"I'm in Las Vegas and will leave immediately for La Puerta. I have a big business deal ready for you and Jose."

"Very good. I'm waiting for you, Boris. Adios."

The Kruchenko call is a surprise until the decoder displays the number.

"Oh, oh!" shouts Tony, "That's a number in La Puerta! Let's go! We don't want Kruchenko to beat us to Manuel."

As they speed towards La Puerta, they pick up Manuel's phone as it rings again. There is no answer.

"Damn!" shouts George, as he floorboards the car, "We've got to get there before he escapes again. And let's hope that there hasn't already been a fatal confrontation between Manuel and Kruchenko."

"No need to floor it, George," states Tony. "If he tries to leave, Ali will take him out."

George eases off ever so slightly. "So, how did he get into the house without Ali's knowledge?"

"No idea. But it's all academic now. He's in there and won't escape."

Ali, watching Manuel's house, calls Jamshid by radio. As planned, the conversation is in Farsi.

"Jamshid, Manuel did not answer Kruchenko's call. He may be preparing an ambush or escape. But don't worry, we have the place surrounded."

"Good. If he comes out - shoot him!"

As they drive up the dirt road to the house, George offers a comment.

"We have one thing in our favor. Kruchenko recently bought this car for Rimma. Manuel won't be able to identify it."

At about 200 yards from the house, Tony gives last minute instructions.

"OK, Jamshid. Knock on the door. If Manuel shows, hand him our authentic looking telegram. If he's holding a weapon, ask to be paid, then walk away calmly. If he's not armed, kill him and move away from the door. We'll cover you if he isn't alone. Remember, don't give the telegram to anyone else. Okay. Let's do it!."

Two minutes later, Jamshid walks briskly to the front door. With telegram in hand and ready to ring the bell, the door flies open and he finds himself looking into the barrel of a shotgun. As an experienced Savak agent, Jamshid remains calm and quickly raises both arms in the air flashing the telegram. As his eyes focus on the gunman, he does a double-take, shouting.

"Boris Kruchenko! It's you!"

George hears the shouting and starts to run towards the house.

Tony yells, "Stop, George! It may be a trap!"

George stops, draws his weapon and begins a slow backward walk to the car.

Kruchenko spots him and moves past Jamshid, shouting, "Felipe, Felipe! Stop. I will not hurt you."

Jamshid takes advantage of his position behind the Russian and shouts, "Freeze, or I shoot!"

Kruchenko freezes but does not drop his shotgun. George, aiming at Kruchenko, pleads with him.

"Boris, please! Put down your weapon. We will not harm you, I promise."

As Kruchenko lowers the gun and walks towards George, Tony rushes out of the car and takes aim at the Russian.

"Boris! Drop that shotgun, now! Or George and I will shoot you!"

Tony's appearance, whom he recognizes as the 'house mover', adds to Kruchenko's confusion. He lays down his weapon and walks to George.

"Felipe, my friend. What are you doing here? Why are you armed? And why does the big man call you George?"

George secures his weapon and gives Kruchenko a bear hug.

"Boris, my dear friend. My real name is George and the big man is my father. I'll explain everything later. But tell me, where have you been and when did you get here? And have you seen or heard from Manuel?"

Kruchenko smiles and leads George towards the front door. Jamshid, weapon in hand, stops them at the door.

"Not yet." he orders. "I enter first!"

Tony pulls George away from Kruchenko and levels his automatic at the Russian.

"Listen very carefully, friend. If Manuel or anybody else is in there waiting to ambush us, you die."

Bewildered and trembling, Kruchenko mumbles, "I guarantee on my life. It is safe to enter."

"OK, Jamshid," orders Tony, "give a look."

Jamshid enters, followed by George.

Kruchenko, face ashen and still trembling, lights a cigarette and asks Tony, "What is your interest here and why did George tell me his name was Felipe?"

"Like George told you. We'll explain later and you better pray he doesn't get hurt!"

"My word is my honor. I said it is safe in there."

George appears at the door.

"OK, Dad. You can enter - and you won't believe what we found."

Tony handcuffs the Russian and orders him to enter first. Jamshid covers the Russian while Tony looks at some familiar photos in the living room.

He calls out, "Where are you, George?"

"In the kitchen, Dad."

Before entering the kitchen, Tony pulls out a business card, writes a note on the back and places it in his shirt pocket. Kruchenko and Jamshid follow him. As Tony enters, the scent of alcohol permeates the air.

"Oh, oh – someone has been drinking."

He takes three steps, sees a body on the floor, pulls out the business card and hands it to George. George looks at it, then at Kruchenko, then at his father and shakes his head in denial.

"Read it aloud, George."

George looks at Boris and reads, "Kruchenko killed Manuel."

"No! No!" shouts Kruchenko, "He committed suicide!"

Manuel is still warm, but very dead. His facial signs are those of a man who died in extreme agony. On the wet floor next to the body is an almost empty bottle of Pisco. The evidence on the table shows that the bottle was recently opened.

Kruchenko pleads, "My friend Felipe - I mean George. Who are you and why you do this to me? Manuel was very evil man. You need to know what bad things he did. He also have evil friends who do drugs and kill people. Please free me. I will tell you who and where they are."

George has become fond of his graying Russian friend. Kruchenko helped him when he was a total stranger, refined his bridge game, taught him how to be a conservative blackjack winner and treated him like a family member. He pats Kruchenko's shoulder.

"Don't worry, Boris, everything will work out for you. We'll talk later; meanwhile, we need to search the house.

As Tony examines the contents of Manuel's briefcase on the kitchen table, Jamshid calls out from the pantry, "Ah ha—I know how Manuel died."

"Good, but wait—look what I found in the briefcase." Tony pulls out a handful of photos. He looks at them, then waves one at Kruchenko. "Tell me, Boris—who is this man?"

"He is Carlo Perez, the leader of many evil men like Manuel. He is a Bolivian who deals drugs and is a hired assassin. Free me and I will tell you how to find him and his partner, Jose."

Tony shows the Russian another very familiar photo. "And who is this man with you?'

Kruchenko looks at it, then lowers his head, closes his eyes and shakes his head. "Manuel used my cousin Katerina and her friend Rosita to get me to introduce him to Carlo and Jose. He is Lee Harvey Oswald - he was used as patsy, like me and others."

As the Russian stands motionless, Tony profiles him. *"His pain appears genuine. I know he's not KGB and I'm sure Manuel hooked him on drugs. I know he was a patsy and I'm convinced he doesn't know Carlo is dead."* "OK, George, I believe your friend is on our side. Un-cuff him."

Kruchenko stands next to the table, looking around while rubbing his wrists, trying to figure out who these men are, how he was discovered and why they are here. The briefcase also contains photos of Jose, Dan Hill, Sammy, Hank, Poncho, Gabriel, Pepe, the lady with the gravely voice in Chile and her accomplice, Oscar, and a young girl (not Rosita) sitting on Manuel's lap. A book includes the addresses and phone numbers of Carlo, Jose, Sammy, Hank and other names unfamiliar to Tony and Kruchenko. In addition to La Paz, Carlo is shown to have an address at Cochabamba, Lake Titicaca and Santa Cruz. Jose is listed in La Paz, Cochabamba, Oruro, Lake Titicaca and Lake San Luis.

"Look at this," observes Tony, "a Bolivian passport, a Panamanian passport and a Cuban passport, all recently stamped. Now let's see what's in his wallet."

Jamshid turns over the body and extracts the wallet. "It's very full."

Tony first removes and counts the money. "1,800 U.S. dollars – a Bolivian pilot license – a Bolivian Driver's License – a safety deposit key, and, look here! More photos!"

Everyone crowds around Tony. "Here's one of me, another of George and me, here's Frank Monti, the Macho boys...and here's one of my buddy, Nunzio!"

"May I see that one of Mr. Addabbo?" asks Jamshid. He examines it carefully. "That's what I thought. This photo has been cut out of his passport."

"It certainly is," confirms Tony. "Several years ago, when I asked Nunzio to meet me in Peru to look at a sulfur mine, he told me his passport was missing and he was waiting for a new one. He thought it might have been stolen at the time. One of the Machos must have stolen it. He'll be relieved to know what happened to his passport...and to Manuel."

Jamshid points to an unopened bottle of Pisco on the kitchen table. "There are more unopened Pisco bottles in the pantry." With questioning looks from Tony and George, he adds, "Examine the bottle. Then examine the body."

"The Pisco looks OK. And you'd need to do an autopsy to determine the cause of death."

Tony hands the bottle to Kruchenko, "Anything wrong with this bottle, Boris?"

He looks at it closely from all angles, "No...it looks good to me." He doesn't look up, however.

Jamshid points to Manuel, "I've seen that look many times in my country. Note the frothing of the mouth. I know how he died."

Kruchenko hands the bottle to George, "Here, Felipe, er, I mean George. You look."

George looks at Tony, then Kruchenko. He raises the Pisco bottle in the air, announcing, "Ladies and gentlemen of the jury, there is not one shred of evidence that this exhibit was planted by my client."

Tony smiles at Kruchenko, "By the way, Boris, my son is not a car mechanic. He's a lawyer."

"George is correct," states Jamshid, "No one can prove who injected cyanide into the bottles."

Tony looks at the body, "My only regret is that I didn't kill the bastard."

Kruchenko, still bewildered by this rapid turn of events, looks at Tony, "Are you all Police?"

"No, my friend. But welcome to the Capture Team!"

"Yes, Boris," adds George, "since we have a common goal and since you know Carlo's partner, Jose Martinez, we need your help in trapping him."

"I will help you find Jose. But what about Carlo and others?"

"Carlo, Dan Hill, Sammy, Hank, Poncho, Gabriel and Pepe are dead. We'll explain the details to you later. For now, tell us where you've been the past month."

The Russian appears relieved.

"Come, I will show you." He leads them out the back door to the adjacent downhill house. "This house has been my secret for more than two years now. Katerina, Rosita and Rimma not know I had it." He walks them around the small, partially furnished house. "I have new car in garage with plenty gas and good food supply in pantry. Come, I will open a bottle of vodka and we celebrate."

Kruchenko hands each a crystal clear glass and opens a new bottle of vodka from a kitchen cabinet, fills their glasses, then raises his glass. Before the Russian can make a toast, Jamshid gets the high-sign from Tony, quickly draws his weapon and aims it at Kruchenko. "Sorry, Mr. Kruchenko. But make a toast and take the first drink."

Kruchenko looks startled and hurt, then puts his glass on the table. He shakes his head in disbelief, slowly pours more vodka into his glass until it overflows, raises it and announces, "Like I told George's father: 'my word is my honor'. I will never harm my friend or the family of my friend."

He chug-a-lugs his drink, pours another and raises his glass. "I make this toast to my new friends, who I will always consider like my family."

Tony raises his glass towards the Russian. "Thank you, Boris. I'm sorry we had to do this, but, when we tell you everything that has happened to us, you'll understand. We've been targets of Los Machos for years. But now we can believe your word is your honor and will drink with you."

They click glasses and drink the vodka. Kruchenko then offers to tell them his story.

"In 1963, I was looking for work in Mexico City while I live with cousin Katerina. Manuel was sometimes friendly with Rosita and knew Rosita was close friend of Katerina. One day, Manuel told Rosita that he has job for me." He pauses, then, "He told Rosita he was working undercover for the Mexican authorities and needed to set-up a spy in a sting operation. Manuel said he needed the spy, a man named Oswald, to meet a Russian diplomat who would introduce Oswald to a man named Carlo for a very special project. He wanted me to act as the diplomat."

"And you agreed?" asks George.

"Not at first. Katerina warned me not to impersonate a Russian diplomat."

"What happened next?"

"Then Manuel started to tell me it would be secret government work in connection with the CIA, with a ten thousand dollar bonus and many more undercover projects. He paid me one thousand dollars in cash to help me while I thought about the job. He took me to the best restaurants and night clubs and started me on drugs. It was not long until I be hooked and agreed to act the part of the diplomat."

"Then Manuel introduced you to Oswald?

"No. Manuel introduced me to a CIA agent by name of Daniel Hill. Hill told me how important I be to the undercover operation. He also say he would have undercover work in Las Vegas and Tucson and gave me another two thousand dollar advance. Then Manuel introduced me to Oswald."

"What were you told to say to Oswald?"

"I told Oswald that I was a KGB agent acting as a diplomat who needed an undercover man for special project. He wanted to know the details. I told him that only a man named Carlo Perez could explain the details and finances with him. He liked idea and agreed to meet with Carlo."

"Did Oswald set conditions to his meeting Carlo?" asks Tony.

"Yes. He said Carlo must agree to meet him in a public place."

"What was your impression of Oswald?"

"He was smart and a careful young man. He spoke fair Russian and some Spanish."

"Did you ask him how he learned Russian?"

"Yes. He said he visited Russia, lived in Minsk and married a pretty girl named Marina."

"How many times did you meet with Oswald?"

"Only twice. First at night and then the next morning. In the morning he wore a fake mustache."

"How did he explain the mustache?" asks George.

"He said it was sometimes his disguise for undercover work."

"Then you introduced him to Carlo."

"Yes, at the Hotel Regina and I know at that moment that Carlo was bad person."

"What did Carlo tell Oswald?"

"I don't know. They told me my services were no longer required and to leave."

"Did you see Carlo or Oswald after that day?"

"Never. Then, when I hear and read that Oswald kill President Kennedy, I know Oswald was set up as patsy."

"What about the other men?"

"I only saw Manuel, Jose and sometimes Pepe and Gabriel in Las Vegas and Tucson. They kept me in drugs and used me to pick up heroin at airports."

Jamshid, an experienced Savak interrogator, smiles at Kruchenko, cracks his knuckles, then politely asks, "Tell us, Mr. Kruchenko, when and how did you break your heroin habit?"

"One day, twenty year ago, I looked in mirror and saw man I did not respect, with no future. I decided to trick Manuel and others to believe I still be addicted. I rented a cabin in Patagonia and, as you call it, I went 'cold-turkey'? It take me over one year to feel human again."

"How did you explain your disappearance?"

"I lied to Manuel. I told him I was in Mexican jail. He believed me, and we continued to do business."

Tony pulls a casino token out of his pants pocket, flips it in the air, looks at it, then flips it to Kruchenko. The Russian looks at it and smiles. "I have many casino tokens I won at blackjack. As young boy, I learn to play cards with my father and mother. My father teach me how to figure odds and manage money. He also teach me to never be greedy and learn when to stop."

"We saw a picture of you between two casino security guards. Were you caught cheating?"

"No, I never cheat. Ask George. One night a dealer recognize me. He catch me wearing a disguise and called the pit boss who called security. They remove my fake mustache, took photograph and told me to stay away from that casino. I never cheated at blackjack. I taught George the techniques for winning play."

"Yes," agrees George, "and I got caught by a sharp dealer, too. You remember, Dad. But that's all behind us now. Boris just confirmed what we have believed for some time. Like Oswald, he was set up as a patsy, realized what happened, how he had been used, and decided to get even."

"Well, now it's time to move on," adds Tony. "We need to go after Jose, the last assassin."

A few minutes later, in Manuel's house, Kruchenko assures everyone he will dispose of Manuel's body, the Pisco bottles and firearms. He agrees to remain in Manuel's house to receive possible phone calls from Jose and maintain radio contact with the Capture Team. Jamshid and another Savak agent bag up all the photos and documents related to the conspiracy and carry them to the car. George pats Kruchenko on the shoulder.

"Boris, I'll assure Katerina, Rimma and Rosita you're safe and will be home soon."

Tony hands Kruchenko a Montico mini transceiver.

"Here, Boris, use this to call us. George will show you how to use it. We're all in this together now. I'll contact you soon for a special assignment."

Two hours later, with the ladies in Rosarita, George assures them that Boris is safe.

"Where is he?" asks Katerina.

"He's in Tucson getting his car fixed and will be home soon for a celebration."

"What about Manuel?" asks Rosita.

"He committed suicide in La Puerta," George replies calmly.

Rimma looks at Rosita, Katerina, then George.

"That makes us very happy, George."

George knew Rimma wasn't deceived but was going along with the story.

JULY 18, 1993, MONDAY MORNING IN CHULA VISTA

From George's apartment in Chula Vista, Tony calls Addabbo.

"Nunzio, how's the book coming?"

"Good. I'm over 300 draft pages but need more data. What's the latest?"

"I have an interesting surprise for you."

"What's that, Tony?"

"Remember a few years ago when you couldn't meet me in Peru because you were waiting for a new passport?"

"Yeah,...I reported a missing passport in Santiago. I believe it was 1986. Why?"

"Do you remember what photo you used in the passport?"

"I've had so many passports I'd never remember that. But, you know something, I remember I also reported a missing passport in 1975 or 1976 when I was living in Mexico City. Are you suggesting they were stolen?"

"I know for a fact that your 1986 passport was stolen. And I'd bet both were stolen."

"You found my 1986 passport?"

"Not exactly. We found a photo from one of your passports. Knowing you so well over the years, I'm sure it was taken out of your 1986 passport. I'll explain where I found it when I see you."

"Where are you?"

"At George's apartment, leaving in about an hour for Los Angeles to meet Dr. Asti. Jamshid and I will leave tomorrow for New York. I'll mail you the photo if you like."

"I have a better idea. I'll drive down to LA and meet you."

"Great! I can give you a lot more information. Meet us at LAX, United terminal, outside check-in at 10 A.M. OK?"

"See you in the morning. By the way, any luck locating Kruchenko or Manuel?"

"Found 'em both."

"Muy interesante! Hasta mañana, viejo." (Very interesting! Until tomorrow, ol' man)

Next morning, the men meet as planed. Nunzio, appalled at Tony's appearance, wastes no time voicing his feelings.

"Tony, you look like hell! You must be down to about 200 pounds. And those black circles under your eyes tell me you need some heavy duty R and R after you see Dr. Asti."

"Nunzio, you worry too much. I can still run circles around guys half my age."

"Sure. I'll remember to tell your grand-kids after your gone."

"Look, I'm okay. Just a little tired from all the recent action. Dr. Asti will be here soon."

"Speaking of Dr. Asti," announces Jamshid, "here he comes."

With the four men in a huddle, inside the terminal, Dr. Asti waves his finger at Tony and repeats, almost verbatim, Nunzio's earlier words.

"Also," continues Dr. Asti, "here's something to help your heart, boost your energy and improve your immune system."

He hands Tony a large bottle of 100mg Coenzyme Q10 capsules.

"What!" complains Tony "More damn pills?"

"Don't argue, macho-man! Take one with every meal. It helps the cells in your body covert food into energy and its antioxidant properties protect your heart against free radical damage. I also prescribe that you visit Carmen ASAP! You need to rest. Doctor's orders!"

Before passing through security, Tony hands Nunzio the photo from his stolen passport, explains how they discovered Kruchenko, what happened to Manuel and outlines the basic plan to trap Jose, the final assassin, in Bolivia.

"Be careful in dealing with Jose," warns Nunzio. "I guess I don't need to remind you, but he masterminded the Grassy Knoll surprise, is an explosives and communications expert. He's avoided capture for years. He's one smart hombre!."

"True, Nunz, but there's a big plus in our favor. He doesn't know Manuel is dead. We plan to send a series of telegrams to him from Manuel. George will do it from Mexico. We'll get him yet - the murdering son-of-a-bitch!"

"We know Jose is clever," reminds Nunzio. "Won't he call the La Puerta house expecting Manuel?"

"No problem with that. Kruchenko is with us. He'll answer the phone. He'll tell Jose that Manuel just left for Las Vegas and will be returning in a few days. Jose knows Manuel and Kruchenko are setting up a deal. He won't be suspicious. George and Ali will remain in Kruchenko's house, next to Manuel's, in case of trouble."

"God, I hope you're right, Tony. It's been going on forever. So, why are you going to New York instead of Mexico for some of Carmen's TLC?"

"Judy is getting married tomorrow and I'm happy to say I'm to be best man."

"I thought her fiancé was in Africa?"

"He was, but he got a temporary assignment in New York. I'll be with Carmen after the wedding and coordinate things from there. Pray for us, Nunz, that this will finally be the end of this nightmare."

"You know I will, Tony. But coordinating things isn't exactly R and R!"

"Nunzio, you worry too much! Everything I do in Manzanillo is relaxing."

"Sure! Follow the doctor's orders and give Carmen a hug for me. She's one hell of a classy lady."

"I know, Nunz," Tony uncharacteristically sighs deeply. "She is one 'hell-of-a-classy lady', and much more! She's given me years of love and support and all I've given her is worry. I can never make it up to her. And I can't wait to spend the rest of my days with her."

CHAPTER 36

EIGHT DOWN - ONE TO GO

In New York, Tony gives the bride away in a civil ceremony. Then, contrary to Dr. Asti's instructions, returns to meet with George in La Puerta, Baja California.

JULY 21, 1993, LA PUERTA, BAJA, CALIFORNIA (MEXICO)

Tony and George prepare the following telegram, from Manuel to Jose: (translated from Spanish to English). "Jose. The business with Kruchenko is on the road. What's up on your end? Your associate, Manuel."

This official looking telegram is sent to Rashid, who has it hand delivered to Jose in Oruro the next day. Rashid reports that Jose has done a professional job in retrofitting the guarded heroin plant to look like a sulfur refinery ready for business.

Pleased with progress, Tony flies to Manzanillo two days later to be with Carmen.

Kruchenko receives Jose's first call the next evening. Jose immediately recognizes Kruchenko's voice and conducts the conversation in English.

"Boris, my dear friend. How are you?"

"Not so good, Jose. I have a high fever and other problems. I could not travel to Tucson with Manuel. He told me to stay here and wait for your calls."

"Why did he go to Tucson?"

"He went to meet a pilot friend at Marana airport, where we do business. Pilot said he flew for C.I.A. and would have no problem at Port of Entry. Manuel is there to negotiate price."

"It is not like Manuel to go and not call me first. When is he returning?"

"He said in few days. He will go to Las Vegas after Tucson to get more money."

"How much does the pilot want?"

"I don't know. He will only make deal with the money man. I have no money," lies Kruchenko.

Monitoring the call from the house next door, George applauds Kruchenko's coolness.

"Manuel wants to know when you will be ready to make first shipment."

"I can be ready in two weeks. But first I need money. Tell Manuel to call me."

"Why you need money?"

"Don't worry about it. And don't ask so many questions! I'll explain it to Manuel."

"Jose, you have no cause to speak to me like that!" Kruchenko sounds offended. "I made good business contact with the pilot. I not your enemy."

"Okay, Boris. Tell Manuel my cash is low. I need $20,000 to pay local officials to be quiet."

The conversation ends with Jose wishing Kruchenko a speedy recovery and the promise of a substantial bonus when the deal is consummated.

George immediately calls Tony.

"Dad, the call came. Jose has a financial problem and needs twenty thousand hush-money. I think we should send it to him."

"Agreed. I'll have Jamshid arrange the cash transfer, ostensibly from Manuel, of course."

"Good. Now, how is Carmen? How do you feel? And are you taking your meds?"

"Who needs meds in this environment. Carmen and I are having a great time."

"Dad, you're impossible! Love ya'. Bye."

Jamshid calls Rashid in Bolivia, advising, in Farsi, that Ali will carry the cash on the first of August. Then Jamshid receives a disturbing call from Rashid on July 30.

"Please tell Mr. Berlotti to hold the money. Jose has just been arrested. I'll give you details later."

Tony then instructs Jamshid.

"Have Ali travel to Bolivia as planned. We can't get to Jose while he's in custody, so find out why he was arrested, what it will take to spring him and hold the money until I can make a decision."

The next day, Rashid advises that Jose was most likely arrested by local police because he didn't have the required cash for a payoff to officials.

AUGUST 2, 1993

A favorable break comes at noon when Kruchenko receives a call from Bolivia.

"Hola, Señor Kruchenko?" Kruchenko does not recognize the voice.

"Si, con quien habla?" (Yes, with whom am I speaking?)

The following is translated from Spanish to English.

"The police in Oruro. One moment, please."

There is a shuffling of paper and whispering in the background, then the familiar voice of Jose.

"Hello, Boris."

"Hello, Jose. What is wrong and where are you?"

There is more whispering and a short pause before the reply.

"I'm with the police, waiting for Manuel and the money."

"Manuel has already sent the money. It is in La Paz and will be delivered to you personally at your Oruro plant, at your convenience. He also said more money is coming soon."

Jose thanks Kruchenko and reminds him to stay near the phone until delivery is made.

The conversations are monitored and recorded by George, who immediately calls Tony.

"Dad, we're ready to deliver the hush-money and I've already prepared a note from Manuel to Jose."

"Read it to me, George."

"Jose. This money is for your local friends. Tell them this amount will be tripled with the first sale now being negotiated. You must be ready to ship within one month. Please keep in contact with Señor Kruchenko for details. I do not want my associates to know the location of our operation."

AUGUST 5, 1993

Ali arrives at the main gate of the Oruro plant. The security guard blindfolds and body-searches him before they drive to the main building. Upon entering, Ali is led to a small room. His blindfold is removed and another guard directs him to open his briefcase. Satisfied that there are no weapons, only papers and bundles of money, the guards lead him to Jose's office.

During his long walk through the plant to Jose's office, Ali notices the absence of plant operators. He sees only two armed guards sitting on a platform, smoking cigars. Upon entering the office, jammed with electronic equipment, Ali greets Jose by name. Sitting on a high back chair, flanked by two police officers, and smoking a long cigar, Jose snarls:

"How do you know I'm Jose?"

Primed for the question, Ali promptly responds.

"Manuel showed me your picture in Las Vegas, to be sure I'm delivering this money to the proper person."

One of the officers rises and walks to Ali with his hand extended. "Show me your passport."

The officer examines it, then in broken English waves it at Ali.

"It show you arrive Bolivia August third. Why you wait two days to come?"

Once again, primed for the question and according to plan, Ali coolly explains.

"I have been sick at the Sheraton Hotel in La Paz with a case of 'puna' (high altitude sickness) and also 'disenteria' (dysentery). I came as soon as possible. I'm very sorry. Here's the money."

Jose counts the money, gives the officers an affirmative nod, then blows smoke at Ali.

"Is that all?"

"No, Sir. He gave me a note for you. Here."

Jose's demeanor changes from confrontational to friendly as he waves the note in the air.

He smiles at the officers, proudly announcing, "See, I told you my friend would deliver. We'll soon be back in business. Here, read it. Return our friend's passport and let's have a drink."

Jose opens a bottle of Pisco. Ali politely declines a drink, citing recent abdominal problems. Jose writes a note, places it in an envelope addressed to Manuel and hands it to Ali.

"Please see that Manuel gets this note as soon as possible and tell him to call me."

Ali is escorted to his taxi at the main gate. Jahangir and another Savak agent, parked a short distance from the main gate and disguised as surveyors, remain to monitor the plant. They wave at Ali as he heads for the Oruro airport for the next flight to La Paz and a meeting with Rashid.

En route to La Paz, Ali, well trained in area-identification, makes a list in Farsi of what he saw and heard during his plant walk and meeting with Jose. Hours later, in the Sheraton Hotel, Rashid and Ali receive a radio call from Jahangir, advising that Jose and two police officers were driven back to town, that Jose returned with a bus load of workers and the plant appears to be operating again. Early the following morning, Rashid calls Jamshid, providing, in Farsi, Jose's latest activities. During breakfast, Jamshid briefs Tony.

"Jose's heroin plant, disguised as a sulfur refinery, is back in business, with two armed guards There are beam antennas and dish arrays on the grounds, including a helicopter pad. Jose's office is clean and orderly but looks like an electronics laboratory, with test equipment, radio transceivers, linear amplifiers, closed circuit cameras and TV's, portable GPS units, two copiers, two FAX machines, two computers and two operating Unicom radios. All other radios were shut-down so Ali was not able to determine operating frequencies. The entire plant reeks of dangerous sulfur dioxide and Ali left with a headache."

Pleased with the report, Tony decides to end his idyll with Carmen and return to New York to plan a strategy to trap Jose. He promises Carmen he will return within one week. Her reaction is swift and firm.

"I'm coming with you!"

"You'll get bored."

"No, I won't! I'll keep you away from chili-dogs and make you take your medicine. Let's pack."

MONDAY, AUGUST 8, 1993, NEW YORK

At his New York office with George, Kruchenko, Jamshid, Judy, Josh and Carmen, Tony asks for suggestions on trapping Jose. Jamshid, Tony's faithful and fearless body-guard, quickly volunteers to fly to Bolivia as Manuel's courier.

"I will avoid the police, kill Jose and this case will be closed at last!"

"Thank you, Jamshid. But this is a family thing," interrupts George. "Jose killed my mother and sisters and I want him! I think we should send him a telegram, from Manuel, stating he will send a female partner to sign the shipping contract. I'll do another female impersonation and lure Jose to a hotel room and our agent Jahangir.

Rashid and Ali will be nearby covering the operation. I guarantee, the S.O.B. will never leave the room alive."

"Sending a female is a good idea," agrees Judy. "But I want to be that lure. Jose doesn't know me. He might recognize George's disguise possibly from photos taken by his dead associates. Besides, I still haven't had my revenge for Peter's death!"

"Wait!" Now it's Kruchenko. "I insist I lure Jose to your agents. Jose still believe I work with Manuel. He also believe I arranged the contract. I would not create suspicion. He would..."

"Hold it!" Josh gets in on the discussion. "I learned many Mossad tricks from my father and know how to eliminate Jose. Judy shouldn't go. I volunteer."

"Well, I won't volunteer," states Carmen. "I'd be too nervous in any cloak-and-dagger scenario, but I will pay for the operation. I want my Tony free of this conspiracy."

Tony raises both arms in frustration. "That leaves me. Unfortunately I can't go because I'm sure Jose has photos of me and my size is a dead give-away. I agree a female would be the best lure. If the police follow Jose to the room, we'll have Rashid, Jahangir and two more agents as back-up in case of trouble. I've made the decision. We'll send Judy."

"Hold it, Dad!" shouts George, "Judy isn't trained to handle a potential crisis. She'd probably freak-out, blow the operation and get herself killed! Sorry, Judy."

"Don't argue with your father, George. I've been waiting a long time for this opportunity. Remember, it was you that taught me how to stay cool under pressure. I'm going!"

"And," continues George, "what will your wonderful new husband think about your mission?"

"Good point," adds Tony. "You must discuss it with David and get his agreement before we agree to send you."

"David just left on a four week field trip to several African nations and can't be reached. I'll discuss it with him as soon as he returns."

George pounds the table. "We can't wait that long for a decision. It's imperative we strike while we have Jose set up in a favorable position. And that's now!"

"George is right. Do whatever you can to contact David, but I'll need your answer within forty-eight hours or Boris gets the nod."

Judy rushes to the door, stops, turns and announces, "If I can't reach David, then I'll go without his okay."

"We all love you, Judy, and appreciate your dedication to the Capture Team, but my decision is final," states Tony."

"And, by the way, Judy," adds George. "We want a recording of all your conversations with David regarding this assignment."

When Judy exits the conference room in a huff, Tony shakes his head.

"George, what the hell is the matter with you! That wasn't necessary!"

"It was very necessary! Her "revenge" statement revealed she'd lie to take the assignment."

"I know Judy, she's like a daughter! She wouldn't lie to me. You owe her an apology."

"You're getting soft, Dad. But I will apologize."

FORTY-EIGHT HOURS LATER, 9 AM

Tony enters Judy's communications room and finds her sobbing in front of her short-wave transceiver. He knows why she's crying, puts his arms around her.

"Sorry, Judy. But you know something? I'm kinda' glad you couldn't reach David. We desperately need you as our communications controller. Another thing, we all agreed you wouldn't freak-out in a crisis. George just said that because he wanted to keep you out of harm's way."

"I know. He already apologized." Judy sniffles. "I'm OK now, Mr. Berlotti."

"That's my girl. Now, after your coffee, tell Rashid and Ali to stand by in La Paz."

An hour later in the conference room, Tony outlines a plan to trap Jose. The meeting comes to an abrupt halt when he puts down his cigar and grabs his chest. He shakes his head and recovers quickly, but George does not allow him to continue. He rushes to his side.

"Dad, this meeting is adjourned and don't even think about arguing about it! Now, let's get you on the couch!"

Carmen, already in tears, is at Tony's side. "I agree with George, darling. You're going to rest."

Josh and Jamshid support Tony in their arms. "Okay, Rais. Let's go, now!"

In earlier days, Tony would have roared like an enraged bull at being ordered around. Recognizing now that he is in his mid seventies with a weak heart, he takes a deep breath. But he wants closure to this conspiracy that has destroyed so many lives.

"Okay, okay. I'll rest. In the meantime, draft a telegram for Jose. Wake me in time for lunch and I'll review it at that time."

Four hours later, Tony awakens and sees Carmen sitting in a chair next to his sofa. She bends over and holds his hand, "My, darling. That was the best sleep you've had in a long time. Hungry?"

"I'm starved. What's for lunch?"

"The others have already eaten. You and I have a meal waiting in the kitchen."

"Where's the draft of that telegram?"

"We knew you'd ask. It's next to your wine glass at the table. Let's go."

The telegram, prepared in Spanish by George, brings a frown to Tony's forehead.

"Jose. Our business partners want Boris to approve your product before agreeing to the contract and delivery. I am sending him to examine the product and explain how it is to be transported. For security reasons, a lady with the contract and cash will travel on a separate flight. Boris will arrive your plant on August 22 with details. Regards, Manuel."

Carmen shrugs her shoulders. "What's wrong, Tony?"

"What's this about a lady going to Bolivia? George isn't going as that woman. Period!"

"We held a meeting while your were sleeping. It was agreed to include the lady associate only as a lure. George doesn't plan to go. Now finish your soup, dear."

A half hour later in the conference room, Tony thanks his staff for their dedication to The Capture Team efforts and their concern over his health. As everyone watches in dismay, he lights a long Macanudo, leans back in his high back executive chair, looking at his cigar.

"I know what you're thinking but I don't care what Dr. Asti says. I gave up a lot and this is one pleasure I won't do without. Now tell me, George, how will Boris explain, to Jose's satisfaction, the way the heroin is to be transported? And how will he lure Jose away from the plant?"

"The bases are covered. Boris will bring Jose a box of cigars, in individual metal containers. The plan, he will explain, will be similar to the sulfur brick operation we had at La Esperanza."

"It won't fly because he'll surely link it to us!"

"Got that covered, too. Boris will tell him it's Manuel's idea; that Manuel, familiar with the sulfur brick operation, made a deal with another Chilean refinery that's in operation to cast and ship the bricks. And that the details are in the contract with the lady in a secret location."

"Excuse me," states Kruchenko, "I know Jose. He'll need the money and will not question what I tell him."

"OK, George," continues Tony. "How does Boris explain the lady's involvement?"

"He tells Jose that the lady associate represents a Las Vegas syndicate with an unlimited cash supply - if the product is good. Jose will get a large advance, in cash, immediately upon signing the contract and that the deal is off if he is followed by bodyguards and/or police."

"Jose is smart," snaps Tony. "He won't go without back-up!"

"Sorry again, Mr. Berlotti," interrupts Kruchenko. "I know Jose. He will want the money and will agree to go alone."

"What is your back-up plan if Jose insists on bringing protection?"

"Boris explains that Jahangir is the only person who knows the lady's secret location and that the deal is off if they are followed."

"And," continues Tony's interrogation, "what will you do if the police do show and order Jahangir to lead them to the lady?"

"Got that covered, too. Jahangir has already promised he will never lead them to any lady. He will make it clear that, even at the risk of being arrested, the deal is off."

"That," states Tony, "could happen."

"Yes, Sir," adds Jamshid. "I have worked with Jahangir many years and can assure you - he will never yield to their threats or torture and is willing to die to uphold his promise. I think you already know that..."

"Please," interrupts Kruchenko, "I will explain all this to Jose in private when I first meet him. I know him and guarantee he will not involve police. He will agree to come alone with me."

Tony leans back, blowing smoke rings. "OK, George. Then what?"

"Boris will examine and approve the quality of Jose's heroin. Then he will signal Ali, waiting nearby, who will make a surprise visit. Ali will state he just arrived with more money for the lady, that the money is with a friend and he needs instructions on where to deliver it.'

"More money," states Kruchenko, ""will appeal to Jose."

"Then," continues George, ""Boris will tell Ali to return to his hotel and wait for directions to the lady. Ali will leave, but wait nearby. After Jose and Boris leave with Jahangir, Ali will enter the plant with the friendly guards."

"That's risky," warns Tony.

"Not really. During the past few weeks, Rashid has succeeded in converting two of Jose's plant guards to our payroll, with salaries beyond their wildest dreams. They have promised loyalty."

"It could backfire on you with a double-cross."

"Extremely doubtful. They understand that we have already contacted their families; that they will be killed if they double-cross us."

"Then what?" questions Tony.

"Ali will pay off the guards, place our remote incendiary units, exit with the guards and trigger the units. Jose's plant will be destroyed."

"Okay. What happens with Jose?"

"We've saved the best for last."

"Tell me about it."

"When Jose, Boris and Jahangir are well away from the plant and in a secret location, Jahangir will subdue Jose with our Montico paralyzer. They continue out of town to Jose's prepared grave. Jahangir will administer a lethal injection. Jose will join Carlo and the rest of Los Machos in Hell."

"You're making this very complicated," waves Tony. "I'm not sure about your 'best for last'. Sounds like Mission Impossible to me."

"Dad, it'll work. What have we got to lose?"

"A couple of precious lives, that's all!"

Jamshid waves his arms and stands. He has been Tony's bodyguard many years, intimately familiar with his devotion, protective nature and how desperately he needs closure to this conspiracy. He stands alongside the boss and places both hands on his shoulders.

"It will be Sunday, with no one in the plant. Rais, you need not worry about our safety. We have agreed that George has the best plan and only seek your approval to execute it."

Tony stands, lights a fresh cigar, smiles grimly at George, then walks slowly out of the room.

"What's wrong with my Dad?" asks George.

"I think I understand," confides Jamshid, "He wants so much to personally conduct this final stage. He's always been the one in charge. It's very difficult for him to admit his health will keep him away from the action. When he returns to us here, George, I assure you, he will give you the go-ahead."

After waiting patiently, several minutes later, Judy states, "I'm going out to check on him."

Seconds later, Judy is heard screaming for help. In the adjoining room. Tony is on the couch, ashen and in a cold sweat. Judy is kneeling beside him, holding his hand. George is first to enter as Tony slowly opens his eyes.

"Dad! What happened? Your heart again?"

"I'm okay, I guess. I took a nitro pill and will feel better in a minute. Then I'll come back to the meeting."

"Dad, you're not moving! That's an order!"

Carmen rushes in with a glass of water and pillow.

"Here, Tony, drink, put your head on the pillow, be quiet and listen to George."

Tony sees himself surrounded. The angina pain does not diminish his sense of humor.

"What the hell is this? Another conspiracy?"

"Yeah, Dad. We're conspiring to keep you alive. Is that Okay with you?"

Tony propped up, and holding Carmen's hand, looks at George.

"Okay, son. Go for it!"

They all take turns hugging the boss. Seconds later Judy enters with a bottle of champagne.

During the next week, plans are finalized to eliminate Jose. Tony prepares a telegram, from Manuel to Jose confirming Kruchenko's arrival date. Jamshid, meanwhile, briefs his Savak team. The team is in place in Bolivia on August 20.

After a stop in Rosarita to bid farewell to Katerina, Rosita and Rimma, Kruchenko departs for Bolivia via Mexico City to do his part for The Capture Team and get his final revenge. Rashid reports that the Oruro police have not interfered with Jose after the payoff and that Jose received the telegram.

Kruchenko arrives at the plant on schedule and is greeted warmly by Jose. Except for the two "friendly" guards at the front gate, the plant is idle. Jose assures Kruchenko that the police will not interfere with their operation but warns of dire consequences if this is a set-up.

Kruchenko assures Jose that this lucrative operation was carefully planned in every detail by Manuel.

"Manuel," assures Kruchenko, "worked many long hours on this contract. He said you will be very pleased with the financial arrangements. Now, let me examine your product. "

Half an hour later, after random sampling, Kruchenko nods his approval but complains about the strong smell of sulfur. Jose apologizes, citing that the sulfur pile and some equipment are necessary decoys. As they walk to Jose's office, Kruchenko signals Ali, who is escorted into the plant by one of the guards.

Jose is pleased to hear that he will receive additional operating funds, then issues another warning, "If this operation fails, you will all have serious problems!"

"No problems, Señor Martinez," states Ali. "Manuel assured us that this is a big contract."

After receiving instructions from Kruchenko, Ali leaves Jose's office, drives away and waits nearby to re-enter the plant.

Minutes later, Jose and Kruchenko leave the building and make their way to the Russian's car. Jahangir is in the rear seat reading a magazine.

"Who's that man?" asks Jose.

"Manuel took special precautions. That man is the only one who has the lady's location. If we see any police, he will not take us to the money."

Satisfied with the arrangement, Jose enters the front seat, with Kruchenko driving. When they are out of sight, Ali enters the plant and begins to set his devices while Rashid remains on guard in a four-by-four near the plant entrance in case of trouble.

Ten minutes later, Jose orders Kruchenko to turn around and return to the plant.

"Why? What is wrong?" asks the Russian.

"I forgot something important. Go back!"

Reluctantly, Kruchenko makes a u-turn. When they stop at the plant gate, the guards are missing. Jose gets out, walks into the guard shack and calls the plant. Kruchenko, nervous, unarmed and suspecting that Jose senses trouble, gets out of the car and waves frantically at Rashid who is already driving towards the gate, flashing his headlights.

Jahangir quickly exits the car and motions to Rashid to stop. Watching from inside, Jose, accurately assessing a double-cross, slams down the telephone and comes out with gun in hand. Before he can ask questions, a loud explosion is heard from within the plant followed immediately by smoke. Kruchenko and Jahangir run towards the plant, knowing that Ali is still in there. Jose jumps in Kruchenko's car and races away at high speed. Rashid, realizing he can't catch the speeding car, meets Kruchenko and Jahangir at the plant door. Entering the building now would be suicide, as sulfur dioxide fumes have already started flowing out of the broken windows.

Praying that Ali could still be alive, Jahangir puts a handkerchief over his mouth and rushes into the smoke filled plant as Rashid and Kruchenko scream at him to stop. In less than one minute, Jahangir staggers out, teary-eyed and gasping for breath.

"It was very foolish of you to go in there," states Kruchenko. "I don't know what happened, but we know Ali is gone."

"Yes," adds Rashid sadly. "So is Jose. Unfortunately he is still alive."

The trio quickly leave the scene, return to Oruro and transmit this sad turn of events to Jamshid.

"Mr. Berlotti," states Kruchenko, "will be very upset when Jamshid gives him the bad news."

In New York the following afternoon, Tony calls his staff for a meeting. His reaction to the news is predictable.

"Saving the best for last, eh? I was right about Mission Impossible."

"Do you suppose," postulates George, "that Ali committed the ultimate sacrifice if he suspected a double cross by Jose?"

"Absolutely not," responds Jamshid. "He was planning to bring his family to Las Vegas."

"That's so sad," states Judy, weeping.

"We'll take good care of his family. It's all we can do. For now what's important," concludes Tony, "is that Jose got away. We have arrived at 'the best for last'. That's yet to come."

George pounds the table. "I'll go to Bolivia, track down and kill the son-of-a—"

"No, George," interrupts Tony. "We now lay low for a while and plan more carefully. We'll keep Rashid, Jahangir and two more agents there until he reappears. Then we'll nail him."

Realizing his father has a serious heart condition and depressed over the loss of another associate, George pulls Carmen aside.

"Carmen, we've got to get Dad away from the office for a rest and you're the only one he'll listen to. Give him an ultimatum; whatever it takes to get him to your place."

"Ultimatums, and confrontations don't work with Tony, George. You know that. He's already said we need to lay low for a while, so I'm sure I can persuade him into coming to Manzanillo for a rest while your men in Bolivia look for Jose."

"You are so right, Carmen. You know him so well..."

"On another subject, George. Your father has been telling me of your growing relationship with Rimma. Bring her to my hacienda for a few days and we four can have some fun and get better acquainted. Does she play bridge?"

"Yes," grumbles George, "but she's a novice."

"Ha! You're just like your father. He doesn't think I play well either. So, just to make it fair, we'll play ladies against men at 25 cents a point, agreed?"

"Carmen, you'll lose a bundle. But I recognize your ploy. I'll make travel arrangements for Rimma and me. You'll love her. "

At Carmen's hacienda, Jamshid screens all communications to Tony and passes them on to George. Leisurely breakfasts on the patio, daily walks and siestas, occasional dinners at Las Hadas and nightly bridge games prove to be Tony's best medicine. He appears re-energized and ten years younger. Carmen approves of Rimma and encourages the relationship. George keeps his father advised on Capture Team activities. Three weeks pass quickly and Tony decides it's time to accelerate the search for Jose. On their final night, Carmen, who seldom holds back on any subject, poses a question to Rimma, but it's primarily aimed to trigger a response from Tony.

"So, tell me, Rima. When are you and George going to marry?"

While Rimma looks perplexed, Tony responds. He motions Rimma to remain silent, places his cards on the table and looks squarely at Carmen.

"Let's not worry about George and Rimma, Carmen. When are you finally going to accept my marriage proposal?"

Carmen screams, throwing her cards in the air, and begins to cry.

George gives his father a thumbs-up as Rimma moves to comfort Carmen, whose tears of joy run down her cheeks.

"Well? asks Tony, moving quickly to her side.

Between sobs of joy, Carmen accepts. "Si, si, si mi amor. Cuando?" (Yes, my love, when?")

"I promise. Just as soon as we close this case."

"Tony! Don't do this to me again." Carmen frowns. "It's been going on forever. Set a date and make me happy. I'll do anything you want - give you anything you want. But set a date!"

George sides with Carmen. "Come on, Dad. Carmen's right. It's already been much too long. You've loved her for years. Enough already! Make a commitment and I'll be best man."

Rimma sides with George. "Yes, Mr. Berlotti. Do it! Carmen loves you."

Tony has been contemplating this scenario for months. He already has a date in mind, but first he cracks a smile and waves his arms. "What's this? Yet another conspiracy?"

"Yes," agrees Carmen. "But you know this is one conspiracy you'll love. Now, when?"

"Well, I've always liked Manzanillo in April and your birthday is April 21. How will that do?"

"You promise? On your life?"

"You know I never renege on a promise."

Carmen embraces Tony, then rings the maid for champagne.

The next morning, Tony and George fly to New York. Rimma, promising Carmen she will return to help with wedding plans, flies to Tijuana.

SEPTEMBER 22, 1993, NEW YORK

Tony is at the conference table in his office with George, Jamshid, Judy, Josh and four agents. "So, what's new, Judy?"

"A slight problem, Mr. Berlotti. Rashid reports that Kruchenko refuses to leave Bolivia. He wants to remain to assist in Jose's capture."

George reacts quickly. "Dad! Boris can't stay! He isn't trained in our business. He'll get killed!"

"You're right. Instruct him to get back to Rosarita and take care of the three ladies until this case is closed. But be sure to thank him for his offer."

George calls Boris. "Hello, my good friend Boris. I understand you want to remain in Bolivia until we get Jose, is that correct?"

"Yes, George. Jose has no reason to kill me. He believes Manuel sent me to him with the big contract. If he finds me, I will explain I was looking for him to find out what he wants me to do with Manuel's contract and money. I can be a decoy for Rashid and Jahangir. I'm not afraid of Jose."

"How will you explain why you ran from the car when the plant exploded?"

"I will tell him I did not run away from him, but ran to the plant because I was trying to save his operation. I will tell him that, without his heroin, we have no business. He will understand."

"I believe you're right, but stay in La Paz with Rashid and Jahangir and I'll get back to you."

Tony agrees to keep Boris in Bolivia. "But he is to follow Rashid's instructions and is to remain out of sight until a plan is developed to trap Jose.

Tony, George, Jamshid, Josh and Judy work 16 hours a day preparing their plan. Seventy-two hours later, Jamshid passes the plan to Rashid, via coded Farsi.

During the next two months, hoping to encounter Jose, Kruchenko is instructed to maintain a high profile, shuttling between hotels and restaurants in La Paz and Oruro. The Savak team, in disguise, is always nearby.

DECEMBER 2, 1993

The first break occurs while Rashid and Kruchenko are in Oruro. Jahangir reports that their La Paz informant saw Jose rush out of the Sheraton Hotel into a taxi when it was announced that Pablo Escobar was assassinated in Columbia. According to the informant, a driver named Luis, parked behind Jose's taxi, knows the driver of that taxi. Rashid and Kruchenko return immediately to La Paz. Luis tells Rashid that the taxi driver, Pedro, has not yet returned to the hotel.

"Why," asks Luis, "are you looking for Pedro?"

"I was told," lies Rashid, "that a friend of mine from Argentina got into his taxi. I need to find him so I want to ask Pedro where he took my friend."

Pedro finally shows up three days later. Rashid introduces himself as Señor Ramsey and advises that he needs to deliver money to Jose from Manuel.

"I'm sorry," states Pedro. "But I never saw your friend before. I drove him to Lake Titicaca where he picked up two suitcases at a small cabin, then we drove back to La Paz where he got three more suit cases from an office. Then we went to a house in Cochabamba for two more suitcases and then to the airport. He said he was going to take a helicopter to Lake San Luis."

"Did my friend say why he was going to the lake?"

"No. He was very angry when he got into my taxi. He said many things would change with Escobar's death. When I asked why, he told me not to ask questions. But he gave me a big tip."

After receiving another big tip, Pedro provides Rashid with Jose's Cochabamba address.

The following afternoon, with Rashid and Jahangir nearby, Kruchenko knocks on Jose's door in Cochabamba, then has a brief conversation with a maid who answers the door.

"I'm sorry," states the maid, "Mr. Martinez didn't say where he was going and Mrs. Martinez is visiting friends in Peru."

The trio drive to the airport. While Rashid and Jahangir wait in the car, Kruchenko learns from the station manager, Rodolfo, that Jose charted a helicopter to Lake San Luis and that the helicopter has not yet returned.

That evening, after being apprized of the latest development, Tony instructs his team to remain in Cochabamba until the helicopter returns. They are to present themselves as land developers wishing to take aerial photos of the Lake San Luis area for a proposed project. The site is adjacent to the Jose Martinez property. If possible, they should try to get the pilot to pinpoint Jose's location.

The following morning, Rodolfo agrees to fly the team to Lake San Juis when the helicopter returns. "The two hour trip requires $600 advance payment, in cash!"

Rashid and his men go into a huddle and come up with only $490. Kruchenko's request that he pay with a credit card is refused. Jahangir proves how easily people can change their minds when presented with an attractive offer. He pulls off his Rolex watch, and hands it to Rodolfo.

"This watch," he brags, "is worth much more than $1000. Will you accept it as down payment?"

Rodolfo examines the watch and obviously knows the difference between the real thing and a fake.

He promptly accepts it as down payment.

"Not yet," states Jahangir. "You get my Rolex[20] when we get on the helicopter."

When yet another day passes without sign of the helicopter, Tony is notified. He issues new instructions.

"Split up. I want Rashid and two agents to return immediately to La Paz and stand by with a helicopter ready to go. Jahangir, Kruchenko and one agent are to remain in Cochabamba and wait for Jose's helicopter. If the helicopter returns to Cochabamba with Jose, follow him and call me. If the pilot is alone, ask him if he left Jose at the lake. If so, charter the chopper and call Rashid immediately, advising him of your estimated takeoff time. Rashid and his crew can take off then within 20 to 25 minutes before Jahangir, which should put both helicopters over the lake about the same time. Once you've located Jose's property, photograph it and the surrounding area, locate a favorable landing site nearby, then return to your respective bases and call me. If the pilots ask questions, tell them you're land developers and will return to the area soon for field work."

As the hours pass without the helicopter's arrival, the team's frustration mounts. The weather is good, there are no reports of downed aircraft and the pilot is experienced. Jahangir presses for information.

"I'm not worried," states Rodolfo, "Ramon is a good pilot and will explain when he returns."

---

[20] Tony had given his Savak team Rolexes several years ago for "No-Ruz" (their New Year, which begins on the first day of spring).

The following noon, Ramon calls Rodolfo from La Paz, explaining that he has been flying Señor Martinez between Lake San Luis, Lake Rogoaguado and La Paz, picking up supplies. They are now headed back to San Luis.

"I'll be back in two days," advises Ramon.

"Good," states Rodolfo, "I have another charter flight waiting for you."

CHAPTER 37

TORCH THE BASTARD

DECEMBER 14, 1993, NEW YORK, TONY'S OFFICE

While Tony, Judy and Josh are in the kitchen having breakfast, George and Jamshid confer in the radio room. "I'm getting tired of this long wait," complains George. "We should act."

"What would you do, George?"

"I'm prepared to go to Bolivia, stake-out Jose's place and burn him while he's asleep. That's how he killed Mom and my sisters. Dad would approve."

"That would place you in a vulnerable position. As much as your father wants to close this case, he also doesn't want you exposed to danger. He can't lose his last child, his only son, George."

"So tell me, Jamshid - what would you do?"

"To be perfectly honest, since I've seen your father endure so much pain and suffering at the hands of these ruthless men for so many years, I would also torch the last assassin."

Delighted with Jamshid's answer, George replies.

"Good. If Dad doesn't make a decision soon, I'll instruct Rashid to torch the bastard."

Jamshid quickly backs off. "I'm sorry, George. Even though I agree with you, I would never issue such instructions without the approval of our 'Rais'."

George persists. "We can't afford to wait. If we don't strike soon, Jose will get away and I won't let that happen."

"Don't let your emotions control your judgment, George. Act like the lawyer you are and follow your father's instructions. I know he will do the right thing."

Realizing he won't get Jamshid's support for his unauthorized preemptive strike, George temporizes his stand. "Well, I'm not going to wait very long."

DECEMBER 17, 1993, NEW YORK

Being glued to her radio station for days pays off for Judy. She receives Jahangir's coded message that the helicopter has arrived and a meeting is planned for tonight.

The following morning, Jamshid is awakened at three in the morning with a disturbing message from Jahangir. "The pilot will not fly us to Jose's ranch until after his Christmas vacation. He will return on January 9, 1994. Please advise."

Jamshid returns to bed.

"Another delay. Rais will be disappointed when I tell him at breakfast and George will surely want to leave for Bolivia immediately."

Jamshid is always first to greet Tony in the morning. Tony enters the kitchen at 7 A.M. and sees the look on Jamshid's face. "Okay, Jamshid. What's happened now?"

"Well, Rais, the news is not altogether discouraging."

As Jamshid explains, Judy pours Tony his morning energizer, a cappuccino. He sips it slowly, lights a cigar and, eyes closed, leans back in his chair. Everyone stops eating. They know Tony is preparing to make a statement. He opens his eyes, sips his cappuccino and smacks his lips.

"Know what we're going to do?"

As always, he gets their attention.

"I've been thinking about my wife and daughters last night. Carlo had Los Machos torch them to death. The arsonists, killers of my family - and President Kennedy, are all gone now except Jose. And, guess what? He was the expert who planned that horrific death by fire of three innocent women." Another satisfying sip of cappuccino. "After thinking about it all night, I made a decision."

Tony picks up his cigar lighter and triggers it's flame. "TORCH THE BASTARD!"

Almost simultaneously, they all rise, shouting. "Yes! Yes!"

Jamshid gets George's attention and nods. *"I told you he'd do the right thing."*

The rest of the day is spent planning the instructions to 'torch'. At nine in the evening, Jamshid passes the instructions to Rashid. The Savak team and Kruchenko are to remain in Bolivia until Jose is eliminated. George, Judy and Josh will remain in New York to monitor messages. George agrees but is disgruntled at not being closer to the action.   Tony and Jamshid will go to Carmen's hacienda where they will join the Brooks' for Christmas and return to New York on January fifth.

Tony returns from Manzanillo on schedule but looks tired. He has suffered another angina attack at the beach in spite of Carmen's loving care. George decides it's time to become more aggressive about his father's medical condition.

"Dad, you should have stayed in Mexico for more rest. There's nothing you can do here until we hear from Rashid. I have everything under control."

"You're probably right.   But I'm here and I sense a final closure soon. Now, let's discuss your future, George. Carmen can set you up with a big-time Mexican law firm whose clients are business men interested in expanding international operations.   It would be a great start. Does that appeal to you?"

"I've been giving my future a lot of thought lately. When this case closes and the story breaks, I know we'll have to change identities and leave the country. I agree that Mexico would be a good start."

"Good. I'll have Carmen set the wheels in motion."

JANUARY 10, 1994, NEW YORK

In Judy's radio room, a message from Jahangir.

"Ramon, the pilot, arrived but the mechanic states the helicopter won't be ready to fly until January fourteenth. We are ready."

Pleased with the news, Tony sends a return message to Rashid.

"Sorry I can't be with you.   Good luck on your final assignment."

When Jahangir and Mehdi arrive at the hanger the following morning, they find Ramon in a heated argument with the mechanic. According to Mehdi, Ramon is demanding that the helicopter be ready to test fly tomorrow morning. The mechanic told Ramon it would be ready when he released it and if Ramon persisted, he would walk off the job. After a fast huddle, Mehdi leaves quickly to find Rodolfo, the manager. Jahangir politely asks Ramon to join him at the car for a confidential advance cash bonus. Jahangir opens his briefcase exposing several rolls of $20 bills.

"Ramon, this is yours if you do two simple things for me, agreed?"

The sight of the money quickly subdues Ramon's anger. "What do you want?"

"First, you are making the mechanic very nervous. He may forget something important on the engine and we would not feel safe flying with you. Please stay away from him until he's finished. Then I need to see if you can identify a person in a photograph."

Ramon curses the mechanic, but agrees. As Jahangir stalls for time while looking for the photo, Mehdi returns quickly to the helicopter when he can't find Rodolfo. He finds the mechanic on a high ladder working on the antenna, cursing Ramon.

Mehdi politely asks. "Sir, I have an important question to ask. Can you come down?"

"I don't need to come down. What is it?"

"I'm sorry Ramon argued with you. He's upset because we told him we would cancel our charter if the helicopter isn't ready on time. I went to see the manager about paying extra to have another mechanic help you - but Rodolfo is gone."

"I'm the only one who works on this helicopter and I don't like to be rushed."

The mechanic puts a wrench in his pocket and climbs down.

"How much were you going to pay Rodolfo?"

"Ahhh," thinks Mehdi, *"he's hooked."* Then, "By the way, what's your name?"

"I'm Pedro."

"My pleasure, Pedro. Listen, we don't want to rush you, but if you get the helicopter ready on schedule, I will give you two hundred American dollars and we won't tell Rodolfo. Can you do it?"

When Pedro sees Mehdi fingering a roll of twenties, he looks around to be sure they're alone. "If you keep Ramon away from me, I can do it."

"I give you my word. Ramon will not bother you and I'll pay you when you're finished."

At the car, meanwhile, Jahangir finally finds the photo and shows it to Ramon.

"Do you know this man?"

"Yes. His name is Jose Martinez. I flew him all over Bolivia before Christmas. He's very rich. I left him at his ranch at Lake San Luis. Why do you ask?"

"As we stated, we're land developers planning a project near his property. We need to discuss local labor prices, easements, and other business matters with him."

"Well, your timing is good because he's planning to relocate soon to Lake Rogoaguado. He wants me to fly him there on February eleventh.

"Why is he moving? Do you think he would sell?"

"He was very nervous and in a hurry. I believe he's running away from something. When I asked him why he is moving he told me not to ask any questions."

"Does he have a large staff?"

"No. He sent everyone to Rogoaguado to build a new ranch house."

"He's alone at the lake?"

"No. He kept his old husband and wife team who cook and clean the ranch house."

Having obtained this valuable piece of information, Jahangir, now well bankrolled, quickly peels off three hundred dollars in twenties and hands it to Ramon.

"Here. This is just a thank you bonus. We want to charter you for all our land development flights. Oh, one special favor. Please don't upset the mechanic. We want a safe helicopter."

Mehdi arrives, holding his right hand over his heart, signaling the crisis with Pedro had been averted. The trio drive back to the hotel and wait for word from Rodolfo or Pedro.

JANUARY 13, 1994

During the afternoon, Rodolfo calls to advise the helicopter will be ready for takeoff at 08:00 in the morning. Jahangir alerts Rashid in La Paz and Rashid alerts Jamshid in New York that they are on schedule.

The following morning, at 07:35, as Rashid and two agents are airborne for Lake San Luis, a crisis develops in Cochabamba. Rodolfo refuses Jahangir's $600 cash.

"No, no," complains Rodolfo. "I want the Rolex you offered."

"Now wait. I offered the Rolex because we didn't have enough cash. Here, take the money."

Rodolfo shakes his head in denial. "The Rolex or you don't fly in my helicopter."

Under normal circumstances, Jahangir would have persisted. Realizing that Rashid was already airborne and that he could not risk a delayed takeoff, he gives Rodolfo his treasured watch.

As they climb to cruise altitude, Ramon shakes his head at Jahangir.

"You should have argued with Rodolfo. I know him. He would have taken the cash."

The two hour flight is routine. When Ramon announces they are over Jose's ranch, Jahangir spots the other helicopter and calls Rashid.

"Rash, we are starting to circle the ranch. We'll pinpoint and photograph the area while you locate the landing site for our base camp."

As Ramon continues to circle the area, he and Jahangir watch Rashid's helicopter land.

Rashid calls Jahangir.

"This is a good site for our camp. Talk to you later."

No longer able to suppress his curiosity, Ramon asks, "Those are your associates?"

"Yes. That's our survey crew from La Paz. They will set up camp and contact Señor Martinez to explain our project. I have taken enough photos of the area, so let's return to Cochabamba."

Two hours later, after Rashid's tent is set up and equipped, he and another agent, carrying survey gear and camera, begin their two kilometer walk to Jose's ranch house. Looking through binoculars at approximately four hundred meters from the house, Rashid sees no sign of life.

He scans the area and identifies what must be Jose's house, four small houses nearby, a barn, an empty corral, a well housing, two elevated water tanks, a wood tower with stacked antennas, a noisy generator with elevated fuel tank and a helicopter pad with wind sock. They circle around, putting the barn between them and the ranch house, and then proceed with caution.

"If anyone stops us," whispers Rashid as they continue, "set up your transit while I ask to see Señor Martinez."

They knock on the barn door. Getting no answer, they enter carefully. They find an old jeep, a D-4 bull-dozer, a 1978 Ford pick-up, a hand mortar mixer, six wheel barrows and an assortment of hand tools. Rashid touches the hoods of the jeep and pick-up.

"This pick-up was driven earlier this morning."

His agent whispers. "Want me to disable it?"

"No. We'll take care of the vehicles and the generator when we're sure Jose is asleep."

Before exiting the barn, Rashid calls his agent at base camp.

"Notify Jahangir that we are on our way to Jose's house."

At approximately fifty yards from the ranch house, an elderly couple walk out and start walking towards one of the small houses. They see Rashid and his agent. Without stopping, the old man waves an arm in the air.

"El patron esta adentro," (The owner is inside) he informs them.

As Rashid approaches the ranch house door, he sees the old couple enter the third small house. Jose's house is a weather beaten structure requiring a lot of work.

"This place is a shambles. Maybe that's why he's moving to Lake Rogoaguado," Rashid reasons as he knocks on the door.

When the door finally opens after six knocks, Rashid is greeted by the sight of a 357 magnum pointed at his chest.

"Ah – it's Jose."

As an ex Savak agent accustomed to facing weapons, Rashid, in disguise, decides to act afraid. He drops his briefcase and trembles.

"Please, Sir, don't shoot. We are surveyors."

"Why were you circling around my ranch? And why are you here?"

After Rashid explains that they plan to develop the adjacent property and wish to discuss possible financial benefits with him, Jose holsters his weapon and invites them in.

"Now," questions Jose, "Just how can I benefit from your development?"

"Actually, our buyers are really interested in your property because it's high and has the best view of the lake. They sent us here to obtain your permission to survey your ranch so we can determine if there is some way they can purchase a piece of it for access to the lake."

Jose lights a long cigar. "Your timing happens to be very good. I'm a business man and I'm always willing to do business for profit. Do your survey. Then have your company make me an offer."

"This is incredible," shouts Rashid, excitedly waving his arms. "Our management will surely want to discuss details with you. Will you permit us to look around your house and make a floor plan? "

"Yes. And you can also look at the other four houses and barn. I own 22 hectares (54.362 acres). I may sell all of it and retire to La Paz. I will get Lucho, my cook, to prepare lunch."

When Jose leaves, Rashid and his agent move quickly around every room, making notes. The house is clean and well furnished, with sealed boxes in every room, obviously ready to move to Lake Rogoaguado. As they place their stage-one fire charges, Rashid whispers.

"This is like a gift from heaven. As George always says - ' a piece of cake'."

They exit the front door just as Jose arrives with Lucho.

"Nice house," praises Rashid. "If our management buys your ranch, we will recommend the house be used for senior staff."

"That's good. By the way, this is Lucho, my cook. He will serve lunch in forty five minutes."

The agents, meanwhile, make notes as they survey the water tower, generator, antennas and barn.

When Rashid and his agent return for lunch, Jose is already seated at the head of the table, lighting a cigar. He looks at his watch, then blows smoke in the air. "You're two minutes late."

"I'm sorry," apologizes Rashid, "we were just..."

"I'm a very punctual person," interrupts Jose. "I expect other people to be just as punctual. Now let me tell you," puffing on the cigar, "I am moving on February eleventh. Your associates need to make me an offer before I move. Make no mistake, I will not delay the move to La Paz."

Rashid nods his head in agreement, thinking, *"Liar. We know why you're running to Lake Rogoaguado. And it's ironic that you're moving on February eleventh. That's the date in 1990 when Manuel tried to kill Mr. Addabbo."*

"I promise," assures Rashid, "we will rush our survey and return soon."

As the sun dips below the horizon, the agents eat a light supper and send the following message to Tony, via Jahangir.

"Mr. Berlotti. Everything very easy and on schedule. We will terminate work in about twenty-four hours. Our main concern is to protect Jose's innocent cook and housekeeper. Stage two could be activated tonight, but our helicopter will not return until 09:00 hours an Monday."

Thirty minutes later, their message is acknowledged by Tony.

"Good work, Rashid. Yes, protect all innocent people. Be careful and good luck."

Before retiring, the agents set and activate their perimeter alarm system and review tomorrow's activities. After an early breakfast, Rashid and one agent return to Jose's property and again pretend to be engaged in a topographic survey.

At eleven in the morning Lucho appears and invites them to join Jose for lunch at one.

Rashid accepts and apologizes that they don't have any wine to bring.

Lucho waves his arms in the air.

"No importa. Tenemos bastante Pisco." (Doesn't matter. We have plenty of Pisco) and walks away slowly, shaking his head.

"Rashid, Lucho appears to be worried or upset about something, don't you think?"

"Yes. There were no moving boxes in his cabin. I bet he's wondering what will happen to him and his wife when Jose moves."

"We can't let anything happen to the old folks or Mr. Berlotti will be very upset."

"I agree. We need to make sure they don't leave their cabin during the blaze. They may even sleep through it as the fire will be concentrated in Jose's bedroom. Besides, we will be right there to keep the fire from spreading."

"If Jose manages to make it to the front door, I'll kill him."

"Of course. But I guarantee, he'll never make it out of bed."

As the "surveyors" set up their level near the house, Rashid decides he needs a glass of water. He knocks on the door. Lucho's wife greets him. She looks as old as her husband, with skin as dry and wrinkly as a dead leaf. The smell of a simmering onion indicates that Lucho is already in the kitchen.

When she returns with the water, Rashid asks, "Donde estan los hombres?" (Where are the men?")

"El patron esta embalajando y Lucho esta en la cocina." (The owner is packing and Lucho is in the kitchen.).

While at the door, Rashid notices more boxes have been packed, ready for transport, in the living room.

At five minutes to one, Lucho appears on the porch hammering a large tin pot.

"Oh, oh," alerts Rashid. "Let's go in before he reminds us how punctual he is." *"He will soon find out how punctual we are, too."*

The agents are surprised to be greeted at the door by Jose. Yesterday he addressed them in English. Today he speaks to them in Spanish.

"Buenas tardes topografos. Adelante por favor." (Good afternoon, surveyors. Come in please.).

In the dining room, Lucho quickly appears with a tall pitcher of Pisco sours. He fills their glasses and departs. Although these agents are Moslems, they are not strict adherents of Islam and join in Jose's toast. Not to do so may cause suspicion.

"Here's to a successful business association."

"Yes, Señor Marinez, we guarantee our business will be successful." *"Ours, but not yours."*

Throughout lunch, Rashid keeps wondering why Jose departed La Paz so quickly after the news of Pablo Escobar's assassination. *"He's surely running away from someone, but who and why? Did he cross Escobar or his associates? After tomorrow, it won't matter."*

Jose fills his wine glass for the fifth time and lights a long cigar.

"Ahhhh - fine Cuban leaf."

He leans back in thought, then makes Rashid an offer.

"I have been thinking. I will sell my ranch - all of it - for one hundred thousand dollars. But, gentlemen, I must have all of the money before February eleventh.

"That, Señor Martinez, sounds like a very generous offer. Knowing how much our management want your property, I can almost guarantee they will pay your price."

"Good! But remember - you don't have much time. I invite you for dinner tonight at eight.

Rashid observes Jose carefully. *"He suddenly appears very nervous. What's going on..."* "You are very kind, Señor, and we accept your invitation."

"Good. Lucho will prepare my favorite, empanadas de pollo (chicken turnovers). You like them?"

"Oh, yes, Sir." *"And we trust you will enjoy your last meal."*

From their base camp at seven, Rashid advises Jahangir they are preparing to dine with Jose and that all systems are ready. He wants to be assured their helicopter will arrive Monday morning and provide a back-up helicopter in the event of a delay. Jahangir confirms the message, then reads a message from Tony:

"Be careful. Take care of yourselves and protect the old people. Good luck tonight. We will celebrate in Las Vegas on your return."

The agents arrive at five to eight and are greeted by Lucho's wife, who whispers that they are early and Jose is not yet ready. She escorts them into the living room, then leaves for the kitchen. Rashid notices more new boxes in the room, including four cases of Pisco. At precisely eight o'clock, Jose appears with a tall drink, smoking a cigar.

"Welcome, amigos. Tonight we have an early celebration."

He then shouts at Lucho for Piscos. Lucho's wife appears, walks directly into Jose's room and returns with a half full pitcher. She places it on the coffee table, gives Rashid a toothless smile and walks back to the kitchen. Jose has obviously had a few but does not apologize for his sudden loss of memory as to the location of the Pisco. He fills their glasses and raises his glass making a toast.

"A la venta." (To the sale).

Rashid is proud to have been selected for this assignment. Unlike his more polite and compassionate assistant, Darius, he has been conditioned to the hard facts of his profession and takes great satisfaction in the fact that this killer is going to die by his chosen kind of hell. The agents raise their glasses to Jose with a smile and slowly sip their Piscos.

"Drink up, assassin. Enjoy your final moments. We're certainly going to enjoy them!"

Lucho limps in carrying a large platter of hot empanadas, places them in front of Jose's seat, lights four candles, and fills their wine glasses.

"Listo" (ready) and the old man hobbles back to the kitchen.

Darius has been thinking about the old man and his wife. *"Lucho and his wife must be devastated wondering what will happen to them after Jose leaves. We can't allow them to die with Jose."*

Jose piles five empanadas on his plate and hands the platter to Rashid.

"Buen provecho" (enjoy your meal or bon appetite).

The rapidly diminishing pile of empanadas is testimonial to Lucho's skill in the kitchen. Darius seizes this opportunity to question Jose's intention with the old couple. He smacks his lips.

"Jose, these are the very best empanadas I have ever eaten. Lucho deserves a medal. Are he and his wife moving with you?"

Jose lights a cigar, then looks suspiciously at Darius.

"Why are you interested? Why should you worry about that old man and his wife?"

"Well," interjects Rashid smoothly. "Who would make your favorite dish and keep your house so neat and clean if you left them behind."

Jose finishes his wine and nods his agreement. Then, increasingly drunk, switches between Spanish and English.

"Si—tienes razon." (Yes—you're right). He does make the best empanadas and my wife is a bad cook."

Darius comments. "A man of your stature should not have his wife cooking anyway. So, you will take them with you?"

Jose blows smoke in the air, slowly pours himself another glass of wine and chugs it, smiling:

"I will sleep on it," then shouts towards the kitchen, "Lucho, mas tinto!" (more red wine).

"Good, drink up, Jose. More wine will make you sleep soundly."

Then Rashid inquires of Jose, "Señor Martinez, we notice you have quite an array of antennas on your tower. But where are your radios?"

"They're all packed. Why do you want to know?" Obviously paranoid, Jose again looks suspicious.

"Sorry for prying. My associate here is an amateur radio operator. We just wondered because we didn't see any radios."

Satisfied with Rashid's explanation, Jose confides, "I'm an electrical and electronic engineer. I experiment with communications equipment." He pours himself another glass of wine and continues, "So, tell me...what will your people build here? And why Lake San Luis?"

"Our managers represent a large U.S. corporation. They specialize in developing exclusive foreign resorts for celebrities and wealthy executives who want to stay away from tourists and paparazzi."

Jose nods his approval, has another drink, stands and lights a fresh cigar.

"Well then, amigos, I think I should raise my price. Que te parece?" (What do you think).

"We are sure management will consider any reasonable offer. It's a good location for them."

"In that case, I double my price. Tell them I want two hundred thousand dollars - in cash."

Rashid stands, finishes his drink and salutes Jose.

"Consider it done, Señor Martinez. Now, it's late and we must go. Our survey must be completed quickly. The empanadas and fine wine were delicious and a pleasant ending to a very productive day."

While walking the agents to the door, Jose's gargantuan appetite, coupled with his overindulgence of Pisco and red wine, finally give rise to a thunderous belch.

"Aaaaaah," he bellows without apology and rubbing his belly, "Now I will sleep soundly all night."

Rashid gives him a deceptively kind smile. "Yes, I'm sure you will."

Forty five minutes later at base camp, the three agents set alarms, gather their gear and quietly move towards the ranch. They stop behind the barn to view the houses. The ranch house lights are still on in the kitchen and Jose's bedroom.

"Lucho and his wife must still be there cleaning up. Let's wait," whispers Darius.

Fifteen minutes later, the kitchen light goes out. The old couple exit and walk towards their cabin. Lucho's wife could be heard complaining about Jose's smelly cigars. Lucho agrees, then prophetically predicts, "Some night when he has had too much to drink, like tonight, he'll set the place on fire with one of those damn Cuban cigars."

When a light appears in the small cabin, the agents move quietly to it and peek in the windows. The old couple are in the bedroom undressing. They put on nightgowns, kneel beside the bed in a long prayer, then turn off the flickering low wattage lamp and retire.

"Now I'm satisfied," whispers Darius. "They will be safe there."

Rashid and agent Mohamad, move to the empty house nearest Jose's. They energize their remote units and pressurize the chemical canisters. Meanwhile, Darius goes to the barn, disables the jeep and pick-up, then pulls the fire hose from the water tower and tosses it to Rashid and Mohamad.

ONE AM SUNDAY, JANUARY 16, 1994

Jose's bedroom light is still on. They wait as Rashid looks at his watch again and again.

Rashid instructs Mohamad, "Approach the house with caution and determine what he's doing. If he comes out - kill him!"

Ten minutes later, Mohamad returns with a thumbs-up.

"He's sound asleep on the bed. Probably passed out – but his .357 is on the night stand."

"I'm ready to shut down the generator," whispers Darius.

"Not yet," orders Rashid. "Since his light is still on, we can't shut it down as planned. The sudden change to darkness could awaken him. Let's wait."

At Two AM, Rashid gives the signal to move. Darius pulls the fire hose to within twenty meters of the house. Rashid and Mohamad move to Jose's corner bedroom walls, spray them and secure the remote ignitor modules. Rashid moves back to Darius, while Mohamad stands at the front door with his gun ready.

Ten minutes later Rashid depresses his remote control button, triggering short time-delay fuses, first in the hall leading to the bedroom, then the two exterior bedroom walls, cutting off any chance for Jose's escape. The result is textbook perfect. Within seconds, the bedroom becomes engulfed in a spectacular blaze. Jose's screams and thrashing around last less than two minutes.

"Yes!" shouts Rashid. "Thanks to Allah - It's over - as planned. Mr. Berlotti will be very relieved." As the bedroom fire rages, Darius moves quickly to the house and begins to douse the roof, other exterior walls, then breaks windows and sprays into the living room and dining room.

The bright blaze, intense heat and odd smell awaken the old couple who scramble out of their cabin with Lucho shouting, "Por Dios! Que paso?" (Good God! What happened?)

With raised arms, Rashid replies, "No sabemos todavia." (We don't know yet).

Lucho quickly analyses the situation, advising that Jose was drunk and smoking a cigar when he went into his bedroom. His wife agrees as she makes the sign of the cross.

The agent's preparations and immediate action prevent the fire from consuming the remainder of the house. The fire is extinguished at approximately four thirty in the morning along with the arrival of an unexpected visitor carrying a lantern.

Rashid, standing behind Lucho, immediately palms but does not draw his hidden weapon when Lucho greets Pedro.

"What happened?" asks Pedro.

"Jose burned in the fire."

"He was drunk and smoking again, right?"

"Yes, like always."

"What a pity, Lucho. Jose was a very intelligent and rich man."

"That's how life is, Pedro."

Rashid remains silent, thinking, *"Mr. Berlotti won't believe it was this easy and I'm sure George will remind everyone that he predicted it would be a piece of cake."*

At five, Lucho's wife informs the men she will prepare breakfast, then apologizes that they will need to eat in shifts because of her very small kitchen. Head bowed, she walks away in tears.

The helicopter arrives on schedule but circles the ranch several times before landing. When the helicopter door opens, Jahangir exits with a smile, followed by a puzzled looking Ramon.

"What happened?" asks Ramon.

"There was a fire in one of the bedrooms."

"Is Señor Martinez OK?"

"There's a lot of damage, but he's OK," lies Rashid. "He's having breakfast with Lucho."

CHAPTER 38

THE ASSASSINS ARE DEAD

JANUARY 16, 1994

The helicopter lifts off on schedule and lands in Cochabamba before noon. Jahangir attempts, unsuccessfully, to negotiate the return of his Rolex already on Rodolfo's wrist. He pays for the balance of the charter and promises more flights to Lake San Luis.

Before leaving, Rashid continues their deception with Ramon. "We will meet with Jose Martinez again in two weeks."

Back in New York, anticipating word from Bolivia, Tony and his team remain silent in the radio-computer room. The fragrance of fresh coffee, cappuccino and Tony's cigars add a Starbucks ambience to the room.

George breaks the silence. "Damn! Look at the time. We should have heard from them."

Judy shakes her head. "I hope they didn't run into trouble."

"Don't worry," assures Jamshid. "My men are professionals in this kind of work."

"Judy may be right," adds Josh. "Jose is the cleverest of the assassins. Remember, it could have been him who had Ali killed in that Oruro fire."

George paces the floor. "What do you think, Dad?"

"I think I need another cappuccino! And we must wait."

This wait is not long. Half an hour later radio silence is broken as the sound of Farsi comes through loud and clear. The message is short, but the look on Jamshid's face, which is generally impassive and serious, needs no translation. The subdued tension in the quiet room erupts into thunderous cheers.

"Tell, tell! What did Rashid say?" demands the excited Judy.

"Success! We have closure."

Tony raises a fist in the air. "Yes, team! Finally, the assassins are dead."

"I told you it would be a piece of cake!" shouts George.

"And I knew justice would prevail in the end," adds Judy. "Peter and Dr. Monti would be proud!"

"Okay, team. Start making arrangements for our celebration in Vegas. I'll call Carmen, Silver Fox and Hal Brooks with the good news.

About an hour later, Judy walks into Tony's office to ask for the celebration date and finds him on the couch, ashen, in a cold sweat and holding his chest. She screams for George.

George knows the problem. He is quietly firm as he takes control.

"That's it, Dad. You are officially retired and going to be with Carmen for some TLC as soon as we pack your bags. The assassins are dead. Your business days are over, period. I'm taking over now!"

"What the hell does a lawyer know about engineering and construction!" snaps Tony, in obvious pain.

"I'll see that your contracts are completed. Then we'll liquidate. You'll have enough to be independent"

As Judy places a cold towel on Tony's forehead, he closes his eyes and raises his arms.

"OK, I'll go to Carmen's and think about it. And don't do anything foolish while I'm gone."

Three days later, Tony calls Nunzio again.

"Couldn't say much the other day because I was feeling lousy and didn't have the final details. Nunz, you already have most of it, but go ahead and record this. Stop me if you have any questions."

The recording lasts about twenty minutes without interruption.

"Now," states Tony, "you can finish the exposé. All of the bastards are gone."

"What are your plans, Tony?"

"George and I will take new identities and relocate out of the U.S. Carmen and I will finally be able to marry, but I don't know where we'll settle. I believe George will marry Rimma and probably practice law in Mexico. Josh will be my personal bodyguard, Judy will join her husband, probably in Africa, Kruchenko refused my bonus. He told me he has plenty of money and will leave Rosarita to start a new life in Guadalajara. I don't know what Rosita and Katerina plan but feel sure Boris will help them. In the future, Jam (Jamshid) or Rashid will contact you with any additional information. As you know, Nunz, this has been one hell of a nightmare. I want nothing more now than peace and quiet with Carmen. I believe I have vindicated Gloria and my daughters.

When the time is right, after you complete the book, I hope we can arrange to meet again."

"Tony, I believe you have also vindicated President Kennedy. And the world needs to know. Damn it, Tony! It isn't fair that you have to leave the country. You deserve a presidential commendation for what you did. You solved the mystery of the century."

"I know, but there are still some V.I. P.'s who want the public to believe the Warren Commission. They'll do anything, as they've already proven, to discredit any other explanation."

"But, Tony, you have the facts. There are witnesses, diaries, tapes, photos, medical reports, hand grenades, fingerprints, my stolen passport photo..."

"That's right, but I can't trust anybody in government. They'd detain me, ask a million questions, want me to prove everything, harass my witnesses, keep me in this country and who knows what else. No, Nunz, my life would be miserable again and I don't need any more misery. I'm out of here! I love my country but can't trust the government in this."

"Where's Rashid going?"

"According to Jam, he wants to try to establish a relationship with Rosita. Jahangir is homesick and will probably return to Iran. I don't know what Darius, Mohamad and the other agents will do. Carmen is giving each of my Savak men a severance pay of twenty grand, except Jam and Rashid. They'll get fifty G's. And I've been paying their expenses as well as salaries all these years and feel sure they have all put aside quite a bit of money."

"Does Brooks know where you'll be?"

"No. Only George, Jam, and Rashid will know. All other lines of communication are off."

"Just like being in the Witness Security Program..."

"No! I'll be a lot safer, Nunz. The Marshal's Service falls under the Department of Justice. And, with Justice, we'd be back to square one with the harassment. I just can't trust them."

"I understand. I received their letter and services information a couple of years ago when I thought that could be an option while Manuel and Jose were still alive. Remember, it was Manuel who tried to kill me in Coloso. Anyway, I couldn't do it because I'd have to reveal too many details, sever all relations with my family and, most important, Tony, I made you a promise."

"Thanks, Nunz. You're one of the good guys that I could trust throughout this ordeal."

"You're 'family', Tony. And you know how we Italians are about family. Hey, that's what family and friends are for, right? I'll be waiting to hear from you. Ciao viejo. (So long old man).

"Ciao, Zorro Plateado." (So long, Silver Fox).

ILLUSTRATIONS

NOTE: Names within dashed boxes on organization charts indicate individuals not on payroll or directly involved in operations or patsies or out of the money flow loop.

Plate 1AB, Conspirators Hit-Team

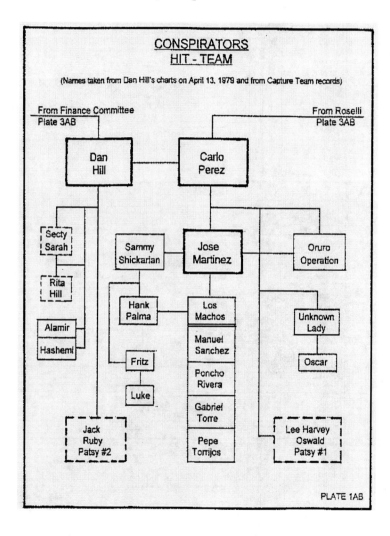

394

Target *JFK*

Plate 2AB, Plan of Dealey Plaza

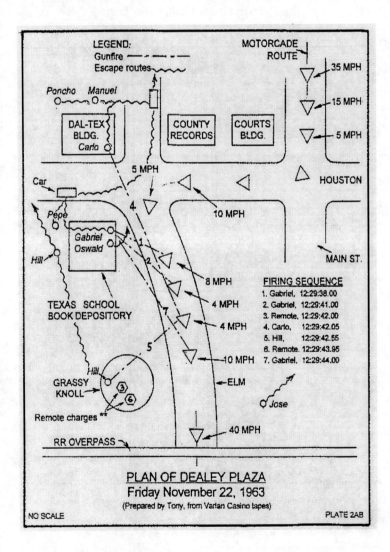

Plate 3AB, Conspirators Assassination/Finance Committee

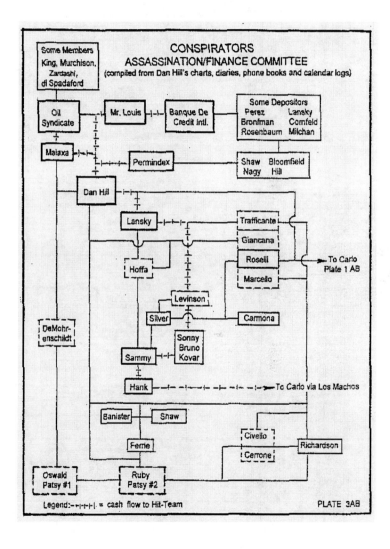

396

Plate 4AB, Plan of Sulfur Plant Ambush

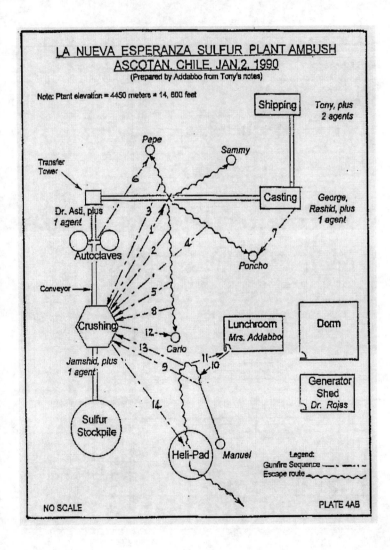

Plate 5AB, Capture Team

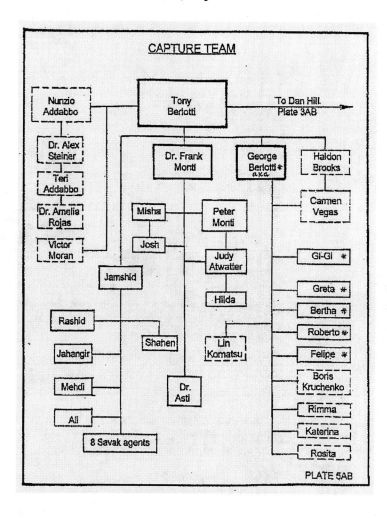

MILESTONES

<u>December 1953</u>   Tony Berlotti and Nunzio Addabbo meet on a Pan Am Flight from Brazil to the U.S.

<u>Pre 1959</u>   Organized crime in Havana, headed by Lansky and Trafficante, enjoy huge casino profits.

1959

<u>January</u>   Fidel Castro takes control of Cuba from Batista.

<u>February28</u>   Marita Lorenz meets Castro on board her father's cruise ship "Berlin" in Havana. They begin a love affair. Marita's father, Heinrich, was a wealthy German Navy Captain and U-boat commander during WW11. Her mother, Alice, was a cousin of Henry Cabot Lodge and began an intelligence career in the French underground, moving up into British intelligence and then to the OSS (now the CIA). After WW11 she worked for U.S. Army Intelligence and at the Pentagon.

<u>Early March</u>   Castro sends a private jet to New York for Marita. She lives with Castro at the Habana Hilton until September.

<u>April</u>   Marita accompanies Castro to the U.S. to meet President Eisenhower who refuses to see him. During that trip she tells Castro she is pregnant.

<u>May</u>   Marita meets Frank Sturgis, Castro's Chief of Air Force Security. Sturgis would later be identified as a CIA Contract Agent and one of the Watergate burglars. Sturgis' given name is Francisco Fiorini.

<u>May to October</u>   Sometime during that period, FBI reports indicate that Marita had one and possibly two abortions or first a miscarriage and then an

abortion. She turns against Castro when Sturgis tells her Castro plans to kill her and her baby. Soon after, she infiltrates Castro's 26th of July Movement in New York and provides membership information to the FBI.

Mid Year   Marita Lorenz is hired as contract agent by a CIA operative to eliminate Castro.

Fall   Judith Campbell has a brief affair with Frank Sinatra. (Judith married Billy Campbell when she was 18, divorced him after JFK was assassinated, then married golf pro Billy Exner).

1960

January   Marita Lorenz fails to kill Castro.

Early February   Training of Cuban exiles by the CIA to invade Cuba is approved by IKE.

February 7   Frank Sinatra introduces JFK and Ted Kennedy to Judith Campbell at the Sands in Vegas.

March 7   JFK and Judith start a 2 ½ year affair at Plaza Hotel in NYC, the night before the NH primary.

Late March   Judith is introduced to Sam Flood at a Sinatra party in Miami.

April 8   Judith meets Sam Flood in Chicago on behalf of JFK, soliciting election help and discovers that Sam is actually Sam Giancana, head of the Chicago mob family.

April 12   JFK meets Giancana at Fontainebleau in Miami.

August to
November   Sturgis introduces Marita to "Eduardo" (CIA's Howard Hunt) in Miami where she becomes trained in Operation 40 (code name to assassinate Castro).

November	JFK wins close election over Richard Nixon. Giancana takes credit for the Cook County swing vote.
December 4	Marita travels to Cuba to see Castro.

1961

Early January	Marita returns to Cuba, carrying two Botulism-Toxin pills to be dropped into Castro's drink. (One pill can kill in 30 seconds). In addition to foolishly hiding the pills in a cold cream jar, causing them to gunk-up, she admitted later that she couldn't carry out her assignment and said she flushed the pills down a bidet.
January 20	JFK sworn-in as President.
March	Robert Maheu (ex FBI), coordinates with Robert Bissell (CIA), Giancana, Roselli and Trafficante, to eliminate Fidel Castro before the planned Cuban invasion, known as "Operation Zapata". Due to poor intelligence reports, the original invasion site at the Bay of Trinidad is scrubbed at the last minute in favor of the Bay of Pigs. Bissell asks for Sixteen B-26's. JFK authorizes only eight. Training for the invasion takes place in Guatemala. During this period, Marita Lorenz meets Marcos Perez Jimenez, ex dictator of Venezuela.
April 4	Carlos Marcello is deported to Guatemala City in military aircraft, ordered by JFK & RFK.
April 17	Bay of Pigs Invasion. JFK refuses to provide military air cover. The invasion fails two days later. Six of the eight B-26's are shot down and many invasion men are killed.
June	Marita becomes Jimenez's mistress.
August 8	Giancana meets JFK at White House.

Mid Year	Judith Campbell makes many trips to the White House, carrying envelopes between JFK, Giancana and Johnny Roselli (Giancana's representative in Las Vegas and Los Angeles).
Fall	JFK approves "Operation Mongoose" to overthrow Castro.
Late Year	FBI puts "tail" on Judith Campbell, Sam Giancana and Johnny Roselli.

1962

March	Marita gives birth in New York to daughter Monica, fathered by Jimenez. (Years later, Monica marries Neil Ortenberg, Publisher of Thunder's Mouth Press in New York).
March 22	J. Edgar Hoover reminds JFK that Campbell's association with Giancana and Roselli is bad news.
April	CIA (Harvey) passes poison pills to Roselli, who will arrange to have them passed on to de Verona in Cuba for contract on Castro, Raul and Che Guevara.
May 7	Robert Kennedy meets with CIA regarding plot to kill Castro.
December	Judith Campbell tells JFK she is pregnant.

1963

January 27	Campbell has an abortion in Grant Hospital, Chicago, arranged by Giancana.
February 15	Phone call to Sammy Shickarian in Las Vegas regarding meeting in Puerto Rico.
February 16	Down payment to assassinate President Kennedy made.
February 27	During Hit-Team meeting in Las Vegas, it is suggested that a poison pen be given to

Campbell to kill JFK. (The pen was originally made to kill Castro. When anyone depressed the top of the pen, a tiny hole would allow a poison needle to pass up into the finger). The idea is scrubbed because the JFK/Campbell affair ended immediately following her abortion.

March 6
Carlo Perez suggested as Hit-Man. Oswald targeted as Patsy.

August 16
Jimenez is extradited to Venezuela. He spends five years in jail, then offered asylum in Spain by Generalissimo Franco.

September 18
Dan Hill meets Jack Ruby in Dallas to set-up Ruby as Patsy #2.

September 25
Tony Berlotti arrives in Mexico City and meets Victor Moran.

September 27
Oswald arrives in Mexico City and, according to Boris Kruchenko, is interviewed at Soviet Embassy by KGB Col. Oleg Maximovich Nechiporenko.

September 28
Dan Hill arrives in Mexico City. Oswald visits Cuban Embassy.

September 29
Jack Ruby arrives in Mexico City and meets Hill.

September 29
Tony takes conspiracy photograph in Sanborn Restaurant.

October 8
Carlo and Los Machos arrive in Dallas.

October 12
Carlo puts "tail" on FBI agent James Hosty.

October 16
Oswald hired by Texas Book Depository.

November 15
Hit ordered on Carlo if he fails to assassinate Kennedy.

November 18
Marita claims she was driven to Dallas with Sturgis, "Ozzie" (who she claimed was

Oswald), Gerry Hemming (long time CIA agent), Pedro Diaz Lanz (former head of Castro's Air Force), two Novo brothers (anti-Castroites) and Orlando Bosch (leader of the anti-Castro movement). They drive all night from Miami and check into two adjoining motel rooms.

November 19   Marita claims that soon after their early morning arrival, Jack Ruby arrives and complains of her presence. Ruby leaves after Sturgis speaks with him outside, then Howard Hunt arrives, hands Sturgis an envelope and goes inside to speak with Oswald. She tells Sturgis she wants out of her deal to act as a "decoy" and is ready to leave.

November 21   Sturgis drives Marita to the airport in early morning for her flight to Miami.

November 21   Carlo settles into his "ambush" position. Jose prepares his "Grassy Knoll" surprise.

November 22   President Kennedy is assassinated.

November 22   Marita flies from Miami to New York, with her child. During the flight the co-pilot announces that President Kennedy has been shot in Dallas.

November 22   Dallas police officer Tippit is shot and dies.

November 22   Oswald is arrested as Kennedy's assassin.

November 23   FBI interrogates Sturgis in Miami. He claims he was home watching TV the day before.

November 24   Jack Ruby shoots and kills Oswald.

1964

January   Jimmy Hoffa's trial begins.

June   Guy Bannister (ex FBI) dies.

July 28   Hoffa is found guilty by Kennedy committee.

1967

January 3	Ruby is reported dead in prison. There are doubts about his death and disappearance.
February 22	David Ferrie is found dead in his apartment. It is called a suicide.
March 7	Hoffa jailed in Lewisburg Penitentiary, PA, with a 13 year sentence.
April	Tony establishes temporary residence in Santiago, Chile.
July	Dan Hill, after locating Tony, moves to Santiago, Chile.
October 9	Che Guevara assassinated in Bolivia.
October 27	Dan Hill visits his friend Sam Giancana, in exile in Mexico and leaves on October29.
December 20	Hill, who claims he is CIA, recruits Tony as a Contract Agent.

1968

January 4	Tony uncovers the conspiracy by identifying Hill, Ruby, Oswald and a man sitting next to Oswald in his Mexico City photograph. The identity of the man next to Oswald is unknown at this time.
March 15	Hill introduces his boss, Mr. Louis, to Tony in Santiago, Chile. Mr. Louis claims he is CIA. (Tony never learned if Louis was a first or last name).
March 24	Tony and Hill meet Addabbo at a fly-in "asado" (barbeque) at the Los Andes Airport, Chile.

<u>June 5</u>	Robert Kennedy assassinated in Embassy Hotel in California.
<u>November</u>	Nixon elected President.

1970

<u>October 11</u>	Tony's husband and wife team are torched in Bolivia by Carlo's hit-team.
<u>Late Oct</u>	Tony opens office in Tehran, Iran.

1971

<u>January</u>	Bill Bonanno begins serving time in Terminal Island Federal Correction Institution in CA.
<u>Mid Year</u>	Tony assembles a team of ex-SAVAK agents.
<u>Mid Year</u>	Johnny Roselli and Bill Bonanno meet in prison.
<u>December 23</u>	Nixon frees Jimmy Hoffa from prison.

1973

<u>February 5</u>	Richard Helms begins term as Ambassador to Iran.
<u>September 11</u>	Chile's President Allende is assassinated. General Augusto Pinochet assumes control.
<u>Fall</u>	Tony's wife and daughters are torched in their home while asleep.

1974

<u>Early</u>	Bill Bonanno meets G. Gordon Liddy in prison.
<u>July 4</u>	Conspirator's hit-team meet in Varian Casino in Iran.
<u>August 9</u>	Nixon resigns.
<u>August 14</u>	Clay Shaw (ex CIA) dies.

September 9	Tony meets Haldon Brooks, via Dan Hill, in Mexico City.
October 20	Tony hires Guy Asti, M.D.
December 21	Tony meets Carmen.

1975

June 18	Hill travels to Chicago.
June 19	Sam Giancana assassinated in his home. He had been slated to testify before the Senate.
July 30	Jimmy Hoffa disappears.
September 20	Judith Campbell Exner testifies before the Frank Church Congressional Committee. Soon after, she fears for her life and becomes a recluse.

1976

| June 24 | Roselli testifies before the Senate. |
| July | Roselli's severed body is found in steel drum floating in Dumfounding Bay, Florida. |

1978

March	Misha, Tony's ex Mossad agent, travels to Bolivia, Paraguay and Brazil in search of Carlo and two Nazi war criminals. He never returns.
April 28	George Berlotti makes his first appearance as Gi-Gi, a female impersonator.
May 31	Marita Lorenz testifies before the House Select Committee on Assassinations in closed secret session, under a grant of immunity. According to Louis Stokes, who chairs the hearing, the Committee concludes that there was probably a conspiracy by two main groups: members of organized crime and anti-Castro Cubans.

1979

<u>January 16</u>	Shah, in failing health, flees Iran.
<u>January 30</u>	Khomeini returns to Iran and assumes control.
<u>April 13</u>	Dan Hill dies in Iran. Tony's SAVAK team obtain his diaries, tapes and phone books.
<u>November 4</u>	Fifty-two hostages taken at U.S. Embassy in Tehran by Islamic rebels.
<u>December 5</u>	Peter Monti assassinated in Bolivia by Carlo's hit-team.
<u>December 27</u>	Russia seizes control of Afghanistan. Pakistan General Mohammad Mustaf predicted the seizure in 1978. No one listened.

1980

<u>August 30</u>	Hank Palma is found dead in his Las Vegas home.
<u>December 5</u>	Sammy Shickarian hires a private detective to locate Tony.
<u>December 6</u>	Tony and Addabbo meet at Marana Air Park, Arizona.

1981

<u>January 15</u>	Gabriel, of Carlo's Hit-Team, dies in ambush in Mexico.
<u>January 20</u>	Tehran hostages released on Reagan's inauguration day after 444 days in captivity.
<u>September</u>	Marita is flown to Havana in a chartered plane to see Castro and visit with her son, Andre. (It's unclear when or if she had Castro's son. He may have been adopted). On her return, she continues doing odd under-cover jobs for the FBI.
<u>October 22</u>	Tony and Addabbo meet at dinner for Barry Goldwater, arranged by Betty Ford and Sammy Davis Jr., at the Tucson Community Center.

1982

| November 14 | Addabbo, on a business trip in Bolivia, is driven to the site of Che Guevara's grave. |

1984

| Fall | Addabbo moves to Santiago, Chile, forms and opens Mountain States Engineers Limitada office for the parent company in Tucson. |

1985

March 3	Tony meets Alex Steiner, M.D. at Addabbo's apartment in Santiago for a game of bridge. Severe earthquake hits the area in afternoon. Epicenter is near Viña del Mar.
May 3	Addabbo and Dr. Steiner hear plot to assassinate Tony.
September 22	George and Judy set-up Sammy Shickarian for a heroin deal.
September 27	Tony and team establish a plan to ambush Carlo and Los Machos in Chile.

1986

| Mid Year | Addabbo's passport is stolen. New passport issued on December 2, 1986. (See July 17, 1993). |

1987

| Mid Year | Jose Martinez, Carlo's partner, starts a sulfur operation in the Cerro Patalani area, Bolivia. |
| November | Dr. Asti and Ali discover, in Boris Kruchenko's Patagonia cabin, a photograph of Oswald and Boris side by side on a sidewalk in Mexico. |

1988

<u>May</u>	Jose Martinez hires Ramsey Rushard (Rashid of Tony's Capture Team) to organize the Patalani sulfur project.
<u>Late Year</u>	Marita's passport shows that she spent 10 days in Cuba, probably to visit her alleged son, Andre, who is working as a medic in Nicaragua and giving aid to Contra victims.

1989

<u>March</u>	Start-up of the Patalani sulfur/heroin plant fails. Carlo's estimated loss is $750,000. The heroin remains on site under guard.
<u>Mid Year</u>	Marita joins a group of ex-spies, such as Philip Agee, in the Association of National Security Alumni.
<u>September</u>	Tony restarts his La Nueva Esperanza sulfur operation to trap Carlo and Los Machos.
<u>December 8</u>	Ramsey (Rashid), meets Carlo, Jose and Manuel at the Sheraton Hotel in La Paz where he proposes a heroin smuggling operation from La Nueva Esperanza plant near Ascotan, Chile.
<u>December 11</u>	Manuel flies Ramsey (Rashid) to Tony's sulfur plant to check out the operation. Manuel is impressed.
<u>December 13</u>	Carlo agrees to visit the sulfur plant on January 2, 1990.
<u>December 18</u>	Amelia Rojas, M.D. invites Teri Addabbo, friend since 1984, to join her on a medical field trip to a burial site near Ascotan in the high Andes.
<u>December 29</u>	Tony and his Capture Team make final arrangements for the sulfur plant ambush.

1990

January 1   Dr. Rojas and Teri Addabbo start their field
                   trip. They spend the first night in Calama near
                   Chuquicamata, the world's largest copper
                   operation.

January 2   Dr. Rojas and Mrs. Addabbo get lost, are
                   captured and handcuffed by Tony's team and
                   led to Tony at the sulfur plant. Moments later a
                   helicopter arrives with five conspirators hoping
                   to consummate a heroin deal. The ambush
                   takes place as planned except that Manuel, the
                   pilot, escapes with the helicopter after
                   exchanging gunfire with Mrs. Addabbo. Carlo,
                   Pepe and Poncho are gunned-down and Sammy
                   dies of heart failure.

January 3   Nunzio Addabbo learns, for the first time,
                   details of Tony's clandestine operation. Tony
                   shows him and Mrs. Addabbo the conspiracy
                   photograph he took in Mexico City.

January 11   Mrs. Addabbo, now a target, is flown out of
                   Chile. Tony sends Rashid to protect her.

January 12   Tony provides Nunzio Addabbo with a
                   briefcase full of conspiracy data and gives him
                   carte blanche to write the exposé. Jose and
                   Manuel are still alive and dangerous.

February 11   Manuel makes an attempt to assassinate Nunzio
                   Addabbo in Coloso, Chile. A dog saves his life.
                   Addabbo spends time in two Chilean hospitals
                   and physical therapy in the U.S.

September 15   George Berlotti, impersonating a Puerto Rican,
                   meets Boris Kruchenko at the Bridge Center in
                   Tucson.

September 22   Tony and Jamshid gain access to Kruchenko's
                   condo. George plays duplicate bridge with
                   Boris at the Bridge Center.

September 23   Tony and Jamshid gain access to Kruchenko's
                   Patagonia cabin.

October 15	George meets Kruchenko's ladies in Rosarita, Baja California, Mexico.
October 30	Ali follows Kruchenko to a house in La Puerta, Mexico. It is learned later that this is one of Manuel's hide-outs.
November 16	George learns Kruchenko's secret.

1991

July 4	Dr. Monti suffers a heart attack.
July 30	Tony suffers a heart attack.
September 5	Mrs. Addabbo diagnosed with severe myelodysplastic syndrome.
Mid Year	Marita, in her studio apartment in Jackson Heights, Queens, NY, begins writing her autobiography.

1992

January 7	Dr. Monti dies.
January 17	Mrs. Addabbo dies.
December 20	Jose and Manuel located in the Dominican Republic.

1993

April 2	Tony has another heart attack.
May 6	George blows his cover at the Tropicana Casino in Las Vegas.
May 15	Jose and Manuel return to the heroin plant in Oruro, Bolivia.
June 8	Manuel receives Kruchenko's telegram to begin Manuel's set-up.
June 17	George and Ali gain access into Manuel's house in La Puerta.

<u>June 25</u>	Tony meets Addabbo at Porky and Glen's Restaurant on Long Island, NY.
<u>July 15</u>	Manuel's apartment is located in Mexico City. He isn't there.
<u>July 16</u>	Manuel calls Kruchenko from his La Puerta house. Kruchenko is missing.
<u>July 17</u>	Tony and his team rush to La Puerta and find Kruchenko in Manuel's house. Manuel has committed suicide. In Manuel's wallet, Tony finds photos of himself, Dr. Monti, George and Nunzio Addabbo. Addabbo's photo is from his passport stolen in 1986.
<u>July 23</u>	Jose is located in Oruro, Bolivia.
<u>July 30</u>	Jose is arrested by Oruro police.
<u>August 5</u>	After a police pay-off by Ali, Jose is released.
<u>August 22</u>	Kruchenko arrives in Bolivia to set-up Jose. Ali is killed in Jose's heroin plant fire and Jose escapes.
<u>December 2</u>	Jose is tracked to La Paz, then disappears.
<u>Late Year</u>	Marita's autobiography is completed, co-authored by Ted Schwartz, titled <u>MARITA</u> and published by Thunder's Mouth Press in New York. Neil Ortenberg, publisher of Thunder's Mouth Press was married to Marita's daughter, Monica.
<u>December 6</u>	Jose is reported to be at his ranch house on Lake San Luis, Bolivia.

1994

<u>January 14</u>	Rashid, Darius and Mohamad charter a helicopter to Lake San Luis.
<u>January 16</u>	Jose, the last assassin, is torched in his ranch house while asleep.

January 19   Tony calls Silver Fox and reports that Jose has
                    been eliminated.

Accident Report

FLUOR DANIEL
CHILE LTDA

CORRESPONDENCIA INTERNA

PARA: L. C. RICHARDSON   FECHA: FEBRUARY 19, 1990

LUGAR: ANTOFAGASTA   REFERENCIA: ESCONDIDA PROJECT
                                                   CONTRACT 8001
DE: MAX DOLLMANN   CLIENTE: MINERA ESCONDIDA LTDA.

LUGAR: ANTOFAGASTA   PROPOSITO: N. ADDABBO'S MEDICAL
                                                   STATUS

                                       MDG/769

Following is the result of telephone conversation with Dr. Ducach.
Please note that Dr. Cassatti is not in Santiago and is expected later
today or tomorrow.

I informed Dr. Ducach of Mr. Addabbo's accident and gave him the
information relative to the Mutual's doctor diagnosis, injuries, spine
problem and present status of the patient.

I also indicated that Mr. Addabbo believed that he needed hydrotherapy
which is not available at mutual Antofagasta. Based on above and
previous discussions of the convenience of transfering Mr. Addabbo to
Clinica Las Condes and have Dr. Weiner and his team treat Mr. Addabbo,
I asked Dr. Ducach to give us his personal opinion. Dr. Ducach
indicated that Clinica Las Condes is probably the best equiped Clinic
and has very good doctors. He indicated he did not know personally Dr.
Weiner, but he has heard that Dr. Weiner is a good professional
traumatologist.

Dr. Ducach also indicated that a reumatologist should be called,
recomending for this matter Dr. Basualdo.

Writer contacted Dr. Basualdo, explained the situation and that
probably Mr. Addabbo would be in Santiago sometime this week. Dr.
Basualdo indicated that upon Mr. Addabbo's arrival to Las Condes Clinic
he should be contacted at telephone # 2273138 and he would treat him.

Finally I asked Dr. Basualdo what his opinion was relative to Dr.
Weiner, his team the Las Condes Clinic facilities, the convenience of
transfering Mr. Addabbo, etc., and he indicated that Dr. Weiner is
excellent and Las Condes Clinic the best equiped in Chile.

Please inform writer if I should make arrangements for Mr. Addabbo's
transfer to the Las Condes Clinic.

Regards,

Max Dollmann
MDG/rumo
cc.: N. Addabbo personal folder

Accident Report 2

**FLUOR DANIEL
CHILE LTDA.**

FE 71 12:50

FACSIMILE LEAD SHEET

Fax Nº FA-F-FR – 583

Date: FEBRUARY 21, 1990
FILE: 1037/180.29

Number of documents
including lead sheet _____ 1

To: Company Name: _____ FLUOR DANIEL

Attn: _____ KAREN SCOTT/JANET CARTER

City: REDWOOD CITY _____ State: CALIFORNIA _____ Country: U.S.A.

Facsimile Number to be called _____ QUICK 4

From L. C. RICHARDSON

Reference : ESCONDIDA PROJECT - CONTRACT Nº 800100

Subject : NUNZIO ADDABBO TRANSFER TO SANTIAGO

PLEASE ADVISE TERI ADDABBO BY PHONE AS WELL AS BY EXPRESS POUCH THAT NUNZIO IS TRAVELLING TONIGHT ON THE 7:00 P.M. PLANE TO SANTIAGO RELATIVE TO HIS TRANSFER TO THE CLINICA LAS CONDES, SANTIAGO.

NUNZIO WILL BE TRAVELLING WITH CHARLES HANNA, WILL BE MET AT SANTIAGO AIRPORT BY THE CLINICA LAS CONDES AMBULANCE AND WILL BE ADMITTED TO THE CLINIC APPROXIMATELY 10:00 P.M. TONIGHT. A DR. ERASMO VERA WILL BE ON HAND TONIGHT RELATIVE TO THE NORMAL ADMITTANCE TEST/EXAMINA-TIONS AND DR. BASUALDO (DOCTOR RECOMMENDED BY DR. DUCACH...) WILL EXAMINE NUNZIO TOMORROW MORNING. THE TELEPHONE NUMBER OF CLINICA LAS CONDES IS (02) 211 1002.

REGARDS,

L. C. RICHARDSON

LCR/sam

cc: C. W. Hanna
　　M. Dollmann
　　N. Addabbo

Department of Justice Letter

U.S. Department of Justice

United States Marshals Service

600 Army Navy Drive
Arlington, VA 22202-4210

Mr. Nunzio Addabbo
519 W. Taylor #210
Santa Maria, CA 93454

November 22, 1991

Dear Mr. Addabbo:

In reply to your recent inquiry concerning the Witness Security program operated by the U.S. Marshals Service, we are enclosing general background information which we feel will answer most of your questions.

Due to the sensitive nature of this program, we must refrain from discussing further specifics.

Your interest in the U.S. Marshals Service is most appreciated.

Sincerely,

William M. Dempsey
Public Information Officer

Encl:
a/s

REFERENCES

1. *ACT OF TREASON* by Mark North.

2. *BOUND BY HONOR* by Bill Bonanno.

3. *CASE CLOSED* by Gerald Posner.

4. *CHILE'S MATES DOWN UNDER* by Tim Duncan.

5. *CONSPIRACY* by Anthony Sommers.

6. *CONTRACT ON AMERICA* by David Scheim.

7. *COUP D' ETAT* by A. Weberman and M. Canfield.

8. *CROSSFIRE* by Jim Marrs

9. *DEFAULT JUDGEMENT* by Michael P. Collins.

10. *HONORABLE MEN* by Wm. Colby & Peter Forbath.

11. *J. EDGAR HOOVER*, The Man and the Secrets by Curt Gentry.

12. *JFK-CONSPIRACY OF SILENCE*, Charles A. Crenshaw, M.D.

13. *LIBRA* by Don DeLillo.

14. *MAFIA KINGFISH* by John Davis.

15. *MARINA AND LEE* by Priscilla J. McMillan.

16. *ON THE TRAIL OF THE ASSASSINS* by Jim Garrison.

17. *PLAUSIBLE DENIAL* by Mark Lane.

18. *SIX SECONDS IN DALLAS* by Josiah Thompson.

19. *THE CIA AND THE CULT OF INTELLIGENCE* by Victor Marchetti (ex CIA) and John D. Marks.

20. *THE DARK SIDE OF CAMELOT* by Kitty Kelly.

21. *THE DARK SIDE OF CAMELOT* by Seymour M. Hersh.

22. *THE DAY KENNEDY WAS SHOT* by Jim Bishop.

23. *THE EXNER FILES* by Liz Smith.

24. *THE HOFFA WARS* by Dan E. Moldea.

25. *THE JOHNSON TAPES* by Michael R. Beschloss .

26. *THE MAFIA ENCYCLOPEDIA* by Carl Sifakis.

27. *THE SPY WHO LOVED CASTRO* by Ann Louise Bardach.

28. *THE VERY BEST MEN* by Evan Thomas.

29. *VEIL* by Bob Woodward.

30. *WILL* by G.Gordon Liddy.

31. *WITNESS* by Mansur Rafizadeh.

Note: Much of the material in the above references support the events, dates, evidence and conclusions in this exposè.

WITNESSES

1.   Tony Berlotti took the Mexico City photograph on September 29, 1963, Showing Dan Hill and Jack Ruby seated at a foreground table, Lee Harvey Oswald and Carlo Perez seated in a background table and Victor Moran standing next to a copper sculpture in the Sanborn Restaurant in the Zona Rosa.

2.   Victor Moran was in the Sanborn Restaurant with Tony on September 29, 1963 and saw Hill, Ruby, Oswald and Perez.

3.   Rosita was dating Manuel in Mexico City in 1963

4.   Nunzio Addabbo met Dan Hill at the Los Andes Airport in Chile on March 24, 1968.

5.   Tony's SAVAK team photographed and taped the Hit-Team reunion in Iran on July 4, 1974.

6.   Haldon Brooks told Tony, on September 9, 1974, that he had known Dan Hill for several years.

7.   Rashid and Ali witnessed the mistaken ambush and death of Gabriel (member of Carlo's hit-team) in Mexico on January 15, 1981.

8.   Nunzio Addabbo and Alex Steiner, M.D. heard plot to assassinate Tony in Santiago on May 3, 1985.

9.   Tony Berlotti, George Berlotti, Tony's Savak Team, Mrs. Addabbo and Amelia Rojas, M.D. were at the La Nueva Esperanza Sulfur Plant in Chile on January 2, 1990 where Carlo and his hit-team were ambushed.   Four conspirators were pronounced dead by Drs. Guy Asti and Amelia Rojas.

10.   Tony showed his Sept. 29, 1963 Mexico City conspiracy photograph to Mr. & Mrs. Addabbo in Antogafasta, Chile on Jan.3, 1990.

11. Tony provided Nunzio Addabbo with diaries, tapes, charts, notes and photos on Jan.12, 1990.

12. Tony, George, Jamshid, Boris Kruchenko and other team members discovered Manuel's dead body in La Puerta, Mexico on July 17, 1993. They collected photographs of Tony, George, Dr. Monti and Addabbo from Manuel's wallet. Addabbo's photo was from his stolen passport.

13. Rashid, Darius, Mohamad, Lucho and Lucho's wife saw Jose Martinez go up in flames in his ranch house at Lake San Luis, Bolivia on January 16, 1994.

EVIDENCE

. Dan Hill's reel tapes 4, 5, 6, and 7 converted to cassette tapes 1, 2, 3,and 4.

. Hill's diaries 1 through 11.

. Hill's private phone books.

. Hill's organization charts.

(Note: Other Hill tapes and diaries which did not contain conspiracy data were not numbered by Tony's Capture Team).

. Hill's calendar logs 1958 through 1979.

. Tony's micro tapes 5 through 44.

. Sammy Shickarian's ledgers (diaries) 12, 13 and 14.

. Sammy's photos.

. Hank's diaries 15, 16, 17 and 18.

. Kruchenko's photos.

. Rosita's photos.

. Katerina's photos.

. Manuel's photos.

. Tony's photos.

. George's photos.

. Rashid's photos.

. Jamshid's photos.

. Ali's photos.

. Jahangir's photos

. Mehdi's photos.

. Montico's micro tapes 45 through 138.

. Jamshid's cassette tapes 139 through 202.

. Hand grenades from the Ascotan ambush.

. Dr. Asti's photos.

. Dr. Rojas's photos.

. Varian Casino photos.

. Manuel's private phone book.

. Manuel's wallet.

. Shickarian's private phone book.

. Shickarian's wallet.

. Hank's private phone book.

. Addabbo's photos.

. Addabbo's stolen passport reported to U.S. Consulate in Santiago, Chile.

. Photo from Addabbo's stolen passport.

. Addabbo's accident and medical records.

Note: The assassins' voices on the tapes, during the Hit-Team reunion at the Varian Casino on July 4, 1974, are, in essence, confessions to JFK's assassination.

CONCLUSIONS

Much of the material in the public domain supports *TARGET *JFK**. What has never been reported, until now, are the correct names of JFK's assassins, their association with the Finance Committee, the money trail, the motives calling for the assassination and how they were finally eliminated.

After reviewing all available notes, interviews, photos, tapes, diaries and personal experiences, there is no credible evidence that the CIA, FBI, S.S., LBJ, Nixon or Castro had any direct involvement in the assassination of JFK. While there were several ex-CIA and ex-FBI individuals directly involved in the conspiracy, the important unresolved questions are: what did LBJ, Hoover, Nixon and other government officials know about a possible hit on President Kennedy and when did they know it?

Lee Harvey Oswald was, as he claimed, a patsy, but never had a chance to tell his story. He was "sheep-dipped" (a term used by the intelligence community to manipulate an individual for a specific purpose) by Carlo, Jose, Shaw, Bannister, Ferrie and de Mohrenschildt. He was seen at the Carousel Club with Clay Shaw, indicating he was wearing several hats, working as a triple agent with ex government men as well as mobsters. Nitrate tests established that he didn't fire a weapon on November 22, 1963; proving he couldn't have shot President Kennedy or Officer Tippit, contradicting the Warren Commission. Some individuals have claimed it was easy for JFK to be hit from the Book Depository; yet the best sharpshooters were unable to replicate what Oswald allegedly accomplished. Another Warren Commission fallacy is their belief that all shots came from the sixth floor of the Book Depository.

Jack Ruby, another patsy brilliantly set-up by Dan Hill, was never permitted to tell his full story. Like Oswald, he realized that he had been set up and could not get a fair hearing in Dallas. He repeatedly requested Chief Justice Earl Warren to allow him to testify in Washington, yet Warren refused without a satisfactory explanation. Neither the FBI nor the CIA knew that Ruby went to Mexico City in September 1963. As Ruby's alibi, Dan Hill arranged to have a man named "Larry" make at least one phone call from Ruby's apartment and office on September 29, 1963. Why did J

Edgar Hoover, in refusing to give Ruby a lie detector test, state that
such tests are unreliable? The questions remaining about Ruby are:
was he intentionally infected with cancer, allegedly dying in prison
on January 3, 1967? Or, as reported by Mrs. Grace Pratt, given
Ruby's connections to the assassination money flow, was he
secretly flown out of the country, possibly to Israel? Had it not
been for John Richardson's untimely accident, Ruby never would
have been involved in the conspiracy.

This writer agrees with Tony Berlotti that Carlo Perez, on the
roof of the Dal-Tex Building and Dan Hill, behind the Grassy
Knoll, fired the fatal shots at JFK and that Gabriel, on the sixth floor
of the Book Depository, missed the motorcade driver and wounded
Governor Connally.

The killer's get-away car, as reported by Jim Garrison, was
confirmed during the Hit-Team reunion in Iran on July 4, 1974. See
Plate 2AB and Chapter 10.

From Dan Hill's diaries, tape recordings and information in
the public domain at the time, Tony Berlotti is convinced that the
conspiracy began with top level associates in finance, politics and
special interest groups seriously concerned over President
Kennedy's plans to pull out of Vietnam, to crush the CIA, "cool it"
with Israel, go after the "Mafia" and the resulting impact those
actions would have on their interests. Those associates formed the
ASSASSINATION/FINANCE COMMITTEE shown on Plate 3AB
and designated Daniel Hill to coordinate the assassination effort,
contracting an "outsider" for the hit.

Hill kept detailed records and recorded most of his phone
calls. Plate 3AB has been prepared from many of his diaries, charts,
telephone books and calendar logs, showing the 'in-the-loop'
COMMITTEE leaders outlined with heavy lines. The conspirators,
who refined "money laundering" to a fine art, deposited their
"Illegal" profits from drugs, Casino skimming, loan-sharking,
prostitution etc., in the Swiss Banque De Credit International and
Permindex.

It is common knowledge that Swiss banks don't reveal the
identities of its depositors, making detection difficult. One of the
conspirator's laundering techniques was the Swiss omnibus
accounts, where depositors anonymously buy stock in the market,
making it easy to avoid paying capital gains while frequently
gaining control of that stock. Another illegal method was the
"mortgage scam" where the conspirator bought, say, a dozen

laundromats or theaters, etc. with, perhaps a 10% down payment and a 40% first mortgage. The buyer then borrows his remaining 50% from the Swiss bank. This means the buyer is paying himself interest and also allows him to deduct that interest on taxes.

According to Tony Berlotti and Dr. Monti, Dan Hill, the articulate snob with a Bostonian accent who claimed to be CIA, was either an agent for a foreign country or ex-CIA hired by the Finance Committee to coordinate the assassination effort. If he was ex-CIA, he used his old contacts to his advantage. He certainly had reliable "inside" sources regarding President Kennedy's travel plans. Dr. Monti claimed that Dan Hill's Remote Farm, demobilized in 1969, was never a CIA Camp Peary Annex. Hill's closest friends in organized crime were Sam Giancana, Johnny Roselli and Meyer Lansky. Sarcastic notes in his diaries indicated he disliked Sammy Shickarian, Carlo Perez and loathed Tony Berlotti. His instructions came down from a Mr. Louis (it is not known if Louis is a first or last name). According to Hill's notes, Louis was the Committee organizer. Louis, along with members of the Oil Syndicate, was determined to keep Khomeini out of power in Iran. (See Plate 3AB). According to Tony's ex-Savak agents in Iran, Hill was murdered for his direct involvement in the anti-Khomeini movement.

Sam Giancana, the notorious Chicago crime boss, who collaborated with JFK, Robert Kennedy and the CIA to remove Fidel Castro from Cuba, was murdered with a .22 caliber handgun with a silencer while preparing a late dinner in the basement of his Oak Park, IL home on June 19, 1975, clearly indicating it was an "inside" hit by a trusted friend. Hill's diary showed he purchased two airline tickets from Santiago, Chile, to Chicago for June 19, another indication that Giancana had to be silenced before his upcoming appearance before the Senate. Hill and Giancana were good friends. (Hill visited him in Mexico in late October 1967 while Giancana was in exile and helped him resolve many legal problems). The second airline ticket was in the name of Guillermo Ruiz, perhaps Hill's back-up or another patsy. Berlotti believes Hill had orders to silence his friend Giancana and that he did not act alone.

Johnny Roselli, Giancana's man in Las Vegas and Los Angeles, and close working friend with Hill, was also involved in the plot to eliminate Castro. He, along with Hill, Sammy Shickarian, Carlo Perez and others, were dealing "outside" the organization in drugs and casino skimming. He informed Shickarian he would be in

Dallas on November 22, 1963, which would have been contrary to assassination instructions. In 1971, Roselli told Bill Bonanno he had shot President Kennedy from within a storm drain. Roselli's storm drain story is an obvious fabrication. Those familiar with storm drain design know that drop inlet boxes, at the curb, would make that almost impossible, except for a midget using a short barrel weapon to take a low angle shot at a moving target. Curbside onlookers might also block the view. Jose Martinez, Carlo's electronic and explosives expert, who planned the Grassy Knoll surprise, recorded seven shots. Roselli's would have made eight. On June 24, 1976, Roselli testified before the Senate. One month later his body was found in a floating 55 gallon drum in Florida waters. Dan Hill's notes indicate that Roselli was silenced for testifying before the Senate on orders from Joe Aiuppa. Could he have been eliminated for announcing he was in Dallas on November 22, contrary to instructions? Was he eliminated because he was accused of skimming? Or, did his friend Dan Hill kill him for what he told the Senate? Dan Hill's notes confirmed that Jimmy Hoffa, contrary to reports accusing him of calling for a Kennedy "hit", wanted no part of the Kennedy assassination. His only link in the loop was his message from the Lansky Group to Sammy Shickarian regarding a five hundred thousand dollar contract. According to Hill's diary, Hoffa was advised that the money was for another attempt to eliminate Castro. On July 30, 1975, Hoffa drove his 1974 Pontiac to the Red Fox Restaurant, seven miles northwest of Detroit, to meet Anthony Provenzano and Anthony Ciacalone. When Provenzano and Ciacalone didn't show, Hoffa walked out of the restaurant and was never seen again. His mysterious disappearance remains unresolved. Provenzano and Ciacalone had air-tight alibis covering that time span.

J. Edgar Hoover was the man with many secrets. He kept files on the private lives of politicians, Hollywood celebrities, communists and others he believed would serve some useful purpose, such as spying on JFK's affair with Judith Campbell and their relationship with mobsters Giancana and Roselli.

It is common knowledge that, until Robert Kennedy became Attorney General, Hoover constantly denied the presence of organized crime. Unknown to most people is that while he had considerable blackmail material in his files against others, he was soft on the "mob" because he knew he was a blackmail target of the mob and feared losing control of the FBI. According to Bill

Bonanno, attorney Roy Cohn showed him photos, taken by Lewis "Louie" Rosentiel, of Hoover dressed in drag and on the lap of an unidentified male. If Hoover was aware of the conspiracy against JFK, he kept silent as a matter of self preservation. Hoover was found dead in his home the morning of May 2, 1972.

On April 4, 1961, Carlos Marcello, organized crime boss in New Orleans, was handcuffed and flown to Guatemala, "kidnap style", on a military plane ordered by JFK and Robert Kennedy, who claimed that Marcello was illegally in the U.S. with a fake Guatemalan birth certificate. It was rumored that Marcello vowed to "get even" for his deportation. According to Hill's notes, Marcello was an active supporter in the conspiracy to assassinate President Kennedy but, like the other mob bosses, he did not initiate the conspiracy or directly handle any assassination money.

Santos Trafficante, Jr., organized crime boss in Florida (headquarters in Tampa), was heavily involved in gambling and drugs. He moved to Cuba in 1946 and, under Meyer Lansky, controlled casino operations in Havana until they were run out of Cuba by Castro in 1959. He was one of the mob's most active supporters in the plot (started by President Eisenhower and the CIA and continued by JFK) to remove Castro from Cuba. He blamed JFK and the CIA for the Bay of Pigs fiasco and his inability to resume Cuban operations. He died of heart failure in 1987.

The ruling members of the crime family were predominantly Sicilian. Meyer Lansky, a Polish Jew, was organized crime's "financial wizard" and probably the most respected of all mob leaders. His uncanny ability to amass millions of dollars for the multi layered national "syndicate" he created afforded him star status in the mafia family. According to Hill's notes and charts, Lansky decided how the "laundered" assassination money should flow to hit-man Carlo Perez. (See Plate 3AB). There was no indication in Hill's notes that assassination money passed through a man called "Eduardo" (identified by several people as E. Howard Hunt, CIA). A note after Lansky's name indicated that he had one million dollars available for the assassination. Lansky died in 1983.

Sammy Shickarian, the hot tempered Armenian, rose from bookie to big-time Las Vegas operative with close ties to professional hit-men. Although his diaries were sloppy and showed many date gaps, they listed many names found in Hill's diaries. He was very friendly with Johnny Roselli, worked with, but despised, Dan Hill and was responsible for selecting Carlo Perez as the man most capable of carrying out the assassination of President Kennedy. Shickarian died of heart failure during the high altitude La Nueva Esperanza ambush in Chile on January 2, 1990. (See Plate 4AB).

Judith Campbell was introduced to JFK, then a Senator, by Frank Sinatra in February 1960. She and JFK immediately began a 2 1/2 year affair. In March 1960, she was introduced to Sam Giancana, after which she began delivering secret messages between JFK and Giancana. It would be learned at a later date that those messages involved plans to have organized crime remove Fidel Castro from Cuba. In late December 1962, Judith advised JFK she was pregnant. She had an abortion in January 1963 and broke off relations with the President. Judith was never involved in the conspiracy to assassinate President Kenney. She died on September 24, 1999.

Marita Lorenz, once Fidel Castro's lover, later CIA contract agent to assassinate Castro and an FBI informant, is one of the most controversial figures in the conspiracy to assassinate President Kennedy. Some of her stories are contradictory, perhaps as carefully orchestrated disinformation to tie Oswald and Ruby directly to the conspiracy. She claims she was driven from Miami to Dallas on November 18th along with Frank Sturgis (alleged CIA), the Novo brothers (anti-Castroites), "Ozzie" (who she claimed was Oswald) and others. She remained in one of two adjoining motel rooms on the 19 and 20 and was told she was there as a "decoy". She claims that Jack Ruby arrived the morning of the 19th and quickly left, then E. Howard Hunt arrived, met with Sturgis and later with "Ozzie". According to Dan Hill, Oswald was being watched by the Los Machos hit-team and there were no notes indicating that Oswald was in Miami on November 18 or that he was in a Dallas motel room meeting with Hunt. If what she stated is true, the person she thought was Oswald had to be an imposter. The real Oswald, hired by the Texas Book Depository on October 16, 1963 was, in fact, working there during the alleged trip to Dallas. Marita did not like the arrangement and flew back to Miami the morning of November 21st. When President Kennedy was assassinated, she was on a flight, with her child, from Miami to New York.

Frank Sturgis (real name Francisco Fiorini), alleged CIA contract agent and one of the Watergate burglars, was questioned by the FBI the day after the assassination. He had an alibi, stating he was home in Miami watching TV, and was apparently believed.

According to the August 20, 1978 Sunday News Journal, a secret CIA memorandum, in the hands of the House Assassination committee, initialed by Richard Helms and James Angelton, placed E. Howard Hunt (CIA) in Dallas on November 22, 1963. Hunt had witnesses placing him in Washington, D.C.

David Ferrie wore many hats. He worked with Clay Shaw (ex-CIA), Guy Banister (ex-FBI) and Carlo Marcello (organized crime boss in New Orleans). He was a competent pilot, actively involved in the plot to remove Castro from Cuba and knew Oswald and Ruby. He, along with Shaw and Banister, with instructions from Dan Hill, "sheep dipped" Oswald for Oswald's meeting with Carlo Perez in Mexico City. Several days before District Attorney Jim Garrison planned to call Ferrie before a grand jury, Ferrie's naked body, along with two unsigned suicide notes and several empty prescription medicine bottles, was found dead in his apartment on February 22, 1967. The coroner ruled that he died of "natural causes".

Was it suicide? Did Clay Shaw have him silenced? Did Dan Hill eliminate him as another dangerous "witness" before he relocated to Chile? Hill's diaries did not show where he was on February 22, 1967.

New Orleans private detective Guy Banister, the alcoholic and hot tempered ex-FBI agent, once in charge of the Chicago FBI office, was also actively involved in the plot to remove Castro from Cuba. His name, Camp Street and Lafayette Street addresses and phone numbers were noted in all of Dan Hill's diaries. Before Oswald moved to Dallas he was passing out pro-Castro literature in New Orleans. When several of Banister's employees reported Oswald's activities, Banister told them, "Don't worry, he's with us." Banister provided Oswald with a third floor room in the Newman Building and, like Shaw and Ferrie, was obviously sheep dipping Oswald. Banister died of a heart attack in June 1964. Tony Berlotti believes that Banister drank himself to death and that Dan Hill had conditioned him to believe Oswald would travel to Mexico as a friend of Cuba and act as a double agent.

Clay Shaw (alias Clay Bertrand), was another controversial member of the conspiracy to assassinate President Kennedy. He was ex-CIA, Director of the New Orleans International Trade Mart, Director of Permindex, Director of Centro Mondiale Commerciale, wealthy real estate developer, close friend of Hill, Banister, Ferrie and members of the Banque De Credit International. On January 29,

1969, Clay Shaw went on trial as a conspirator in the assassination of JFK. Jim Garrison's case against Shaw did not convince the jury of his guilt and on March 1, 1969, he was found innocent. Like Banister, Hill used him to condition Oswald as a double agent. Hill's notes show that Shaw, "Mr. Louis", Zardashi and Malaxa were associates. (See Plate 3AB). He died of lung cancer on August 14, 1974.

Con artist and ladies-man Enrique "Hank" Palma, Sammy Shickarian's leg-man, was in the loop because of his fluency in English/Spanish and association with Los Machos. He was responsible for the transfer of assassination money from Sammy to Carlo. On August 29, 1980, he was at the Jockey Club in Las Vegas with female impersonator George Berlotti and drinking heavily. While in the men's room, one of Tony Berlotti's Savak agents slipped a "mickey" in his drink. The next day, after missing a meeting, Sammy and Los Machos went to his townhouse and found Hank dead. He left a scribbled note, "get Gi-Gi – bitch!" According to Tony, his high alcohol level, coupled with the mickey, killed him.

George de Mohrenschildt, the white Russian with close ties to the CIA, was an intellectual. He spoke English, Russian, Spanish, German, Polish and French, had a PhD in International Commerce and a Masters in Geology and Petroleum Engineering. As shown in Hill's notes, he was closely associated with Malaxa, P. di Spadaford and King in the Oil Syndicate. He frequently visited Lee and Marina Oswald in Fort Worth and Dallas. It is believed that the words "baby sitter" in one of Dan Hill's diaries, connecting Oswald and de Mohrenschildt, was another intelligence term, like "sheep dipping", that was used to have an agent condition someone for a particular mission. On March 29, 1977, several hours after agreeing to meet a House Select Committee investigator on Assassinations, de Mohrenschildt allegedly committed suicide with a shotgun. If it was suicide, Tony Berlotti believes that Dan Hill never told him why he was "baby sitting" Oswald and that his suicide was after years of guilt for Oswald's death.

Nicolae Malaxa, was a wealthy Romanian industrialist and key player in the Oil Syndicate. During WWII he was in business with Albert Goring, brother of Field Marshall Herman Goring. In 1946, he entered the U.S.A. on a trade mission and sought all means to remain. For him, the ends justified the means. He deposited $100,000 in Richard Nixon's Bank of California account in

Whittier, California, as an obvious quid pro quo for Nixon's efforts to keep him in the United States. In 1951, Nixon, then a California Senator, urged the Immigration and Naturalization Service to grant Malaxa permanent status to build a plant, in Whittier, to produce tubing for oil drilling. It was the height of the Korean War and Nixon stated the essential plant could not be built without Malaxa. The "essential" plant was never built, Malaxa never became a citizen and remained in the U.S.A. until he died in New York in 1972.

The name Levinson, without a first name, appeared many times in the notes of Dan Hill, Sammy Shickarian and Dan Hill's organization chart. The clue to Levinson's identity was determined from one of Sammy's phone books showing Levinson's unlisted phone number at the Horseshoe Casino in Las Vegas. According to Dr. Monti's investigation, Edward Levinson, originally with the Flamingo and Sands Casinos, was major stockholder in the Fremont Hotel and part owner of the Horseshoe Casino. Levinson was a big-time casino owner/operator, bookmaker and associate of many organized crime leaders, especially his friend and boss Meyer Lansky. He also had close ties to Bobby Baker, LBJ's protégé aide. Given Baker's known connection with organized crime, the question remains, was LBJ compromised for what he may have known from Baker? Because Levinson's name box in the organization chart is not outlined in bold line, it is believed he, like Hoffa, was told that the money was for another attempt to eliminate Castro. (Note: In the plot to eliminate Castro, the code words for assassination were: "Executive Action").

Sonny (no last name) was obviously a trusted lieutenant of Trafficante. He was in the "need to know" money loop and dispatched to transfer cash from Levinson to Bruno and Kovar. Bruno (no last name) and Kovar (no first name) were obviously trusted soldiers under Sonny. They transferred cash to Sammy Shickarian for the JFK assassination, but didn't know who originated the conspiracy.

According to Dan Hill, John Richardson, whose name and phone numbers in Dallas and Miami appeared in Hill's diaries, was a DEA agent taking money from Carlos Marcello for special assignments. Richardson was paying Ruby for information on police and other activities in Dallas. Dan Hill originally selected Richardson, a sharp-shooter, to gun down Oswald at the Texas

Book Depository; unfortunately, his untimely accident (Chapter 3) forced Hill to develop a plan to use Ruby, which he did with remarkable success. According to Tony Berlotti, Richardson's phone numbers were "pay phones" and he was never able to determine Richardson's true identity.

Hill showed the names of mobsters Joe Civello and John Cerrone, on his chart, between Richardson and Ruby. Civello was Marcello's man in Dallas. Cerrone was an old Chicago friend of Ruby. It is not known how Hill used them with Ruby.

The Banque De Credit International, Permindex and Oil Syndicate, from Dan Hill's charts, obviously were laundered money conduits to Dan Hill for the $700,000 assassination contract on President Kennedy. The only known names in those organizations and the "zigzagging" money flow, as listed on Hill's charts, are those shown on Plate 3AB. Since it was never determined if Louis was a first or last name, the identity of Mr. Louis has never been established. Dan Hill introduced Tony Berlotti to Mr. Louis, who claimed to be CIA, in Chile in March 1968. Tony learned that Hill was receiving payments from Louis to maintain offices in Mexico, Chile, Iran and U.S. Haldon Brooks was receiving payments from Louis to operate an office in Mexico City for "insider" information on Pemex (Mexico's National Oil Company). Louis's mysterious disappearance from Switzerland surprised Hill and Brooks. Tony does not believe Louis was CIA and that he probably died of old age.

There was no indication in any of the conspirator's notes of how much of the $700,000 contract came from individuals or from each of the three money sources shown on Plate 3AB.

Jose Martinez was Carlo Perez's "think tank". He planned the Dealey Plaza ambush and Grassy Knoll surprise and claimed he recorded seven shots in six seconds. According to instructions, Oswald's contract was to shoot JFK's driver to stop or slow down the motorcade. When Oswald realized he was being used as a patsy in the plot to assassinate the President, he left the building via the front door. Gabriel, who was with Oswald as back-up, rushed the first shot and missed the driver. Carlo Perez, sharp shooting leader of the hit team and mountain climber, was on the roof of the Dal-Tex Building. He was the first to hit President Kennedy from the rear. Less than one second later, Dan Hill, from behind the Grassy Knoll, hit Kennedy from the front. Gabriel's second or third shot hit

Governor Connally. The other two shots from the Grassy Knoll were remote charges placed by Jose Martinez, which were observed by several people as puffs of smoke. (See Plate 2AB).

According to Tony Berlotti, Haldon Brooks, who was on Mr. Louis's payroll in Mexico City, until Louis disappeared suddenly, was never in the assassination loop. Brooks knew but did not like Dan Hill and eventually became Tony's confidant. He retired to Mexico's Lake Chapala.

After reading diaries, listening to tapes and researching the listed "references", what emerged as perplexing dichotomies were the Marita Lorenz story of her trip to Dallas on November 18, 1963 and the Johnny Roselli story reported to Bill Bonanno. The Lorenz story would place a second assassination team in Dallas. If such a hit team existed, they never moved into designated ambush positions. Only three firing positions were witnessed and recorded: the sixth floor of the Book Depository, the Grassy Knoll and the Dal-Tex building, all occupied respectively by Oswald and Gabriel, Dan Hill and Carlo Perez. Roselli told Bonanno he shot JFK from a storm drain inlet, yet no shots were heard or recorded coming from any storm drain. E. Howard Hunt (CIA) stated he was not in Dallas on November 22, 1963 and had an alibi for being elsewhere. Frank Sturgis denied being in Dallas on November 22, 1963 and also had an acceptable alibi.

What makes the Warren Commission Report a colossal disaster was its rush to judgment. They miserably failed to examine all available evidence. Warren, for example, did not call Marita Lorenz to testify or allow Jack Ruby, at Ruby's fervent request, to tell the truth in Washington. He relied heavily on information from Hoover. Hoover, unfortunately, and for reasons already explained, withheld critical evidence. Releasing the implausible "magic bullet" theory and quickly naming Oswald the " lone gunman" is proof that Warren, Hoover and President Johnson wanted rapid closure to the case. If they knew the truth, they covered it up.

Tony Berlotti strongly believes, and this writer agrees, that there may well have been a second team in Dallas to assassinate JFK, but their ambush was called off when they learned another team was already in place. The only person who had a good reason to tip-off the second team was Dan Hill.

CIA official James Angleton agreed with one of the theories that Oswald was a "pro Castro agitator" who met a KGB assassination expert in Mexico. What the CIA didn't know was that Oswald met Boris Kruchenko in Mexico City. Kruchenko was never KGB nor an assassin. He was being used by the Hit-Team to set-up Oswald. Following his guilt feelings over Oswald's death, Kruchenko assisted Tony's Capture Team in pursuit of the assassins.

Several people saw two men on the sixth floor of the Texas Book Depository just before the shooting began. Ms. Tonie Henderson saw two men, describing one as possibly a Mexican or Negro. Actually, one was Oswald, the other was Gabriel, a dark skinned Bolivian and member of the Hit-Team. It was Gabriel who fired the first shot and missed the motorcade driver. It is believed Gabriel's second or third shot hit Governor Connally. (See Plate 2AB).

The FBI reviewed a film by Charles Bronson (not the movie star), taken minutes before the shooting, showing two men on the sixth floor. The FBI returned the film without taking action because Hoover had already presented the "lone assassin" theory. Robert Hughes gave his film, showing two men on the sixth floor, to CBS for evaluation. There was no productive follow-up on that film.

Ms. Beverly Ellis took movies with her new camera showing shots from the Grassy Knoll. The FBI took her film and have not yet, to the best of our knowledge, returned it to her.

Charles Breem, standing next to Ms. Ellis, also heard shots from the Grassy Knoll and Lee Bowers, a RR yard worker, saw two men behind the Grassy Knoll fence just before the shots were heard.

Ed Hoffman, a deaf mute, saw two men behind the Grassy Knoll. He told the FBI that one of the men had a gun. He was told to be quiet about it, that the FBI didn't want to hear anything else from him.

Ms. Jean Hill, standing curbside on Elm as the motorcade passed, saw a gunman fire from behind the Grassy Knoll fence. She was taken by Secret Service men for interrogation in a nearby building. She said she was followed for years by the FBI.

Mary E. Woodward, a journalist, saw JFK's head explode. Her statement was dismissed and not reported by the FBI and the Warren Commission.

As JFK's motorcade approached Houston Street, Oswald realized he had been set up as a patsy. He ignored Gabriel, rushed down to the lunch room for a drink and, after being questioned by police, left the building from the front door instead of the rear door as planned. Angered, he rushed to his room, pocketed his revolver and went to the Texas Theater determined to take, by force if necessary, the money promised him by Carlo and Jose. Oswald's "negative" nitrate tests, indicating he didn't fire a weapon on November 22, 1963, were kept secret for ten months by the Warren Commission.

FBI ballistics lab reports showed that none of the four bullets found in Officer Tippit's body were fired from Oswald's revolver. Although there is no evidence, it is Tony Berlotti's assumption that two of the Los Machos hit-team raced to eliminate Oswald at his boarding house, were stopped by Tippit, then panicked, shot him and fled the scene. This explains reports that two men were seen at the scene and that two types of bullets were used in killing Tippit. There can be no doubt that Oswald was a patsy.

According to many witnesses, shots were heard from the sixth floor of the Book Depository, the Grassy Knoll and the roof of the Dal-Tex Building. Gabriel fired three shots from the sixth floor. Two shots from the Grassy Knoll were "remote charges" planted and triggered by Jose, one shot from behind the Grassy Knoll fence was by Dan Hill and one shot from the roof of the Dal-Tex Building was by Carlo.

Gabriel repelled down the rear wall of the book Depository. Hill, posing as Secret Service, rushed to the rear of the Depository to kill Oswald, then left the scene on Houston Street. Carlo repelled down the rear wall of the Dal-Tex building and rushed, with Manuel and Poncho, to the get-away car parked between the Dal-Tex Building and County Records building. (See Plate 2AB for assassins escape routes).

Mrs. Teri Addabbo and Dr. Amelia Rojas were witnesses to the sulfur plant ambush on January 2, 1990. Teri exchanged gunfire with Manuel before his escape. Four assassins died in the ambush and were pronounced dead by Drs. Asti and Rojas. Their bodies were cremated in the autoclaves.

Nunzio Addabbo, this author, became an assassination target when it was known he could identify Manuel and Jose, the remaining assassins. On Sunday February 11, 1990, when Manuel attempted to eliminate him in Coloso, Chile, a dog saved his life. He spent time in two Chilean hospitals and physical therapy in the U.S. His stolen passport is a matter of record with the U.S. Consulate in Chile.

In 1991, with two killers remaining and being on their hit-list, Nunzio Addabbo considered a name change, relocation and "witness protection". He abandoned that idea when severing all ties with family and friends was not an acceptable option. See Department of Justice letter.

In reviewing the References, we found that while each presented many correct conclusions, they were unable to include critical names and or events in the conspiracy. Some suspected the existence of a conspiracy organization and a hit team but could not name them. They did not know whom Oswald met in Mexico City before and after he went to the Russian and Cuban Embassies. They did not know who was on the sixth floor of the Texas Book Depository with Oswald or why Oswald went to the Texas Theater with a gun. They certainly didn't know who set up Ruby to assassinate Oswald. The majority rightly concluded that it was a conspiracy. We believe that much of the "evidence" presented to the Warren Commission, including some found in several of the JFK conspiracy and assassination books, contain deliberately developed misinformation and disinformation by those who wanted to cover-up the facts and confuse the public. Some who supported the Warren Commission Report, believing in the "lone assassin", "magic bullet" theory, were probably given false information and/or brainwashed by government officials.

New Orleans District Attorney Jim Garrison was definitely hot on the trail of the assassins; but, unfortunately, concentrated almost exclusively on the case against Clay Shaw. As a result, he lost focus on the big picture. He failed to investigate such operatives as Marita Lorenz, E. Howard Hunt, Frank Sturgis and others who were reported to be in Dallas for the assassination. He knew that Oswald's nitrate tests were negative but failed to challenge J. Edgar Hoover. We can only surmise that Garrison knew how Hoover would react to being challenged and didn't pursue the matter.

Pertinent unanswered questions are:

- Acccording to Dr. Crenshaw, trauma doctor examining JFK's wounds, there was a frontal head entry wound and a neck wound. We conclude that the neck wound was Shot #4 from the rear by Carlo on the roof of the Dal-Tex building and the frontal head wound was from Shot

#5 by Dan Hill on the Grassy Knoll, confirming the forward, then backward thrust of JFK's head. Also, according to Dr. Crenshaw, two days later when he was examining Oswald, near death, he was called to the phone. The caller was LBJ, the new President of the United States, with the following message: "I want you to obtain a bed-side confession from Oswald that he was the lone gunman. The Secret Service agent in the room with you will be your witness." Dr. Crenshaw said, "Yes, sir." Oswald died before uttering any words.

- Why did our "Government Doctors" disagree with Parkland Hospital staff doctors regarding the wounds to JFK's head? According to Paul Peters of Parkland hospital, Dr. Rose, a forensic expert, wasn't allowed, by Secret Service Agents, to complete an examination of JFK's wounds. Naval doctors Humes and Boswell, inexperienced in forensic examinations, performed the autopsy. That was a blatant manipulation of critical medical evidence.

- During the July 4, 1973 Hit-Team reunion, Carlo stated that when Manuel was watching the FBI office in Dallas on November 20, 1963, he saw a woman with Dan Hill. Hill stated he was with Ruby. If Manuel was correct, could that woman have been Marita Lorenz? If there was a second assassination team in place, Hill was the only person in-the-loop who had reason to call them off and obviously did.

- Why did J. Edgar Hoover quickly name Oswald the "Lone Gunman" and agree with the "Magic bullet" theory when he had evidence that Oswald didn't fire a weapon on November 22, 1963?

- Why did FBI agent James Hosty, in Dallas, receive orders from counterintelligence superiors (Sullivan and Angleton) to avoid Oswald just days before JFK's assassination?

- Why did the FBI fail to report, to the Warren Commission, Hosty's name and phone numbers found in Oswald's phone book?

- Why were Oswald's prints found on his bolt action rifle after original tests did not show his prints? Unknown to the FBI, the original unidentified prints belonged to Gabriel, who fired 3 shots at the motorcade from the sixth floor.

According to the funeral director, Secret Service men pulled his prints in the funeral parlor and he had to clean Oswald's fingers before burial. If the original rifle tests showed prints, they were Gabriel's and the FBI could not identify them.

- Why did the Warren Commission fail to mention that Oswald was, and had been for over a year, a "Confidential Agent" for the FBI on November 22, 1963?

- Why didn't Earl Warren allow Ruby to testify in Washington?

- Why didn't the Warren Commission call many key witnesses to testify?

The reasons for the above and other investigative anomalies in the tragic assassination of JFK were, in our opinion, deliberate actions to cover-up the truth or, in some cases, attempts to develop and present plausible denial "evidence" to shield their ignorance for not knowing the facts and obtaining immediate closure to the assassination. Either scenario is cause to ponder "why?".

This author has interviewed many of the principals, seen the photographs, transcribed the tapes, diaries, ledgers, calendar and phone logs, and seen the devastating effect the long and expensive manhunt had on Tony Berlotti. Although his innocent involvement ruined his life and fortune, Tony has no regrets. Unfortunately, neither he, nor we, will be around when the "official?" JFK assassination records are made public on November 22, 2038.

We are proud to dedicate this book to Tony Berlotti. He avenged the senseless murders of his wife and daughters and finally eliminated JFK's assassins.

EPILOGUE

We believe readers want to know what happened to Tony Berlotti and the surviving members of his courageous Capture Team after the last assassin was eliminated in 1994.

For security reasons, some locations cannot be revealed at this time.

Victor Moran, Tony Berlotti's Mexican engineering consultant who was standing next to the copper sculpture when Tony took the incriminating conspiracy photograph in Mexico City, is retired with his wife in a Mexico City district. Victor is in his mid eighties.

Computer whiz Judy lives and works with her husband, David, somewhere in Africa.

Boris Kruchenko retired to Guadalajara, Mexico. He lives alone, enjoys playing bridge on the world wide web (www), remains drug free and has never returned to Las Vegas.

Katerina, Kruchenko's cousin, moved into a Mexico City condo owned by Carmen. She lives alone.

Rimma, Katerina's daughter, married George Berlotti.

Rosita moved from Rosarita to Cuernavaca, Mexico where she met and married a wealthy rancher. She and Katerina, separated by only a one hour drive, remain good friends.

Haldon Brooks and his wife are retired at Lake Chapala, Mexico. Their occasional house guest for a weekend of bridge is Boris Kruchenko.

Rashid, the most daring of Tony's Savak agents, who rushed into the line of fire to protect Tony in Las Vegas, is retired in Las Vegas and remains a close friend of Jamshid. He received a large retirement bonus. He reported, without details, that Fritz and Luke have died.

Jamshid, Tony's Savak team leader and loyal bodyguard who also put himself in the line of fire to protect Tony, is retired in Las Vegas. Tony and Carmen provided him with a sizeable retirement package.

Jahangir, Mehdi and the remaining Savak agents have relocated to California. Each of them received retirement bonuses.

Dr. Asti sold his internal medicine practice and is retired with his wife in a southwestern state.

George (Tony's son), is married to Rimma, practices international law in a foreign country and manages Tony's and Carmen's legal and financial matters. They have two children, visit frequently with Tony and Carmen and enjoy vacations at Carmen's Manzanillo hacienda.

Tony has relocated out of the U.S. with Carmen, content now that he has accomplished the mission that was thrust upon him. It was not the life he would have chosen to live. He changed his name again and at last report was undergoing speech therapy after suffering a stroke. He and George edited and approved this author's first draft of this book and subsequent revisions. According to Tony, his September 29, 1963 incriminating conspiracy photograph taken in Mexico City will be released upon the death of his friend Victor Moran. All remaining conspiracy photos, tapes, diaries, logs and notes, now in his and George's possession, will be released in accordance with George's instructions.

"Zorro Plateado", Spanish for " Silver Fox", was the code name for this author, Nunzio Addabbo, who lives with his co-author wife, Elizabeth, in North Carolina. This author has been the grateful beneficiary of the loyal friendship of this remarkable man since 1953. While his story had to be told, I will protect Tony's privacy and anonymity for the balance of my life. We pray for his health and happiness with Carmen.

If it were not for Tony's wealth and tenacity to seek justice after the murders of his wife and daughters, friends and President Kennedy, this story may never have reached the public.

In closing, we find it fitting to repeat that line from the Bible, familiar to the CIA:

"And ye shall know the truth..."

ACKNOWLEDGMENTS

With the exception of the Introduction, written by Colonel David Andre[21], the authors prepared the entire contents of TARGET *JFK*. If there are any errors and/or omissions, they are inadvertent and we apologize. In order to maintain total control over all aspects of an admittedly controversial book, we avoided conventional publishing houses and selected Third Millennium Publishers, an "electronic book" and " print-on-demand" publisher.

We have had carte blanche from Tony Berlotti to produce this exposé; but it is Tony's story and based entirely on information obtained from him. Words are inadequate when it comes to "thanking" Tony, one of life's true heroes. He has shunned exposure or praise for the monumental mission he undertook and completed, but the nation should be grateful to him and his Capture Team. When his wife and daughters were murdered by JFK's assassins, he dedicated his life and fortune to tracking and eliminating them at a great physical and financial cost. His mission was personal but the results are of international impact.

Tony's son, George, a lawyer, deserves high praise as well. His young life was put "on hold" while he joined in his father's mission. He reviewed and approved the manuscript along with his father and provided additional material and insight. Dr. Monti provided invaluable technical information, security systems and background data on the CIA, FBI, MOSSAD and KGB.

Tony reserves the highest praise for Carmen, a lady in the finest sense of the word, making it possible for Tony to persevere when the odds became overwhelming. She filled a void in Tony's heart and life, cared for him, provided refuge, and critical financial support for the Capture Team.

Many thanks to all in the Capture Team, especially to Tony's bodyguard, Jamshid, who supplied data on SAVAK and Iranian operations and to Rashid, who like Jamshid, stood in the line of fire to protect Tony. They also maintained communications with this author during Tony's 'silent' periods.

---

[21] Retired and decorated WWII Marine pilot.

We thank Michael McCollum, CEO of Third Millennium Publishing, for his personal hands-on assistance in producing our book.

Nunzio thanks his dearest wife, Elizabeth, whose perseverance, even during her long and painful chemo therapy treatments never diminished. She was the only editor and made this true story read more like a suspense novel than another ho-hum documentary, of which there are dozens.

Due to the sensitive nature of this material and in order to protect certain individuals, Tony instructed the authors to 'hold' all sources and evidence confidential until he or George release the material.

Authors' Biographies

Nunzio Addabbo

Nunzio Addabbo is the TARGET*JFK* Capture Team "insider" with the secrets and survivor of an attempt on his life by a member of the Hit-Team who assassinated President Kennedy. He is a retired international engineering/construction management consultant on some of the largest worldwide projects. Addabbo speaks English, Spanish, Italian and some Farsi. He is an experienced technical writer, holds a U.S. pilot's navigation patent, commendations from the National Academy of Sciences and Smithsonian Astrophysical Observatory and a instrument rated commercial pilot with licenses in the U.S., Canada, Chile and Iran. Addabbo, a licensed amateur radio operator, has been approved for entry into the 2002 Who's Who in America and is a member of MOAA, The Military Officers Association of America and AFIO, the Association of Former Intelligence Officers.

Elizabeth Addabbo

Elizabeth Addabbo is a well-traveled free-lance writer, photographer and lecturer. Her weekly column, AT YOUR REQUEST, tying food preparation to history and culture, was one of the most popular ever published on the California Central Coast. Her various travel articles were enthusiastically received. She has been District, Regional and National Director of Member Services for two major real estate franchises and the owner/teacher of her own real estate licensing school. Elizabeth has served as an Ambassador for an important California HMO and has been a promotional artist for several major cosmetics companies. In addition to co-authoring TARGET*JFK* , she is completing an important historical novel, THE LIBERATION OF VIVIENNE and co-authoring THE EPONYMOUS COOKBOOK with Allan Amenta.

TARGET*JFK* has been registered with the Writer's Guild of America west. Elizabeth and Nunzio have been interviewed several times on television and radio and reviews of TARGET*JFK* have appeared in several local publications.

INDEX

Names with asterisks (*) have been fictionalized to protect the innocent.

450

Target *JFK*

Broadway, 100, 159, 245
Broe, Bill, 62
Bronfman, 227
Bronson, Charles, 434
Bronx, 126
Brooks Brothers, 15, 47
Brooks*, Alice, 112, 140, 141, 142, 144, 145, 150, 152, 153,
    156, 157, 161, 171, 217, 243, 244, 288, 318, 338, 398
Brooks*, Haldon, 104, 106, 107, 108, 109, 110, 111, 112,
    126, 128, 136, 137, 138, 139, 140, 141, 142, 143, 144, 145,
    146, 148, 150, 151, 152, 153, 154, 155, 156, 157, 158, 161,
    171, 173, 174, 217, 239, 243, 244, 288, 318, 338, 339, 389,
    406, 419, 432, 433, 440
Brown, Janice, 208
Bruno, 10, 11, 12, 13, 431
Bush, George (CIA), 163

C

C.I.A., 12, 15, 16, 18, 21, 23, 34, 40, 41, 42, 43, 47, 48, 50,
    52, 53, 55, 57, 60, 62, 63, 66, 70, 75, 78, 82, 83, 87, 96,
    100, 104, 117, 128, 137, 163, 180, 242, 251, 266, 348, 354,
    398, 399, 400, 401, 403, 404, 405, 417, 423, 424, 425, 427,
    428, 429, 430, 432, 433, 441, 442
Calama, 248, 252, 254, 257, 263, 410
California, 6, 26, 101, 111, 161, 163, 167, 175, 238, 244, 270,
    271, 282, 285, 290, 291, 315, 318, 325, 405, 431, 440
Camp Peary (CIA), 53, 55, 425
Camp Street, 429
Campbell, Judith, 19, 399, 401, 406, 426, 428
Canada, 155
Cananea, 209, 217, 218
Capture Team, 4, 104, 134, 160, 163, 165, 167, 177, 192,
    193, 194, 197, 198, 201, 203, 204, 210, 211, 212, 217, 219,
    220, 228, 238, 240, 243, 246, 257, 261, 271, 273, 274, 313,
    320, 322, 324, 326, 329, 333, 339, 341, 347, 350, 360, 361,
    365, 367, 392, 397, 409, 421, 434, 440, 442
Cardonian*, 252, 253
Carmen, 140, 141, 142, 143, 144, 145, 146, 147, 148, 149,
    150, 151, 152, 153, 154, 155, 156, 157, 158, 160, 162, 163,
    171, 172, 173, 174, 175, 179, 182, 183, 184, 191, 207, 210,

D

E

F

H

I

L

M

N

O

Q

R

Rashid, 5, 79, 80, 82, 88, 91, 92, 95, 96, 97, 106, 107, 108,
109, 111, 112, 138, 163, 192, 193, 194, 196, 197, 200, 204,
205, 210, 214, 215, 216, 217, 229, 231, 232, 233, 234, 238,
240, 242, 243, 244, 245, 246, 248, 251, 252, 253, 254, 256,
259, 260, 261, 263, 264, 267, 270, 272, 312, 313, 314, 315,
316, 322, 324, 326, 329, 330, 336, 337, 338, 339, 354, 355,
357, 358, 359, 360, 363, 365, 366, 367, 369, 370, 371, 373,
374, 375, 377, 378, 379, 380, 381, 382, 383, 384, 385, 386,
387, 388, 389, 390, 409, 410, 412, 419, 420, 421, 440, 442
Reagan, Ronald (President), 407
Real del Monte, 26, 27
Red Fox Restaurant, 426
Regina* Hotel, 25, 27, 29, 349
Remote Farm, 47, 52, 53, 55, 425
Reno, 279
Renzetti, Bert, 61
Reza, 66, 205
Rhonda, 182, 183, 184
Ricardo, 157, 158, 162, 222
Ricardo Lyon Ave., 222
Richardson*, John, 4, 14, 22, 23, 25, 26, 27, 28, 29, 30, 32,
37, 38, 39, 64, 81, 180, 417, 424, 431, 432
Richardson, Laddy, 270, 414, 415
Rimma, 298, 299, 300, 301, 302, 303, 304, 305, 307, 308,
309, 310, 315, 316, 317, 318, 319, 322, 324, 326, 327, 328,
329, 331, 332, 333, 334, 338, 341, 342, 343, 347, 350, 351,
365, 367, 368, 389, 440, 441
Rincon Gaucho Restaurant, 111, 140
Rio Plata, 106, 111, 179, 181
Rivera, Poncho, 17, 18, 28, 29, 30, 35, 86, 156, 167, 168,
169, 170, 192, 193, 194, 195, 196, 197, 198, 199, 203, 204,
218, 259, 261, 263, 323, 335, 346, 347, 410, 435
Rodolfo, 370, 371, 372, 375, 376, 377, 378, 388
Rodriguez, Antonio, 33
Roemer, Bill (FBI), 67, 70
Rojas, Amelia, M.D., 256, 257, 258, 259, 261, 262, 263, 264,
265, 266, 323, 409, 410, 419, 422, 435
Rosario, 246
Rosarita, 285, 292, 293, 302, 303, 304, 316, 322, 327, 328,
330, 331, 332, 338, 339, 341, 342, 350, 365, 369, 389, 411,
440

S

T

U

V

W

Y

Z

Zahedan, 64, 68, 130, 142, 145, 146, 154, 173
Zaire, 173
Zangi*, 142, 151
Zardashi, 430
Zona Rosa, 25, 30, 33, 106, 110, 419
Zorro Plateado*, 163, 238, 391, 441
Zurich, 48